I0197788

Election Management Bodies in Southern Africa

Comparative study of the electoral commissions' contribution to electoral processes

A review by
**Open Society Initiative for Southern Africa
and ECF-SADC**

2016

OSISA
Open Society Initiative
for Southern Africa

ECF
ELECTORAL
COMMISSIONS
FORUM OF SADC
COUNTRIES

Published by the Open Society Initiative for Southern Africa (OSISA) and African Minds

OSISA
President Place
1 Hood Avenue
Rosebank
Johannesburg, 2196
South Africa
www.osisa.org

African Minds
4 Eccleston Place, Somerset West, 7130, Cape Town, South Africa
info@africanminds.org.za
www.africanminds.org.za

ⓒ 2016
All contents of this document, unless specified otherwise, are licensed under
a Creative Commons Attribution Non-Commercial 4.0 International Licence

ISBNs
Print: 978-1-928332-17-6
EBook: 978-1-928332-18-3
e-Pub: 978-1-928332-19-0

Copies of this book are available for free download at www.africanminds.org.za and www.osisa.org

ORDERS
To order printed copies within Africa, please contact:
African Minds
Email: info@africanminds.org.za

To order printed copies from outside Africa, please contact:
African Books Collective
PO Box 721, Oxford OX1 9EN, UK
Email: orders@africanbookscollective.com

CONTENTS

PREFACE

To the extent that elections determine how political power is allocated and dispersed, and the related management of public resources, they are high-stakes events and high points in the political history of any country. In many countries around the world, disputed or failed elections have been the cause of much human insecurity, deaths and destruction of lives and property. Against this background, over the past two decades or so, Southern African countries have entrenched the use of elections as the only means and medium for electing governments and representative institutions in governance. As a region, the Southern African Development Community (SADC) has been spared the ignominy and spectre of military rule. The question is no longer whether or not elections regularly and periodically take place to enable citizens the exercise of their constitutional authority as envisaged in Article 21 of the Universal Declaration of Human Rights. Rather, it is the quality of the elections that is at issue. The primary question today is whether elections are inclusive and fair, and produce truly legitimate outcomes. Experiences from the region and elsewhere have shown that when an electoral process fails to produce credible outcomes, the legitimacy of institutions of governance is brought into question, with declining citizen confidence in electoral processes.

Central to elections are electoral management bodies (EMBs). These institutions, which are creatures of national constitutions or statute, are mandated to manage most, if not all, aspects of the electoral process, including but not limited to: the registration of voters; preparing and updating of voters' registers; the registration of political parties – in general or for elections; civic and voter education; the nomination of candidates for elections; the enforcement of electoral codes of conduct; regulating media coverage of elections; the accreditation of party agents and observers; polling and announcement of results; and recommending electoral reforms.

Informed by the political history, constitutional traditions of the country and lessons from regional and international best practice, the design, mandate, extent of powers and even the number of institutions responsible for electoral matters in each country, vary. For example, while some countries have one EMB for all electoral matters, in some countries these functions, especially those relating to the registration of voters, the registration and regulation of political parties, and the regulation of media coverage of elections may be dispersed among more than one institution. Whatever the design and context, credible elections are dependent on an electoral management process that is faithful to the principles of 'independence, impartiality, transparency, professionalism, and sustainability'.[1]

---

1 See https://aceproject.org/ero-en/misc/egypt-principles-for-independent-and-sustainable [accessed 6 August 2016].

As organisers and referees of highly contested, sometimes zero-sum contests on the transfer of citizens' trust to elected representatives and institutions, EMBs are every loser's worst enemy. They are generally misunderstood institutions, sometimes suffering serious stakeholder trust deficits, and often criticised for that which they are not mandated or even permitted to do. If they are not fighting off possible manipulation by vested interests – such as incumbent governments, and powerful political and business interests – EMBs may have to deal with an unfavourable political and legislative environment or deliberate or unavoidable financial asphyxiation, all of which limit their capacity to deliver credible elections.

This study, which is a collaborative effort between the Open Society Initiative for Southern Africa (OSISA), the Open Society Foundation's Africa Regional Office (AfRO) and the Electoral Commissions Forum of Southern African Development Community Countries (SADC-ECF), builds on similar work undertaken by AfRO together with the Open Society Initiative for East Africa (OSIEA) in 2015 and the Open Society Initiative for West Africa (OSIWA) in 2011. Findings and recommendations from this pan-African initiative are expected to increase information and knowledge on the strengths, weaknesses and workings of EMBs in sub-Saharan Africa with a view to facilitating peer learning among African election managers, as well as informing policy-makers, legislators, governments and civil society on a progressive reform agenda to strengthen inclusive electoral processes and democratic practice.

In Southern Africa, EMBs whose states are members of the SADC are organised under the SADC-ECF. Established in 1998, the SADC ECF seeks to strengthen EMBs in the SADC region as well as promote conditions conducive to free, fair, credible and transparent elections. This it does primarily through peer learning and capacity building of its membership. Pursuant to this mandate, in 2003, the SADC-ECF partnered with the Electoral Institute for Sustainable Democracy in Africa or the Electoral Institute for Southern Africa (EISA), as it was known then, to develop and adopt Principles for Election Management, Monitoring and Observation in the SADC Region (PEMMO). Since then, the PEMMO have been the guiding principle of the SADC-ECF's work on the management, monitoring and observation of elections in SADC member states. In 2007, the SADC-ECF added to its toolbox, the Principles on the Independence of EMBs in the SADC Region. By establishing and nurturing this partnership with the SADC-ECF (and its 15 EMB membership), both OSISA and AfRO seek to not only promote co-ownership of the research process by EMBs, but also, very importantly, ensure that findings and recommendations from the study are fed directly into the formal decision-making processes of the organisation and through it the respective EMBs' national-level processes, as necessary. Through its membership, the SADC-ECF is well placed to bring regional best practices to bear at the national level.

This study, the largest of the three studies covering East, West and Southern Africa covers Angola, Botswana, Democratic Republic of the Congo (DRC), Lesotho, Malawi, Mauritius, Mozambique, Namibia, Seychelles, South Africa, Zambia and Zimbabwe.

While Tanzania is a member of the SADC-ECF, the country was not included in this study as it was covered in the East African study. For each of the 12 countries, researchers focused on:

- A comparative analysis of the legal frameworks the EMBs operate under and of the historical and political contexts they function within;
- A comparative study of the institutional nature of the EMBs;
- An assessment of the powers vested in the EMBs in the conduct and management of electoral processes with particular reference to the preparation, management and updating of electoral registers; the identification and updating of electoral constituencies; roles in the drafting of electoral laws; the conduct and management of electoral operations; roles in certifying and proclaiming electoral results; roles in ensuring that electoral results are credible; and roles in electoral conflict resolution;
- A comparative assessment of the independence of the EMBs with particular reference to funding and relationships with the executive, political parties, parliament and the judiciary (electoral justice mechanisms).

Siphosami Malunga
Executive Director, OSISA

ACKNOWLEDGEMENTS

This book benefited from the partnership of the Electoral Commissions Forum of the Southern African Development Community (ECF-SADC), the Open Society Initiative for Southern Africa (OSISA) and the Africa Regional Office (AfRO), who worked collaboratively with all the election management bodies in Southern Africa to bring this publication to fruition.

We thank the following persons for their contributions to this publication: Hilda Modisane, ECF-SADC Programme Manager; Siphosami Malunga, OSISA Executive Director; Ozias Tungwarara, Programme Support Division Director AfRO; Takawira Musavengana, OSISA Democracy and Governance Cluster Team Leader, Lusako Munyenyembe, OSISA Democracy and Governance Programme Officer, and Glen Mpani, OSISA Democracy and Governance Programme Manager.

Special mention goes to Benedict Komeke, OSISA Democracy and Governance Programme Associate, who assisted in organising the review and related meetings.

We also extend our gratitude to all the chapter authors: Dr Nuno de Fragoso Vidal (Angola); Prof. Emmanuel Botlhale with Dr Onalenna Selolwane (Botswana); Dr Joseph Cihunda Hengelela (the DRC); Prof. Mafa M Sejanamane (Lesotho); Ms Ann Maganga (Malawi); Dr Roukaya Kasenally (Mauritius); Dr Domingos M do Rosário (Mozambique); Mr Moses Ndjarakana (Namibia); Dr Nandini Patel (Seychelles); Dr Collette Schulz-Herzenberg (South Africa); Dr Njunga-Michael Mulikita (Zambia); and Dr Charity Manyeruke (Zimbabwe); and the editor, Prof. Mcebisi Ndletyana.

This project would not have been possible without the leadership of the respective chairpersons and senior management of EMBs as well as that of the ECF-SADC under its President, Hon. Justice Rita Makarau and the Chairperson of the ECF-SADC Executive Committee, Hon. Justice Mahapela Lehohla.

OVERVIEW

The 21st century has seen electoral democracy flourishing in Africa. Countries located in the southernmost region of the continent have been no exception. The Freedom House, the global body that rates the democratic status of the various countries, affirms this. Reporting on the year 2015, the organisation's report, 'Freedom in the World 2016', cites member countries of the Southern African Development Community (SADC) largely in approving terms. Only two countries in the region, for instance, are rated 'not free', whilst the rest range between 'partly free' and 'free'.[1]

Today's picture is drastically different to what prevailed in the immediate 30 odd years following decolonisation. Independence was soon followed either by one-party states, sheer authoritarianism or a descent into civil war. Post-colonial leaders had become a reincarnation of their colonial oppressors. Just as the former colonial subjects thought they had finally realised the dream of democracy, it was once again deferred and seemed never to return.

Whilst lasting almost two generations, the nightmare of post-colonial oppression did pass. It ended just as the 20th century was coming to a close. By the early 1990s, undemocratic independent Africa was also swept up in what the American scholar, Samuel Huntington, dubbed, 'the second wave of democracy'.[2] The catalyst came outside the continent, set in motion by the end of the Cold War and the consequent rise of the unipolar world-order dominated by the United States of America and her West European allies.[3]

America adopted democratisation as its mission to spread throughout the un-free world. Joining America in her quest were global lending institutions, namely the International Monetary Fund and the World Bank. In addition to the structural adjustment of the economy, these lending institutions insisted on democratisation. That pre-condition found resonance in the pro-democracy movements that were emerging throughout the continent, largely spurred by the relatively low standards of life. To save their economies, and partly hoping to thwart the loss of their political power, Africa's undemocratic elite acceded to democratisation.

Thus the last decade of the 20th century ushered in competitive politics. Once again elections quickly became a regular feature of Africa's post-colonial politics. In some instances, old regimes made way for new governments. Whilst laudable, the excitement

---

1   Available at https://freedomhouse.org/report/freedom-world/freedom-world-2016 [accessed 26 july 2016].
2   Huntinton SP (1991) *The Third Wave: Democratization in the Late Twentieth Century.* Norman, Oklahoma: University of Oklahoma Press.
3   Diamond L & Plattner MF (eds)(1993) *The Global Resurgence of Democracy.* Baltimore: John Hopkins University Press.

with elections betrayed a flawed fascination with mere compliance with procedures. Little attention was given to electoral governance. This is quite different to mere electoral processes. It focuses more on the institutional structures that administer the elections to ensure that they are configured in a manner that imbues them with integrity and thus enable them to deliver credible elections. In turn, credible elections go a long way in enhancing the political institutions and the system.[4]

From the early 2000s, therefore, the institutional structures that administered the elections became just as important as the occurrence and process of elections. Particular attention was focused on both the legislative and institutional framework, especially to achieve uniformity in the region. To this end, and among other instruments, SADC's Electoral Commissions Forum (here-after referred as the 'Forum'), adopted the document: 'Principles for Election Management, Monitoring and Observation in the SADC Region', on 6 November 2003.[5]

The foregoing document underscored a number of principles on electoral governance. On the election management bodies (EMBs), for instance, the document stipulated that they should be:

- Funded adequately to undertake their legislated or prescribed functions;
- Representative of society, especially women and that care be taken to appoint independent individuals, some of whom should be competent in legal issues;
- Accountable only to parliament, and not a ministry, enhancing their prospects of being independent; and
- Funded directly by parliament through a budget vote.

That said, the Forum didn't prescribe the form of the EMB. This was an acceptance that they do and can take various shapes. As a principle, EMBs are generally made up of a Commission, which is an executive body, and the administrative section that attends to the day-to-day logistical issues related to the elections. This combination has given rise to three forms of EMBs: stand-alone, statist and mixed. A stand-alone EMB not only has an independent institutional location, but also has its own staff serving as the administrative arm. Conversely, a statist EMB is part of the state machinery, located within a particular ministry, and uses civil servants to undertake the actual work. A mixed EMB entails a commission that plays a supervisory/executive role, whilst civil servants constitute the administration.

In other words, each country adopts the form that best suits it. Whilst allowing for variety, however, the Forum has repeatedly emphasised the importance of internalising the above-mentioned principles, and others, in the configuration of EMBs and running

---

4   Lindsberg S (2009) Democratisation by elections: A mixed record. *Journal of Democracy* 20(3): 86–92.
5   Available at http://www.idea.int/africa/southern/upload/The-SADC-ECF-EISA-Principles-document.pdf [accessed 26 July 2016].

of their elections. In undertaking this study, with the explicit support and cooperation of the Forum, the Open Society Initiative for Southern Africa (OSISA) underscores the importance of EMBs in delivering credible elections. Their functions straddle the multiple phases that characterise the electoral process, from the campaign, to the election-day and counting of ballot papers, and to the announcement of results.

For example, some of the EMBs key functions include compiling and updating the voters' roll, registering political parties and candidates, drawing-up and enforcing a code of conduct, setting up voting stations and delivering the election material, counting the ballot papers, arbitrating over disputes and announcing the election results. All these functions are critical to the fairness of the electoral process and general acceptance of the outcome and, ultimately, the stability of the country.

The study was done in 12 countries, all within the SADC region. They are:

- Angola
- Botswana
- Democratic Republic of Congo
- Lesotho
- Malawi
- Mauritius
- Mozambique
- Namibia
- Seychelles
- South Africa
- Zambia
- Zimbabwe

As noted earlier, members of SADC Forum collaborated with OSISA and the team of researchers from the conceptualisation of the research guide, to alerting the various member countries of impeding visits from researchers and urging them to cooperate. Their representatives were present, for instance, at the inception workshop held in Harare in August 2015 to conceptualise the research guide. The inception workshop was also attended by the representatives of the various electoral commissions. The idea was to ensure transparency of the process, and to enhance the rigour of the research questions and methodology. In this way, the EMBs and commissioners, who are the subject and respondents of the research, could develop confidence in both the integrity and utility of the research papers for their own work.

The research team was made of researchers drawn from each country. Care was taken to appoint individuals who are not only resident in their countries of study, but were also intimately knowledgeable about the EMBs, the electoral process and the general history of the country. Researchers had either published and/or been involved in electoral work of their country of study. Overall, the team was multiracial and gender-representative, and with mostly one researcher from each country.

The research questions covered a number of aspects. They related to, among others:

- History of the country: colonial and post-independence;
- General socio-economic profile of the country;
- Electoral system;
- Legislation, both domestic and international, and the institutional framework;
- Form of the EMB and level of independence: legislatively, institutionally and financially;
- Structure and operation of the EMB;
- Gender make-up;
- State of relations with stakeholders; and
- Funding of political parties.

In other words, the study adopted a case-study approach. This entailed field-work, which included interviews with a number of respondents who are knowledge about the subject either from actual involvement, academic study or through media coverage. Secondary literature was consulted to provide historical background and context. Most importantly, researchers made extensive use of primary documents, such as legislation, government and observers' reports, and surveys.

The research exercise span over a period of roughly eight months. In addition to Harare's inception workshop, another was held in Johannesburg in November 2015 to discuss draft papers. Researchers not only got feedback on their papers from each other, the editor and the OSISA team, but also from the representatives of each commission. The purpose was to ensure that none of the emerging drafts suffered from any factual errors or omissions, whilst maintaining their intellectual integrity.

The rigour of the methodology shows in the richness of the chapters. Each chapter makes for an interesting read, providing very useful insight. A few points about the findings are worth noting here, whilst leaving the rest to the reader to study further. Whilst all these countries share a common history of colonial oppression, they are also different. The peculiar history of each country has shaped the EMB, giving it a unique identity. Thus the electoral commissions are, by and large, different from each other.

Whilst most countries believe in and do appoint individuals of integrity as commissioners, the vibrancy and level of independence of each commission vary from country to country. This variation is occasioned by the state of democracy in a particular country. In vibrant democracies, characterised by absolute acceptance of democratic principles and competitiveness, commissions tend to be highly independent, with their own staff.

Where power between the executive and parliament is lopsided, commissions face some notable challenges. Founding legislation for the commission is absent and the executive meddles in the appointment of the administrative staff. The absence of the legislation is deliberate to allow for executive intrusions, and insecurity of tenure, which makes commissioners susceptible to official influence. The situation is worse in quasi-democracies. There's no pretense at independence. The monarch appoints commissioners of his own choosing, who are answerable to him.

Equally noteworthy is that countries with a history of civil war and still gripped by tension, have an appointment process that, albeit unconventional, reveals a careful attempt at fairness. They give direct representation to each rival, based on the strength of their parliamentary representation, and to civil society. Whilst this measure goes a long way in pre-empting any grievance that could arise from a sense of exclusion, it doesn't give the appointed commissioners agency and independence. Commissioners appointed by civil society constitute a minority. As for those appointed by parties, they are affectively accountable to them. When parties are unhappy about their performance, they are removed. This makes not only for a fractious commission, but also an unstable one.

The use of information technology also varies from one commission to another. This is largely a function of each country's developmental profile. Whilst the latter factor is true of most countries, recurrent electoral disputes can be a sufficient trigger to secure sophisticated technology, even though a country may not necessarily be wealthy. Namibia is one such country, with a distinction of being the only country with e-voting. It was prompted by perennial disputes over electoral results.

Namibia is an illustrative example of the general disposition towards innovation. But, elections are treated largely as a seasonal pre-occupation. Electoral matters attract attention only during an electoral season, but ignored soon thereafter.

Some EMBs suffer from critical vacancies, others do not compile reports on elections, and the few that do are not invited to parliament to account. This limits the possibility of commissions improving on their performance and operations.

Media access remains a serious challenge in most countries. Elections and parties are guided by a code of conduct, but its not always easy for commissions to ensure equal and fair access to media by all parties. Public media tends to be dominant in the region, and is often prone to control by the party-in-government. This means the contest is uneven, with the field tilted towards the incumbent. Opposition parties in some countries are further disadvantaged by lack of public funding towards political parties. Parties-in-government often find it easy to raise funding from the private sector, which courts favour with government. Opposition parties don't have such sources, and thus their party machinery is not fully developed and their campaigns are not highly effective.

The various EMBs that are presented in this volume, therefore, reveal an informative array of experiences, dynamics and challenges. Collectively, the EMBs in the region represent a marked improvement. They underscore the general acceptance of competitive electoral democracy in the region and that a legitimate electoral outcome is crucial for creating healthy political institutions and a stable society. Each case study below makes specific and detailed recommendations to improve the EMBs. A lot more remains to be done, which will not only to improve the EMBs themselves, but also enhance prospects of stability, peace and the general betterment of the human condition.

1

ANGOLA

Dr Nuno de Fragoso Vidal

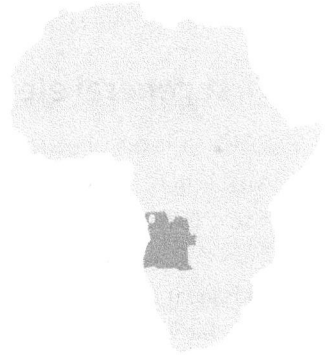

Introduction

This chapter provides an analysis of the Angolan electoral processes since the transition to a multiparty democracy in the 1990s. The focus is primarily on the electoral management body, in consideration within the whole evolving and dynamic political context and its interaction with other electoral organs, structures and actors.

The chapter is structured in three major parts, each one dedicated to one of the three elections that occurred since the transition. The first section deals with the first multiparty elections of 1992, the major electoral organs, the legislation endorsing them and their performance within the context of a troubled transition that was halted by the resumption of civil war right after elections. The extra ten years of civil war and its outcome in 2002, within a different international and domestic context, determined the new electoral structuring that set the stage for the following electoral process in 2008. Such a new context and setting majorly contributed to a qualified majority victory of the party in power. These issues are analysed in the second section. The third and final section is dedicated to the period evolving from the 2008 elections to the third electoral process of an Angolan multiparty system in 2012. Here attention is focused on the new constitution of 2010, which favoured an age-old concentration of powers in the presidency; the ensuing electoral engineering; and the renewed qualified majority in 2012.

In order to allow for a comparative perspective on the evolution of the electoral structures, their impact on reality, and how they were in turn influenced by such reality, the sections follow a similar thematic analysis. Different sections consider the historical-political context, the structuring of the electoral organs through political negotiation and endorsing legislation, the state power (mainly focusing on the legislative and the judiciary), access to the media, electoral observation, reported problems in each election and the financing of political parties. The chapter ends with recommendations and suggestions that could contribute to the more effective performance of electoral organs, structures and procedures.

First general elections and structures in 1992

Political and economic context

Angola has a long tradition of conflict and authoritarianism. Even after colonialism, peace, freedom and democratisation have been hard to realise. The first elections after the transition to a multiparty system (1992) were traumatic and plunged the country into an additional ten years of war, adding to the previous 16 (from independence in 1975 to the 1991 Bicesse peace-agreements).

The nationalist war against the Portuguese (1961–1975) promised freedom from a long colonial repression, but independence in 1975 marked the beginning of a civil war (which had effectively started even before) with major foreign involvement right from the start. With few interruptions (1991–1992; 1994), the war lasted for almost 27 years – up to February 2002 – when the rebel leader of the National Union for the Total Independence of Angola (UNITA), Jonas Savimbi, was killed in action and a peace memorandum was signed in March that year.

Between 1975 and 1977, there was a period of relative freedom in Angola. However, in 1977 an aborted coup resulted in a major purge with massive killings all over the country. An authoritarian and repressive one-party socialist regime was put in place by the Popular Movement for the Liberation of Angola (MPLA), ruling the country since independence. Paranoid state security bodies were in charge of surveillance and political repression. Non-state media were closed down and the right to association was limited to the party and mass organisations, such as the labour union of Angolan workers (UNTA), organisation of Angolan Women (OMA) and MPLA's youth league (JMPLA).[1]

The judicial system became 'militarised', combining civilian and military courts with the ability to impose heavy penalties, including the death penalty (mainly for political and security crimes) and functioning under a vague and almost limitless revolutionary legitimacy. This system was politically dependent, being under the direct influence of the party and ultimately of the president. A culture of fear, intimidation and repression became entrenched.[2]

In a country with a weak sense of nationhood at the time of independence, the civil war became a main factor of further social and economic fragmentation. Resources became more and more absorbed by the war effort. The economy was almost exclusively dependent on oil revenue, and agriculture and industrial production dropped precipitously. The conflict increasingly assumed an ethnic overtone and accentuated the urban/rural divide. The developmental gap between Luanda and the provinces, as well as between the coast and the interior also widened. In the early eighties, the majority of the population was

---

1   Vidal N (2004) The genesis and development of the Angolan political and administrative system from 1975 to the present. In: S Kyle (org.) *Intersections between Social Sciences*. Cornell, NY: Cornell University. pp. 1–16.

2   Vidal N (2007) Social neglect an the emergence of civil society. In: P Chabal & N Vidal (eds) *Angola: The Weight of History*. London: Hurst. pp. 200–235.

already facing extreme poverty, aggravated by the disruption of health and educational services.[3]

Violations of human rights by both sides of the conflict became common, as well as impunity for the perpetrators of those crimes, as reported by several international organisations throughout the entire war.[4] Priority given to defence and internal security stood in the way of democracy, transparency and accountability.[5]

With no freedom of expression and no civil society organisations (CSOs) or legal opposition allowed, inefficiency and corruption thrived. The increasing intensity of the war in the 1980s reinforced the whole system: the decline in public services; repression and authoritarianism; centralisation and the concentration of power; the disruption of internal production resulting in increasing economic dependency on oil revenues; intensifying social fragmentation, insofar as people resorted more and more to personal and informal solutions for their growing problems; and the erosion of state institutions and collective/public consciousness.[6]

In the mid-80s, the regime had reached the peak of power concentration and administrative centralisation: the country was run by President Eduardo dos Santos, exerting to the full his functions as president of the party, head of state, head of government and commander-in-chief of the armed forces.[7]

Increasing imports to feed an expanding war and to compensate for disrupted agriculture and industry, along with the fall in oil prices in 1986, created serious problems for the balance of payments. Together with the Union of Soviet Socialist Republics' (USSR's) decreasing capacity to carry on supporting the war effort, these problems led to cautious economic reforms from 1987 onwards.[8] Officially, the socialist model lasted until the third MPLA Party Congress of December 1990. Complex negotiations with South Africa, the US and Cuba led to the withdrawal of Cuban troops and Namibia's independence, paving the way for the 1991 Bicesse peace agreement between the MPLA and UNITA and the 1992 multiparty elections — the first ever in Angola.

General elections in 1992

The MPLA had to quickly make massive changes before the elections to help the party come to terms with the new multiparty framework and the market economy. A constitutional revision of law 12/1991 in 1991 simply approved the basic principles of a

3   Ibid.
4   Human Rights Watch (1994) *Angola: Arms Trade and Violations of the Laws of War Since the 1992 Elections – Report*. NY, USA: Human Rights Watch.
5   Human Rights Watch (1999) *Angola Unravels: The Rise and Fall of the Lusaka Peace Process – Report*. NY, USA: Human Rights Watch.
6   Vidal N (2003) Modern and post-modern patrimonialism. In: M Newitt, P Chabal & N MacQueen (eds) *Community & the State in Lusophone Africa*. London: King's College London. pp. 1–14.
7   Vidal N (2007) The Angolan regime and the move to multiparty politics. In: P Chabal & N Vidal (eds) *Angola: The Weight of History*. London: Hurst. pp. 124–174.
8   Ferreira ME (1995) La reconversion économique de la nomenklature pétrolière. *Politique Africaine* 57: 11–26.

multiparty democracy, defining Angola as a democratic state based on the rule of law, enshrining key civic and human rights, as well as the basic principles of a market economy. The laws of association (14/1991), freedom of the press (22/1991), the permission to go on strike (23/1991) and independent radio broadcasting (9/1992), opened the space for the emergence of opposition political parties and civil society – church organisations, private media, independent labour and professional unions, and CSOs and non-governmental organisations (NGOs). State radio, television and newspaper became somewhat more pluralist and a wave of strikes took place in 1991 and 1992.

Nevertheless, the presidency and the MPLA's top echelons retained tight control over the state's resources (mainly the oil revenues) and institutions, with special emphasis on the state media. The private media were also kept under close surveillance, especially the new private commercial radio stations, which started broadcasting in 1992, each one kept within the sphere of influence of the party in power through their boards of directors.[9]

In this favourable position – controlling the state institutions, administration and resources – the MPLA led the transition process. The party managed to unilaterally change most of the new legislation (with several of the new laws approved between March 1991 and September 1992 by the People's Assembly – the parliament of the single party system). The state's administration capacity was used to for the party's electoral campaign and a significant amount of funds were gathered for electoral purposes, including for the general distribution of material benefits.[10] Brazilian experts in political marketing were hired to manage the party's campaign and a major investment was made to increase party membership, which saw a dramatic increase from 65 362 members in 1990 to 544 639 by the end of 1992.

Besides UNITA (funded by the US and several Western countries, along with its own diamond revenues), emerging opposition parties and CSOs faced severe constraints and were extremely fragile and dependent. Minor opposition parties were easily manipulated and their activities disrupted, such was the case of the Party for Democratic Renewal (PRD), initially established by MPLA dissidents.[11] The so-called privatisation process mainly benefited the same old political elite, which was now transformed into an entrepreneurial class dominating the new private sector.[12]

---

9   Without exception, all the new private radio stations were indirectly controlled by the MPLA; broadcasting licenses were conceded to MPLA members that were supposed to assume a pro-governmental stance in face of forthcoming elections: LAC – Luanda Antena Comercial (Luanda); Rádio 2000 (Lubango); Rádio Morena (Benguela) and Rádio Comercial (Cabinda). UNITA's radio Voz do Galo Negro (Voice of the black cock), unauthorised during the civil war was then authorised but again declared illegal as soon as the war resumed in October 1992.

10 Messiant C (1995) Angola les voies de l'ethnisation et de la décomposition: Transition à la démocratie ou marche à la guerre? L'épanouissement des deux 'partis armés' (Mai 1991–Septembre 1992). *Lusotopie* 3: 181–221.

11 Ibid.

12 See Aguilar R (2003) Angola's private sector: rents distribution and oligarchy. In: K Wohlmuth, A Gutowski, T Knedlick, M Meyn & S Pitamber (eds) *African Development Perspectives*. Germany: Lit Verlag; Aguilar R (2005) *Angola: Getting off the Hook*. Gothenburg, Sweden: SIDA Gothenburg University, in particular pp. 13–18.

In compliance with the Electoral Law (5/1992, 16 April) the National Electoral Council (CNE), already planned at the Bicesse peace agreements of 1991, was created and went into operation on 11 May 1992. The CNE hierarchic structure comprised a president, general director and provincial electoral commissions to be run by provincial electoral directors and provincial electoral cabinets. Under the Electoral Law, political parties had the right to supervise the electoral registry, but besides the MPLA, none of them had the capacity to do so, not even UNITA.

In accordance with the law, the Supreme Council of the Judiciary elected the president of the CNE – which was one of its members, Judge Caetano de Sousa – to be appointed by the President of the Republic. A former member of the National Front for the Liberation of Angola (FNLA), Onofre dos Santos, was chosen and appointed by the President of the Republic to the position of general director of the elections. Besides those two positions, the CNE also included five citizens of recognised public merit chosen by the President of the Republic and the Minister of Territorial Administration; one representative from the National Council for the Media;[13] and one delegate from each of the political parties and coalitions contesting the elections. Presidential candidates could also have a representative at the CNE if they wished to.

According to the Bicesse agreements and the Electoral Law (5/1992), the CNE was supposed to direct the electoral process and was conceived as an organ independent from the government and the political parties, deemed competent to coordinate, direct and assume the electoral registry and all other activities related to the electoral process (art. 13). It was also responsible for processing the electoral results and their public announcement, complying with constitutional prerogatives to assure the freedom, justice and transparency of the electoral process.

Despite all the tasks mandated to the CNE, several electoral activities had to count on the support of the state administration, especially the maintenance of the electoral registry. The government – through the Ministry of Territorial Administration – took over the administration of the electoral process from the Bicesse agreements to the constitution of the CNE, with the Minister of Territorial Administration becoming a permanent member of the CNE.[14] The government was also responsible for the informatics system for processing the electoral data and results received from 5 800 polling stations all over the country. Such governmental control was criticised by several opposition parties, namely UNITA and its leader, which became louder after the first electoral results were announced pointing to the MPLA's victory.[15]

Despite all the criticism that later arose from the opposition, the CNE and its director were able to acquire a considerable degree of credibility throughout the whole process,

---

13 The National Council for the Media (CNCS) was conceived in accordance to the first press law of 1991 (law 22/1991, 15 June) as a media regulating body basically conceived to safeguard the freedom of expression, with its regulation set in 1992 by a specific law (7/1992, 16 April).
14 From a private interview with Onofre dos Santos, Luanda, 21 September 2015.
15 Albuquerque C (2002) *Angola, a cultura do medo* [Angola, the culture of fear]. Lisbon: Livros do Brasil.

especially within the international community and with the UN Special Representative, Dame Margaret Anstee.[16] The strong presence of the international community, the considerable bargaining power of UNITA, the presence of a delegate from each party at the CNE, and the nomination of Onofre dos Santos (former member of the FNLA and long-time counsellor of the historical nationalist leader Holden Roberto) as General Director, all afforded some credibility to the CNE and restrained the political criticism of the MPLA's control over the council.

Massive UN assistance with electoral logistics and organisation was a key feature of the first general election and, according to several of the interviewees, seems to have been responsible for dissipating the initial political tension and mistrust among the opposition.[17] The electoral hardware logistics were mainly assumed by the United Nations Angola Verification Mission II (UNAVEM II), involving 25 000 people (national and foreign) in one of the largest UN electoral support operations, with costs of about USD 40 million, paid by international donors. There was also a strong and significant presence of international observers (about 800), half of whom were chosen by the UN. The other half was selected by parliaments, governments, specialised organisations, the European Parliament, 13 observers from the Organisation of African Unity (OAU) and MPLA and UNITA invitees, among other foreign personalities. International observation was determined by its own law (6/1992, 16 April).[18]

In Angola's first nationwide multiparty elections ever, a turnout of more than 91% (4.4 million) registered voters gave the MPLA candidate, President Dos Santos 49.57% of the vote against 40.07% for Savimbi, while the legislative elections resulted in UNITA getting 34.10% of the vote against 53.74% for the MPLA.

Despite a so-called Joint Declaration of Angolan Political Parties issued on 2 October 1992 by UNITA with seven other opposition parties declaring the elections fraudulent, the UN and other foreign observers considered them 'generally free and fair'.[19] According to the law there should have been a presidential election run-off, but the civil war immediately resumed, plunging the country into a new decade or conflict.

Transition towards a multiparty system

Lusaka Peace Protocol 1994–1998

Increasing US pressure seems to have led to the Lusaka peace agreement of November 1994 and the implementation of a Government of Unity and National Reconciliation

---

16 Anstee M (1996) *Orphan of the Cold War: The Inside Story of the Collapse of the Angolan Peace Process, 1992–1993.* London: Palgrave.
17 From private interviews with Onofre dos Santos, Abel Chivukuvuku, Lucan Ngonda, Sediangany Mbimbi, Adalberto da Costa Júnior, Filomeno Vieira Lopes, in Launda, September 2015.
18 Albuquerque C (2002) *Angola, a cultura do medo* [Angola, the culture of fear]. Lisbon: Livros do Brasil.
19 Ibid.

(GURN), inaugurated in April 1997, whereby the MPLA government integrated members of UNITA and other political parties represented at parliament.[20]

Amidst several recurrent military incidents, the Lusaka protocol was partially implemented until 1998, when the government decided to suspend it due to UNITA's repeated failure to hand over the administrative control of municipalities in the areas it still dominated. At the fourth MPLA congress of December 1998, a decision was made in favour of a military solution.

The resumed war resulted in another contraction of the political and civil space that had partially relaxed during the 1994–1998 period.[21] Political pressure on the private media was reinforced through state security and judicial activity, which resulted in several arrests and lawsuits against journalists.[22] A multitude of opposition political parties had to face the challenge of internal factions contesting the legitimacy of their respective leaders – the so-called phenomenon of Renovadas – which, according to all the affected opposition leaders, were instigated and sponsored by the MPLA to foment division and weakness.[23] The party most affected was UNITA, whose deputies in Luanda were split between those who supported Savimbi and those who did not. Among the latter, a clearly government-sponsored group of defectors was formed (UNITA-Renovada or Renewed-UNITA), which took the parliamentary seats reserved for Savimbi's party, but without any domestic or external credibility.

Electoral restructuring in the late 1990s

In the meantime, amidst this worrisome context, during the Lusaka protocol period (1994–1998), and even after that, in 1999, discussions were taking place between the MPLA and the opposition concerning the new legislation that had to be approved, including the new constitution and the electoral package of laws. By then the MPLA was considering the possibility of elections, even in a situation of conflict, in order to further isolate Savimbi's UNITA.

---

20 UNITA headed the ministries of Commerce, Tourism, and Health, and had five vice-ministers at the ministries of finance, defense, social reinsertion, agriculture, and information, and integrated provincial governments, with the governors of Cuando Cubango, Uige, Lunda Sul, and the vice-governors of Kwanza Sul, Benguela, Huambo, Bie and Luanda.

21 Within the period of 1994–1998 there was a boom in private newspapers (e.g. *Folha 8, Actual Fax, Agora, Comércio & Actualidade, O Independente* and *Angolense*, joining *Imparcial Fax*, which had existed since 1991). A labour union federation emerged in 1996 (General Centre of Independent and Free Labour Unions of Angola – CGSILA), ending the monopolistic status of the MPLA's federation (UNTA), allowing representation of other independent labour unions (e.g. teachers – SINPROF; Journalists – SJA). The state monopoly on radio broadcast also came to an end in 1997 with the re-opening of the Catholic Church's Radio Ecclesia in Luanda (closed in 1977).

22 See Amnesty International (AI) (1999) Angola, Freedom of Expression under Threat. Index AFR 12/016/1999, 1 November 1999. Available at https://www.amnesty.org/en/documents/afr12/016/1999/en/ [accessed 23 June 2016]; also Amnesty International (AI) (2000) Angola: Unfair trial of Rafael Marques. Index AFR 12/004/2000, 30 March 2000. Available at http://web.amnesty.org/library/index/ENGAFR120161999/en/ [accessed 20 November 2015].

23 Vidal N (2007) The Angolan regime and the move to multiparty politics. In: P Chabal & N Vidal (eds) *Angola: The Weight of History*. London: Hurst. pp. 124–174.

Those first discussions in the late 1990s left no doubt about the intentions of the party in power to reinforce government influence on the electoral management body, especially on the electoral registry through the Ministry of Territorial Administration. The opposition contested this, reaffirming the politically independent character of that organ. In January 1999 an executive decree approved the internal regulation of a planned National Direction of Electoral Processes with the competence to organise and execute all procedures for electoral processes, including the much disputed electoral registry (decree 7/1999, arts 1 & 2). In June 1999 a new decree placed that planned organ under the coordination of the Ministry of Territorial Administration (86/A-99, art. 1). In the same year a new statute of the Ministry of Territorial Administration, approved by the Council of Ministers (decree-law 19/1999), defined the National Direction for Electoral Processes as one of the central executive services of the ministry (art. 18) and attributed to the ministry the competence to create all the necessary organising and technical-administrative conditions for the electoral process, including the electoral registry (art. 1).[24]

Such discussions were put aside as the war raged on and the military defeat of UNITA became the priority, an objective achieved in February 2002 with the killing of Savimbi in combat. After several attempts by the international community and Angolan social movements (e.g. the Pro Pace Movement[25]), the cease fire and the Luena Peace Memorandum (4 April 2002) were signed by the victorious MPLA and the defeated UNITA without any external or internal participation. This relationship imbalance would from then on characterise the Angolan multiparty system.

With the end of the war, new legislative and presidential elections were expected to occur and talks on the electoral process regained importance. However, by then the political and military context had radically changed in favour of the MPLA, victorious from a long and exhausting civil war, with its main rival killed in action and UNITA's army in disarray and starving. The international community had long abandoned Savimbi and explicitly or implicitly supported the MPLA's political quest to legitimately govern the country. Even UNITA's long-time ally, the US, had normalised diplomatic relations with the MPLA, recognising its government in 1993 and taking full advantage of new business opportunities in the country.

In the face of such a favourable context, the party in power carefully prepared an electoral strategy designed at the fifth congress in 2003, again taking advantage of its dominance over other state structures —the legislative, the executive and the judicial, along with the public and private sectors of the economy and, last but not least, the state media.

---

24 Gomes C (2010) *Gestão da dissensão: a comissão nacional de eleições no processo eleitoral angolano de 2008* [Managing Dissent: the National Electoral Commission in the Angolan Electoral Process]. *Oficina do CES* 357: 3–4.

25 In the late 90s, myriad projects and initiatives for peace emerged between churches and CSOs: Pro Pace movement; Angolan Group Reflecting for Peace (GARP); Programme for Peace Building (PCP); and a number of others. For a detailed analysis of these initiatives, see Comerford M (2005) *O Rosto Pacífico de Angola*. Luanda: Author's edition, especially the end of chapter 2 and chapter 4.

Legislative power and elections

Confident of its electoral prospects after a major military achievement and the weakening of the opposition, the MPLA lost interest in the negotiations about the future constitution after several deadlocks with the opposition in 2004–2005.[26] The party believed it could achieve a two-thirds majority in the legislative elections, following the examples of the Mozambique Liberation Front (FRELIMO) in Mozambique and the African National Congress (ANC) in South Africa, and therefore approve the new constitution at will.

New electoral legislation had to be approved before elections, but considering the new internal and international context and the MPLA's parliamentary majority (129 seats out of 220, against UNITA's 70 seats and the remaining dispersed through smaller parties[27]), the positions of the party in power would prevail, mainly establishing the centrality of government and the Ministry of Territorial Administration in the electoral process.

The first electoral calendar was presented in 2004 with legislative elections expected to occur in 2006 and presidential elections one year later. A proposal for the electoral registry came before parliament for discussion, presented by the MPLA, which established its previously exposed intention to place the responsibility for the registry in the hands of the government through the Ministry of Territorial Administration. The opposition complained again, insisting on the need to assure compliance with the above-mentioned law of 1992 (5/1992) determining that the CNE was a politically independent organ, competent to coordinate, execute, conduct and operate all activities related to the elections, as well as the superintendence and supervision of the electoral registry (art. 154).

The MPLA only conceded on recognising the role of the CNE to supervise the whole electoral process and to check the registry. Political parties were also allowed to check the registry if they wished to do so. Nevertheless, the organisation of the registry was to be the responsibility of the government administration (Ministry of Territorial Administration) under the argument that only the state administration had the structure and logistics to meet the demands of such task.[28]

The new electoral law was approved in August 2005 (6/2005, revoking the old 5/1992) stating the independence of the CNE, which was deemed responsible for coordinating the execution of all activities related to elections, as well as the supervision of the electoral

26 Vidal N (2007) The Angolan regime and the move to multiparty politics. In: P Chabal & N Vidal (eds) *Angola: The Weight of History.* London: Hurst. p. 162.

27 PRS – *Partido da Renovação Social* [Party of Social Renewal], six MPs; FNLA – *Frente Nacional de Libertação de Angola* [Front for the National Liberation of Angola], five; PLD – *Partido Liberal Democrata* [Liberal Democratic Party], three; PRD – *Partido Renovador Democrático* [Party of Democratic Renewal], one; PAJOCA – *Partido da Juventude Operários e Camponeses de Angola* [Party of Youth, Workers and Peasants], one; PDP-ANA – *Partido Democrático para o Progresso da Aliança Nacional* [Democratic Party for Progress of the National Alliance], one; PNDA – *Partido Nacional Democrático de Angola* [Angolan National Democratic Party], one; FDA – *Forum Democrático Angolano* [Party of Angolan Democratic Fórum], one; AD – Coligação, *Aliança Democrática-Coligação* [Party of Democratic Alliance], one; PSD – *Partido Social Democrata* [Social Democratic Party], one.

28 Gomes C (2010) *Gestão da dissensão: a comissão nacional de eleições no processo eleitoral angolano de 2008* [Managing Dissent: the National Electoral Commission in the Angolan Electoral Process]. *Oficina do CES* 357: 3–4.

registry (art. 154, 1). A new electoral registry law (3/2005, 1 July), stated that it was up to the CNE to approve and supervise the electoral registry programme presented by the competent organ of the government (art. 13). The old National Electoral Council of 1992 (Conselho Nacional Eleitoral – CNE) was transformed into the National Electoral Commission (Comissão Nacional Eleitoral – CNE).

The Electoral Registry regulations were later approved by the Council of Ministers and left no doubt about the centrality of the government and the Ministry of Territorial Administration, defining the three organs responsible for the central coordination of the electoral registry, namely the Council of Ministers, the Ministry of Territorial Administration and the Inter-ministerial Commission for the Electoral Process (CIPPE).[29] According to the regulations, it was up to the Ministry of Territorial Administration to conceive, programme, organise, coordinate and execute the electoral registry (art. 6), up to the Council of Ministers to define the guiding principles and main tasks (art. 4), and up to the CIPPE to prepare the technical, material and administrative conditions for elections.

The CNE could still check the registry and officially 'supervise' it, but was clearly demoted in the decision-making and main operative tasks, devoid of several of its previous powers and main role in the 1992 electoral process. In the end, as concluded by the EU Electoral Observation Mission (EU EOM) to the 2008 elections, 'the CNE's role as supervisor of the registration process was at best limited'.[30]

The new criteria for the CNE's composition established the principle of proportionality. Such a principle was already present in the old 5/1992 law, but had not been strictly enforced in the 1992 process, as those had been the first inaugural elections of the multiparty system and it had not been not possible to establish what the proportion of parliamentary forces was at that time. Therefore, the principle of proportionality was not applied and all the political parties running for the 1992 elections were represented at the CNE (even though it must be noticed that most of the important decisions were taken outside of the CNE, at the level of the Political-Military Joint Commission[31], comprising only the MPLA, UNITA and representatives of the Troika – US, Russia and Portugal).

According to the MPLA, it was now possible to enforce the proportionality principle in the selection of commissioners and avoid the 1992 'chaotic' meetings with representatives of all parties. On the opposition side the counter-arguments pointed out that the proportion of forces in parliament was again vitiated since parliament had been elected in 1992 for only five years and had since been operating without an electoral mandate.

---

29 CIPPE in the Portuguese acronym; previously created by a resolution of the Council of Ministers of 21 December 2004 as a government organ responsible for the technical, material and administrative conditions for elections, comprising representatives of the Ministries of Territorial Administration, Interior, Post Offices and Telecommunications; Council of Ministers Resolution 34/2004.

30 European Union Election Observation Mission (2008) *Angola Final Report: Parliamentary Elections, 5 September 2008*. Brussels: European Parliament. p. 15. Available at http://eeas.europa.eu/eueom/pdf/missions/fr_eueom_angola_08_en.pdf [accessed 23 June 2016].

31 From private interview with Onofre dos Santos, general director of the 1992 elections, Luanda, 21 September 2015.

Despite the opposition's arguments, the MPLA's majority in parliament approved the new composition of the CNE as having 11 members: comprising two citizens appointed by the President of the Republic; six citizens appointed by the majority of MPs at the National Assembly proposed by the political parties represented at the parliament, three of which were to be appointed by the majority party and the other three by the remaining parties and coalitions (two from the first most popular opposition party and one from the second); one judge of the Supreme Court elected by the Supreme Council of the Judiciary (Caetano de Sousa was once again nominated and elected as president of the CNE, who also happened to be deputy-president of the Constitutional Court); one representative of the Ministry of Territorial Administration; and one member of the National Council for Media elected by its members.

At local level, the CNE was composed of the provincial electoral commissions (made up of nine members, six to be elected by the parliament, three of which appointed by the majority party and three from the rest of the opposition, one judge nominated by the Supreme Council of the Judiciary, one citizen appointed by the provincial government and one representative of the Ministry of Territorial Administration). The municipal electoral cabinets replicated the composition of the provincial cabinets (except for the citizen, who was supposed to be appointed by the municipal administrator) and, whenever necessary, communal electoral cabinets were nominated at will by the CNE.[32] Representatives of political parties and coalitions in parliament and up to five representatives of the political parties and coalitions without parliamentary seats could attend the CNE deliberative meetings, but could not participate in discussions. Only presidential and MP candidates could not be members of the CNE.[33]

The opposition complained that such composition allowed the MPLA and its president to directly and indirectly appoint eight out of 11 members to the new CNE (including the president of the CNE), also ensuring the same proportional majority at the CNE local structures. The MPLA would directly and indirectly control a two-thirds majority in the CNE, given the party and presidential influence over the other state organs such as the Supreme Court (judges were appointed by the President of the Republic), the National Council for the Media (itself majorly directly and indirectly appointed by the MPLA, its president and government; see below) and the Ministry of Territorial Administration (MPLA's government). The opposition was unyielding in its proposals that also included one representative of civil society organisations and one representative of the churches, and other proposals comprising nine independent personalities voted by a two-thirds parliamentary majority[34] that would force the MPLA to negotiate.

---

32 Arts 156 to 161, Law 6/2005, *DR, I*, 95, 10 August 2005 (Electoral Law, revoking law 5/1992).

33 Art. 156, 3 & 4, Law 6/2005, *DR, I*, 95, 10 August 2005 (Electoral Law, revoking law 5/1992).

34 Gomes C (2010) *Gestão da dissensão: a comissão nacional de eleições no processo eleitoral angolano de 2008* [Managing Dissent: the National Electoral Commission in the Angolan Electoral Process]. *Oficina do CES* 357: 7.

Fearful of another deadlock (after the constitutional deadlock of 2004/2005) the MPLA again rejected the opposition's proposal and approved its own plans. Executive commissions were created by the Council of Ministers to effectively manage the electoral process on a daily basis, with members exclusively appointed by the majority party.[35] The approval of the new electoral legislation brings to mind the old socialist days when the People's Assembly behaved as an echo-chamber for laws approved by the Council of Ministers, which was presided over by the president of the party/President of the Republic.[36] Mistrust in the process resurfaced and led the main opposition party to question the legitimacy of any future elections, seeing as they could not be considered democratic, free and fair by international standards.[37]

In the end, the whole context favoured the MPLA government – the civil-war winner with a weak opposition and no longer subject to the influence and watchdog role of the international community as had been the case in 1992. The party took over the organisation of the electoral process (through the Council of Ministers and the Ministry of Territorial Administration), especially taking control of the long-disputed electoral registry and the CNE's composition and competences. The MPLA effectively controlled the entire electoral process, from the registry to the planning, management, operation, execution and, last but not least, the CNE, the supposedly independent organ expected to exert some supervisory role over the registry and the electoral process.

The MPLA's shenanigans did not pass unnoticed by the Southern African Development Community (SADC) Parliamentary Forum 'Voter Registration Observer Mission Report' one year prior to elections, pointing out that:

> The fact that 6 of the 11 NEC [CNE] members were nominees of political parties, raised questions on the extent to which the NEC could be viewed as impartial in managing the electoral process and in this case voter registration. This also raised questions on the extent to which other stakeholders, especially political parties, could trust the voter registration exercise to be free from interference by the key player.[38]

---

35 Compare the electoral law approved by the National Assembly, Law 6/2005, *DR, I*, 95, 10 August 2005 (Electoral Law, revoking law 5/1992) with the Council of Ministers Decree 63/2005, *DR, I*, 111, 16 September 2005 and the Council of Ministers Decree 62/2005, *DR, I*, 107, 7 September 2005.

36 In the same sense, see Human Rights Watch (2004) *Some Transparency, No Accountability: The Use of Oil Revenue in Angola and its Impact on Human Rights*. HRW Report 16(1). NY, USA: Human Rights Watch, pp. 76–77; also, Miranda A (2004) *Angola 2003/2004: Waiting for Elections*. Norway: Christian Michleson Institute. pp. 25–26.

37 Statements and arguments produced by UNITA's secretary for information, Adalberto da Costa Júnior, in a press conference. See Da Costa Júnior A (2005, 7 December) Alert on the legitimacy and dangers of the electoral process. Press Conference, Hotel Trópico, Luanda.

38 SADC (2007) *Voter Registration Observer Mission Report – Angola 2007*. Windhoek: SADC Parliamentary Forum. p. 18.

Concerning the accumulation of functions, the SADC mission recommended that:

> In order to enhance transparency and accountability, the CIPPE and the NEC [CNE] should ensure that none of their officials performed both registration and supervisory functions. This recommendation stemmed from the concern raised by some stakeholders of instances where CIPPE officials at provincial level also worked for the NEC.[39]

Concerning the involvement of the Ministry of Territorial Administration, the SADC observation mission recommended that:

> For future voter registration and elections management, Government should seriously consider using a single independent electoral management body to avoid confusion and to enhance transparency and credibility as opposed to the current arrangement where both the MAT and the NEC [CNE] were involved in the process.[40]

Executive power and elections

Despite the existence of the so-called Government of Unity and National Reconciliation (GURN), comprising members of the opposition and having power since 1997 (see above), all the major positions were occupied by MPLA members and the government was effectively led by the party in power. As stressed by all the opposition leaders, every governmental position occupied by their representatives at the GURN had been emptied of any effective power; no matter what position was attributed to the opposition – minister, vice-minister, governor, administrator – each and every politically sensitive duty was in practice transferred to the nearest position occupied by an MPLA member in the same ministry. Thus, if the governor was from UNITA, the effective powers, such as budget management, rested with a vice-governor belonging to the MPLA.[41]

Despite this, most of the opposition remained in the GURN, fearing retaliation from the majority party in terms of the cancellation of state budget funds and the loss of other benefits related to the positions occupied. There was also difficulty in obtaining a consensus within and among opposition parties in favour of abandoning their positions at the GURN, as that could be seen again, internationally and domestically, as anti-national reconciliation. Without much success, UNITA's new leader, Isaias Samakuva, tried to replace some of his party's representatives, in parliament and in government, who had been occupying their posts since the days of *UNITA-Renovada*.[42]

---

39 Ibid.: 22.
40 Ibid.
41 From private interviews with leaders of opposition parties occupying positions in GURN, Luanda, May–June 1998; Abel Chivukuvuku and Alcides Sakala (UNITA); Ngola Kabango and Holden Roberto (FNLA); Anália Vitótia Pereira (PLD); Eduardo Kwanga (PRS).
42 On this subject, see articles *Substituição de parlamentares aquece debate na Assembleia Nacional*

The combination of party, state, president and government is as old as the regime, but at elections they become one solid team. Party events made use of state administration logistics and resources, while government events were overwhelmed with party symbols and the party faithful from MPLA mass movements. Accordingly, the party made sure that its ministers, provincial governors and administrators (who in most cases were also top members of the party at national and provincial levels) were seen to inaugurate public infrastructure projects financed with public money in ceremonies where state and party symbols were often combined to give credit to the MPLA for such achievements. MPLA flags were everywhere in the provinces and are very similar to the Republic's flag. Such events were manipulated by the state media in order to give as much political credit as possible to the party in power.[43]

Judicial power and elections

Political control over the judiciary remained as strong as ever. The President of the Republic, who is also president of the MPLA, maintained significant power over the judiciary, including the power to appoint Supreme Court judges without confirmation by the National Assembly.

The opposition regularly accused the judicial system of being politically influenced in cases involving factions within their parties (*Renovadas'* phenomena), often resulting in judicial decisions to suspend the state subsidy to those parties and serving the general purpose of dividing and weakening the opposition (see above). Several of these parties also pointed to the Supreme Court's decision, on 22 July 2005 not to consider Dos Santos' presidential administration since 1992 as presidential terms, as an example of presidential influence over the judicial system. Such a decision was seen as a way to circumvent the constitutional decree that limited presidential mandates to three five-year terms.[44]

As rightly stressed by the opposition (so-called group of seven),[45] the Supreme Court judges appointed to the CNE structures did not stand down from their duties at the Supreme Court (e.g. Caetano de Sousa, president of the CNE for the 1992 and 2008 elections). This was not only unconstitutional (according to art. 131 of the Constitutional Law on the incompatibility of functions), but also legally and politically unacceptable since the Supreme Court acted as the Constitutional Court, to which parties appeal in instances of electoral disputes. The same person (or persons) could rule as CNE commissioners at the first instance, and then again as judges at the second instance (Constitutional Court).

[Replacement of MPs warms up debates in the National Assembly] (2006, 1 February) *Jornal de Angola*; *Sem consenso* [Without consensus] (2006, 1 February) *Jornal de Angola*.

43 European Union Election Observation Mission (2008) *Angola Final Report: Parliamentary Elections, 5 September 2008*. Brussels: European Parliament. p. 21. Available at http://eeas.europa.eu/eueom/pdf/ missions/fr_eueom_angola_08_en.pdf [accessed 23 June 2016].

44 From private interviews of the author with N'Gola Kabango (president of the FNLA), Isaias Samakuva (president of UNITA) and Eduardo Kwangana (president of PRS) in October 2008.

45 Group composed of UNITA, FNLA, PLD, PAJOCA, PDP-ANA, FpD and POC's (Parties of Civil Opposition, not represented at parliament).

Financing of political parties

Moving on from the previous practice whereby the Supreme Court assumed the role of Constitutional Court, a new Constitutional Court was appointed in late July 2008,[46] and on 25 July ruled on which political parties were authorised to run for the elections. Insofar as the distribution of public funds for political campaigning depended on such authorisation, the amounts of funding were only approved at the end of July by the Council of Ministers, in a clear violation of the law determining parliament as the competent organ for such an approval. The funding was only made available to political parties in early August, less than 30 days before the elections scheduled for 5 September, while the law established that 90 days was the rule. The opposition campaigns were obviously compromised (especially those of the smaller parties) while the MPLA campaign was far ahead.

The Council of Ministers approved USD 17 million to all ten political parties and four coalitions, but the effective disproportion of means became evident in favour of the MPLA's heavily funded campaign, allegedly supported by donations from Sonangol (the national oil company), Endiama (the national diamond company), private companies and investors.[47]

In fact, the main problems for the opposition were financial. Membership fees were merely symbolic at around USD 1 per month, and even then most members did not usually pay their dues.[48] Those opposition parties represented in parliament before the 2008 elections survived essentially on funds coming out of the state budget (about USD 10 per vote obtained in the 1992 election), which in 2006 worked out at around USD 14 million/year for UNITA and sums that varied between USD 100 000 and USD 900 000 for the rest of the opposition, with the majority situated within the USD 100 000 and USD 200 000 range.[49] Opposition parties without exception complained that this was far from sufficient and was also paid irregularly (sometimes even suspended) so as to disrupt their activities or apply pressure on them at key moments, such as during the constitutional deadlock in 2004/2005 (see above).

In view of such financial restrictions, it was extremely difficult for the opposition to expand activities outside provincial capital cities. UNITA was the only opposition party with an effective national presence outside the provincial capitals. Some parties, such as the Democratic Party for Progress–Angolan National Alliance (PDP-ANA) and the Party of the Alliance of Youth, Workers and Farmers of Angola (PAJOCA), were still struggling

---

46 The new Constitutional Court is composed of 11 judges; four of which (including the court's president) are appointed by the President of the Republic, four are elected by a 2/3 qualified majority vote at parliament (including the court's deputy-president), two are elected by the Supreme Council of the Judiciary and one is selected through curricular application in an open public call. Law 2/2008, *DR, I,* 17 June 2008 (Constitutional Court Organic Law).

47 Roque PC (2013) *Angola's Second Post-War Elections: The Alchemy Of Change.* Institute for Security Studies (ISS) situation report. Pretoria: ISS. p. 7.

48 From private interviews of the author with all the political leaders of the opposition in October 2008.

49 For the exact number of votes obtained by each party in the 1992 elections see, Marques S (1993) *Angola: da Guerra à Democracia.* Luanda: Edipress. p. 43.

to get an office in the capital city of Luanda. The situation was far worse for parties without parliamentary representation and without access to state budget funds.

In absolute contrast to the opposition stood the MPLA, with an impressive collection of buildings throughout the country, with a presence in each and every village. The party had the largest state subsidy of around USD 21.5 million and membership fees obtained at source from salaries at some state companies. Moreover, it controlled directly or indirectly the most significant private companies and their funding for the campaign, which was managed through a special holding created for that purpose – the Society for Management and Financial Participation (GEFI).

Access to the media

In view of the stated compliance of the electoral process with international and regional norms and standards, the opposition's access to the state media (national radio, television and daily newspaper) remained a major problem.

A new press law enacted in 2006 (7/2006, 15 May) maintained the monopoly of long and short wave frequencies exclusively for the public radio station, Rádio Nacional de Angola (RNA), leaving only medium and FM waves for the use of private radio stations. The installation of provincial radio transmitters implied the provision of local content, which effectively meant that private radio stations were not allowed to broadcast nationally or across provincial boundaries (arts. 52 to 54). The only relatively independent radio station — the Catholic Church Radio Ecclesia — was therefore denied from broadcasting outside Luanda, this despite having installed a network of re-transmitters in several provinces since 2003.

The new law abolished the state monopoly over television broadcasting, but as happened with commercial radio stations in 1992, no politically independent television channels emerged. In 2008 a new TV channel, Zimbo, was licensed, initiating its broadcasting in 2009 but was again related to a financial group proximate to the regime – *MediaNova* (see below). Private weekly newspapers, in their low thousands, were basically restricted to Luanda and a few capitals of the most accessible provinces (coastal). The only daily newspaper was still the government-owned *Jornal de Angola*, with a circulation of around 40 000 and reaching every provincial capital.

Contradicting the recommendations of the Declaration of Principles on Freedom and Expression in Africa of the African Commission on Human and Peoples' Rights, state-owned media (television, radio, newspaper and news agency) continued to operate under exclusive governmental control, without a governing board protected against editorial interference from the government.[50] International reports stressed the regime's intimidation of journalists by either forcing them to practise self-censorship or by co-opting them into the state media.[51]

---

50 African Commission on Human and Peoples' Rights (2002) *Declaration of Principles on Freedom of Expression in Africa,* 32nd Session, 17–23 October 2002, Banjul, The Gambia.
51 See Human Rights Watch (2004) *Unfinished Democracy: Media and Political Freedoms in Angola – Report.*

As monitored by the EU EOM between 11 August and 3 September, airtime and space on the public media (TPA 1, RNA, and *Jornal de Angola*) was majorly devoted to MPLA activities (57% to 65%), while UNITA had 12–19%, and the rest of the opposition combined had less than 4.8%. Needless to say, most of that airtime allocated to the MPLA had a positive and supportive tone (75% and 32% of the news at TPA 1 and RNA, respectively) while more than 46% and 41% of the news allocated to UNITA (TPA 1 and RNA respectively) was presented in a negative tone. The same happened at the *Jornal de Angola*, where 36.1% of MPLA news was presented in a positive tone and 28.1% of UNITA news was presented in a negative tone.[52]

In the face of such biased election coverage by the state media, the role of a media regulatory body would obviously be important. However, insofar as the new press law (7/2006) was not regulated (clarified and specified in several of its sections) as was supposed to happen within 90 days from its publication (art. 87), several important procedures were left up to subjective interpretation (eventually to be settled by the National Assembly, art. 88), leaving the media regulatory body – the National Council for the Media (CNCS) – without rules on its organisation, composition and mandate.[53]

The CNCS continued to be regulated by the old law (7/1992), with a total of 23 members mainly appointed by the government and the majority party, although also comprising members appointed by the opposition parties (according to the 1992 legislature), journalists and the churches. Above all, it maintained its somehow previously harmless role, more educational than proactive, with a mandate limited to making recommendations or requests to the media to provide answers when complaints were received. The opposition blamed the MPLA's influence for the organ's lack of effectiveness. In fact, it was unable to make a single pronouncement during the electoral period in the face of a series of outright violations of the law by the state media in favour of the party in power.

NY, USA: Human Rights Watch; also news report Media Institute of Southern Africa (2005, 23 February) Director of government news agency threatens to shoot journalist. IFEX. Available at https://www.ifex.org/ angola/2005/02/23/director_of_government_news_agency/ [accessed 23 June]; also Human Rights Watch (2006) *Human Rights Watch World Report* 2006. NY, USA: Human Rights Watch & Seven Stories Press, pp. 74–79; European Union Election Observation Mission (2008) *Angola Final Report: Parliamentary Elections, 5 September 2008*. Brussels: European Parliament. p. 23. Available at http://eeas.europa.eu/eueom/pdf/ missions/fr_eueom_angola_08_en.pdf [accessed 23 June 2016].

52 European Union Election Observation Mission (2008) *Angola Final Report: Parliamentary Elections, 5 September 2008*. Brussels: European Parliament. pp. 25–29. Available at http://eeas.europa.eu/eueom/ pdf/missions/fr_eueom_angola_08_en.pdf [accessed 23 June 2016]; also European Union Election Observation Mission Angola (2008) *Preliminary Statement: Legislative Election, September 2008*. Brussels: European Parliament. p. 9. Available at http://eeas.europa.eu/eueom/pdf/missions/eueom_angola_2008_ ps_en.pdf [accessed 23 June 2016].

53 As previously referred, the CNCS was originally created in sequence of the first press law (Law 22/1991, *DR, I*, nº25, 15 June 1991 (Press Law)) with its first regulation set by a specific law (Law 7/1992, *DR, I*, 16 April 1992 [National Council for the Social Media – CNCS]).

Electoral observation and reported problems

Important to the credibility of the electoral process was international and domestic observation. A specific law on electoral observation had been enacted on 4 July 2005 (4/2005), allowing civil society organisations to observe parliamentary elections for the first time. However, in practice several problems emerged, with difficulties arising around the accreditation of civil society observers.

The largest and most soundly structured civil society initiative to observe the elections was a coalition platform mainly funded by the US National Democratic Institute – *Plataforma Nacional da Sociedade Civil Angolana para as Eleições* (PNASCAE) – which trained 2 640 observers, but only managed to get accreditation for 1 300, and in the end only 28 observers (out of the proposed 370) were allowed to observe the elections in Luanda,[54] where 30% of the electorate was concentrated. The CNE justified the refusal of these and other CSO observers' applications on procedural grounds, incomplete applications or forged documents.[55]

The international observation teams comprised the European Union, the European Parliament, Pan-African Parliament, Community of Portuguese Speaking Countries (CPLP), SADC, the US diplomatic mission in Angola and the African Union.[56] The European Union, with the largest contingent of observers was able to get reasonable coverage of the whole country, having deployed 108 observers (long-term and short-term observers) in teams of two across all 18 provinces of Angola, spanning 46 of the country's 164 municipalities and producing the most reliable, data-based report ever written on Angolan elections.[57]

Besides the aforementioned problems regarding access to the media and the accreditation of civil society observers, other sets of problems reported by electoral observers focused on several logistical problems during election day, especially in the outskirts of Luanda (concentrating most of the Luanda voters). Of the 1 522 polling stations of Luanda, 320 did not open due to the lack of election material, and others opened late for the same reasons, which led the head of the EU EOM, Luisa Morgantini, to make a first statement characterising the situation as chaotic. Due to these problems and in compliance with

---

54 From private interview with Onésimo Setecula, coordinator of the Civil Society Observation Platform (PNASCAE), September 2008.

55 European Union Election Observation Mission (2008) *Angola Final Report: Parliamentary Elections, 5 September 2008*. Brussels: European Parliament. pp. 13–14. Available at http://eeas.europa.eu/eueom/ pdf/missions/fr_eueom_angola_08_en.pdf [accessed 23 June 2016].

56 The European Union (108 observers, comprising long-time and short-time observers, joined by a 7-member delegation from the European Parliament, headed by Ms. Fiona Hall, MEP), the Pan-African Parliament (27), the Community of Portuguese Speaking Countries – CPLP (17), SADC (90), the US diplomatic mission in Angola (40); the African Union (40); Japanese embassies (6). See Hall F (2008) *Report of the Delegation to Observe Parliamentary Elections in Angola*. Brussels: European Parliament. p. 2. Available at http:// www.europarl.europa.eu/intcoop/election_observation/missions/2004-2009/20080905angolareport.pdf [accessed 23 June 2016].

57 European Union Election Observation Mission (2008) *Angola Final Report: Parliamentary Elections, 5 September 2008*. Brussels: European Parliament. Available at http://eeas.europa.eu/eueom/pdf/ missions/fr_eueom_angola_08_en.pdf [accessed 23 June 2016].

the law, the election was extended for a second day (the 1992 election had also taken place in two days) with some polling stations remaining closed on the second day.[58] Other problems included late accreditation of party delegates and polling station staff, insufficient distribution of ballot papers, the absence of voters' rolls in most of the polling stations under observation, and the absence of independent scrutiny of vote counting in the Luanda central headquarters.[59] The absence of voters' rolls clearly contradicts the SADC guidelines requiring the existence of an updated and accessible voters' roll.[60]

The EU EOM remarked on the exceptionally high turnout in some provinces where many voters live in remote areas, such as Moxico, Cuando Cubango and Lunda Sul. In addition, they noted –the turnout was 108% in the province of Kwanza-Norte, and that in the province of Cabinda – despite the FLEC campaign to boycott the election – the turnout was 87.7%.[61]

As election day approached, several logistical problems started to accumulate: the fact that no proper and comprehensive voters' rolls were made available on time by the CNE; the confusing, complex and too large system of 12 400 polling centres subdivided into 50 195 polling stations throughout the country to allow for a limited number of voters per polling station (no more than 250 voters in each); the late training of polling staff; the late or no accreditation of party delegates and observers; and so on and so forth.

Due to such problems, the CNE allowed people to vote away from their place of registration. On 2 September, just three days prior to the election, the CNE announced that voters could vote normally anywhere within their municipality and that the tendered ballots should only be used for people voting from outside that area. As explained by the EU EOM, the instruction was given to the polling staff only on the morning of election day in Luanda and even later or not at all in some provinces, leading to obvious confusion and varied interpretations. As a consequence, the majority of polling stations were unable to reconcile the number of ballots used with the number of people who had voted in their municipalities.[62]

58 Hall F (2008) *Report of the Delegation to Observe Parliamentary Elections in Angola*. Brussels: European Parliament. p. 6. Available at http://www.europarl.europa.eu/intcoop/election_observation/ missions/2004-2009/20080905angolareport.pdf [accessed 23 June 2016].

59 European Union Election Observation Mission (2008) *Angola Final Report: Parliamentary Elections, 5 September 2008*. Brussels: European Parliament. Available at http://eeas.europa.eu/eueom/pdf/ missions/fr_eueom_angola_08_en.pdf [accessed 23 June 2016].

60 SADC (2004) *Principles and Guidelines Governing Democratic Elections*. Gaborone: SADC; also SADC (2015) *Principles and guidelines governing democratic elections*; adopted by the Ministerial Committee of the Organ (MCO) on Politics, Defence and Security Cooperation on 20 July 2015, Pretoria, Republic of South Africa, Section 13.4.1, 2015.

61 There were 145 067 registered voters in Kwanza-Norte, but 156 666 people voted, of which 144 055 votes were valid. European Union Election Observation Mission (2008) Angola Final Report: Parliamentary Elections, 5 September 2008. Brussels: European Parliament. p. 44. Available at http://eeas.europa.eu/ eueom/pdf/missions/fr_eueom_angola_08_en.pdf [accessed 23 June 2016].

62 European Union Election Observation Mission (2008) *Angola Final Report: Parliamentary Elections, 5 September 2008*. Brussels: European Parliament. p. 13. Available at http://eeas.europa.eu/eueom/pdf/ missions/fr_eueom_angola_08_en.pdf [accessed 23 June 2016].

Such flexibility and the consequent confusion would eventually explain a turn-out above 100%, as happened in the province of Kwanza-Norte. However, such events are detrimental to the transparency and credibility of electoral processes and should be avoided in future elections, starting with proper voters' rolls being made available in time as determined by law. Unfortunately, as we will see in the next section, the problem with the availability of voters' rolls repeated itself in the 2012 election.

Although several cases of violence and intimidation by MPLA supporters in rural areas of Huambo, Benguela, Bié and Cabinda had been reported in months prior to the elections by the Human Rights Watch team visiting the country,[63] most of the international and national observers to the elections stressed and praised the peaceful environment in which the elections took place.

The 2008 qualified majority vote

Within the above characterised general context, when the 2008 elections finally took place, the internal and external situation was totally favourable to the MPLA and the party managed to achieve a resounding victory with more than 81.64% of the vote against 10.39% of UNITA (in a turnout of 87.36% of 8 256 584 registered voters).

According to the voter registration law (art. 9, 3, law 3/2005)[64] the Council of Ministers decided in May 2007 that it was not possible to organise the registry and voting process to the Angolan *diaspora* due to lack of administrative capacity and therefore (as happened in 1992) those voters were excluded. The decision seems to have mainly benefited the MPLA, since most of the *diaspora* is thought to hold resentments towards the party in power.

Considering the logistical problems on election day and alleged procedural illegalities, UNITA demanded the annulment of elections and filed a complaint with the CNE on the following day (7 September), asking for a re-run in eight days. The complaint was refuted in the first instance by the CNE and in the second instance by the Constitutional Court for lack of sound proof.[65] Other complaints at national level were later filed by other opposition parties such as the Front for Democracy (FpD), PDP-ANA, the Liberal Democratic Party (PLD), and Democratic Angola – Coalition (AD-Coligação), but were also dismissed.

The EU and the Pan-African Parliament recognised several shortcomings, but generally accepted and approved the electoral results along with the other international

---

63 Human Rights Watch (2008) Angola: Doubts over free and fair elections. Intimidation of opposition, media before first poll since 1992. Available at https://www.hrw.org/news/2008/08/13/angola-doubts-over-free-and-fair-elections. [accessed 1 November 2015]. See also Human Rights Watch (2009) Angola democracy or monopoly? Angola's reluctant return to elections. pp. 32–42. Available at https://www.hrw.org/sites/default/files/reports/angola0209webwcover.pdf [accessed 1 November 2015].

64 Such article stipulated in article 9, 3, (Law 3/2005, *DR, I,* 1 July 2005 (Voter Registration Law)) that Angolans living outside the country were to be registered 'as far as material conditions and accompanying mechanisms by the competent entities were established'.

65 Constitutional Court Decision [*Acórdão*] nº 74/2008, 16 September 2008. Available at http://www.tribunalconstitucional.ao [accessed 1 September 2015].

observers. The EU Parliament delegation went even further, considering such a qualified majority as the logical consequence of the MPLA's control over the state's structures [66]

On the other hand, the most influential parties of the opposition considered the whole electoral process fraudulent and a farce. Nevertheless, they still accepted the electoral results and occupied their seats at parliament under the argument that this was the better way of showing the Angolan society and international community its commitment towards peace consolidation and the democratisation process.[67]

In the end, it became clear that the whole electoral process of 2008 lacked pluralism, with too much state control by the party in power using and abusing its prerogatives as civil war winner in control of the legislative, the executive and the judiciary (more than in the 1992 elections). As rightly summed up by the EU Parliament delegation, 'Angola should move to a true multiparty system; this implies a change towards a culture of pluralism'.[68]

Electoral restructuring for the 2012 elections

The new Constitution of the Republic established the administrative independent electoral organs (art. 107). A new Organic Law on the Organisation of General Elections was approved on 21 December (36/2011) as well as a new Organic Law on the Organisation and Functioning of the National Electoral Commission (12/2012, 13 April).

Registry

Under the new law, the CNE kept its statute as independent body responsible for organising, implementing, coordinating and conducting elections and even recovered some control over the database of the previous registry process. It was now up to the CNE 'to maintain and manage the data of voters obtained from the civil identification database and from information provided by voters and prepare voters' rolls based on that information' (art. 144, law 36/2011).

It was up to the public administration (Ministry of Territorial Administration) to undertake the electoral registry and its update under the supervision of the CNE. The Ministry of Territorial Administration had until 15 May 2012 to hand over to the CNE the custody and management of the Central Informatics Files of the Electoral Registry (FICRE), its informatics programs, database, institutional records and other elements of the electoral registry in its possession. Before the transfer, all the material should be

---

66 Hall F (2008) *Report of the Delegation to Observe Parliamentary Elections in Angola*. Brussels: European Parliament. p. 8. Available at http://www.europarl.europa.eu/intcoop/election_observation/missions/2004-2009/20080905angolareport.pdf [accessed 23 June 2016].

67 From private interviews with Isaias Samakuva (UNITA), Eduardo Kwangana (PRS) and Sediangani Mbimbi (PDP-ANA); September 2008.

68 Hall F (2008) *Report of the Delegation to Observe Parliamentary Elections in Angola*. Brussels: European Parliament. p. 9. Available at http://www.europarl.europa.eu/intcoop/election_observation/missions/2004-2009/20080905angolareport.pdf [accessed 23 June 2016].

audited by an independent company chosen and hired by the CNE (art. 211, law 36/2011). This process took place between 29 July 2011 and 15 April 2012.

However, the process did not exactly follow this path. The electoral registry effectively started on 29 July 2011 and officially closed on 15 April 2012, but unexpectedly reopened in early August to allegedly register 1.5 million voters that still needed to collect their voter cards.[69] The registry and FICRE were supposed to have been independently audited by Deloitte, but no audited and accurate electoral rolls from the registry were ever made available and there was no published or publicly known audit report on FICRE. A Deloitte report on its review of the registry (not an official audit report and not on FICRE) leaked to the press, exposed several detected flaws such as the fact that 6.5 out of the 9 million registered voters had been registered without presenting identity cards and therefore could not have their identity checked at polling stations. The same document also expressed concerns regarding the data centre and data systems operated by sub-contracted entities.[70]

A new party, the Electoral Coalition for the Salvation of Angola (*Convergência Ampla de Salvação de Angola – Coligação Eleitoral* [CASA-CE]) and UNITA alerted the CNE in July that electoral rolls made available by then were incomplete and incorrect, and even the names of key opposition leaders were missing.[71] The opposition condemned these flaws for blocking its ability to observe most of the polling stations, again casting doubt on the transparency and credibility of the elections.[72] In the end, no proper, audited and full electoral rolls were publicly made available by the ministry or the CNE for public consultation.

The SADC parliamentary forum observation mission referred to those facts recommending:

> The need to avail the report produced by independent auditors on the Voters' Roll to all electoral stakeholders in order to improve stakeholders' confidence in the electoral process. (...) [and] The need to avail the voters' roll in good time for the Angolans to verify their information in line with the law.[73]

Problems related to the management of electoral data and electoral rolls were attributed by UNITA to a Portuguese company, SINFIC. UNITA accused SINFIC of complicity in FICRE management malpractices. Such accusations were based on the leaked 'Deloitte report' of June 2012, according to which SINFIC, at the service of the Ministry of

---

69 Roque PC (2013) *Angola's Second Post-War Elections: The Alchemy Of Change.* Institute for Security Studies (ISS) situation report. Pretoria: ISS. p. 7.

70 *Novo Jornal,* 28 September 2012.

71 Roque PC (2013) *Angola's Second Post-War Elections: The Alchemy Of Change.* Institute for Security Studies (ISS) situation report. Pretoria: ISS. p. 7.

72 Smith D (2012) Angolan president expected to win another term in 'flawed' election. *The Guardian,* 31 August 2012. Available at http://www.theguardian.com/world/2012/aug/31/angolan-president-win-term-election [accessed 1 December 2015].

73 SADC (2012) *Parliamentary Forum Election Observation Mission to the Angola 31st August 2012 General Elections – Interim Mission Statement.* Gaborone: SADC. p. 13.

Territorial Administration, was the effective manager of the system of electoral registry, the main file of FICRE.[74]

UNITA had already complained that the electoral logistical structures were partly replicating the ones of 2008. According to them, the same companies hired in 2008 were once again being hired for the 2012 elections. This was the case with the Spanish company, INDRA, hired to supply all the voting materials and scrutinising equipment, and the Angolan companies, LTI and BECOM, hired to provide logistical support and the transport of that material.[75] According to UNITA, LTI and BECOM were owned by generals close to the MPLA and the Presidency and once again, as in 2008, these companies were supervised by the Military/Security House of the Presidency of the Republic.[76]

CNE composition

There was some organisational re-arrangement, but essentially the CNE maintained its three main structures at national, provincial and municipal levels: the Plenary of the National Electoral Commission at the central level and the provincial electoral commissions and municipal electoral commissions at local levels. There were also three technical directorates at the three levels to help with the implementation of the decisions and policies of the commission – administration, finances and logistics; electoral organisation, statistics and information technologies; civic and electoral education and information.

The CNE composition was expanded to comprise 17 members. The president is still a judge chosen and appointed by the Supreme Council of the Judiciary. The other 16 members are appointed by the National Assembly by majority vote, on the basis of proposals by the parties and coalitions represented at parliament in line with the principles of majority rule and respect for minorities, which for the 2012 elections worked as follows: nine members for the MPLA; three for UNITA; two for the Social Renewal Party (PRS); one for the FNLA and one for the New Democracy (art. 209, law 36/2011).

Members of the CNE are appointed for up to two five-year terms. The new law kept the possibility of political parties' official representatives and government members to attend the CNE plenary sessions, under the category of 'permanent participants', but now with the ability to intervene, although still without a vote (art. 145, law 36/2011), which somehow represents an advancement on the transparency of the CNE plenary meetings.[77] The

---

74 'Complaint of Crime' [Queixa-Crime] presented by UNITA to the Angolan General-Attorney on 27th March 2013.

75 See UNITA (2008) *Relatório de auditoria às eleições legislativas de 5 de setembro. Uma contribuição para a realização de eleições livres, justas e transparentes em Angola* [Audit report to the legislative elections of September 5. A contribution to free, fair and transparent elections in Angola] Luanda: UNITA; references to the role of INDRA in the 2008 elections can also be found in European Union Election Observation Mission (2008) *Angola Final Report: Parliamentary Elections, 5 September 2008.* Brussels: European Parliament. pp. 12–13. Available at http://eeas.europa.eu/eueom/pdf/missions/fr_eueom_angola_08_en.pdf [accessed 23 June 2016].

76 Roque PC (2013) *Angola's Second Post-War Elections: The Alchemy Of Change.* Institute for Security Studies (ISS) situation report. Pretoria: ISS. p. 7.

77 According to the law, 'permanent participants' would include: one representative of the executive to support the electoral process; one from each political party or colligation represented at parliament; up to five

same composition was replicated at the Electoral Provincial Commissions and Electoral Municipal Commissions.

The law states the political independence of the CNE and its members through the appointment criteria, based on civic and moral responsibility as well as technical competence, along with the rule determining that CNE commissioners cannot be members of the executive bodies of political parties (the same principles applying to the selection of the CNE members to the local structures at the provincial and municipal levels).[78] As a positive step towards probity, the new law forbade members of the CNE to accumulate other functions while conducting the role of commissioners, namely magistrates and deputies who held other positions in several other administrative bodies at central and local level.[79] This was a response to the criticism expressed by the opposition in the 1992 and 2008 electoral processes and the SADC mission in 2007, against judges (namely the president of the CNE in both elections, Caetano de Sousa) who kept conducting their functions as magistrates after being nominated to the CNE (see above).

Nevertheless, the opposition was still critical of the majority of the MPLA appointees to the CNE, and the appointment of its president by the Supreme Council of the Judiciary (itself an organ mainly appointed by the President of the Republic).

The problem immediately emerged after the approval of the Law on the Organisation of Elections (36/2011), with the selection of Suzana Inglês on 17 January 2012 by the Supreme Council of the Judiciary. Considering that she had been occupying the position since 2010, it was in fact a re-appointment to comply with the new law. According to several opposition parties and civil society organisations such an appointment once again violated the recently approved law (in its art. 143, 1), clearly stating that the new president had to be a judge at the time of appointment and that he/she had to suspend this role with the nomination to the CNE. Suzana Inglês had been a magistrate since 1994 and was a well-known leader of the MPLA's Organisation of Angolan Women.

UNITA and the PRS applied to the Supreme Court which ruled in favour of the complainants on procedural grounds. Suzana Inglês left the position on 17 May 2012. UNITA and the PRS had also sought to nullify all the decisions taken by Suzana Inglês while at the CNE, but the Supreme Court denied this request. In June the new CNE president was nominated, André Silva Neto, and UNITA's selected commissioners to the CNE were finally sworn in, accepting the Supreme Court's decision and the new president.

---

representatives of political parties and colligations not represented at the parliament; one of each political party running to elections after the definite approval of candidates, excluding those already represented under the previous criteria (art. 145, law 36/11, *DR, I*, 21 December (Organic Law on General Elections)).

78 Art. 7, Law 12/2012, *DR, I*, 13 April 2012 (Organic Law on the Organisation and Functioning of the National Electoral Commission).

79 The role of commissioner at the CNE cannot combine with the position of President and Deputy-President of the Republic; minister of parliament; ambassador; magistrate; general attorney and deputy general attorney; provincial governor and deputy provincial governor and any other positions at local administration; positions at local autarchies, art. 44, Law 12/2012, *DR, I*, 13 April 2012 (Organic Law on the Organisation and Functioning of the National Electoral Commission).

In the end, both the MPLA and the opposition do seem to consider their nominated commissioners as their representatives and it is hard to see how the political independence of the organ can be strengthened by such an attitude.

The SADC Parliamentary Forum mission of observation to the Angolan 2012 elections reported 'shortcomings in the selection process for CNE Commissioners',[80] suggesting that:

> [...] in addition to appointing the Chairperson of the CNE, it will be in line with the Norms and Standards for Elections in the SADC Region if the Supreme Council of the Judiciary is mandated to appoint all other commissioners of the CNE before ratification by the National Assembly in order to guarantee greater independence of the Commission [emphasis mine].[81]

Despite those shortcomings, the mission still expressed the:

> [...] overall view that the legal framework within which the CNE is established and operates generally augurs well for the independence and autonomous functioning of the Commission in line with the Norms and Standards for Elections in the SADC Region and the SADC Principles and Guidelines for Democratic Elections [emphasis mine].[82]

Accreditation of party delegates

Again replicating the 2008 elections, problems arose with the accreditation of opposition delegates to the polling stations. For several weeks prior to the election, opposition parties repeatedly accused the CNE of deliberately delaying the accreditation of their delegates, while the CNE alleged that their accreditation did not comply with the established deadlines and procedural requirements. On the Thursday before the election, several members and a candidate of the new party coalition, the Broad Convergence for the Salvation of Angola–Electoral Coalition (CASA-CE), tried to force entry into the CNE building in Luanda to demand their accreditation and ended up being arrested by the police.[83]

Contradicting the law, the CNE did not send the list of registered delegates to each candidate ten days before the election (n4, art. 94, law 36/2011), alleging that parties did not provide the required documents in time. Several parties only received accreditation for their delegates on the eve of election day, which rendered it impossible to dispatch accredited

80 SADC (2012) *Parliamentary Forum Election Observation Mission to the Angola 31st August 2012 General Elections – Interim Mission Statement.* Gaborone: SADC. p. 7.
81 Ibid.
82 Ibid.
83 Coligação para a Observação Eleitoral (COE) (2012) *Relatório Final de Observação das Eleições Gerais de 2012 da Coligação para a Observação Eleitoral 2012* [Final report of observation on the 2012 Angolan general elections, of the Electoral Observation Coalition]. Luanda: COE. p. 5; also Smith D (2012) Angolan president expected to win another term in 'flawed' election. *The Guardian*, 31 August 2012. Available at http://www.theguardian.com/world/2012/aug/31/angolan-president-win-term-election [accessed 1 December 2015].

delegates throughout the whole country.[84] Later, the Constitutional Court referred to these problems while ruling on the complaints of the PRS, CASA-CE and UNITA, and actually recognised the non-compliance of the CNE as well as the complainants (see below).

Although the law provided for each party to have delegates at each polling station, only a small percentage of stations in fact had opposition delegates. On election day (repeating events of 2008) only the MPLA had delegates at each of the 10 349 polling stations and 25 359 polling tables[85] at the 18 provinces and 170 municipalities throughout the country, along with the CNE, which had 170 000 people (comprising 16 000 presiding officers and 12 000 logistical supervisors)[86] to staff all those polling stations and tables. In a few provinces the opposition tried to combine efforts and send out delegates to get larger coverage, but most of the polling stations and tables were left without opposition delegates.[87]

Access to the media

From 2008 onwards, the Angolan media underwent a process of deep restructuring following the new increased economic growth of the country resulting from the oil boom. New pro-regime media corporations owned by the regime elites (e.g. *MediaNova*) developed well-funded, modern outlets, attracting several of the best journalists and opinion-makers[88] and suffocating smaller and relatively independent newspapers, which went bankrupt for lack of advertising (mainly controlled by the regime itself). The Union of Angolan Journalists referred to this fact in a report issued during the electoral campaign, stressing that most of the private newspapers belonged to sectors related to the governing party, and as such represented the oligopoly and monopoly prohibited by the press law.[89]

---

84 Coligação para a Observação Eleitoral (COE) (2012) *Relatório Final de Observação das Eleições Gerais de 2012 da Coligação para a Observação Eleitoral 2012* [Final report of observation on the 2012 Angolan general elections, of the Electoral Observation Coalition]. Luanda: COE. p. 5; also Episcopalian Conference of Angola and São Tome (CEAST) *Report of the CEAST to the 2012 elections.* Available at: http://club-k. net/index.php?option=com_content&view=article&id=13011:conferencia-episcopal-de-angola-e-sao-tome&lang=pt [accessed 25 October 2015].

85 Each polling table had a maximum of 500 registered voters, while in 2008 they had 250.

86 Roque PC (2013) *Angola's Second Post-War Elections: The Alchemy Of Change.* Institute for Security Studies (ISS) situation report. Pretoria: ISS. p. 7.

87 Coligação para a Observação Eleitoral (COE) (2012) *Relatório Final de Observação das Eleições Gerais de 2012 da Coligação para a Observação Eleitoral 2012* [Final report of observation on the 2012 Angolan general elections, of the Electoral Observation Coalition]. Luanda: COE. p. 20; also Episcopalian Conference of Angola and São Tome (CEAST) *Report of the CEAST to the 2012 elections.* Available at: http://club-k. net/index.php?option=com_content&view=article&id=13011:conferencia-episcopal-de-angola-e-sao-tome&lang=pt [accessed 25 October 2015].

88 From the 2008 elections onwards, the group MediaNova launched several new media outlets in Angola besides the TV channel Zimbo – a weekly newspaper *O País* and the radio station *Rádio Mais* in Luanda. On the characterisation of this and other economic groups on their relationship to prominent personalities of the regime see Filipe C (2013) *O Poder Angolano em Portugal* [Angolan Power in Portugal]. Lisboa: Planeta; Costa J, Teixeira Lopes J & Louçã F (2014) *Os Donos Angolanos de Portugal* [The Angolan Owners of Portugal]. Lisbon: Bertrand: Lisbon; Soares de Oliveira R (2005) *Magnificent and Beggar Land: Angola since the Civil War.* London: Hurst.

89 Sindicato de Jornalistas Angolanos (SJA) (2012) *Monitoria da Mídia em Tempo de Eleições.* Luanda: SJA. p. 14.

The strategy went even further, with the new media corporations investing in several of the most important Portuguese media corporations, where criticism of the regime had been common for years as a space used by Angolan critics to voice their complaints and to reach the international arena.[90]

Consequently, the tone of criticism in the private media in Angola and Portugal towards the government was less aggressive. A more professional display was put on, integrating several reports on positions assumed by the opposition but always keeping them from detracting from the image of the party in power and its candidate.

In view of the 2012 elections, once again all the usual tactics and strategies were set in motion with the state administration, resources and logistics at the service of the MPLA and its candidate, especially the state media (TPA 1, RNA and *Jornal de Angola*). As previously mentioned, a new private TV channel, Zimbo, was created in 2008 and started broadcasting in 2009 but, as reported, it was owned by *MediaNova*, and therefore closely related to the regime and with an editorial line within the limits of 'political correctness' to the party in government and its candidate.

The 'new' private media introduced modern layouts and attractive design. They hired several expatriate cadres recruited in Portugal, and added a more professional tone to the reports, which complied with the appearance of respect for pluralism, but were still effectively under close control of the regime. Ironically, the new private newspapers indirectly contributed to the extinction of the most politically inconvenient 'old' private press, which had been left without advertising, were printed badly and full of careless mistakes.

Although it must be recognised that the old private press had serious financial handicaps and editorial flaws, they nevertheless partially filled the void by voicing criticism of the regime.

In a few cases, the new private media did actually escape central control, proving at times the 'danger' of hiring professional journalists used to operating according to standard reporting procedures with some autonomy. Such was the case, for instance, of the previously mentioned Deloitte review of the flaws in the electoral registry, which was leaked and published by *Novo Jornal*.[91] Nonetheless, these episodes were the exception.

In the end, the party and its government greatly reinforced their influence over the public and private media. National radio broadcasts remained exclusive to the state-owned RNA, and the Catholic Church Radio Ecclesia abandoned its quest for national broadcasting rights when in December 2012 (three months after elections), they announced the decision to drop their petition and give up on their protracted battle to expand their broadcast coverage. Although it is true that this radio station had in recent years (mainly

---

90 Filipe C (2013) *O Poder Angolano em Portugal* [Angolan Power in Portugal]. Lisboa: Planeta; Costa J, Teixeira Lopes J & Louçã F (2014) *Os Donos Angolanos de Portugal* [The Angolan Owners of Portugal]. Lisbon: Bertrand: Lisbon; Soares de Oliveira R (2005) *Magnificent and Beggar Land: Angola since the Civil War.* London: Hurst.

91 *Novo Jornal*, 28 September 2012.

from 2011 onwards) been changing its editorial line, stressing religious issues over more politically sensitive issues, it was nevertheless a good source of non-partisan information. The focus of the editorial line on religious issues and the decision to give up on expanding their broadcast coverage gave rise to enormous political speculation[92] and certainly paid lip service to pluralism of opinion in the media and to the democratisation process itself.

In compliance with the law, during the month-long electoral campaign all candidate parties had access to five minutes of national television airtime and ten minutes of radio broadcasting (art. 73, n1, law 36/2011). However, obviously reflecting a difference in funding, there was a stark contrast between the technical quality, editorial structuring and production of the MPLA radio and television programmes and those of the opposition.

The 2012 public media coverage of the elections was undoubtedly biased in favour of the MPLA and its candidate. The public media coverage reached the level of propaganda, prior to and especially during the electoral campaign, with endless and constantly repeated reports on each and every ruling party, state and presidential event, giving them an incredible amount of airtime and space.[93] National television and radio reports went back and forth from a party event to a state event to a presidential event, from declarations made by government officials to party officials (sometimes the same person at different events), further confusing party and state and thereby directly helping the campaign of both the MPLA and its presidential candidate.

Once again in a repeat of 2008, as elections drew closer, the party, state, government and president became one, as reflected in the public media and some of the private outlets, reporting on the massive programme of public works inaugurated by government officials/ party candidates and the president, also inaugurating private buildings and projects with visible impact on society (especially hotels in the provinces, along with major industrial and agricultural private-investment projects). Again, at these inaugural events it was commonplace to see symbols of the party and the Republic mixed up together on caps, t-shirts and banners.

The public newspaper *Jornal de Angola*, the most read in the whole country and with the largest number of printed copies, reaching all the provinces, followed its television and radio counterpart's bias in favour of the MPLA as reported by the Angolan Journalists' Union Media Monitoring Report. According to the Union only the MPLA had access to prominent space and the use of photographs on the front page. The rest of the candidates only appeared in small, marginal spaces on the front page or if they were being reported

---

92 See article Angolan government tightens its grip on Radio Ecclesia (2014, 28 March). Angolan News Network. Available at http://www.angolanewsnetwork.com/news/2014/3/28/angolan-government-tightens-its-grip-on-radio-ecclesia.html [accessed 1 December 2015].

93 Sindicato de Jornalistas Angolanos (SJA) (2012) *Monitoria da Mídia em Tempo de Eleições*. Luanda: SJA. This monitoring report analysed 11 newspapers (*Folha 8, O País, A Capital, Agora, Semanário Angolense, Angolense, Novo Jornal, Jornal de Angola, O Independente, Continente, Factual*), five Rádios (*RNA, LAC, Mais, 2000, Morena*), representations of the National Radio in four provinces (Huíla, Huambo, Benguela and Cabinda) and two TV channels (National Television – TPA 1 and *Zimbo*).

on negatively, 'especially UNITA which is frequently dealt with in a negative tone'.[94] The same report criticised two specific sections of *Jornal de Angola*, '*Ditos & Feitos Eleitorais*' (elections, all said and done) and '*Diários da Campanha*' (election campaign diary), associated with opinion and editorial articles, saying that those spaces,

> [...] can demonstrate deep hate and favour the MPLA. Therefore, in general, the readers and potential voters do not have the opportunity to observe debates between candidates (complete absence of opposing views) and can only access one program of government and one electoral manifest: the one from the party which ended its mandate.[95]

Contrary to their silence during the 2008 elections (see above), the Journalists' Union issued a statement during the 2012 electoral campaign accusing the private and public media of gross and intolerant violation of the laws regulating journalism, especially in the electoral period.[96]

The same type of criticism, denouncing the partiality of the public media, was expressed by the Episcopalian Conference of Angola and São Tomé (CEAST) report,

> The state media, namely the Angolan Public Television, Angolan National Radio and Angolan Newspaper *Jornal de Angola*, were not impartial prior, during or after elections, clearly favouring the party in power and conceding little space to opposing perspectives. Guest commentators had usually and excessive uniformity of language and perspectives. *Jornal de Angola* was too hostile to the opposition parties, without discerning between information service and propaganda.[97]

Prior to the elections, the National Council for the Media (CNCS) praised the President of the Republic's decision to dismiss the Councils of Administration of the National Radio and Television (deliberation of 29 of June). The measure was in accordance with the Council's previously expressed concerns, seen as an attempt to improve the quality of those public services in respect of plurality and impartiality. However, after the elections, the CNCS ended up criticising the public media's behaviour.

---

94 Sindicato de Jornalistas Angolanos (SJA) (2012) *Monitoria da Mídia em Tempo de* Eleições. Luanda: SJ. p. 14.
95 Ibid.: 14–15.
96 Coligação para a Observação Eleitoral (COE) (2012) *Relatório Final de Observação das Eleições Gerais de 2012 da Coligação para a Observação Eleitoral 2012* [Final report of observation on the 2012 Angolan general elections, of the Electoral Observation Coalition]. Luanda: COE. p. 15.
97 Episcopalian Conference of Angola and São Tome (CEAST) *Report of the CEAST to the 2012 elections.* Available at: http://club-k.net/index.php?option=com_content&view=article&id=13011:conferencia-episcopal-de-angola-e-sao-tome&lang=pt [accessed 25 October 2015].

The New Year's message of the CNCS president warned of the 'worrying evaluation' of the Angolan public media's performance during elections, with its 'lack of impartiality as mentioned in the totality of electoral observation reports produced by national and foreign entities'.[98]

At the end of 2012, and in compliance with the new law (art. 8, n2, law 7/2006, replacing law 22/1991), new regulations for the CNCS were to be approved that would increase its powers of intervention and specify its mandate, composition, organisation and functioning. However, the new regulatory law has not been implemented and the CNCS still has the same composition as set by the regulatory law 7/1992 and the mandates of its members have long since expired.

The new law reduces the number of members to be appointed by the opposition, preventing the Journalists' Union from appointing a member and imposing the selection of the president by MPLA-appointed members only. The CNCS would be reduced to seven members appointed by parliament (three by the majority party, two by the opposition in general, one by a journalists' assembly organised by the ethics commission – no longer appointed by the Journalists' Union as in the previous CNCS law – and one from the Conference of Angolan Christian Churches – CICA). The president of the CNCS is chosen by the majority party (no longer by the Judiciary Council) and the deputy-president is elected from among the general council's members (art. 13. n1 & 2). Probity rules attempt to sustain the independence of the CNCS by stating that its members cannot have business interests in media corporations and, in the two years prior to their appointment, cannot have had positions in the journalists' union, editorial desks of media corporations, political parties or political associations, state organs, or have been members of any national security forces (art. 12. n1).

According to journalists interviewed in the course of this research, given the majority party's control over the ethics commission and the reduced number of members chosen by the opposition, the council would become much more politically influenced by the majority party than it is already. The spokesperson of the CNCS, Joaquim Paulo, explained that there has been some resistance to renewing the composition of the CNCS' general council under the new law, insofar as the opposition would lose relevance in it. According to him, the CNCS should be much more technical than political.[99] Such statements reveal the effective political dependency of the organ under the old and new regulations, the difference being the degree of influence by the MPLA, which has increased as a result of the new regulations.

It must be noted that CNCS regulations and composition were the same in 2008 (with its toothless behaviour in the face of outright violations of the press law by the public

---

98 New Years's message from the CNCS president (2012, 27 December). CNCS-Angola. Available at http://cncs-angola.blogspot.com.br/ [accessed 1 December 2015].

99 Voice of America Radio News (2012) *CNCS em Angola com mandato expirado*. 9 April 2012. Available at http://www.voaportugues.com/content/conselho-nacional-de-comunicao-social-em-angola-com-mandato-expirado/2713053.html [accessed 1 December 2015].

media) and in 2012, with relatively more powers of intervention, providing a few critical deliberations as previously mentioned, but still unable to issue any direct appraisals during the electoral period (August 2012) when it was most needed. On June 2012 the council approved a deliberation on the correct media procedures for covering the campaign, but remained silent through the entire campaign, issuing a new deliberation only in October, after the elections, when it was already irrelevant to the process. In the end, the real issue at stake in this discussion is not very different to the discussion on the CNE's composition and the battle over the political influence of such organs.

Given all the problems with the operation of the CNCS, it is important to stress that The Declaration of Principles on Freedom of Expression in Africa recommends self-regulation as a preferable solution to the establishment of such a regulatory body.[100] Therefore, in view of the 2017 elections, it would probably be much more fruitful for this recommendation to be acted upon as part of an eventual media-regulation restructuring process.

Electoral observation and reported problems

The lack of opposition party access to the media was noted by the majority of national and international election observers, but this was more of a problem than in the previous (2008) election, especially at international level.

In general terms, the new law on electoral observation (11/2012, 22 March) complies with SADC norms and rules on electoral observation, which was ratified by the Angolan state as a member of SADC.[101] However, taking advantage of large prerogatives permitted by that same law, the CNE took several decisions that in practice constrained international and national observers.

As a result of the quality and credibility of the 2008 EU EOM report, there was no invitation to an observer mission from the EU for the 2012 elections. International observers were basically limited to SADC, the Community of Portuguese-Speaking Countries and the African Union (AU), which from the 2008 experience could be seen as much more government-friendly than other international electoral observation missions, such as the EU.

The law allowed diplomatic missions accredited in the country to appoint any of their members to observe the elections (art. 18, law 11/2012). Nonetheless, the government reminded those missions of a set of rules determined by law that they had to respect, which included a ban on public statements about observations on the process (art. 33 p. & e., law 11/2012), the need to communicate in advance their mission's objectives (art. 3, law 11/2012), the intended areas of observation (art. 28, n3, law 11/2012), and the responsibility of the state to assure the security of all national and international observers (art. 6 n2, law

---

100 African Commission on Human and Peoples' Rights (2002) *Declaration of Principles on Freedom of Expression in Africa*, 32nd Session, 17–23 October 2002, Banjul, The Gambia.

101 Including the SADC Principles and Guidelines Governing Democratic Elections, the SADC Parliamentary Forum Norms and Standards for Elections in the SADC Region, and the SADC Election Commissioners' Forum (SADC-ECF) and Electoral Institute of Southern Africa (EISA) Principles for Election Management, Monitoring and Observation in the SADC Region.

11/2012). Any malpractice or complaints observed should be reported first to the CNE before any other entity (art. 33 c., law 11/2012) via a report template supplied by the CNE to all national and international observers; all observation reports had to be first sent to the CNE before being made public (art. 33 f.). Observers' accreditation could be revoked at any time if compliance with the established rules wasn't followed (art. 33 n2, law 11/2012).

Finally, despite the evident problem of access to the public media, international observers and their reports basically praised the peaceful and mature way in which the elections took place, generally considering them transparent, 'free and fair' with an extremely government-friendly tone.[102] The head of the AU mission, Pedro Pires (former president of Cape-Vert), was the only one who pointed out the problems observers had attaining accreditation, besides the more commonly mentioned problem of unequal access to the state media.[103]

As for national observers, accreditation became an even more tortuous and difficult process at central and local level than in 2008. At central level several difficulties arose due to procedural and technical issues, and were aggravated at local level by the CNE's decision to centralise the whole process by insisting all applications should be directly sent to the CNE in Luanda. This decision came about late in the process and the provincial electoral commissions that had already received applications could not forward these to Luanda and only informed the applicants after the deadline had expired, preventing many observers from getting their accreditation. Another contested decision of the CNE was the limiting of the number of national electoral observers to 3000, a number far below the 10 349 polling stations.[104] All these problems were later heavily criticised in the civil society organisations' reports as well as in the CEAST report.[105]

Only two groups of national observers managed to have a minimally structured observation team, covering more than a couple of provinces and showing a methodological commitment towards impartiality: namely the previously mentioned reports of the CEAST[106] (covering 12 of Angola's 18 provinces with 13 observers, but unable to get accreditation for the remaining five observers initially allowed by the CNE)[107] and the

102 SADC (2012) *Parliamentary Forum Election Observation Mission to the Angola 31st August 2012 General Elections – Interim Mission Statement.* Gaborone: SADC. p. 14.
103 Angola election judged 'free and fair' by African Union. (2012, 2 September). BBC News online. Available at http://www.bbc.com/news/world-africa-19460914 [accessed 13 December 2015].
104 Coligação para a Observação Eleitoral (COE) (2012) *Relatório Final de Observação das Eleições Gerais de 2012 da Coligação para a Observação Eleitoral 2012* [Final report of observation on the 2012 Angolan general elections, of the Electoral Observation Coalition]. Luanda: COE. p. 18.
105 Ibid.; also Episcopalian Conference of Angola and São Tome (CEAST) *Report of the CEAST to the 2012 elections.* Available at: http://club-k.net/index.php?option=com_content&view=article&id=13011:confere ncia-episcopal-de-angola-e-sao-tome&lang=pt [accessed 25 October 2015].
106 We are here considering CEAST as a national observer insofar as most of its observers and coordinators were Angolan.
107 CEAST could not get accreditation for observers in the provinces of Cabinda, Zaire, Namibe, Lunda Sul and Huambo.

Coalition to Electoral Observation (COE 2012) (a group of seven credible civil society organisations who observed the elections in nine provinces).[108]

Despite all the difficulties in getting accreditation as well as the limited numbers of observers, it must be stressed that these organisations' reports were much more incisive and reliable than the international ones. They courageously reported on: the accreditation problems for observers and opposition delegates; the unavailability of voters' rolls; the non-compliance with the law on electoral conduct by several candidates (mentioning the MPLA, UNITA and CASA-CE); and the intolerance, intimidation and violent incidents occurring during the months prior to elections. Moreover, the CEAST report abstained from calling the process free and fair, while the COE 2012, despite acknowledging the incidents affecting the transparency and credibility of the process, did consider the elections free, fair and peaceful. It is worth noting that none of these organisations observed in the problematic province of Cabinda, which according to the opposition repeated the malpractices of 2008 (reported by the EU EOM; see above) with allegations that foreigners were voting in that province, as well as in Lunda-North and Kwando-Kubango.[109]

As reported by most international and national observers, behaviour was a generally peaceful behaviour during the campaign and on election day. However, one cannot ignore the numerous incidents of violence, political intolerance and arbitrary arrests in 2012, before and after the elections, several of which being mentioned in the national observers' reports.

The police prevented the majority of peaceful anti-government demonstrations from taking place and made use of excessive violence to crack down on several actual demonstrations. Selecting only the most noteworthy reports, on 10 March 2012, security agents in plainclothes attacked a crowd of 40 demonstrators in the Cazenga neighbourhood on the outskirts of Luanda. On the same day security agents in plainclothes brutally assaulted a senior opposition politician from the Democratic Bloc, Filomeno Vieira Lopes, during a demonstration in the city centre.[110] On 12 March, police raided the newspaper *Folha 8*'s office, run by William Tonnet, a journalist known for his criticism of the regime (who later adhered to CASA-CE) and confiscated the paper's equipment on charges of 'outrage against the president', an offence under the 2010 crimes against the security of the state.[111] On 10 May 2012, a UNITA municipal secretary in Huambo was killed in a sequence of attacks by alleged MPLA supporters, who also allegedly destroyed a UNITA convention area.[112]

---

108 COE was able to monitor nine provinces and 28 municipalities (presumably with 28 observers, although that is not specified in their report): Benguela (3 municipalities); Cuanza Sul (5); Huambo (5); Huila (3); Luanda (5); Lunda Norte (1); Lunda Sul (3); Mexico (1); Uíge (2).

109 From private interview with Isaias Samakuva, president of UNITA in September 2012.

110 Human Rights Watch (2013) *World Report 2013: Angola: Events of 2012.* p. 4 Available at https://www.hrw.org/sites/default/files/related_material/angola_4.pdf [accessed 30 September 2015].

111 Ibid.: 3.

112 Voice of America Radio News (2012) *Huambo: Violência entre elementos da UNITA e do MPLA faz 1 morto e vários feridos* [Huambo: violence between members of the MPLA and UNITA ends up with one death and several wounded]. Available at http://www.voaportugues.com/content/angola-violencia/1659634.

Finally, the most publicly known cases of the so-called 'revolutionary youth' cannot go without mention. This movement spread via social networking sites, gathering together urban/suburban students and singers of rap, hip hop and *kuduru* to publicly speak out against the president and the regime. The movement slowly emerged after the end of the war, gaining increased inspiration and motivation in 2010/2011 from the so-called Arab Spring. Several opposition political parties hoped to attract a few of these new leaders and their rebelliousness to their ranks in view of the 2012 elections. However, besides denouncing the political manipulation of the public and private media, the judicial and legislative systems, and of the electoral process and results, they also rejected the dynamics of partisan politics.[113]

Several public demonstrations by these groups of youngsters took place, mainly in Luanda since the first trimester of 2011, through 2012 and afterwards, involving between a dozen and a hundred people depending on the occasion.[114] The regime has always reacted with disproportionate violence despite there being a relatively small number of dispersed young individuals or small groups of individuals who are very active in web-based social networks, but don't have any significant mass mobilisation capacity. Several members of those groups have been arrested, beaten, questioned and released at several of those demonstrations, especially in 2011 and 2012 as elections approached.[115]

After elections, the violent break up of this youth movement's demonstrations took place between 20–24 June 2015. The National Directorate for Criminal Investigation raided several of their members' homes in Luanda and arrested 15 of them after they had attended a meeting to discuss politics and governance in the country. The country's Interior Ministry released a public statement on 20 June saying they were suspected of planning to disrupt public order and security. On 16 September 2015 the 15 detainees and two others were formally charged with preparing for a 'rebellion' and 'plotting against the president'. The trial of the 17 activists, which began on 16 November 2015, had enormous international repercussions. A verdict is expected sometime in 2016.[116]

This repressive attitude towards dissident socio-political movements does not augur well for the democratisation process in view of the anticipated 2017 elections. Such repression should be challenged with reference to the human rights' principles largely protected by

---

html [accessed 30 September 2015].

113 For a comprehensive analysis of this movement see Vidal N (2015) Angolan civil society activism since the 1990s: reformists, confrontationists and young revolutionaries of the 'Arab spring generation'. *Review of African Political Economy*, 42(143): 77–91.

114 Demonstrations of these youngsters occurred on several occasions, the most relevant as follows: 7 March, 3 September, 3 December 2011; 10 March (Luanda and Benguela), 14 July, 22 December 2012; 30 March, 27 May, 19 September 2013; 23 November 2014.

115 See Human Rights Watch (2012) Angola: Violent crackdown on critics; Increasing violence and threats raise concerns about 2012 Elections. Available at https://www.hrw.org/news/2012/04/02/angola-violent-crackdown-critics [accessed 30 Setptember 2015].

116 See Amnesty International coverage on this case at https://www.amnesty.org/en/latest/news/2015/12/angola-kangaroo-court-undermines-judicial-independence-as-trial-of-activists-enters-fourth-week/ [accessed 22 December 2015].

the constitution and Angolan law in conformity with the international and regional treaties of which Angola is a signatory.

Financing of political parties

Despite the economic oil boom and the massive availability of funds for public investment, funding for the electoral campaigns of political parties and coalitions (provided for by Law 10/2012, 22 March) was significantly reduced. On 12 July 2012, the President of the Republic (head of the government) approved an amount of about USD 800 000 of public funding for each of the nine contesting political parties and coalitions, while in the 2008 elections the public funding approved by the Council of Ministers had been about USD 1.2 million for each of the ten political parties and four coalitions (USD 17 million in total).

Not only did the campaign funds decrease, but they were only made available to the opposition a month prior to elections, as had happened at the 2008 elections. This delay again significantly crippled the opposition's already meagre capacity to campaign outside the capital city and the main provincial capitals. Campaign materials could not be ordered and made available in time for the campaign.

In addition to the funding issues, internal factionalism within opposition parties weakened their preparedness, with the most affected parties being the FNLA, PRS and the PDP-ANA. Factions aggressively contested the leadership of their parties, accusing them of being funded and supported by the MPLA.

In the case of the PRS, the challenger, António Muachicungo, was expelled from the party, but he applied to the Constitutional Court and got a favourable decision that ruled for his re-admission into the party in May 2011. Still unable to get enough internal support to depose the incumbent president (Eduardo Kwangana), Muachicungo decided to create his own party, the United Front for Change in Angola (FUMA), which was cleared by the Constitutional Court and authorised to participate in the 2012 elections. The FNLA president, NGola Kabango (whose leadership had been under attack since the death of former president, Holden Roberto, in August 2007, but recognised as legitimate by the Supreme Court in 2008), ended up being deposed in a sequence of a new decisions by the same Supreme Court in 2011, which ruled him out in favour of the long-time contestant Lucas NGonda. Despite the fact that Kabango's faction managed to collect 21 304 signatures, well beyond the 15 000 required by law, the Constitutional Court did not authorise his faction to run for the elections. In the case of the PDP-ANA a contestant failed to depose the president Sediangani Mbimbi, but even so, the Constitutional Court excluded the party from the elections on procedural grounds (see below).[117]

Aside from UNITA and CASA-CE, the rest of the opposition had poorly funded and poorly organised campaigns: they lacked advertising material, were unable to campaign

---

117 From private interviews with Ngola Kabango (FNLA), Eduardo Kwangana (PRS), Sediangani Mbinmi (PDP-ANA); Luanda, September 2012.

outside the main provincial capital cities, and several of them even lacked the capacity to campaign in the 18 provincial capitals. Although far behind the MPLA campaign, UNITA and CASA-CE were nevertheless able to cover all the provinces and to present a minimally organised campaign with supporting logistics, advertising material for scheduled events, and with political plans and policies presented clearly as a coherent programme. Their airtime broadcasts were professionally edited and structured, although still lacking the quality presented by the MPLA.

UNITA showed that despite all the difficulties affecting the movement following its military defeat in 2002, it managed to re-organise and re-activate itself in the provinces, especially in its historical strongholds on the central plateau. The movement managed to imbue its structures with a civilian character, leaving behind its image of an armed movement/party of the Savimbi period. As for CASA-CE, presided over by UNITA dissident, Abel Chivukuvuku, the coalition was in fact the new big thing on the opposition. It managed to absorb several smaller political forces and even dissidents from the MPLA into a new political project that grew in organisation and reach all over the country throughout the 2012 elections and afterwards.

Once again, in stark contrast with the opposition, the MPLA campaign was even more ostentatious than in 2008. It was professionally organised by Brazilian political marketing companies. It had a presence in each and every municipality and village, hosted major events and demonstrations, was extremely well-funded with loads of widespread campaign material, it subsidised food and drink during the mega-events of the party campaign and hired popular music celebrities to perform. The entire campaign was once again carefully articulated through the inauguration of intensive public works programmes in all the 18 provinces by government officials/party officials and the President of the Republic/ president of the party. The inaugurations involved the party's mass organisations, which used state administration resources and logistics. All the events were fully and intensively covered by the public and private media (see above).

Despite the massive investment by the government in public works, infrastructure and even social programmes, the electoral victory of 2012 was smaller than in 2008. Nevertheless, the MPLA was still assured of a qualified majority of 71.84% of the votes (corresponding to 175 parliamentary seats) against 18.66% for UNITA (32 seats). An 'unexpected' 6% achieved by the CASA-CE electoral coalition (eight seats) transformed it into the third political force in Angola. The remaining seats were distributed between the PRS (three seats corresponding to 1.7% of the vote) and the FNLA (two seats corresponding to 1.13% of the vote). Abstention tripled to 37.2% compared to 1992 (12.5%) and 2008 (12.64%), with a turnout of only 62.77% of the 9 757 671 registered voters out of a total population estimated by the UNDP to be about 19.6 million.

Judicial power and the 2012 electoral process

Once again the opposition complained about the political influence exerted by the MPLA over the judicial system, especially over the Constitutional Court. Alleged examples of such influence were the decisions of the Constitutional Court to reject the applications of well-known parties to run in the elections: the PDP-ANA led by Sediangani MBimbi (with a significant constituency among the Bakongo returnees group in Luanda and in the northern provinces); the FNLA group led by NGola Kabango in favour of the FNLA section led by Lucas NGonda, thus contributing to split an historical party and its constituency (see above); the *Bloco Democratico* (BD) led by Justino Pinto de Andrade (a party of intellectuals and opinion-makers with deep influence among the urban milieu); and the *Partido Popular* (PP) led by David Mendes (a well-known human rights' lawyer, facing the regime in numerous politically sensitive lawsuits).[118]

The Constitutional Court rejected a total of 18 applications, but the trials involving those parties raised serious concerns about political interference due to the potential impact on electoral results and especially on the abnormal levels of abstention (37.2%; see above). The Constitutional Court decisions in each case were mainly based on procedural grounds, usually alleging non-compliance with the number of endorsing signatures required by law. The law requires that, up to 60 days before elections, all political parties have to present documentary proof of a minimum of 14 000 supporters (500 in each of the 18 provincial circles and 5 000 for the national circle) and the same citizen cannot endorse more than one party (art. 51, 4 & 5, law 36/2011). The court alleged that the signatures presented by most of those parties were not properly documented and validated and therefore did not comply with the law's requirements.

However, it is hard to understand how those parties with a relatively long existence, with previous experience in parliament and proven constituencies in several provinces, did not manage to get the sufficient number of signatures while other newcomers that no one had ever heard of did manage to get them.[119] Speculation increased when it became clear that most of the newcomers were not credible opposition parties. When observing the radio and television airtime of parties such as the United Front for Change in Angola (FUMA), the Council for Political Opposition (CPO), the Popular Party for Development (PAPOD) and the New Democracy (ND),[120] it became clear that they essentially used their

---

118 From private interviews with Sediangani Mbimbi (PDP-ANA), Justino Pinto de Andrade and Filomeno Vieira Lopes (FpD), Ngola Kabango (FNLA), David Mendes (PP), Luanda, September 2012.

119 The exception was the PP, created prior to the 2012 elections, but even in this case there was a proven constituency in several provinces due to the path of its leader and the Human Rights association that he led for so many years – *Mãos Livres*. As for the BD, it was a reformulation of the previous FpD, which held a parliamentary seat from 1992 to 2008 and was extinct by law for not having achieved the minimum number of votes required by law in the 2008 election. A new party congress transformed the party into BD.

120 From these parties the only one that was not a newcomer was New Democracy, which had surprised everybody in 2008 coming out of the blue and getting one parliamentary seat, by then also raising serious suspicions of being sponsored by the party in power. Once again in 2012, the party had a weak electoral performance and from its airtime confirmed its proximity to the party in power. However, this time it could not get any seat and according to the law it was extinct. Contrary to what happened to BD in 2008, which went through an extinction process but was transformed by its members into BD, the ND did not transform itself under a different denomination, its leaders and members simply and quietly vanished from the political scene after the 2012 elections, again adding suspicions about its credibility and mentoring. The author interviewed the leader of ND, Quintino Moreira, in September 2008 and

time to attack other opposition parties (mainly UNITA and occasionally the CASA-CE, the major MPLA challengers). They often praised the MPLA government and its deeds, limiting their campaign to a few vague slogans instead of presenting their own political programme. Their campaigns were virtually non-existent and without supporters in the field.

The requirement that the same citizen cannot support more than one party significantly restricts gathering the required number of properly authorised signatures. The party is unable to check if the supporter had not previously signed for a different party, rendering his second signature invalid by the time the Constitutional Court pronounces on applications and processes (art. 51, 5, law 36/2011). Moreover, within a system so deeply permeated by the same party dominating the state and administrative structures since independence, with a long tradition of clientelism and decades of civil war, it is understandable that many citizens might fear reprisals for endorsing an opposition party. The suppression of the rule that one citizen can only endorse one party would be a major advance for the democratisation and peace-making process.[121]

Evidence of alleged electoral fraud and malpractices occurring in several provinces besides Luanda were filed by three opposition parties – the CASA-CE, UNITA and the PRS – and they all laid complaints with the CNE. The FNLA that did not file their own fraud complaint, but expressed their agreement with the fraud complaints presented by UNITA and the CASA-CE and corroborated the evidence with reports from their delegates at several polling tables.[122] The CNE dismissed this evidence and ruled the complaints as unfounded. The three parties appealed to the Constitutional Court as the final court of appeal, which ruled in favour of the CNE in all three cases.

Surprisingly, for usually the judiciary is in full support of the executive, one of the judges – Maria da Conceição Melo — voted against the majority decision in all three cases. She explained that some of the allegations and evidence could not simply be dismissed, and that there were several flaws in the CNE procedures with serious implications for the safeguarding of citizens' fundamental rights that should have been taking into account by the court. She therefore demanded further investigation.[123]

was impressed with the lack of party structure, organisation, cadres, political message or program. The president of the party could not even provide any specific explanation on votes obtained according to provinces, the campaigning events, number of members in each province, names of provincial representatives and so on and so forth. In 2012, as in 2008, the author monitored almost every day of the national television and radio broadcasting campaign of political parties throughout August 2012. The same opinion to the 2012 elections was expressed by other authors, see Roque PC (2013) *Angola's Second Post-War Elections: The Alchemy Of Change*. Institute for Security Studies (ISS) situation report. Pretoria: ISS. pp. 5–6.

121 Standing for the suppression of that rule see also Coligação para a Observação Eleitoral (COE) (2012) *Relatório Final de Observação das Eleições Gerais de 2012 da Coligação para a Observação Eleitoral 2012* [Final report of observation on the 2012 Angolan general elections, of the Electoral Observation Coalition]. Luanda: COE. pp. 10–11.

122 From private interview with Lucas Ngonda, Luanda September 2015.

123 See Constitutional Court Resolution 226/2012, Process 294-D/2012 [presented by UNITA]; Constitutional Resolution 225/2012, Process 293-D/2012 [presented by PRS]; Constitutional Resolution 224/2012,

The position taken by the judge was mostly unexpected. It might simply be an isolated judge who refused to go with the consensus in the face of what she considered to be a gross misevaluation of the facts; or it could be seen as the first breach of political influence over the judiciary that might eventually lead to the necessary and constitutionally protected separation of powers and the independence of the judiciary. However, given the Angolan political, institutional and constitutional context and remembering recent history, expectations must be kept low.

The fact that it was a female judge who spoke out is even more striking and leads us to make a final observation on gender. The 2012 elections saw an increase in the number of women elected to parliament, currently occupying 29% of the seats, with special reference to the MPLA, UNITA and CASA-CE comprising 25–30% of women in their parliamentary caucuses.[124]

Conclusion

From the analysis provided we can clearly observe two different dimensions that need addressing: one at the macro-level, comprising structural and long-term issues; and a second dimension at the micro-level, with the more specific, short-term issues to deal with.

Starting with the macro or structural-level, we should refer to the more general question of the conflation of state, party and government structures. This conflation was also noticed by the SADC mission that observed the voters' registry in 2007, recommending that the 'government should seriously consider the separation of powers between the state, government and the party to avoid conflicts of interest in resolving electoral disputes'.[125]

Or as also noticed by the EU parliamentary delegation to the 2008 elections, 'Angola should move to a true multiparty system; this implies a change towards a culture of pluralism'.[126]

The immediate consequences of such structural problems can be seen at the micro-level, with the ongoing power struggle, disputes and consequent suspicion to control each and every step and organ related to the electoral process: namely the voters' registry; the electoral management body (composition and mandate); the National Council for the Media (composition and mandate); the public and private media administration boards; the logistics and supporting services to elections; the accreditation of party delegates to polling stations; the accreditation of national and international observers; the financing of political parties; the judicial power related to electoral disputes; and to the nomination of

Process 295-B/2012 [presented by CASA-CE].

124 See Human Rights Watch (2013) *World Report 2013: Angola: Events of 2012*. Available at https://www. hrw.org/sites/default/files/related_material/angola_4.pdf [accessed 30 September 2015].

125 SADC (2007) *Voter Registration Observer Mission Report – Angola 2007*. Windhoek: SADC Parliamentary Forum. p. 22.

126 Hall F (2008) *Report of the Delegation to Observe Parliamentary Elections in Angola*. Brussels: European Parliament. p. 9. Available at http://www.europarl.europa.eu/intcoop/election_observation/missions/2004-2009/20080905angolareport.pdf [accessed 23 June 2016].

members to electoral organs. Both the government and the opposition are still primarily focused on (i) disputes and negotiations to get 'their' representatives into all the organs related to the elections; and (ii) keeping legislation that supports their objectives.

In the end, the reputational and procedural damage to the electoral process as a result of this squabbling illuminates the contested legitimacy of the party in power, all state institutions and the entire political system.

Recommendations: 2017 elections

Judicial power

An important first step would be to follow the SADC recommendations to the CNE in 2007, whereby:

> ... in addition to appointing the Chairperson of the CNE, it will be in line with the Norms and Standards for Elections in the SADC Region if the Supreme Council of the Judiciary is mandated to appoint all other commissioners of the CNE before ratification by the National Assembly in order to guarantee greater independence of the Commission.[127]

Accordingly, it would also be important to have new legislation that strongly reinforces in practice the independence of the judiciary through self-regulation mechanisms that deal with the selection and appointment of judges.

Registration

Although it was not taken into consideration for the 2012 election, the SADC mission's recommendation about the 2007 registry is still valid today:

> For future voter registration and elections management, Government should seriously consider using a single independent electoral management body to avoid confusion and to enhance transparency and credibility as opposed to the current arrangement where both the MAT and the NEC [CNE] were involved in the process.[128]

After two peaceful elections (2008 and 2012), it is about time the CNE effectively assumed the leading role in the management of elections by preparing a properly and timely audited voters' register, and by thoroughly training electoral staff and observers at polling stations, as well as parties' delegates at polling stations and tables. Flaws within these processes have

---

127 SADC (2012) *Parliamentary Forum Election Observation Mission to the Angola 31st August 2012 General Elections – Interim Mission Statement.* Gaborone: SADC. p. 7.

128 SADC (2007) *Voter Registration Observer Mission Report – Angola 2007.* Windhoek: SADC Parliamentary Forum. p. 22.

been noticed by international and national observers (as well as the Constitutional Court during the 2012 election) in every election. These flaws have detrimental consequences for the credibility and transparency of the process. These recommendations were once again rightly stressed by the CEAST report on the 2012 elections, but have not been taken into consideration three years after the elections and less than two years before the 2017 elections.

Effective permanent structures between elections

It is important to remember that according to the law, CNE structures at central and local levels should be: permanent and have premises in Luanda and the provinces; provided with adequate equipment and supporting services; and funded with an annual budget of USD 300 million per year. Nevertheless, there is no visible activity between elections, as bemoaned by some CNE members[129] and observed by the author. This lack of activity between elections seems to be even more striking at local levels where it has been most needed.

Another possible measure for reinforcing CNE effectiveness and credibility would be to recover the 1992 role of National Director of the Elections. The director would implement and coordinate procedural tasks and mechanisms between elections, namely: the much-needed training of polling staff and national observers; an audit of the voters' registry and of the information system; communication between central and local CNE structures (administrative and supportive services as well as data communication systems); the training and accreditation of parties' delegates to the polling stations and tables; and the accreditation of national and international observers.

The candidate for such a position should be chosen by two-thirds of parliamentarians from a list of names of well-known personalities and based on their work experience and recognised merit. An innovative way to add to the credibility of the position, and to the electoral management process in general as well, would be to nominate a regionally (Southern African or African) and internationally respected personage.

The suppression of the rule that one citizen can only endorse one party would also be a major advance for the democratisation and peace-making process.[130]

National Council for the Media

The National Council for the Media experiences the same problems, with political parties struggling to influence its composition and mandate. Here, once again, it would be important to follow the recommendations provided by The Declaration of Principles

---

129 From private interviews with CNE members in Luanda, September 2015.
130 Standing for the suppression of that rule see also Electoral Observation Coalition (COE) (2012) Final report of observation on the 2012 Angolan general elections, of the Electoral Observation Coalition. Luanda: COE. pp. 10–11.

on Freedom of Expression in Africa, which recommends self-regulation as a preferable solution to the establishment of a regulatory body.[131]

A restructuring in line with the recommended self-regulated body, but still maintaining sanctioning powers, should be taken into consideration in the run up to the 2017 elections, insofar as the new regulations for the CNCS have been fiercely resisted, as we have seen.

Access to the media

Access to public media has been totally unbalanced in favour of the party in power and its candidate and, since 1992, has been getting worse, reaching the level of outright propaganda – a fact noticed by just about everyone in all the election observation missions.

A restructuring of the CNCS with sanctioning powers intact is a necessary step, but must be complemented by the approval of proper legislation to protect the public media boards' editorial decisions from political interference. As we have seen, contradicting the recommendations of the Declaration of Principles on Freedom and Expression in Africa of the African Commission on Human and Peoples' Rights, state-owned media (television, radio, newspaper and news agency) have continued to operate under exclusive governmental control, without a governing board to protect them from governmental interference.[132]

Electoral observation

In accordance with SADC principles and guidelines, as well as international norms and standards, electoral observation is important for the credibility of an electoral process. As we have seen, the new Angolan law on electoral observation complies in general terms with the SADC norms and rules on electoral observation that have been ratified by the Angolan state as a member of SADC. However, using the wide prerogatives given by that law, the CNE has taken several decisions that, in practice, have constrained and restricted international and national electoral observation.

For the sake of credibility and transparency, the government and the CNE should obviously abstain from any such discriminatory actions against respected and credible international observers. The same goes for the national observers, whose importance was proven during the 2012 elections. Some of these organisations' reports were the only relevant source of credible information. The international ones made their observations in a very government-friendly tone, passing over all the problems and therefore simply paying lip service to their stated objective of providing credible and reliable observation.

Financing of political parties

As was obvious in 1992, 2008 and 2012, the financing of political parties has not been made transparent. Public funding for the electoral campaign of 2008 and 2012, contrary

---

131 See African Commission on Human and Peoples' Rights (2002) *Declaration of Principles on Freedom of Expression in Africa*, 32nd Session, 17–23 October 2002, Banjul, The Gambia.
132 Ibid.

to what is required by law, was made available to the opposition less than a month prior to elections, thereby significantly crippling their campaign.

Although private funding is allowed by law, it must also be acknowledged that within the Angolan political-economic context, most of the private sector is also extremely dependent on the government.[133] Therefore, it is potentially easy to be seduced into funding the party in power.

The law should be amended to force parties' annual financial statements to specify the source of all their funding. Private funding should be limited to proscribed amounts and subjected to rigid criteria (e.g. companies and individuals whose business activities have not involved state contracts for the last five years; companies who donate above certain amounts should be blocked from public contracts for five years). In the same terms, the audit court's explicit approval should be mandatory before the statements are sent to parliament and the minister of finance for publication. Failure to obtain the audit court's approval should accordingly be sanctioned by the law.

---

133 Vidal N (2004) The genesis and development of the Angolan political and administrative system from 1975 to the present. In: S Kyle (ed.) *Intersections between Social Sciences*. Cornell, NY: Cornell University. pp. 9–66.

2

BOTSWANA

Prof. Emmanuel Botlhale, with Dr Onalenna Selolwane

Introduction

Botswana held its first general elections in March 1965, but would continue as a British Protectorate until 30 September 1966 when it was granted full sovereignty. It has had ten post-independence elections between 1969 and 2014. The first six of these were managed by the office of the president until that responsibility shifted to the Independent Electoral Commission (the IEC) which was set up in 1997 following a growing clamour for more credible institutional arrangements. The IEC managed its inaugural elections in 1999 and has therefore had experience of four rounds of election management so far.

The formation of Botswana's IEC and its institutional entrenchment are a reflection of the extent to which Botswana's political practice has evolved since 1965 from a background that had no precedent of universal suffrage in the immediate colonial administrative system or the longer standing customs and traditions of the citizenry. Its inauguration, coming more than three decades after the first general elections, was a milestone in the trajectory of embracing and domesticating competitive elections as a source of legitimating government power. So while this chapter focuses on the character and performance of the IEC from its formation in 1997, it is important also to highlight the historical context that gave birth to its formation and which has shaped its direction, content and dynamic institutionalisation. Historical antecedents are critically important for enhancing understanding of the context in which political and institutional developments happen as well as the drivers that shape the course of change.

The management and outcomes of elections have been a source of discontent among contesting political parties in all post-independence elections. This is because of:

- Allegations by losing parties that ballot boxes were tampered with in the past before they reached the central point where they would be counted. This, together with attempts to conform to international best practice, prompted calls for the counting of the ballots to be done at the polling stations.

- Complaints by opposition parties that the delimitation of electoral constituencies and wards was done in a manner that favoured the ruling Botswana Democratic Party (BDP) and perpetuated its monopoly of majority votes.
- Complaints that the financial playing field was uneven and the elections therefore unfair because the BDP received massive financial support from big business eager to secure its capitalist interests.
- Criticisms from researchers and opposition parties that the ruling party uses incumbency to access state resources (from media coverage to transport) that other contesting parties do not have access to for their campaigns.
- Concern over the integrity of the IEC's independence when its executive secretary is appointed by the president and the fact that the IEC reports to a minister in the office of the president instead of directly to parliament.

The longevity of Botswana's uninterrupted electoral history under universal suffrage provides a unique opportunity to examine the functioning and evolution of its electoral management body within the context of other significant socio-political developments such as the evolution of the electoral civic culture and increasing capacity of the populace to demand accountability. This contrasts starkly with the usual tendency to use the standards of western political systems as reference points while ignoring the specificity of their historical evolution. The uninterrupted history of the rule of law in Botswana similarly gives us a context not found in those African countries where one-party or one-man authoritarian rule displaced democratic governance from independence until the return to multiparty politics in the 1990s.

The chapter contends that the formation of Botswana's IEC was a function of the onset of a competitive electoral system, more than the inauguration of democracy itself. It was spawned by a demand made by opposition parties for an independent election management body (EMB), rejecting the status quo wherein elections were run by the state since independence. From inception, Botswana's IEC has been incrementally evolving, with each innovation spurred by both an increasingly demanding voting public and opposition parties' suspicion of the governing party manipulating elections.

A product of increasing competitiveness in Botswana's politics, the IEC composition, functioning and mandate has consequently remained a subject of contention between the governing BDP and opposition parties. Rival parties disagree on the said issues. This has served to limit the credibility of both the IEC and the electoral process, which could otherwise be enriched by consensus on the issues that are presently marked by discord.

History, society and economy: Political practice and electoral management

From protectorate to constitutional polity

The Bechuanaland Protectorate, which would later become Botswana, was established on 31 March 1885 by the United Kingdom.[1] By 1960, however, in the context of (i) growing nationalism across the African continent, (ii) the threat of the spread of communism, as well as (iii) pressure for decolonisation from the United States of America which sought greater access to markets and raw materials in colonised territories, the United Kingdom government began to accept the need to prepare for relinquishing direct control of colonial territories. Between January and February 1960 the then British premier, Harold Macmillan, visited several African territories to acknowledge the inevitability of the wind of change that had precipitated British acceptance to relinquish territorial control of its empire. That journey began in Ghana (which had committed itself to the territorial liberation of the whole continent following its own independence in 1957) and ended in South Africa whose institutionalisation of racial discrimination precluded the acceptance of extending universal franchise to the native African majority.

In the specific context of the Bechuanaland Protectorate, that wind of change had actually started with the formation of the first legislative council in 1959 and the beginning of constitutional talks which would culminate in the conferment of self-government to the territory. In 1963 the constitutional talks that took place in the town of Lobatse would produce the draft constitution that would be the foundation of the birth of the Republic of Botswana: incorporating a bill of rights, freedom of speech, multiparty democracy and a multiracial society of equals before the law.[2] The final constitutional talks took place in London in 1966 and produced the national constitution whose powers came into effect with the formal transfer of power at midnight 30 September of that year.[3] The constitution of Botswana provided for a multiparty democracy, based on the basic democratic tenet of regular free and fair elections; equality of all citizens; freedom of association, assembly and belief; and the rule of law.

Not surprisingly, given that the constitutional negotiations were between the colonial government and nationalist interests with limited background in constitution making, the choice of model was to some extent a foregone conclusion: the electoral system and constitution would draw heavily on the British model of first past the post legitimation of government power. As in most colonial African territories other than settler regimes, the founding fathers of Botswana had only had since the 1959 legislative council to gain practical experience in the western type of law making and public administration before

---

1   Parsons N (1999) *A Brief History of Botswana*. Available at http://www.thuto.org/ubh/bw/bhp1.htm [accessed 27 August 2015].

2   Sebudubudu D (2009) *Leaders, Elites and Coalitions in the Development of Botswana*. Birmingham: The Developmental Leadership Program (DLP).

3   Benson E & Conolly LW (eds) (2004) *Encyclopaedia of Post-Colonial Literatures in English*. London: Routledge.

they were actually managing the affairs of the state, starting with the internal rule phase of 1965 and then complete sovereignty from 1 October 1966. In that short time from the first sitting of the legislative council to independence they managed to bridge a gulf that had existed between white settlers and local leaders to build trust and a political party that would give them common ground of aspirations for a materially richer, non-racial society; hence the birth of the Bechuanaland Democratic Party (later Botswana Democratic Party) from among the members of the legislative council.

But the BDP was not Botswana's first national party. It was the Bechuanaland People's Party (BPP) that had been founded first to agitate for independence and to represent the territory in the pan-African anti-colonial struggles of the time. But the BPP splintered on the eve of the first general elections in what would be the first of many such splits that came to characterise oppositional politics for decades to come, thus facilitating the consolidation and growth of the BDP's hold onto power and the cementing of its legitimacy as government. The birth of the Botswana National Front (BNF) after the 1965 elections would also give rise to another aspect of opposition politics: that of attempts at reconciling oppositional differences, but repeatedly failing to hold factions together decade after decade. Botswana's political firmament has thus been characterised by a single dominant party and an array of ever changing, ineffectual opposition parties. But that too seems to be changing in tandem with other social changes.

People, civic culture and electoral patterns

Voters are a major stakeholder in the legitimation of government power and the building of political parties that compete for the governing mandate. And Botswana voters have returned the same political party to power over and over again since the first elections in 1965. This has prompted debate on whether the electoral system adopted by Botswana is implicated in perpetuating this state of affairs. However, it is useful to briefly review the rise of civic culture among the voters to appreciate their role in the changing electoral patterns and support for party politics in Botswana.

Because of the disjuncture between actual votes cast and the seats won due to the electoral system, our analysis will focus on actual votes to indicate patterns of change. When we look at voting trends through actual votes, a notable feature to comment on is the fact that after the 1965 general elections, voter turn-out declined until after the death of the founding president. This was Sir Seretse Khama, who had also been a hereditary ruler of the largest traditional polity in Botswana: Gammangwato, which had been called the Central District by the colonial administration. It can be argued that having voted for Seretse Khama's party (which is how most elders referred to the BDP) to take over from the colonial government many voters presumed they had done their civic duty and did not have to vote again until after the chief died. Khama died in office in 1980 and was automatically succeeded by the vice president, Quett Masire, until the next elections in 1984. Voter turn-out that year was significantly higher than in the past three post-independence elections.

The 1980s mark a period of change among Botswana's voting public. After two decades of economic change, rapid rates of urbanisation and considerable developments in access to education, the Batswana (the people of Botswana) had changed from a predominantly rural population with an ideology of leadership by birthright to a more western educated, urban based society beginning to understand the significance of electoral legitimation of leadership. But it still required the interventions of radical civic organisations to drive home the message that electoral processing of power required equal opportunity to contest for that power as well as an engaging voting public capable of demanding accountability. This differed from the traditional cultural perspective that authority ought to be respected by not questioning its decisions. Radical women's groups emerged to challenge government policies and laws which they felt did not give women equal rights with those conferred on men. Emang Basadi Women's Association and Metlhaetsile are two such examples. Other interest groups (youth, ethnic minorities, business interests, and the media) took to increasingly challenging the government monopoly of decision making through the courts, social mobilisation and lobbying.

For instance, a Motswana woman, Unity Dow, took government to court and successfully sought relief from contradictory constitutional provisions which conferred an equal bill of rights on the one hand and, on the other, protected the right of customary law to discriminate on the basis of gender. Ethnic minority groups would similarly seek relief from legal provisions that conferred on them a minority status relative to historically dominant Tswana speaking ethnic groups, even taking the challenge to international forums where Botswana was signatory to international conventions. The media has similarly sought the protection of the courts against attempts by the executive government to silence them. Each successful challenge led to amendments and legal reforms that entrenched the rule of law and the right of citizens to demand accountability from the state.

The Emang Basadi Women's Association went a step further by initiating a political education program to raise awareness among female voters of the link between their votes and the policy and social outcomes of government decision making. They mobilised to develop broad based ownership of the first Women's Manifesto which took the challenge to all political parties, calling on them to make commitments to women's demands for equal rights and protection to win the female majority votes. The first such manifesto was developed in time for the 1994 general elections and before the political parties developed theirs. This ensured the parties would take women's demands into account when developing their own political manifestos. By the 1999 elections the culture of civic organisations challenging government legitimately had come to be accepted as part of democratic culture and would become more and more entrenched as various groups of citizens took to giving voice to grievances through various lawful channels.

This culture is reflected in changing patterns of voting where the ruling party's monopoly of the popular vote declined from 55% in 1994 to 47% in 2014. The highest support was in 1965 when the ruling party garnered 80% of the popular vote. By contrast, the opposition BPP vote has been in terminal decline since the ascendance of the Botswana

National Front as the main opposition party. The BNF's star as the main opposition rose from their first contest in 1969 elections, but was undermined 30 years later by a major split before the 1999 elections, spawning a new rival in the form of the Botswana Congress Party (BCP). In the run up to these elections there was much uncertainty in the ranks of the ruling party over the outcome of the elections given the waning popular vote.

In May 2010 the BDP experienced its first split, thus ending the opposition parties' monopoly of this characteristic with the birth of the Botswana Movement for Democracy (BMD). The split had been brewing for some time on account of increasing factionalism within the party. The BDP had walked away with 53% of the popular vote in 1999 while the main opposition gain of 41% was split between the BNF (22%) and its splinter BCP (19%). In the tide of rising public awareness, voters began to clamour for opposition party unity to consolidate the votes that they had been giving to the fragmented units. That pressure would rise considerably up to the 2014 elections, with the BDP splinter BMD responding by joining ranks with the BNF and others to form an umbrella body (the Umbrella for Democratic Change [UDC]) unifying votes against the ruling party. However, the BCP, which held 19% of the popular vote in 2009, refused to play ball. So once again, while the Umbrella for Democratic Change (a registered party) made historic inroads into the traditional citadels of BDP support, split opposition votes ensured several seats still went to the BDP despite the historic drop of the popular vote to 47%. There were seven parliamentary constituencies where the combined BCP/UDC votes were more than 50%, but which went to the BDP because of the BCP stand not to join ranks with other opposition parties. The BCP increased its popular vote to 20%, while the UDC took 30%, which was 7% lower than the 1994 electoral peak of 37% of the popular vote.

An unprecedented development in the testing of Botswana's legal framework for democratic rule has lately come from the current executive. Following the 2014 elections president Ian Khama wanted to secure full support for his choice of parliamentary speaker and vice president by seeking to reverse set parliamentary electoral procedures based on a secret ballot. The president went to court to see if he could reverse the secret ballot and have parliamentarians voting by show of hands. He lost the court case which was vehemently defended by the opposition members of parliament. But, determined to win, he then wrung concessions from his party majority to vote in support of his choice while using the secret ballot. So parliament could not sit until the courts had settled the matter. This was the first time in the annals of Botswana's parliamentary history where the attorney general, as the legal representative of the state and its constituents, had to defend a sitting president's right to challenge the powers of parliament dominated by his own party! But, even this has served to demonstrate respect for the rule of law by a president desiring more power than the restrictions imposed by law.

What has raised concern in the executive's attempts to control other arms of government, however, has been the president's unprecedented rejection of the recommendations of the Judicial Services Commission (JSC) to appoint a certain Omphemetse Motumise as a high court judge. Although the framers of the constitutional provision to instate the JSC envisioned it as a body that would reinforce the independence of the judiciary and insulate it from interference from other arms of government,[4] they did not in fact make the JSC's recommendations for the appointment of judges to be binding on the part of the appointing authority: the president.

So although its responsibility is to assess and recommend officers to be appointed for judicial posts, and although the president should make appointments only on the basis of the JSC's recommendations, the constitution does not specifically oblige the president to accept such recommendations. And while all other presidents had respected this provision as implicitly binding, the current president has taken a different interpretation and chosen to reject the recommendation. The result has been growing unease over the extent to which the Botswana judiciary is in fact independent from the executive, particularly since, within the executive, the president is not obliged to accept the position of the majority in cabinet.

Economy, inequality and demographic shifts

The BDP government's management of the national economy and the success of its development strategies in transforming Botswana from extreme poverty to middle income status have earned the country well-deserved accolades for good governance. In particular, at a time when most economies on the continent foundered under the heavy burden of debt and economic mismanagement, Botswana's economy went through the era of structural adjustment (dubbed the lost decade of development) practically unscathed. A major problem that has persisted through the transformation to middle income has been the blight of social and economic inequality.

Until the late 1980s and early 1990s, government was able to reduce the sting of inequality through a number of income support programmes as well as macro-economic policies that reduced inflation while pushing high growth rates.[5] But Botswana's economy peaked in the 1990s and began to show signs of inefficiencies in resource allocation and gaps between planned interventions and implementation. Income inequality began to rise again after a period of decline.[6] Similarly employment creation also saw incline and decline before and after the economic liberalisation policies of the 1990s. For example, between 1980 and 1991 when the Botswana economy averaged 10% annual growth rate, the employment growth rate was just slightly lower at 9% per annum.[7] But, in the following decade when economic growth declined to 6% growth rate, the employment growth rate declined more drastically to just 2.2%, suggesting a widening gap between income and

---

4   Government of Botswana (2011) *Administration of Justice (AOJ)*. Available at http://www.gov.bw/en/ Ministries--Authorities/Ministries/Administration-of-Justice-AOJ/ [accessed 13 September 2016].

5   Selolwane O (2012) Welfare, social protection and poverty reduction. In: O Selolwane (ed.) *Poverty Reduction and Changing Policy Regimes*. Basingstoke: Palgrave MacMillan and UNRISD.

6   Mogotsi I (2012) Wealth and Income Inequalities. In: O Selolwane (ed.) *Poverty Reduction and Changing Policy Regimes*. Basingstoke: Palgrave MacMillan and UNRISD.

7   Siphambe H (2012) Development strategies and poverty reduction in Botswana. In: O Selolwane (ed.) *Poverty Reduction and Changing Policy Regimes*. Basingstoke: Palgrave MacMillan and UNRISD.

job creation. This persistent job deficient growth seems to have had some impact on the popularity of the ruling party. High youth unemployment in particular, coinciding with demographic shifts that have seen increased share of youth in the voting population, have not augured well for the ruling party.

The 2011 population has seen the share of children under the age of 15 decreased from 48% in 1971 to 33% while youth increased their share from 22% to 31% in the same period, and those aged 30 to 44 increased from 13% to 20%. So altogether the population aged 15 to 44 years now accounts for 51% of the national population compared to just a third 40 years ago. Unlike earlier age cohorts, this cohort has received near universal access to secondary education but is constrained by limited artisanal and professional skills from enjoying the benefits of employment and contributing to productivity. The increasing gap between employment creation and economic growth therefore hits hardest on the lower end of this population group. They expect, but cannot get, accelerated and sustained employment. Without jobs, youth increasingly turn to antisocial behaviour such as crime, drug and substance abuse, and violence. The question is: to what extent can Botswana youth continue to respect the rule of law and democratic processing of power when their basic needs are not met? What impact could the youth unemployment problem have on party politics and electoral processes? In 2014 some of them mobilised to form a youth party, but then moved into the Umbrella coalition when they could not meet the official registration deadline.

Constitutional and legal framework

The key legal instruments that govern the conduct and administration of elections in Botswana are the 1966 constitution and 1968 Electoral Act (as amended). Before the creation of the IEC in 1997, election management was the portfolio responsibility of the office of the presidency under the direction of the permanent secretary to the president. But there were concerns that as an interested party in the elections, the president could use his authority over the permanent secretary to influence the electoral process in his favour. A referendum was held on 26 October 1987 to ask voters whether they were in favour or against creating the Office of the Supervisor of Elections.

The 'yes' vote was 78%[8] and, subsequently, the Supervisor of Elections was introduced under section 66(1) of the constitution. Section 66(2) provided that the Supervisor of Elections shall be appointed by the president. The Supervisor of Elections conducted elections from 1987 to 1997. Opposition political parties were, however, still dissatisfied with this change, arguing that the Supervisor of Elections was not independent of the office of the presidency. The matter was discussed at an all-party conference, a forum where

---

8   African Elections (2015) *Botswana referendums.* Available at http://africanelections.tripod.com/bw_2.
     html#1997_Referendum [accessed 31 August 2015].

political parties met to discuss issues of mutual interest.[9] The government accepted the resolution of the forum and facilitated yet another national referendum to seek the views of the voters. So on 4 October 1997 voters were asked the following three questions:

- Whether they approved of amending the constitution to replace the post of Supervisor of Elections with an Independent Electoral Commission.
- Whether they approved of amending the constitution to allow Batswana living abroad to vote.
- Whether they approved of amending the constitution to lower the voting age from 21 to 18.

Even though the voter turn-out was low, 16%, all three proposals were approved with 'yes' votes of 73%, 70% and 59% for questions 1, 2 and 3 respectively.[10] The constitution was therefore amended to accommodate the establishment of the Independent Electoral Commission (IEC); allowing Batswana living abroad to vote; and lowering the voting age from 21 to 18. The IEC was established by section 65A of the Constitution of Botswana in 1997, under the section, *'Appointment of Independent Electoral Commission'*. It provides that there shall be an Independent Electoral Commission which shall consist of:

- A chairman who shall be a judge of the High Court appointed by the Judicial Service Commission;
- A legal practitioner appointed by the Judicial Service Commission; and
- Five other persons who are fit, proper and impartial, appointed by the Judicial Service Commission from a list of persons recommended by the all-party conference.[11]

Section 65A(2) provides that 'where the all-party conference[12] fails to agree on all or any number of persons referred to in subsection (1)(c) of this section up to dissolution of parliament, the Judicial Service Commission shall appoint such person or persons as are necessary to fill any vacancy'. To provide context, section 103 of the Constitution of Botswana provides for the creation of the Judicial Service Commission. It provides that there shall be a Judicial Service Commission for Botswana which shall consist of: (i) the Chief Justice who shall be chairman; (ii) the president of the Court of Appeal (not being the Chief Justice or the most senior Justice of the Court of Appeal); (iii) the attorney-general; (iv) the Chairman of the Public Service Commission; (e) a member of the Law Society

---

9   The forum has not been convened since 2005 and the opposition has been calling for its resuscitation.
10 African Elections (2015) *Botswana referendums.* Available at http://africanelections.tripod.com/bw_2. html#1997_Referendum [accessed 31 August 2015].
11 Republic of Botswana (2006) *Constitution of Botswana.* Gaborone: Government Printer.
12 'All-Party Conference' means a meeting of all registered political parties convened from time to time by the minister (65A(3) of the Constitution of Botswana; *Appointment of Independent Electoral Commission*).

nominated by the Law Society; and (f) a person of integrity and experience who is not a legal practitioner appointed by the president.

Beyond the constitution, the Electoral Act (1968; as amended) guides the management of elections. The Act consolidates certain laws relating to elections of the National Assembly and councils; for the qualification and registration of voters; for the conduct of such elections and for other purposes in relation to such elections.[13] It was last amended in 2012 in respect of section 13 to provide for the alphabetical listing of voters' names in the roll. The Act is divided into 12 parts: Introductory (Part I); Disqualification of Voters (Part II); Registration of Voters and Preparation of Rolls (Part III); Appeals, Objections and Cancellations (Part IV); Supplementary (Part V); Elections (Part VI); Polling (VII); Election Expenses and Election Agents (Part VIII); Corrupt and Illegal Practices (Part IX); Election Petitions (Part X); Offences (Part IX); and Miscellaneous (Part XII).

Institutional framework and functioning

While the 2000 all-party conference to propose names of persons to be appointed as election commissioners went on smoothly, the one held in July 2004 was riddled with controversy.[14] The Botswana National Front (BNF), Botswana Congress Party (BCP), Botswana People's Party (BPP), then Botswana Alliance Movement (BAM) and then New Democratic Front (NDF), boycotted the conference. Opposition parties boycotted the conference for a number of reasons. Amongst others was their contention that they were not given sufficient time to scrutinise the names of applicants. They also contended that the government rejected all the suggestions they put to the 2000 all-party conference, including public funding of political parties, introduction of proportional representation, declaring voting day a public holiday, counting of ballots at polling stations, direct election of the president and strengthening the independence of the IEC.[15] The disaffected parties contended that the all-party conference meeting on 27 July was illegitimate. For instance, Dick Bayford, the leader of the New Democratic Front (NDF), denounced the meeting as 'unlawful'.[16] In response, Daniel Kwelagobe, the presidential affairs and public administration minister, stated that the attorney general, Ian Kirby, had advised that the decisions made by the all-party conference meeting were lawful despite a boycott by the main opposition parties.

Since the boycott the BDP-led government has not been keen to reconvene the all-party conference. Past ministers of presidential affairs and public administration, Phandu Skelemani and Daniel Kwelagobe, avowed that they believed in the importance[17] of the

---

13 Republic of Botswana (1996) *Constitution of Botswana*. Gaborone: Government Printer.
14 Sebudubudu D (2004, 4 November) Botswana's main opposition parties boycott the all-party conference. *EISA Newsletter* No 16. Available at www.content.eisa.org.za/pdf/et16.pdf [accessed 31 August 2015].
15 BPP will not honour all party conference (2012, 27 July) *Daily News*. Available at http://www.olddailynews. gov.bw/cgi-bin/news.cgi?d=20040727 [accessed 31 August 2015].
16 Selepeng W (2004, 28 July) All-party meeting proceeds without opposition. *Mmegi*. Available at http:// www.mmegi.bw/2004/July/Wednesday28/912724551923.html [accessed 31 August 2015].
17 Gabathuse R (2007, 30 November) Skelemani, Kwelagobe bury all-party conference. *Mmegi*. Available at

forum but neither convened the forum during his term in office. When the matter was put to then Minster of Presidential Affairs and Public Administration, Mokgweetsi Masisi, in August 2011, he stated that the government had no intention of reconvening the forum.[18] As a result, other than for the selection of commissioners, the all-party conference does not meet. The convening of the all-party conference ensures fairness in the appointment of commissioners because all registered political parties agree on the final selection of candidates and this also lends legitimacy and credibility to the IEC and ownership of the IEC to relevant stakeholders. On the other hand, the government's reluctance to convene the all-party conference for purposes other than the appointment of commissioners is problematic in that opposition political parties, very important stakeholders in the electoral process, feel disaffected and have expressed a consensus opinion that the fact that the government is reluctant to convene the all-party conference derogates from the credentials of Botswana as a model democracy[19] in the sub-continent. One opposition political party interviewee put this in concrete terms saying 'the BDP government does not want to convene the all-party conference for purposes other than the appointment of commissioners because it wants to control the electoral process'.[20] Another interviewee opined that 'the current minster of presidential affairs and public administration has got no interest in the opposition parties, and thus tends to think that the opposition will embarrass the BDP (Botswana Democratic Party) if he convenes the all-party conference'.[21]

It is important to note that, although five commissioners are selected by consensus during an all-party conference, they are not sponsored by any political party or formation. These are apolitical citizens who would have expressed a wish to serve in the IEC as commissioners. They respond to an advertisement for positions of commissioners and this advertisement attracts thousands of applications yet there are only five slots. Regarding gender parity, there is no stipulated gender proportion of the commissioners. With the current commission, there are four males and three females (which almost translates into gender parity). Furthermore, there is no consideration made for social groupings, for example marginalised groups,[22] when appointing the commissioners.

The first appointments of the chairman and the members of the IEC were done by 31 January 1999 in preparation of the 1999 general elections. Subsequent appointments were made at the last dissolution of every two successive terms of parliament. The chairman and the members of the IEC hold office for a period of two successive terms of parliament.

---

http://www.mmegi.bw/index.php?sid=1&aid=43&dir=2007/November/Friday30/// [accessed 31 August 2015].

18 No plans to convene all-party conference (2011, 11 August) *Daily News*. p. 2.

19 There is no legal compulsion to convene the all-party conference other than for the appointment of commissioners. The all-party conference was an initiative of the government to enhance the contours of democracy in Botswana but was discontinued when the BDP government felt that it was being abused by opposition parties.

20 Interview, 25 September 2015.

21 Interview, 9 September 2015.

22 This is a contentious term in Botswana although groups such as Baswara (San) are considered as marginalised (for example, see Saugestad S (2011) *The Inconvenient Indigenous*. Uppsala: Nordic Africa Institute).

The disqualifications for appointment to the IEC are provided for in section 65A (6) of the constitution of Botswana: a person shall not be qualified to be appointed as a member of the Independent Electoral Commission if (i) he or she has been declared insolvent or adjudged bankrupt under any law in force in any part of the Commonwealth and has not paid his or her debts in full; or (ii) he or she has been convicted of any offence involving dishonesty in any country.

Section 65A(7) of the constitution of Botswana provides that 'a person appointed a member of the commission shall not enter upon the duties of the office of commissioner until he or she has taken and subscribed the oath of allegiance and such oath for the due execution of his or her office as may be prescribed by an Act of Parliament. Operationally, the commission is independent because it regulates its work as provided in section 65A (8) of the constitution of Botswana: 'the commission shall regulate its own procedure and proceedings'. All the commissioners and IEC staff that were interviewed expressed the view that the IEC was 'operationally independent'. One interviewee put it in concrete terms saying that 'there is nobody who tells the IEC what to do. There is no interference from the government'.[23] In a similar vein, another stated that 'even the President of the Republic of Botswana does not have the authority to direct the IEC in terms of what it does'.[24] And while it is normal for the president to issue directives to government departments, one respondent asserted that 'we do not receive directives from the president, let alone orders from the minister of presidential affairs and public administration'.[25] Finally, the case of the ruling Botswana Democratic Party's Ignatius Moswaane, whom the IEC refused to register to stand as member of parliament for the Francistown West by-election in November 2013 due to a court order, was given as a foremost example of the IEC's independence.[26]

To summarise the Moswaane case, in September 2013 one of the Botswana Democratic Party's (BDP) primary election candidates, Whyte Marobela, made an urgent court application to bar any BDP candidate from submitting nomination forms to the IEC on 1 November 2013[27] until the BDP central committee had given him a hearing pertaining to his loss to Moswaane. The BDP, through its lawyers, Collins and Newman, instructed the IEC to accept the name of its candidate, Moswaane, for the Francistown West by-election nominations. The IEC refused to do so because doing so would be in contempt of the court. At the end of 1 November 2013, when nominations were closed, Moswaane's name could not be submitted to the IEC and, thus, the following were confirmed as by-election candidates: Habaudi Hobona, Shatiso Tambula, Joseph Mabutho and Kago Phofuetsile. The BDP sought to overturn the IEC's decision through the courts but the IEC unwaveringly stuck to its position and was, finally, vindicated by the court of appeal on 11 December 2013.[28]

---

23 Interview, 9 September 2015.
24 Interview, 28 September 2015.
25 Interview, 28 September 2015.
26 BDP wants IEC to accept Moswaane (2013, 3 November) *Daily News*. p. 1.
27 Nominations for by-election candidates were to be submitted to the IEC on 1 November 2013.
28 End of the road for Moswaane (2013, 17 December) *Botswana Guardian*. p. 1.

Section 65A(12) of the constitution of Botswana provides for the responsibilities of the IEC as follows:

- The conduct and supervision of elections of the elected members of the National Assembly and members of a local authority, and conduct of a referendum;
- Giving instructions and directions to the secretary of the commission appointed under section 66 in regard to the exercise of his or her functions under the electoral law prescribed by an Act of Parliament;
- Ensuring that elections are conducted efficiently, properly, freely and fairly; and
- Performing such other functions as may be prescribed by an Act of Parliament.

Upon the completion of any election, 65A (13) provides that the commission shall 'submit a report on the exercise of its functions under the preceding provisions of this section to the minister for the time being responsible for matters relating to such elections, and that minister shall, not later than seven days after the National Assembly first meets and he or she has received the report, lay it before the National Assembly'.

Finally, section 66 of the constitution of Botswana provides for the appointment of a secretary to the Independent Electoral Commission:

- There shall be a secretary to the Independent Electoral Commission referred to in section 65A (in this section referred to as 'the secretary').
- The secretary shall be appointed by the president.
- The actions of the secretary shall be subject to the direction and supervision of the Independent Electoral Commission.

The IEC is responsible for a number of activities, including but not limited to: establishment of polling districts and stations, registration of voters, allocation of voting symbols to new political parties and independent candidates, registration of candidates, conduct of poll (National Assembly, local government and referenda), vote counting, announcement of results and recruitment and training of registration and poll staff. The commission further undertakes civic and voter education even although this is not its constitutional mandate. To enable the IEC to carry out its jobs of work, it is fully funded by the government in accordance with the laid down procedures applicable to all the ministries and departments. The IEC formulates its budget and the submission is made to parliament by the minister of presidential affairs and public administration. The IEC, as per the Public Financial Management Act,[29] must account for the use of public funds. The IEC secretary is the accounting officer, therefore, he or she appears for the Public Accounts Committee's (PAC) examinations in respect of the IEC's use of public funds. In addition, the IEC must, at the

---

29 Republic of Botswana (2011) *Public Financial Management Act*. Gaborone: Government Printing and Publishing.

end of each financial year, submit books of accounts to the accountant general for onward submission to the auditor general for auditing. If there are any audit queries, IEC secretary must respond to them during PAC examinations and take action.

In terms of staffing, the IEC recruits its staff under delegated authority from the Directorate of Public Service Management (DPSM). The DPSM is the public service employer and its employees are subject to the Public Service Act (2008).[30] The employees of the commission are therefore public servants and this means that they can be transferred in and out of the IEC by the DPSM. However, over time, there has developed an understanding that in transferring staff out of the IEC, the DPSM has to consult the IEC Secretary to minimise disruptions. On the other hand, the IEC secretary is appointed by the President in terms of section 66 of the Constitution of Botswana. This method of appointment notwithstanding, the IEC secretary is accountable to the commission; for example, his/her job assessment is done by the commission. Due to this arrangement, there were confused lines of command. Particularly, in the past, the Office of the President was of the view that the IEC secretary was under its purview. This, however, has been resolved and the understanding is that the officer reports to the commission although he or she is appointed by the president.

The IEC has established two standing committees with membership from commissioners: Legal Affairs and Dispute Resolution; and Information, Education and Research. These were established to give policy direction on legal matters affecting the commission and civic and voter education policies and programmes respectively. The commission develops and implements a five-year strategic plan after each general election. Alongside the electoral cycle, it develops an annual performance plan and is cascaded to the divisions for implementation.

In its portfolio of work, the IEC works with an array of stakeholders. Some of the stakeholders are: voters (principal stakeholders), political parties, traditional leaders, parliament, the executive arm of the government (particularly ministries, for example, Office of the President, finance and development planning, education and skills development, local government and rural development), government departments (for example, Botswana police service), judiciary (in respect of disputes that reach the courts of law), local non-governmental organisations/civil society (for example, Botswana council of non-governmental organisations; election observation) and media. It is important to note that the media are essential to democracy, and a democratic election is impossible without the media[31], because they provide coverage of electoral matters throughout the electoral cycle. Although there is no right to information (RIA) law – the government rebuffed attempts by the opposition to introduce an RIA act in August 2012[32] and despite

---

30 Republic of Botswana (2008) *Public Service Act*. Gaborone: Government Printing and Publishing (This act became operational in 2010).

31 ACE (2015a) *The importance of media to the elections*. Available at http://aceproject.org/ace-en/topics/me/onePage [accessed 1 December 2015].

32 Botlhale E & Molefhe K (2013) The death of the Right to Information Bill in Botswana. *IFLA Journal* 39(3): 204–213.

the existence of restrictive acts such as the Media Practitioners' Act (2008), the media, both public and private, is relatively free to report on anything, including electoral coverage.

However, concerns have been raised by opposition political parties that the public media, particularly Radio Botswana 1 and Botswana Television, disproportionately cover BDP electoral events and give the opposition limited coverage.[33] These charges, however, have to be seen in a wider context: there is no public broadcaster in Botswana, therefore the state broadcaster has a mandate to promote government policies, inadvertently or otherwise, inclusive of covering BDP events. Thus, the absence of a public broadcaster in the mould of the British Broadcasting Corporation poses challenges for the holding of free, fair and credible elections. On the other hand, the government has often attempted to withdraw adverts from the private media, which the courts condemned as attempts to muzzle the private media.

To illustrate, two private newspapers (The *Botswana Guardian* and *MidWeek Sun*) approached the courts in response to an advertising ban in 2001. On 24 September 2001, the High Court declared the ban unconstitutional because it violated the newspapers' constitutional rights to freedom of expression.[34] Similarly, in late December 2014 the government reportedly, through an intercepted unofficial memo, issued a secret directive to its various ministries and parastatals to stop advertising in some private newspapers, among them *The Sunday Standard*, *Mmegi*, *The Botswana Guardian*, *Weekend Post* and *The Patriot on Sunday*.[35] After impassioned denials, then permanent secretary to the president, Carter Morupisi, confirmed in an interview that the ban 'was nothing sinister but a cost-cutting measure'.[36] While the ban has been abandoned, the threat remains that the government may, at any time, use its financial muscle to whip 'recalcitrant' media outlets into line, hence compromising their constitutional rights to freedom of expression, including reporting on incidences of electoral misdemeanour by the BDP government.

There are international stakeholders and some examples are: SADC Electoral Commissioners Forum (for capacity-building and election observer missions), SADC Council of Non-Governmental Organisations (elections observation); United Nations Development Programme (capacity-building), International IDEA (capacity-building, e.g. BRIDGE training); Electoral Institute of Sustainable Democracy in Africa (capacity-building, performance audits and advisory role) and Friedrich Ebert Foundation (capacity-building).

The IEC manages relations with stakeholders through regular consultation forums on issues of elections and democracy. Among these, the SADC Electoral Commissioners Forum deserves a brief mention due to its mandate over EMBs in the Southern African Community's

---

33 ECF-SADC (2009) *Observer Mission Report: Botswana General Elections, 16 October 2009*. Gaborone: ECF-SADC.

34 IFEX (2015) *High Court declares advertising ban against newspapers unconstitutional*. Available at https://www.ifex.org/botswana/2001/09/28/high_court_declares_advertising/ [accessed 4 December 2015].

35 Ontebetse K (2014, 15 December) Govt bans advertising on critical media houses. *The Sunday Standard*. Available at http://www.sundaystandard.info/govt-bans-advertising-critical-media-houses [accessed 4 December 2015].

36 Advertising ban unconstitutional (2015, 4 March) *Mmegi*. Available at http://www.mmegi.bw/index.php?aid=49620 [accessed 4 December 2015].

grouping. The forum, established in July 1998, is an independent organisation in which each country in the SADC region is represented by its electoral management body. Its mandate is: (i) to strengthen co-operation amongst electoral commissions in the SADC region; and (ii) to promote conditions conducive to free, fair, credible and transparent elections in the SADC region.[37] To implement its mandate, the forum undertakes the following: training; orientation of new commissioners and chief executive officers; staff attachments (staff from one EMB are attached to another EMB).[38] The forum also arranges for the sharing of resources and expertise among EMBs in the region and undertakes country-specific projects, organising study tours (beyond the SADC region, for example, Ghana), and helps with the formulation of conditions of service for commissioners.[39] The IEC benefited and still benefits from some of from these services.

In terms of assessing performance, the IEC uses many tools, among them the following: performance audits;[40] stakeholder evaluation workshops;[41] election observer reports; and media reports. To illustrate, some examples are given. In 2004, the IEC requested the International Institute for Democracy and Electoral Assistance (IDEA) to undertake an audit of the 2004 general elections 'with a view to assessing how it carried out its mandate to organise and conduct free and fair elections in Botswana'.[42] IDEA came up with 12 key findings, among them that the mandate of the IEC be extended and that the IEC 'could be more independent if it had unfettered control over the recruitment, discipline and removal of its staff'.[43] It also gave a raft of 12 recommendations, among them that 'evaluation workshops for returning officers should be re-scheduled for November of each election year so that their experiences could form part of the data for the audit exercise';[44] that the IEC should conceptualise and fund exit polls; and that parliament must abolish the Delimitation Commission and, therefore, assign the task to the IEC. In addition, there are reports to the minister of presidential affairs and public administration on general elections. These reports are issued in terms of section 65(13) of the constitution of Botswana and they contain information on activities and processes leading to the preparation for and conduct of general elections. They also contain information on challenges. For example, the 2014 report addressed challenges relating to the legal framework, logistics, human resources and stakeholder involvement.[45]

The IEC, as the sole manager of elections, takes it upon itself to be the forerunner in the matter of electoral reforms. In this regard, the IEC generates and compiles recommendations,

---

37 SADC Electoral Commissioners Forum (2015) *Welcome*. Available at http://www.ecfsadc.org/ [accessed 10 September 2015].

38 Interview, 28 September 2015.

39 Ibid.

40 Independent Electoral Commission (2005) Audit of the IEC's Preparedness to Conduct Legitimate and Credible Elections in October 2004. Gaborone: IEC.

41 Independent Electoral Commission (2005) 2004 Elections Evaluation Report. Gaborone: IEC.

42 Ibid.: 1.

43 Ibid.: 20.

44 Ibid.: 25.

45 Independent Electoral Commission (2014) *Report to the Minister of Presidential Affairs and Public Administration on the 2014 General Elections*. Gaborone: IEC.

giving the status quo and its position in relation to each recommendation and forwards them to the executive and parliament. Immediately upon its inception, the IEC had to grapple with the definition of the descriptor 'independence'. Fundamentally, what does it mean? In the words of one former commissioner, 'the issue of independence was the most topical in terms of what it meant and ways to enhance it during the life of the first commission'.[46] He noted that section 65(a) of the constitution of Botswana states that 'there shall be an Independent Electoral Commission' and ends there, and that 'the thrust of the debate on the independence stemmed from section 65(a) of the Constitution of Botswana'.[47]

Arising from this, both during the formative years and today, one of the reforms that the IEC recommended was the definition of the independence of the IEC. In the main, this conviction was born of the firm and considered belief within the IEC, particularly the commissioners, that the IEC was a body provided for separately and distinctively from other organs of the state, meaning that the IEC was a structurally and operationally independent entity.[48] On the other hand, it was asserted that 'within government circles, the term 'independence' was more of an adjective than a descriptor'.[49] Ultimately, the IEC recommended to the government that there be a specific IEC Act that would, amongst other things, define the independence of the IEC. Furthermore, it recommended that the proposed Act should establish the IEC as a body corporate that had the ability to sue and be sued.

As it is, the IEC is not a body corporate even though it behaves like one. In the normal workings of things, the IEC should be sued through the office of the attorney general like all other government departments but it has resisted this arrangement over the years. Therefore, it is conceived as a body corporate by aggrieved parties and it is often sued in its own right, as happened in the *Whyte Marobela vs. Ignatius Moswaane* case where the IEC was cited as one of the parties in the suit. There has been little movement in this direction and the delay is caused by protracted consultations within and outside government structures. Furthermore, the minister for presidential affairs and public administration is yet to table the matter to cabinet. When the cabinet agrees on the bill, it will be tabled in parliament and follow the normal law-making process.

Overall, disappointment was expressed about the slow progress in finalising the IEC bill before it could be tabled to parliament. Some quotations are instructive:

> I doubt that the government is really committed to granting the IEC the independence that it deserves because the thinking is that 'the IEC is already independent, therefore, what more independence does it want?'[50] ...
> Independence induces a sense of fear among some in the government, hence, the delay.[51]

---

46 Interview, 24 September 2015.
47 Ibid.
48 Ibid.
49 Ibid.
50 Interview, 28 September 2015.
51 Ibid.

In the thinking of some in the government, 'independence' in the IEC acronym is not a descriptor but a word like a person could be called *Bonolo*[52] but the person is not necessarily of a cool temperament. Therefore, there is no hurry to clothe the IEC with the independence it needs.[53]

Others expressed the view that the government was generally reluctant to devolve powers from the government enclave (read the executive arm of the government), as instanced by continual fights between the executive arm of the government and legislature over the independence of parliament and the surreptitious re-centralisation of activities such as primary health and primary education despite the government's avowal to decentralisation. However, one respondent took a positive view: 'consultations take time, therefore, the government is still consulting'. However, she noted that 'on a balance of probabilities, this is taking rather too long if one considers the fact that the IEC was established in 1997'.[54]

To foster continual learning and continuous improvement, the IEC interfaces and benchmarks with regional EMBs (e.g. Republic of South Africa, Lesotho, Namibia, Zambia and beyond for example, Ghana, Kenya and Mexico). Beyond the preceding measures, the IEC is a signatory to various election management protocols. Examples are some of the following: African Union's Charter on Democracy, Elections, and Governance; Southern African Development Community's Principles and Guidelines Governing Democratic Elections; and Southern African Development Community Parliamentary Forum's Norms and Standards for Elections in the SADC region.

Finally, elections, as noted by Akanyang Magama, then Botswana's leader of the opposition when supporting calls for the independence of the Electoral Commission in August 2005, 'are highly emotive'.[55] They produce both winners and losers and others who are dissatisfied with the electoral process; hence, disputes are a natural consequence. The IEC is not mandated by law to adjudicate on election disputes. However, out of its own agency, it has developed alternative dispute resolution mechanisms such as the party liaison committees and the legal affairs and dispute resolution committee. The legal affairs and dispute resolution committee deals with legal issues assigned by the commission and advises the commission on legal matters to enable it to make informed decisions. The chairperson is the deputy chairperson of the commission (legal practitioner). If petitioners are not happy with the decisions of the committee, they can approach the courts of law. Therefore, the Botswana judicial system is the only means of legislated dispute resolution mechanisms in place where registration of objections and petitions are lodged. However, due to high costs involved with litigation, most would-be litigants are dissuaded from approaching the courts for relief.

---

52 *Bonolo*, a verb, denotes a mellow temper.
53 Interview, 24 September 2015.
54 Interview, 10 September 2015.
55 Molaodi P (2005, 3 August) PHK calls for total independence of IEC. *Mmegi*. p. 4.

IEC and fair, free and credible elections

Before assessing the performance of the IEC in regard to the overarching research question 'how does the Independent Electoral Commission contribute to the management of fair, free and credible elections in Botswana?', there is a need to have an understanding of the environment conducive to the holding of free, fair, and credible elections. This chapter argues that the holding of free, fair and credible elections is only possible under one condition: competitive electoral process. Vitally, what is a competitive electoral process? The literature on the theory of elections is voluminous[56] and therefore it is not possible to exhaustively cover it within the confines of this space, but suffice it to summarise key points relating to democratic elections. Theories about elections define expectations about how elections should be carried out and set conditions for evaluating performance.[57] These are both descriptive (what must be done in particular circumstances) and normative (what must be done given specific ideals and norms about elections).[58] The basic principles and expectations of competitive elections are:

- All law-abiding adult citizens are entitled to vote;
- Political parties are free to put up candidates, debate their merits freely, and criticise opponents;
- Political organisations campaign with the objective of winning;
- Each voter casts one vote (preferably in secret) and is not hindered in expressing a choice;
- Votes are honestly counted and the results faithfully reported;
- The candidate, party, or coalition with the most votes wins;
- The losing individual or party does not try to use force to alter the outcome or prevent the winner from taking office; and
- The party in power does not restrict political participation and competition which are within the parameters of existing rules.[59]

It is important to note that the preceding scheme constitutes a competitive democratic ideal that seldom obtains in practice. In this regard, it is 'more fruitful to conceive of electoral systems as ranging along a continuum from this idealised democratic type to authoritarian regimes at the other end'.[60]

While there is universal agreement about the usefulness of competitive electoral process, a competitive electoral process neither defines democracy nor can it be equated with democracy. However, a competitive electoral process 'is a cardinal percept of liberal

---

56 Hayward F (ed.) (1987) *Elections in Independent Africa*. London: Westview Press.
57 Ibid.
58 Kirkpatrick JJ (1981) Democratic elections, democratic government, and democratic theory. In: D Butler, HR Penniman and A Ranney (eds) *Democracy at the Polls: A Comparative Study of Competitive National Elections*. Washington DC: American Enterprise Institute for Public Policy Research. p.326.
59 Hayward F (ed.) (1987) *Elections in Independent Africa*. London: Westview Press. p. 3.
60 Ibid.

democratic theory and practice'.[61] Liberal democracy involves, among other things, free, fair and credible elections. As such, the actual form and content of the electoral process is one aspect by which one can gauge the extent to which liberal democracy is realised.[62] In this regard, one cannot plausibly talk about liberal democracy in the absence of free, fair and credible elections, alongside the rule of law, democratic freedoms of speech, thought, etc.

In analysing competitive elections in Botswana, Holm[63] argues that a democratic electoral system requires institutional conditions, some specified in law and others being born of customs which govern political practice such as: (i) all potential candidates can run for office; (ii) citizens' votes have equal influence; (iii) the contest is governed by rules which insure political freedom and fair voting procedure; and (iv) elected representatives make laws by majority vote. In his summative evaluation, he concluded that 'Botswana shows definite movement toward fulfilling these conditions of a liberal democracy'[64] and 'in contrast to other African countries, Botswana has had much more success with elections in that it is institutionalising a broad range of democratic practices in a context of stability'.[65]

Thus, on a balance of probabilities, an argument can be made that a competitive electoral process exists in Botswana to make it possible to hold free and fair elections. Admittedly, the system is not perfect and, employing the Hayward framework,[66] it can be argued that Botswana's electoral system is more to the left of the continuum (idealised democratic regimes) and less to the right of the continuum (authoritarian regimes). Thus, such a system would be amenable to the holding of free and fair elections. Although there is less emphasis on 'free and fair' elections in favour of credible, legitimate and participatory elections,[67] quality of elections etc.,[68] the criterion of free and fair elections is vital. That is, free and fair elections are necessarily credible, legitimate and participatory. As a result, this chapter will zero in on free and fair elections.

Free and fair and elections mean different things to different people and 'there are no precise definitions for regular, free, and fair elections'.[69] Nonetheless, international human rights conventions, for example article 21 of the Universal Declaration of Human Rights, state that such elections must be periodic, genuine, organised according to universal suffrage, and by secret ballot'.[70] For expositional clarity, this chapter relies on the Inter-

61 Cowen M & Laakso L (2002) Elections & election studies in Africa. In: M Cowen and L Laakso (eds) *Multi-Party Elections in Africa*. New York: Palgrave. p. 1.
62 Ibid.
63 Holm J (1987) Elections in Botswana: Institutionalisation of a new system of legitimacy. In: F Hayward (ed.) *Elections in Independent Africa*. London: Westview Press. pp. 121–147 Ibid.
64 Ibid.: 125.
65 Ibid.: 143.
66 Ibid.: 3.
67 ACE (2015b) *Less talk about 'free and fair' elections?* Available at http://aceproject.org/electoral-advice/archive/questions/replies/54818966 [accessed 5 September 2015].
68 Kelley JG (2012) *Monitoring Democracy: When International Election Observation Works, and Why it Often Fails*. Princeton: Princeton University Press.
69 ND Democracy Web (2015) *Free, Fair & Regular Elections: Essential Principles*. Available at http://democracyweb.org/node/23 [accessed 10 October 2015].
70 United Nations (1948) *Universal Declaration of Human Rights*. Available at http://www.un.org/en/

Parliamentary Union (IPU)'s definition of free and fair elections that relates to rules and standards of international law and state practice.[71] Similarly, Goodwin-Gill, writing under the auspices of the IPU, says that, "'free" is about participation and choice; "fair" is about equality of participation and of the vote, and about impartiality and non-discrimination'.[72]

On a practical level, Sylvia Bishop and Anke Hoeffler[73] have developed ten indicators to judge the quality of election in terms of freeness and fairness. Six pertain to the freeness of the election (i.e. rules of the election and the process prior to the election day) and four indicators score the fairness of the elections relating to voting and events on or immediately after the election day.[74] If a criterion is completely fulfilled, this variable is scored 1 and if on the other hand the variable is not completely fulfilled, this is scored 0. The indicators are:

- Legal framework (the legal framework guarantees the right to vote and run for office and that elections are run at regular intervals);
- Electoral management bodies (Elections have to be managed independently, otherwise they are deemed to impact on the quality of the election);
- Electoral rights (Equal suffrage is in place for citizens of voting age (e.g. no voter group is systematically disadvantaged [de facto]);
- Voter register (e.g. voter registers are accurate: without false names, lack of correct names of individuals, inclusion of name of non-eligible voters (e.g. the dead or children) and multiple entries
- Ballot access (e.g. citizens eligible to stand are able to compete in the election [de facto])
- Campaign process (e.g. no violence, bribery, intimidation or any other unequitable treatment of voters occurs during the process (either threatened or carried out));
- Media access (e.g. all parties/candidates are provided with access to the media; and all parties/candidates have equitable treatment and time on government owned media and the ruling party does not get disproportionately large media coverage in the name of news/editorial coverage);
- Voting process (one voter, one vote that is cast in secret);
- Role of officials (the officials adhere to the election procedures, e.g. they have been trained adequately and know which procedures to follow; they do not interfere in the voting process and file complaints made to them, etc.);

documents/udhr/ [accessed 10 October 2015].

71 Inter-Parliamentary Union (1994) *Declaration on Criteria for Free and Fair Elections.* Paris: IPU.

72 Goodwin-Gill GS (2006) *Free and Fair Elections; New Expanded Edition.* Paris: IPU. p. 73.

73 Bishop S & Hoeffler A (2014) *Free and Fair Elections – A New Database.* Oxford: Centre for the Study of African Economies.

74 Ibid.: 9.

- Counting of votes (tabulation of votes can be tracked from polling stations up through intermediate centers and to the final processing station).[75]

In this regard, this chapter uses the Sylvia Bishop and Anke Hoeffler framework to judge the freeness and fairness of the management of elections by the IEC as illustrated in Table 1. Based on the Sylvia Bishop and Anke Hoeffler framework, and using our own evaluations, the freeness and fairness of Botswana election is ranked at 0.855 (or 86%). It is notable that this scoring is, overall, consistent with assessments by external assessors; for example, the Commonwealth, African Union and Electoral Commissions Forum of SADC Countries (ECF-SADC).

The same sentiment has been expressed by election observers such as the Botswana Electoral Support Network (BESNet) that consists of the Botswana Council of Non-Governmental Organisations, *Ditshwanelo*, *Emang Basadi* Women's Association,[76] the Media Institute of Southern Africa (Botswana chapter) and the ECF-SADC. For example, after observing the 2009 general elections, the ECF-SADC Observer Mission stated its overall impressions as: the mission observed that generally the preparations for the conduct of elections were in place and this assisted the people of Botswana to exercise their constitutional right to vote.[77] The ECF expressed the same sentiments after observing the 2014 elections. In its preliminary statement it noted 'the impartiality and transparency of the IEC, both in law and practice'.[78]

However, this is not to say that there are no problems. To illustrate, when giving its preliminary statement on the 2014 general election, the ECF-SADC Observer Mission recommended some of the following: strengthen the advance voting by introducing application forms for anyone to be eligible to vote; ensure that there are spacious polling stations; consider the use of translucent ballot boxes as provided for in the SADC principles governing democratic elections.[79] In summary, the collective view was that these above issues do not detract from the IEC's ability to deliver free, fair and credible elections. However, this line of thought differs from that of opposition political parties. To illustrate, one respondent contended that 'the playing field is not level and the BDP abuses incumbency as instanced by its use of state resources to campaign and its monopoly use of Botswana Television'.[80] In terms of self-assessment, the IEC respondents expressed the view that, overall, the IEC, within its limited resources, managed elections in a free, fair and credible manner. However, they conceded that there were 'gaps that needed to be filled'.[81]

---

75 Ibid.: 9–13.
76 These are rights groups; *Ditshwanelo* is a human rights group and *Emang Basadi* is a women's advocacy group.
77 ECF-SADC (2009) *Observer Mission Report: Botswana General Elections, 16 October 2009*. Gaborone: ECF-SADC.
78 ECF-SADC (2014) A preliminary statement to the Independent Electoral Commission by the Electoral Commissions Forum of SADC Countries. In: *Observer Mission Report: Botswana General Elections, 24 October 2014*. Gaborone: ECF-SADC. p. 4.
79 Ibid.
80 Interview, 23 September 2015.
81 Interview, 28 September 2015

Table 1: Assessment: IEC contribution to the management of fair, free and credible elections

Variable	Score, max = 1, min = 0	Comments
Legal framework	1.0	The Constitution of Botswana, the Electoral Act and the Local Government Act govern the conduct of elections and these three instruments are implemented in both spirit and letter by the IEC.
Electoral management bodies	1.0	Section 65A of the constitution of Botswana provides that there shall be an Independent Electoral Commission. The Independent Electoral Commission is operationally independent, therefore, it runs elections without interference from outside parties (for example, see the *Ignatius Moswaane vs. Whyte Marobela* case).
Electoral rights	0.7	The constitution of Botswana provides for a multiparty democracy which is based on the basic democratic tenet of regular free and fair elections, equality of all citizens etc. All eligible citizens have the right to vote. However, there are issues around extending the franchise to prisoners and the hospitalised; as a consequence, this results in a score of 0.7.
Voter register	1.0	The voters' roll is updated and it is also available for inspection by the public. Furthermore, there is a provision for objections in the Electoral Act (for instance, a petitioner can object to the registration of a voter in a particular ward).
Ballot access	1.0	There are no obstacles to voting; hence, voters freely exercise their franchise.
Campaign process	1.0	There is no intimidation or unequal treatment of voters.
Media access	0.05	Overall, the state media coverage; radio (Radio Botswana 1), state newspapers (Daily News) and television (Botswana Television), is biased towards covering the ruling Botswana Democratic Party (particularly during elections); hence this low score.
Voting process	1.0	One voter is entitled to one vote and the secrecy of the vote is ensured through the use of polling booths.
Role of officials	1.0	Officials, both IEC and non-IEC (for example, members of the Botswana Police Service and Office of the District Commissioner's staff), adhere to election procedures and they are properly trained in their jobs of work pertaining to election management.
Counting of votes	0.8	There is a transparency in the counting process. However, some advocate for the counting of ballots at polling stations.

Overall score = 1+1+.7+1+1+1+.0.05+1+1+.8 = 8.55/10 = 0.85

Source: Author's evaluation, with reference to Bishop S & Hoeffler A (2014) *Free and Fair Elections – A New Database*. Oxford: Centre for the Study of African Economies.

Challenges

The IEC faces a number of challenges that have serious implications for its independence and operational efficiency and effectiveness. The key ones are enumerated below.

Lack of IEC Act

The foremost challenge that the IEC faces is the lack of an enabling legislation in the form of an IEC Act. While the creation of the IEC is provided in the constitution of Botswana, this is cast in broad outlines that do not explicitly identify the creature that is called the IEC. It is desirable that there be a specific law that defines the IEC; specifically, what its independence means. It is notable that from the inception of the IEC, the commission clamoured for the promulgation of the Act; 18 years later this is yet to be done. However, the absence of a legal framework in the form of the IEC Act does not derogate from the IEC's ability and capability to run free, fair and credible elections. Moving forward, the independence of the IEC can be only be spelt out and legally provided for and protected in the IEC Act.

Lack of definition of the independence descriptor

It is instructive that Botswana's electoral management body is called the Independent Electoral Commission. It would seem from a cursory glance at its name that the creators of the IEC had in mind an independent entity. That is, independent of the executive arm of the government even though it is 100% funded by the government. All evidence suggests that there is a disputed understanding of independence by the government on the one hand and the IEC on the other. While the IEC is wedded to the belief that independence means unfettered independence in terms of carrying out its mandate, the government's interpretation of independence is one which is truncated. During the formative years of the IEC, these different philosophies led to strained relationships. For example, the then permanent secretary to the president (PSP) insisted that the IEC secretary was responsible to the office of the president while the commission contended that the secretary was responsible to it. Matters came to a head when it was contended that the secretary's leave and travel outside the country had to be sanctioned by the PSP. Due to this disputed interpretation of the IEC's independence, 'some in the commission were contemplating seeking the courts' intervention in order to explicitly define what the IEC's independence meant but, nonetheless, this action was stayed'.[82] In the subsequent discussion, an understanding emerged that that the IEC's independence meant, among other things, that the IEC secretary was responsible to the commission. While this is the understanding, some contended that it stood to common reason that interpretations of the IEC's independence should not be premised on a gentleman's agreement between the IEC and government but, rather, on what the law set down in a specific IEC Act.

---

82 Interview, 23 September 2015.

Perceptions that the IEC is not independent

Among non-IEC respondents, there is a perception that the IEC is not independent, even operationally. One respondent stated that 'it is the view of our political party that there is no difference between the IEC and a government department'. The self-same respondent claimed that the IEC members were controlled by the directorate of public service management, and that therefore they could be transferred outside the IEC, thus causing a lot of disruption. He also stated that IEC staff could be disadvantaged in terms of career progression because some might hit a dead-end and would not be able to progress unless they were timeously transferred outside the IEC. Related to this are the politics that surround the hiring of staff at the IEC. One respondent gave the example of the recruitment process for the position of deputy IEC secretary – a post that was vacant for a very long time during which there was a long acting appointment. He stated that the recruitment took too long 'because the government could not find the right candidate for the job although it is not very clear what they wanted because this is an administrative job'. Another candidate also faulted the appointment of the IEC secretary by the state president who also happens to be the leader of the ruling political party as per the dictates of the first past the post electoral system that is used in Botswana. He put this in concrete terms saying that 'President Ian Khama, as the leader of the ruling Botswana Democratic Party, is an interested party in electoral matters, therefore it is problematic that he appoints the chief manager of elections'. The same respondent took issue with the setting of the election day by the president. He contended that 'the president only announces the election day once he is satisfied that his party, the Botswana Democratic Party, is ready. Thus, if the president is satisfied with the readiness of his party, he sets the election date'. In a related vein, he faulted the practice whereby the minister of local government and rural development issues the election instruments for council by-elections and asked 'what informs him/her that a certain date is suitable other than an instruction from above?'

Lack of conditions of service for commissioners

While the non-commissioner staff are governed by terms and conditions as stipulated in the public service act, the same is not true of commissioners. At the same time, there is no provision for the removal of commissioners from office for good cause. In this regard, one respondent remarked that 'were the commission to be faced with a situation where it had to take action against a commissioner for an actionable offence, it is very difficult to imagine what provisions of the law the IEC would use'. He thus asserted that the IEC could find itself in a lot of legal trouble.

Staffing shortage

The IEC faces a staffing shortage although it has devolved its functions to the periphery through the creation of outstations. It was stated that the staff complement at outstations is, at most, 'four officers, including a driver'. In this regard, the IEC secretary stated that 'for the IEC to be felt at outstations, we need between 8 and 11 officers'.

Inadequate resourcing

Like other government departments, the IEC would like to have more resources allocated to it, but it has to contend with reduced subventions. For example, it was stated that one out-station was supplied with one vehicle which was said to be inadequate. The IEC secretary stated that 'one tends to be sympathetic to this situation due to resource constraints'. One respondent took a different view stating that 'the running of elections should not be viewed as a cost item but an investment whose returns are incalculable'. However, another respondent stated that the government made efforts to adequately finance the IEC during election years. To illustrate, he stated that due to a revenue stress, there was a need for cutback budgeting resulting in reduced subventions during the 2014/15 financial year and the IEC was equally affected. This prompted it to appeal to the minister of finance and development planning and the president because 'we could not run a credible election on a shoe-string budget and, at the end, the IEC budget was increased'.

Voter Apathy

As documented by a 2002 IEC study, voter apathy is a problem in Botswana. Although the IEC has, subsequent to the study, intensified voter education and other out-reach programmes, voter apathy is still a problem, particularly among the youth. This is most problematic as Botswana has one of the youngest populations in Africa. Beyond voter apathy is the issue of voter disengagement. This means that voters cannot lobby their representatives on electoral reforms.

Low levels of active citizenship

This is strongly related to civic engagement and it means 'people getting involved in their local communities and democracy at all levels, from towns to cities to nationwide activity'.[83] In this regard, one respondent proposed that 'Batswana should emulate the Americans who generally have an understanding that to be an American is a 24-hour job'. Another lamented that 'some Batswana do not know anything about elections and tend to think that *nna dilo tse ga di nkame* (these things do not affect me)'.

Not-so-vibrant civil society

In the literature, civil society in Botswana is perceived as 'weak' and less vibrant. Some respondents expressed a view that civil society was too passive to engage in lobbying and advocacy in regard to electoral reform. In this regard, a comparison was made with South Africa's chapter 9 institutions that are at the forefront of lobbying and advocacy, including electoral reform.

---

83 Andrej Nosko & Katalin Széger (2013, 25 February) *Active Citizenship Can Change Your Country For the Better.* Available at https://www.opensocietyfoundations.org/voices/active-citizenship-can-change-your-country-better [accessed 13 September 2016].

Slow uptake of IEC's recommendations

The government was faulted for its slow uptake of electoral reforms, principally that of ensuring the total independence of the IEC, despite its public avowals that it believes in its total independence and easy-to-implement reforms such as electronic voting, the counting of ballots at the polling stations and levelling the playing field.

Lack of control over campaign finance

There is no law on the disclosure of sources of campaign funds. Thus the sponsorship of political parties by businesses remains largely secretive. For example, the BDP, riding on the wave of incumbency, has been a favoured beneficiary of secretive private financing, as sufficiently instanced by the P2.4 million (USD 0.22 million) donation it got from 'from friends and the business community'.[84] The opposition also gets funding from undisclosed sources although not on as big a scale as the BDP does. In the final analysis, this situation results in an unlevelled playing field and matters are not helped by the fact that there is no public funding for political parties and that the BDP has resisted this over years.

Conclusion

Elections are critical in a democracy and, therefore, it is vital that they are managed in a free and fair manner. Two things are critical; (i) the rules of engagement; and (ii) election management bodies (EMBs). EMBs are the locus of the electoral process and they play a big role as instruments of governance.[85] This study investigated the overarching research question: How does the Independent Electoral Commission contribute to the management of fair, free and credible elections in Botswana? It used a conceptual framework of free and fair elections. It further asked sub-research questions concerning: (i) the meaning of independence in as far as it relates to the IEC; (ii) independent decision-making and action by the IEC; (iii) impartiality; (iv) integrity; and (v) transparency. To answer the overarching research question, it used the Sylvia Bishop and Anke Hoeffler tool (see Table 1) and assessments by external assessors, for example The Commonwealth and African Union, and local election observers. The study concluded that there is a legal-institutional framework that enables the IEC to contribute to the management of fair, free and credible elections in Botswana. Regarding the five sub-research questions, the study concluded that: the meaning of IEC's independence is not defined; there is independent decision-making and action by the IEC; the IEC is impartial in its job of work; the IEC lends integrity to the electoral process; the IEC is transparent in its job of work. In conclusion, although the

---

84 Molomo M & Sebudubudu D (2006) Funding of political parties; levelling the political playing field. In: Maundeni, Z (ed.) *40 Years of Democracy in Botswana.* Gaborone: Mmegi Publishing House. pp. 147–162.
85 López-Pintor R (2000) *Electoral Management Bodies as Institutions of Governance.* New York: Bureau for Development Policy.

constitution does not define the meaning of the IEC's independence, this lacuna does not detract from the IEC's ability to manage elections in a fair, free and credible manner in Botswana.

Recommendations

Constitutional and legal framework

There is a need for the long-delayed promulgation of the Independent Electoral Commission (IEC) Act that will, among other things, provide for the following:

- The establishment of the IEC as a body corporate.
- The explicit definition of the *independence* of the IEC.
- The explicit definition of reporting lines; i.e. the IEC must report to parliament.

Election management

The mandate of the IEC should be expanded to include, among other things, voter and civic education, control over campaign funds.

- The IEC must have total control of its staff, including the appointment of the secretary.
- Dispute resolution mechanisms should be clearly spelt out in the IEC Act.
- There is a need for the creation of an Independent Media Commission to regulate media during election periods.[86]

Wider constitutional issues

It is notable that the above recommendations will be of no use if some thoroughgoing constitutional reforms are not affected. Therefore, if the IEC and other oversight bodies such as the office of the ombudsman are to report to parliament effectively, the executive-legislature relationship has to be re-aligned to ensure parliamentary supremacy. As it is, the parliament is subservient to the executive arm of the government.[87] Thus, parliament must be strengthened to enable it to exert accountability from the executive.

---

86 There is a precedent for this practice; for example, an independent media commission was established by the Independent Media Commission Act (149/1993).

87 See Emmanuel Botlhale E & Lotshwao K (2013) The uneasy relationship between parliament and the executive in Botswana. Botswana Notes and Records 45: 40–52; and Molomo MR (2012) *Democratic Deficit in the Parliament of Botswana.* Cape Town: The Centre for Advanced Studies of African Society.

List of interviewees (anonymous)

Organisation/ Designation	Narrative	Identifier and dates
Independent Electoral Commission	Personal interviews with 5 * sitting commissioners.	X1, X2, X3, X4, X5; 10, 21 and 22 September 2015
Independent Electoral Commission	Personal interviews with 3 *administrative staff.	X1, X2, X3; 28 and 29 September 2015.
Former commissioners	Personal interviews with 3 * former commissioners.	X1, X2, X3; 22, 23 and 24 September 2015.
SADC Electoral Commissioners Forum	Personal interview with 1 *administrative staff.	X1; 29 September 2015.
Political parties	Personal interviews with 3 * representatives of political parties.	X1, X2; X3; September 2015.

3

DEMOCRATIC REPUBLIC OF CONGO

Dr Joseph Cihunda Hengelela

Introduction

The idea of creating an independent institution responsible for organising elections in the Democratic Republic of Congo (DRC) dates back to the Sovereign National Conference (SNC), which took place from 1991 to 1992. It was a key outcome of the work conducted by the National Electoral Commission (NEC).[1] Once established, the planned institution could not organise elections because of the numerous instances of government interference that occurred until the end of the regime of President Mobutu.[2] However, the need to establish a new independent body to organise elections came to the fore during the Inter-Congolese Dialogue (ICD) held in Sun City in South Africa in 2002, and a resolution was passed to that effect.

An Independent Electoral Commission (IEC) was thus created shortly after the ICD talks were concluded. It was one of several institutions supporting democracy during the transitional period of 2003–2006. This Commission was tasked with identifying and registering voters, and with organising the 2005 constitutional referendum. It also prepared and organised the presidential, parliamentary and provincial elections of 2006 and the Senate elections of 2007. The National Independent Electoral Commission (NIEC or CENI as per its French acronym), created by the constitution of 18 February 2006, replaced the IEC in 2011. The NIEC organised presidential and parliamentary elections in 2006, in 2015 and is currently preparing the 2016 elections.

The establishment of the NIEC and its predecessor the IEC has not solved the problems related to holding free, democratic and transparent elections. The NIEC has not hitherto provided convincing evidence that it is truly fulfilling the expectations of the Congolese people about its mission. There seem to be two problems facing the NIEC. The first concerns the difficulties inherent in the NIEC itself, and the second is a political

---

1   Mudaba YL (2003) La préparation et la gestion des échéances électorales: Cas de la Commission Nationale des Elections (CNE). *Afrique et Développement*. Kinshasa: CNE pp. 89–96.
2   Nzongola-Ntalaja G (2015) *Faillite de la gouvernance et crise de la construction nationale au Congo-Kinshasa. Une analyse des luttes pour la démocratie et la souveraineté nationale.* Kinshasa-Montréal-Washington: ICREDES. pp. 276–281.

environment hostile to democratic elections in the DRC and, indeed, to the birth of a true democracy.

In considering the NIEC's challenges, it is crucial to point out institutional instability as the primary factor negatively affecting the NIEC's ability to carry out its duties. This is evidenced by the delay in setting up the institution itself, five years after it was established by the constitution, on the eve of an election. This institutional instability is also reflected in the electoral legal framework. Over three election cycles in nine years, the election administration went through three configurations and two amendments of the electoral laws. It would appear that these amendments had more to do with protecting vested political interests than with responding to any societal changes.

The crucial element in the various reforms of the NIEC is its composition. It is essentially biased towards the ruling party, despite the return of civil society amongst its members, and the fact that the latter holds the presidency of the NIEC. The NIEC's composition acts as a limitation on its independence from the executive. Financial dependence of the NIEC is glaring and often results in it being incapable of fulfilling its mandate when funds are not made available by the government in accordance with the electoral calendar.

Historical, political, economic, social and cultural context

In order to understand the challenge of organising elections in the DRC, it is essential to take into account the country's political and constitutional history. In this regard, it is interesting to see how Congo's history has influenced the current electoral system, as well as the weight of political, economic, social, cultural and religious factors.

Electoral practices in the DRC: A retrospective look

The history of elections in the DRC goes back to the era of political emancipation, while the country was still under Belgian colonial rule. Though grievances were occasionally expressed by the population during colonial rule, voting as a political right was only granted to the indigenous people of Congo in 1957, in a context of growing momentum towards independence.

In March 1957, a royal decree on urban management was adopted containing provisions for local elections. Following this decree, the first elections in Congo's urban centres of Leopoldville (Kinshasa), Elizabethville (Lubumbashi) and Jadotville (Likasi) were held under Ordinance No. 12/295 in December 1957. Further local elections took place the following year in the remaining provincial capitals of Coquilhatville (Mbandaka), Stanleyville (Kisangani), Bukavu, and Luluaburg (Kananga), as well as Matate and N'djili, two new additional municipal districts in Leopoldville.[3]

---

3   See Ndaywel è Nziem I (2012) *Nouvelle histoire du Congo. Des origines à la République Démocratique du Congo.* Brussels: Le Cri. pp. 428–429.

In the absence of formal professional political structures, voters had little choice but to rely on structures and candidates that were largely organised along ethnic or tribal lines. In Leopoldville and Elizabethville, the two main cities of the colony, the electoral contests pitted the main tribal groupings against each other: the Bakongo vs. the Bangala in Leopoldville, the Kasai (Luba) vs. Katanga natives in Elisabethville. The elections 'took place in an atmosphere of tribal antagonism between leaders of the Alliance of the Bakongo people (*Alliance des Bakongo* – ABAKO) on the one hand, and leaders of 'Liboke lya Bangala' on the other; or between native Katangans and the 'diaspora' from Kasai. The election results led to higher levels of ethnic consciousness, which then became entrenched through the creation of ethnically based political groups.[4] This strong ethnic dimension has remained a factor in the history of elections in the DRC.

Following the inaugural local elections, national pre-independence elections were scheduled for December 1959. A royal decree issued on 7 October 1959, however, generated controversy. It granted the franchise to Belgian and Congolese nationals.[5] The leaders of the ABAKO, PSA (*Parti Solidaire Africain*) and MNC-Lumumba parties refused to recognise the Belgians' franchise, because they did not want a multiracial independent Congo that might be similar to South Africa. When their demands were not heeded, they called on their supporters to boycott the elections. This resulted in a high rate of abstention in the elections, mainly in Leopoldville (70%), in Kongo Central (100%) and in some other territories.[6]

The 1959 elections were followed by a series of laws aimed to prepare Congo for genuine decolonisation. A new constitution was promulgated, which granted the political rights to vote and to be elected. Section 1 of the Decree of 7 October 1959 setting the regulations on the constitution of councils granted mainland Belgians the right to vote.[7] Section 2 of the Fundamental Law of 17 June 1960 enshrining public freedoms granted political rights only to the Congolese, except if otherwise provided by law. In subsequent constitutions, political rights would be granted to the Congolese only.

The election campaign and the elections themselves were marked by a climate of ethnic conflict, sometimes accompanied by the contesting of election results in the courts.[8] In many polling stations around the country, electoral fraud was claimed by some quarters and acknowledged by the Belgian authorities. However, pressed by the 30 June deadline

---

4   Mantuba-Ngoma PM (2013) *Les élections dans l'histoire politique de la République Démocratique du Congo (1957–2011)*. Kinshasa: Konrad-Adenauer-Stiftung Publications. p. 18.
5   Decree of 7 October 1959 determining the rules on the establishment of councils. In: M Katsuva, I Moju-Mbey & I Kambere-ng'Ise (1994) *Régimes électoraux en République du Zaïre: textes législatifs d'organisation.* Kinshasa: ISE Consult and ACCT. pp. 11 and 17.
6   Mantuba-Ngoma PM (2013) *Les élections dans l'histoire politique de la République Démocratique du Congo (1957–2011)*. Kinshasa: Konrad-Adenauer-Stiftung Publications. p. 23.
7   Decree of 7 October 1959 determining the rules on the establishment of councils, section 1. In: M Katsuva, I Moju-Mbey and I Kambere-ng'Ise: *Régimes électoraux en République du Zaïre: textes législatifs d'organisation.* Kinshasa: ISE Consult and ACCT.
8   Mantuba-Ngoma PM (2013) *Les élections dans l'histoire politique de la République Démocratique du Congo (1957–2011)*. Kinshasa: Konrad-Adenauer-Stiftung Publications. p. 26.

for independence, they did not have time to organise new elections.[9] Regardless of the conditions in which the vote took place, the general elections resulted in a parliament controlled mainly by the MNC-Lumumba and its allies, who formed the first government, led by Patrice Emery Lumumba.

Congo's independence was proclaimed on 30 June 1960, but celebrations were short-lived. Indeed within the space of a few days, a political and institutional crisis ensued. Hostility between the head of state, President Joseph Kasavubu, and his prime minister, Patrice Lumumba, plunged the country into a chaos, an impasse that was resolved only by the adoption of the final constitution which ended the crisis in 1964. The political and physical elimination of Lumumba had been envisaged as a solution to the Congolese crisis. This took place through an unconstitutional termination of his mandate as prime minister, and then through his assassination on 17 January 1961.

Even before the 1964 constitution was adopted on 1 August that year, Moise Tshombe became head of a government whose main task was to end the insurgency raging in the country and to hold new parliamentary elections.[10]

Organised in terms of the decree of 6 October 1964 on the organisation of national and provincial elections (*Décret-loi du 6 octobre 1964 portant organisation des élections nationales et provincials*),[11] the elections (despite numerous irregularities that were later confirmed by the appeals court in Leopoldville),[12] strengthened Prime Minister Tshombe's popularity by producing a large majority in parliament for his National Convention of Congo (CONACO).

The new government had barely started to put in place democratic institutions created by the constitution of 1 August 1964 when a new conflict broke out between Prime Minister Tshombe and President Kasavubu, still head of state.[13] This conflict prompted yet another military intervention, with the high command of the army carrying out a coup on 24 November 1965 under the leadership of General Mobutu.

The intervention of the military suspended all institutions created by the constitution of 1 August 1964, and marked the start of the Second Republic. Two years after coming to power, on 20 May 1967, General Mobutu created the Popular Movement of the Revolution

---

9   Ibid.: 27.
10 Ibid.: 35.
11 Katsuva M, Moju-Mbey I & Kambere-ng'Ise I (1994) *Régimes électoraux en République du Zaïre: textes législatifs d'organisation.* Kinshasa: ISE Consult and ACCT. p. 68.
12 Following the numerous election irregularities brought before it, the Leopoldville Court of Appeal cancelled the election results for the voting districts of the Central Basin, Fizi, Kwilu and Maniema. These irregularities were related among others to the lack of ballot boxes in some polling stations, authorities' refusal to let some candidates enter polling stations, authorities' refusal to post candidates' pictures in some polling stations, and attempts by some political party activists to skew the results. With particular regard to the Central Basin, the Appeal Court held further that the authorities had been unable to ensure the safety of members of election commissions and ensure their freedom of movement. See Gérard-Libois J and Van Lierde J (1965) *Congo 1965.* Brussels-Kinshasa: CRISP-INEP. p. 224.
13 Punga Kumakinga P (2005) *Constitutions et constitutionnalisme en Afrique. Cas de la République Démocratique du Congo,* LL.B. dissertation, Law Faculty, University of Kinshasa. p. 119.

(*Mouvement Populaire de la Révolution* – MPR), the political party that became the Mobutu regime's key political tool for nearly a quarter of a century.[14]

To strengthen his political legitimacy, Mobutu announced elections in 1970. This was preceded by a new constitution on 24 June 1967,[15] which made provisions for the extension of the franchise to women.[16] The 1967 constitution is different from the 1964 one in that it prohibited multiparty democracy, which had been in place since 1957. Its section 4 set the MPR up as the only political party in the republic.

Under the second republic, electoral practice came to be entirely characterised by militancy and partisanship. Indeed, candidates were chosen and imposed by the party organs. During the 1970 presidential election, Mobutu was the sole candidate presented by the MPR, the party he had himself created as founder-president. Another feature of electoral practice under the second republic was the 'vote by acclamation during people's assemblies',[17] a practice adopted during the general elections of 2 November 1975, in accordance with section 25 of Act No. 75/009 of 2 April 1975 on the Organisation of Elections (*Loi n°75/009 du 2 avril 1975 portant organisation des élections législatives*).[18] The introduction of this measure was justified as an innovation aimed at empowering the Congolese people and ensuring closeness to their political representatives.

In any event, the legislature established after such atypical elections was interrupted two years later by the Shaba war,[19] which nearly caused Mobutu's downfall. Mobutu announced internal reforms on 1 July 1977, which included the liberalisation of the political system and the decentralisation of economic management and public affairs.[20] The year 1977 also marked the end of his first presidential term which had started on 5 December 1970. The electoral reforms included the dropping of the closed list system that had been in place since the strengthening of the regime in early 1970. According to Mabiala Mantuba-Ngoma,[21] the new Electoral Act granted the right to any eligible Zairian[22] the right to submit their candidature in the constituency of their choice, if he or she was permanently residing in that constituency, or had long-term interests in that constituency such as a

---

14 N'Gbanda H & Ko Atumba N (1998) *Ainsi sonne le glas! Les derniers jours du Maréchal Mobutu.* Paris: Ed. Gideppe. p. 36.
15 Mantuba-Ngoma PM (2013) *Les élections dans l'histoire politique de la République Démocratique du Congo (1957–2011).* Kinshasa: Konrad-Adenauer-Stiftung Publications. p. 39.
16 Ibid.: 119–128.
17 Ibid.: 44.
18 Ibid.
19 The Shaba war refers to two military incursions which took place in March 1977 (Shaba I) and in May 1978 (Shaba II) and which were led by Congolese refugees in Angola, organised under the historic name of the 'Katanga gendarmes', and constituted as FLNC. See Nzongola-Ntalaja G (2015) *Faillite de la gouvernance et crise de la construction nationale au Congo-Kinshasa. Une analyse des luttes pour la démocratie et la souveraineté nationale.* Kinshasa-Montréal-Washington: ICREDES. p. 242.
20 Mantuba-Ngoma PM (2013) *Les élections dans l'histoire politique de la République Démocratique du Congo (1957–2011).* Kinshasa: Konrad-Adenauer-Stiftung Publications. p. 44.
21 Ibid.: 45.
22 The DRC had been renamed 'Zaire' in 1971, to follow the philosophy of 'authenticity'. Through that name change, the Congolese had become Zairian. See section 1 of Act 71-006 of 19 October 1971 amending the constitution.

home or any agricultural or commercial activity. Voters, meanwhile, had the right to vote for any of the candidates endorsed by the MPR, the party state, and appearing on an open list. These relaxed rules, however, did not apply to the presentation of candidates for the presidential election, where the system was designed to support a single candidate in the form of the founding president of the MPR, who was also *ex officio* president of the republic.

Parliamentary and local elections took place on 15 and 16 October 1977, followed by presidential elections on 2 December 1977. While he was satisfied with the manner in which the elections took place in a context of reform, President Mobutu pointed to a number of remaining problems that had, in his view, to be resolved. He criticised the lack of an endorsement mechanism of candidates by the MPR, the impact of money, tribalism, regionalism in the choice of some voters, voting procedures in a largely illiterate society, the verification procedures of vote counting and the publication of results, and finally the mechanism aimed at resolving disputes and conflicts.[23]

The pressure on the regime as a result of the Shaba war resulted in further constitutional reforms and attempts to liberalise the regime, as exemplified by Act No. 78-010 of 15 February 1978.[24] [25] However, changes turned out to be cosmetic and short-lived. Indeed, two years later, in February and November 1980, the regime tightened the screws again with the creation of the central committee, tasked with providing inspiration, giving guidance and making decisions within the MPR.[26]

As might have been expected, the Ordinance-Law No. 82-007 of 25 February 1982 on the organisation of elections of the legislative council, regional assemblies, area councils and local wards (*Ordonnance-loi n°82-007 du 25 février 1982 portant organisation des élections des membres du Conseil législatif, des Assemblées régionales, des Conseils de zone et des Conseils de collectivité*) made it more difficult for candidates to apply. The application process became subject to an endorsement procedure by the central committee. For example, in the case of candidatures for the legislative council (i.e. parliament), applications had to be examined in hierarchical order by the local people's committee, the deputy regional party committee and the regional party committee. Following that, they were submitted to the central

23 Mobutu SS (1983) *Discours, allocutions, messages 1976-1981, Volume 1: 1976–1978.* Kinshasa. p. 121.
24 Kilombo N (1991) *Congo-Zaïre. De la Charte coloniale à la Constitution de la troisième République.* Kinshasa: Ed. Secco. p. 149.
25 These reforms included the amendment of the mechanism granting exclusive allocation of power to the ruling party. The Act used to read 'the people exercise power through the President of the Popular Movement of the Revolution, with the support of the organs of the Revolutionary Popular Movement' and was changed to read 'the exercise of power is executed through the President of the Popular Movement of the Revolution in conjunction with the organs of the movement, each respecting the distribution of powers and functions'. The chairman of the MPR and of the republic maintained the power to initiate legislation and constitutional amendments; he remained the head of government despite the establishment of a first state commissioner; the limitation of presidential terms was abandoned, and the review of the candidates to the presidential election continued to be the sole responsibility of the president's office. The right to vote was granted to all Zairians from 18 years of age.
26 Punga Kumakinga P (2005) *Constitutions et constitutionnalisme en Afrique. Cas de la République Démocratique du Congo,* LL.B. dissertation, Law Faculty, University of Kinshasa. p. 125.

committee by the minister for territorial administration.[27] This mandatory endorsement procedure for candidates was motivated by a need for control, or, as Mabiala puts it, to 'prevent a situation in which just anyone could play a role in society and do whatever they wanted'.[28] The growing influence by the party on electoral matters was further evidenced in Law No. 88-004 of 29 January 1988, which transferred competence to rule in the matter of electoral disputes from the Supreme Court of Justice to the central committee of the MPR.[29]

The 1984 presidential elections[30] and the 1987 parliamentary elections[31] were the last elections of the second republic. They were characterised by the strong influence of the central committee of the MPR. Following many irregularities and improprieties during the 1987 regional and local elections, the central committee took a series of measures to ensure the objectivity of national polls. This included the establishment of election monitors for candidates in each region during the polling and vote counting, and the establishment of regional commissions of the central committee responsible for monitoring the conduct of the elections.[32]

After it was deemed that the above measures were insufficient to ensure the integrity of election results, a far more drastic step was taken by the disciplinary commission of the central committee, which became an exceptional political jurisdiction of the MPR.[33] It consisted of the central committee of the MPR simply cancelling the legislative and municipal elections of 1987 altogether across the entire territory.[34] In his historic speech of 24 April 1990, President Mobutu decreed a democratic transition that consisted of a return to multiparty politics, the abolition of the institutionalisation of the MPR, and consequently a clear separation of party and state, as well as the restoration of the three traditional branches of power: legislative, executive and judicial.[35] A week later, on 3 May 1990, the president announced in the legislative council that the transition would lead to presidential elections after 4 December 1991 (the end of his seven-year term) and to parliamentary elections in 1992.[36] Following procrastination and political conflicts between the president

27 Katsuva M, Moju-Mbey I & Kambere-ng'Ise I (1994) *Régimes électoraux en République du Zaïre: textes législatifs d'organisation*. Kinshasa: ISE Consult and ACCT. p. 163.
28 Mantuba-Ngoma PM (2013) *Les élections dans l'histoire politique de la République Démocratique du Congo (1957–2011)*. Kinshasa: Konrad-Adenauer-Stiftung Publications. p. 46.
29 Eseng'Ekeli JD (2013) *Droit constitutionnel. L'expérience congolaise (RDC)* Paris: L'Harmattan p. 139.
30 Organised by Act 84-001 of 20 January 1984. In: M Katsuva, I Moju-Mbey and I Kambere-ng'Ise (1994) *Régimes électoraux en République du Zaïre: textes législatifs d'organisation*. Kinshasa: ISE Consult and ACCT.
31 Organised by Ordinance-Law No. 87-002 of 10 January 1987. In: M Katsuva, I Moju-Mbey and I Kambere-ng'Ise (1994) *Régimes électoraux en République du Zaïre: textes législatifs d'organisation*. Kinshasa: ISE Consult and ACCT.
32 Mantuba-Ngoma PM (2013) *Les élections dans l'histoire politique de la République Démocratique du Congo (1957–2011)*. Kinshasa: Konrad-Adenauer-Stiftung Publications. p. 48.
33 Kamukuny Mukinay A (2011) *Contribution à l'étude de la fraude en droit constitutionnel congolais*. Belgium: Academia-L'Harmattan, Louvain-la-Neuve. p. 277.
34 Mabanga Monga Mabanga G (1999) *Le contentieux constitutionnel congolais*. Kinshasa: EUA. p. 45.
35 Discours présidentiel d'avènement de la troisième République (April–May 1990). *Zaïre-Afrique* 244–245: 197–203.
36 Mantuba-Ngoma PM (2013) *Les élections dans l'histoire politique de la République Démocratique du Congo*

(and his successors) and opposing political forces committed to change, it took almost 17 years for the planned elections to take place.[37]

The general elections of 2006–2007 formally rekindled the electoral practice that had been initiated on the eve of independence. Even though the polls were organised with significant involvement from the international community, and were rightly qualified as transitional elections by Ngoma Binda,[38] the poll also revived all of the old demons that had characterised election campaigns since independence: regionalism, tribalism, patronage and nepotism. In the presidential elections, for example, voting patterns largely followed language and provincial fault lines, ultimately leading to a polarisation of the spatial distribution of votes between the top two candidates. Money and ethnicity played significant roles in the election campaign.[39]

The legal,[40] and arguably even institutional,[41] frameworks of these elections bear the mark of the post-conflict consensus-seeking context of a fragile state, in a country emerging from a long political and military crisis, coupled with a legitimacy crisis affecting all the individuals and institutions that had ruled the country since independence. These elections were intended to end this crisis. It is for this reason that the electoral system based on the constitution of 18 February 2006 and on the electoral legislation in force at that time was consensual and inclusive, combining both majority voting for single-member constituencies, and proportional systems of open lists with the largest remainder rule (sic) applying for multi-member constituencies.[42]

Key factors influencing the electoral system

The success of an electoral process can depend on several factors that have a direct influence on the elections. These factors are essentially political and economic. But the experience of electoral practice reveals that both social and cultural factors can also determine the organisation and the success of an electoral process. The electoral history of Congo has been marked by one or the other factor, depending on the degree of political openness.

(1957–2011). Kinshasa: Konrad-Adenauer-Stiftung Publications. p. 51.

37 Minani-Bihuzo R (2008) *1990–2007. 17 ans de transition politique et perspectives démocratiques en RDC. Document d'éducation civique.* Kinshasa: CEPAS-RODHECIC.

38 Ngoma-Binda P (2015) Elections transitionnelles dans un contexte d'extrême fragilité et de taux élevé d'espoirs, de méfiance et de craintes. In: Phambu Ngoma-Binda (ed.) *Les élections en RDC. Un regard transversal et prospectif sur les élections législatives et présidentielles de 2006.* Kinshasa: IFEP. pp. 11–23.

39 Mantuba-Ngoma PM (2013) *Les élections dans l'histoire politique de la République Démocratique du Congo (1957–2011).* Kinshasa: Konrad-Adenauer-Stiftung Publications. p. 71.

40 The primary provisions regulating the elections were, among others, the constitution of 18 February 2006, Act 04/028 of 24 December 2004 on the identification and enrolment of voters, and Act 06/006 of 9 March 2006 on the organisation of presidential, parliamentary, provincial, urban, municipal and local elections.

41 The Independent Electoral Commission, regulated by Act 04/009 of 5 June 2004 on the organisation, powers and functioning of the IEC.

42 Ngoma-Binda P Mandefu O, Yahisule J and Moswa Mombo L (2010) *République Démocratique du Congo. Démocratie et participation à la vie politique : une évaluation des premiers pas dans la IIIe République.* Johannesburg: OSF. p. 69.

Political factors

The ardent desire to gain power or to retain it at all costs is an incentive for political actors to spare no effort in winning elections, regardless of the costs involved. This inevitably has an impact on the actual management of the electoral process. Since 1960, the political will of those in power (and therefore of election organisers) to not lose elections drives them to control the entire voting process, starting from voter registration and election campaigning, all the way to controlling the litigation process in case of any dispute over the fairness of the election. Electoral tampering to win at any cost can even impact the drafting of electoral legislation in order to tailor the law in favour of the candidate of the party designated, by the establishment, to win.

Under the one-party regime, a single-candidate poll for the presidential election ensured victory for Mobutu, even though what the law actually stipulated was that only the founding President of the MPR was eligible as President of the Republic. However, for legislative, regional (provincial) and local elections, a proportional representation system with either open or closed lists favoured regime cronies, the only ones to have access to political mandates, thanks to the resources provided by Mobutu's aristocracy to maintain illusions in their electoral strongholds.[43]

The advent of democracy has not fundamentally changed this. However, tampering now takes other forms of electoral fraud and manipulation organised by the governing party, with or without the complicity of the body in charge of organisation the elections. This includes the politicisation of the commission in charge of organising the elections, the appointment of people regardless of qualifications, the involvement of people with vested interests in the deployment of election logistics, the tabulation of election results outside of polling stations in conditions of total opacity, and the manipulation of the judiciary. These are all politically devised strategies aimed at influencing the electoral process, in order to align it with the wishes of the established holders of political power, which also unfortunately corresponds to vested economic and financial centres of power.

Economic and financial factors

Organising elections requires significant financial resources. The logistics and campaigning are two key factors that determine success or failure of the electoral process for the organisers on the one hand and the candidates on the other.

The lack of resources necessarily plays a significant role in the manner in which elections are managed, including the choices made by the organising authority. When the country entered a recession at the end of the copper boom,[44] the option of voting by acclamation

---

43 For more insight, see Mampuya Kanunk'a-Tshiabo A (2005) *Espoirs et déception de la quête constitutionnelle congolaise. Clés pour comprendre le processus constitutionnel du Congo-Kinshasa.* Nancy-Kinshasa: AMA Ed-BNC. p. 159.

44 Punga Kumakinga P (2012) Les interventions du Fonds Monétaire International en République Démocratique du Congo: base juridique, bilan et perspectives. *Librairie africaine d'études juridiques.* Nairobi, Juillet 2012. p. 50.

during rallies was lifted for the general elections of 1975.[45] Although this choice was presented as an innovative measure to empower the Zairian people, the president himself, in a moment of self-criticism, justified the new system as a way of reducing unnecessary government expenses.[46]

The financial argument was again, in a rather questionable manner, used in January 2011 to justify yet another change to the electoral system, reducing presidential elections to a single ballot majority poll. Economic reasons are also behind the DRC's economic dependence to ensure adequate electoral logistics, contributing greatly to the elections fiasco of 28 November 2011.[47] Similarly, the organisation of local elections has been deferred indefinitely since 2006, for lack of funding. Currently, ever more political figures from the government's side are heard using financial arguments to justify their choices.

Social and cultural factors

The organisation, operation and outcomes of elections in the DRC have often been marked by socio-cultural phenomena. In contrast to international norms, electoral competitions are considered in the DRC as competitions between persons rather than between ideas and political programmes. During electoral contests, the identity and origins of a candidate can be used as a political tool, especially when it hampers the popularity of political opponents. The discussion about 'Congolese identity' which was prominent in the 2006 election is a clear manifestation of that reality.

The separatist and exclusivist narratives of election campaigns inevitably produce ethnic violence that taints electoral processes in the DRC,[48] and irreversibly leads to fragmented outcomes along regional lines.[49] According to Ngoma-Binda,[50] the lack of economic development, coupled with society's limited access to knowledge, turn ethnic and/or provincial origin into a key factors in determining voters' choices. Tribalism, ethnicity and regionalism have significantly impacted the organisation and the conduct of elections since 1960, even during the second republic, which was supposedly the high-water mark of national unity over regional and ethnic identities.

45 See Act 75/009 of 2 April 1975 on the organisation of parliamentary elections, section 25.
46 Mobutu cited by Mantuba-Ngoma PM (2013) *Les élections dans l'histoire politique de la République Démocratique du Congo (1957–2011)*. Kinshasa: Konrad-Adenauer-Stiftung Publications. p. 44.
47 Boisbouvier C (2011) RD Congo. Autopsie d'un fiasco. *Jeune-Afrique*, Paris, 18 to 24 December 2011. pp. 10–12.
48 At the 1960 general elections, ethnic divisions appeared between the Bakongo (ABAKO) and the Bangala (UNIMO) in Léopoldville, whereas the divisions in Katanga were between CONAKAT (Confederation of Katanga Associations) and the Baluba from Kasaï. Four decades later, during the 2006 and 2011 elections, the division between eastern and western ethnic groups could still be felt.
49 The regional vote meant that the outcome of the October 2006 presidential election was as follows: the eastern part of the DRC voted for Joseph Kabila and the western part of the DRC voted for Jean-Pierre Bemba, in effect dividing the territory in two.
50 Ngoma-Binda P (2015) Elections transitionnelles dans un contexte d'extrême fragilité et de taux élevé d'espoirs, de méfiance et de craintes. In: P Ngoma-Binda (ed.) *Les élections en RDC. Un regard transversal et prospectif sur les élections législatives et présidentielles de 2006*. Kinshasa: IFEP. p. 21.

Legal framework

The DRC's electoral administration has a national and international legal framework.

National legal framework

The National Independent Electoral Commission (NIEC) was created by the constitution of 18 February 2006, on the recommendation of the Sun City Global and Inclusive Agreement of 2002.[51] According to section 211 of the constitution, the NIEC 'is responsible for the organisation of the electoral process, including voter registration, the maintenance of the voter rolls, and vote and ballot counting during elections and referenda. The NIEC is responsible for the holding of electoral and referendum processes, in compliance with relevant legislation and regulations'.

The constitution makes provision for an organic law to establish the NIEC and describes its organisation and functioning. This organic law was adopted as Act 10/013 of 28 July 2010, amended and supplemented by Act 13/012 of 19 April 2013.[52] This organic law determines the:

- Mission and functions of the NIEC;
- Composition and status of members of the NIEC;
- Organisation and operation of the NIEC;
- Administrative and financial management of the NIEC; and
- Legal and disciplinary status of its members.

The organic law is complemented by the rules of procedure of the NIEC that describe, in great detail the:[53]

- Mission and functions of the NIEC;
- Institutional structure of the NIEC and their respective responsibilities;
- Organisation and functioning of the NIEC's committees and structures;
- Administrative organisation (status of staff members) of the NIEC;
- Collaboration of the NIEC with its partners;
- Rights, benefits and obligations of members of the NIEC; and
- Legal status and disciplinary regime of the members of the NIEC.

---

51 Resolution no. DIC/CPJ/09 on the National Independent Electoral Commission, April 2002.
52 Act 13/012 of 19 April 2013 amending and complementing the Organic Law 10/013 of 28 July 2010 on the organisation and functioning of the National Independent Electoral Commission (consolidated and updated version). *Congolese Official Gazette* (JORDC), special issue of 10 July 2014.
53 Rules of procedure of the national Independent Electoral. *Congolese Official Gazette* (JORDC), special Issue of 10 July 2014.

The current NIEC leadership structure was approved on 7 June 2013 by the National Assembly under resolution 04/CAB/P/AN/AM/2013.[54] The resolution appointing them was confirmed by presidential order on 12 June 2013.[55] The main provisions of the relevant laws were therefore given practical effect, in particular by the establishment of NIEC and its operations. The NIEC was established in 2011, during which it organised the presidential and legislative elections of 28 November 2011.

International legal framework

The DRC has opted for a monist approach to international law, meaning that treaties and international agreements adhered to in compliance with domestic provisions are part of the country's legal framework. These treaties and agreements, once published, supersede all other legislation.[56] The DRC's international legal obligations are universal, continental or regional.

National Independent Electoral Commission

The National Independent Electoral Commission (NIEC) was established in 2011 in accordance with Section 211 of the constitution of 18 February 2006. It replaced the Independent Electoral Commission (IEC),[57] which oversaw the 2005 constitutional referendum and the presidential, parliamentary, senatorial and provincial elections of 2006 and 2007. The IEC was dissolved by the constitution of 18 February 2006 as it was a transitional institution. The task of organising the elections was then vested in the NIEC. Its structure is different from that of the IEC in that it has two bodies: a plenary assembly and a bureau.

Composition, designation and status

The NIEC is composed of 13 commissioners. Ten of those are appointed by the main political groups represented in the National Assembly: six commissioners, including two women, are designated by members of the parliamentary majority and four, including one woman, by the members of the opposition. The three remaining commissioners are designated by members of civil society: religious groups, women's rights organisations and voter education organisations.[58] In terms of section 10 of the NIEC organic law, the criteria for appointing NIEC commissioners include their political representation at the

---

54 Resolution 04/CAB/P/AN/AM/2013 of 7 June 2013 confirming the appointment of members of the National Independent Electoral Commission 'NIEC'. *Congolese Official Gazette* (JORDC), special Issue of 10 July 2014.
55 Ordinance 13/058 of 12 June 2013 on the swearing-in of the members of the National Independent Electoral Commission. *Congolese Official Gazette* (JORDC), special issue of 10 July 2014.
56 Constitution of the Democratic Republic of Congo, section 215.
57 Transitional constitution. *Congolese Official Gazette* (JORDC), special issue of 5 April 2003, Section 155.
58 Act 13/012 of 19 April 2013 amending and complementing the Organic Law 10/013 of 28 July 2010 on the organisation and functioning of the National Independent Electoral Commission. *Congolese Official Gazette* (JORDC), special issue of 10 May 2013, section 10.

National Assembly, gender and their prominence in civil society. The gender criterion plays a role in all three categories of NIEC commissioners (majority, opposition and civil society).

Table 1: Breakdown of seats at the NIEC

	Category	Breakdown of seats according to gender		Total number of seats per category	Percentage
		Male	Female		
1	Majority	4	2	6	46
2	Opposition	3	1	4	31
3	Civil society	2	1	3	23
Total		9	4	13	100
Percentage		69	31	100	100

Source: Act 13 (012 of 2013)

Considering the above, a few observations are warranted. The first is that women are the only social category specifically represented in the NIEC. The youth, people with disabilities and other minority groups are not specifically represented. However, the law provides that the appointment of NIEC commissioners needs to take into account national representation. One may ask what exactly this concept of 'national representation' means. The second observation is that if national representation is deemed to mean that the composition of the NIEC should reflect the diversity of the Congolese nation, then this criterion is not easily applied. The third observation is that as an institution supporting democracy, the composition of the NIEC should primarily reflect neutrality. It should follow that there is an equal distribution of seats among political forces.[59]

Although a significant number (ten out of 13) commissioners at the NIEC are political appointments, the law requires that the NIEC commissioners be chosen from among independent personalities known for their competence, moral integrity, probity and intellectual honesty.[60]

To be a member of the NIEC, the candidate must:

- Be a Congolese national;[61]
- Be at least thirty years of age;[62]
- Be physically and mentally fit, have no criminal record, and be a holder of a certificate of good standing;[63]

---

59 In that scenario, the ruling coalition and the opposition would each have five seats, and civil society would have three.
60 Act 13/012 of 19 April 2013, section 12.
61 Ibid.: section 16(1).
62 Ibid.: section 16(2).
63 Ibid.: section 16(3). The certificate of good standing is issued by the Registrar of births, marriages and deaths in each city, *commune*, sector or chiefdom in the DRC.

- Hold at least a bachelor's degree or an equivalent degree, or provide evidence of at least ten years of professional experience in a field relevant to the NIEC;[64] and
- Enjoy full civil and political rights.[65]

Membership of the NIEC is incompatible with any national, provincial, urban, municipal or local elected office.[66] It is also incompatible with any of the following positions or mandates:

- Membership of the government;[67]
- Magistrate, member of the constitutional court or of the court of auditors;[68]
- Membership of another institution supporting democracy;[69]
- Membership of the economic and social council;[70]
- Cabinet membership or membership of the office of the president of the republic, the speaker of the National Assembly, the president of the senate, the prime minister, members of the government or any other political or administrative authority of the state;[71]
- Membership of the armed forces, national police and security services;[72]
- Career civil service in any of the state utilities or public services;[73]
- Political and administrative office bearer;[74]
- Public office bearer;[75]
- Employee of a public enterprise or mixed enterprise;[76]
- Any office bearer within a political party or political grouping;[77] and
- Any other remunerated functions conferred by a foreign state or an international organisation.[78]

Any person appointed as a member of the NIEC must, within eight days after being

---

64 Ibid., section 16(4).
65 Ibid.: section 16(6).
66 Ibid.: section 171.
67 Ibid.: section 17 (2)(1).
68 Ibid.: section 17 (2)(2).
69 Ibid.: section 17 (2)(3).
70 Ibid.: section 17 (2)(4).
71 Ibid.: section 17 (2)(5).
72 Ibid.: section 17 (2)(6).
73 Ibid.: section 17 (2)(7).
74 Ibid.: section 17 (2)(8).
75 Ibid.: section 17 (2)(9).
76 Ibid.: section 17 (2)(10).
77 Ibid.: section 17 (2)(11).
78 Ibid.: section 17 (2)(12).

appointed, specifically renounce any position, office or function incompatible with membership of the NIEC. Beyond that time limit, the appointee is deemed to have waived his or her appointment with the NIEC.[79]

NIEC commissioners have a six year non-renewable term. At the expiration of their term, NIEC commissioners remain in office until the new commissioners effectively start their mandate.[80] The mandate of NIEC commissioners can end as a result of:

- End of their term;[81]
- Death;[82]
- Resignation;[83]
- Permanent inability to carry out functions;[84]
- Permanent disability;[85]
- Unjustified absence from more than a quarter of sessions during a trimester;[86]
- Acceptance of an incompatible function;[87] and
- Final sentencing to imprisonment as a result of a criminal offence.[88]

A commissioner's permanent inability to carry out his or her functions is determined by the constitutional court at the request of the chairperson of the NIEC, upon recommendation of the Plenary Assembly. In case of a vacancy, a new commissioner is appointed following the same procedure that led to the designation of the commissioner being replaced. The replacing commissioner remains in office for the remainder of the original term.[89]

Before they start exercising their duties and at the end of their mandate, NIEC commissioners are required to submit personal asset declarations in writing to the constitutional court, listing all personal property and family assets.[90] Family assets include spousal assets held under the matrimonial regime, as well as the assets of children who are minors and the assets of any adult children who are dependents of the couple.[91] The constitutional court then passes on this declaration to the tax administration.[92]

Failure to file this declaration within thirty days will result in the said commissioner being deemed to have resigned. Within thirty days following the end of the commissioner's duties, if he or she failed to produce the declaration of assets, is suspected of having filed a

---

79 Ibid.: section 18.
80 Ibid.:
81 Ibid.: section 14 (1)(1).
82 Ibid.: section 14 (1)(2).
83 Ibid.: section 14 (1)(3).
84 Ibid.: section 14 (1)(4).
85 Ibid.: section 14 (1)(5).
86 Ibid.: section 14 (1)(6).
87 Ibid.: section 14 (1)(7).
88 Ibid.: section 14 (1)(8).
89 Ibid.: section 15.
90 Ibid.: section 21 (1).
91 Ibid.: section 21 (2).
92 Ibid.: section 21 (3).

fraudulent declaration, or is suspected of undue enrichment, the matter will be referred to the court of cassation.[93][94] It is important to note that the law does not state who should make the referral. Logic suggests that the tax administration has the means to detect fraud and undue enrichment. The tax administration should therefore report any false or fraudulent declaration of assets by a member of the NIEC to the constitutional court. It is at this level that action may be initiated. Under the principle of unity of the public prosecution service, the attorney general of the constitutional court can transfer the file to the attorney general of the constitutional court in order to take legal action against any member in breach of the legal obligations outlined above.

In carrying out their tasks, NIEC members may neither seek nor receive instructions from any outside authority. They enjoy total independence from the political powers that designated them.[95] They receive a fair allowance in order to guarantee their independence.[96] Together with the officials, commissioners are sworn to a code of conduct before assuming duty. In instances of infringements, they are referred to the court of cassation.[97]

Powers, functions and responsibilities

The constitution provides that the NIEC is mandated to organise the electoral process, including registering voters, maintaining the voters' roll, organising the elections and the vote counting and organising referendums. It must ensure the regularity of the electoral and referendum processes.[98] According to section 9 of the organic law, the NIEC's mission is to organise free, democratic and transparent elections that abide by the principles of independence, neutrality and impartiality.[99]

To achieve this mission, the NIEC is required to:

- Organise and manage the pre-electoral, electoral and referendum-related operations, including the identification and registration of voters, the establishment and publication of party lists, the voting, the counting of votes, the centralisation and announcement of provisional results;[100]

---

93 Under article 153 of the constitution, the court of cassation hears cassation appeals lodged against judgments rendered as a last resort by the civil and military courts. It hears, as a court of first and last instance, of offences allegedly committed by national MPs, senators, members of the executive except the prime minister, judges of the constitutional court, judges of the court of cassation and the prosecutor's office attached to it, members of the state council and the prosecutor's office attached to it, members of the court of auditors and the prosecutor's office attached to it, the first presidents of the appeal courts and the prosecutor's office attached to them, the first presidents of the administrative courts of appeals and the prosecutor's office attached to them, provincial governors and deputy governors, provincial ministers and the presidents of the provincial assemblies.
94 Act 13/012 of 19 April 2013, section 21(4).
95 Ibid.: section 22.
96 Ibid.: section 23.
97 Ibid.: section 49.
98 Constitution of the DRC, section 211.
99 Act 13/012 of 19 April 2013, section 9(1).
100 Ibid.: section 9(1)(1).

- Forward provisional results to the jurisdiction that is competent to announce the final results; [101]
- Issue tenders relating to the pre-electoral, electoral and referendum-related operations, in compliance with relevant legislation; [102]
- Contribute to the establishment of the legal framework applicable to the electoral and referendum-related processes;[103]
- Develop a budgetary forecast and calendar relating to the organisation of the electoral and referendum-related processes; [104]
- Simplify, in French and in national languages, the laws relating to the electoral and referendum-related processes;[105]
- Coordinate the voters' education campaign on election-related matters, including by developing an information and awareness-raising programme for voters in French and in national languages;[106]
- Ensure the training of national, provincial and local authorities responsible for the preparation and organisation of elections and referendums;[107]
- Develop and simplify a code of conduct and regulations on electoral deontology;[108]
- Apportion electoral districts according to updated demographic data;[109]
- Determine and publish the number and location of voting and counting stations as well as local data collection centres for each electoral district;[110]
- Ensure that election and referendum campaigns are compliant with applicable laws and regulations;[111]
- Examine and publish candidates' lists;[112] and
- Accredit witnesses and national and international observers.[113]

The NIEC is also mandated to facilitate and support the resolution of electoral disputes. It develops and simplifies the judicial guidelines on the resolution of electoral disputes.[114]

---

101 Ibid.: section 9(1)(2).
102 Ibid.: section 9(1)(3).
103 Ibid.: section 9(1)(4).
104 Ibid.: section 9(1)(5).
105 Ibid.: section 9(1)(6).
106 Ibid.: section 9(1)(7).
107 Ibid.: section 9(1)(8).
108 Ibid.: section 9(1)(9).
109 Ibid.: section 9(1)(10).
110 Ibid.: section 9(1)(11).
111 Ibid.: section 9(1)(12).
112 Ibid.: section 9(1)(13).
113 Ibid.: section 9(1)(14).
114 Ibid.: section 25(1) (2).

How is the NIEC funded?

The NIEC's resources originate from:

- The state budget;
- Donations and bequests; and
- Assistance and support from bilateral and multilateral partners as well as other funders.

The NIEC has the ability, through the government, to request the necessary assistance and support from international partners for the organisation and smooth conduct of electoral and referendum processes, in compliance with relevant legislation.[115] It sets up its budget in compliance with financial legislation. This budget is sent to the government in order to be included in the state budget. It includes budgetary provisions for salaries, the ordinary conduct of affairs, investment and pre-electoral, electoral and referendum-related operations.[116]

That said, the government's financial commitment towards the NIEC has not been without consequences for the activities of the institution.[117] The funds are allocated in small tranches, which, at times, leads to a lack of compliance with the planned schedule of activities, and has in turn negatively influenced the electoral process.[118] It appears that the government, by failing to make funds available on time, is responsible for the NIEC's difficulties in implementing its planned activities within its own timeframes.

Administrative structure and staff

The NIEC relies on a national executive secretariat (NES), provincial executive secretariats (PES) based in each provincial capital, and a satellite office in the administrative seat of each territory. Because of its specific size and status, Kinshasa has a high number of satellite offices, the number of which is determined by the president of the NIEC after deliberations by the Plenary Assembly. The national executive secretary, the provincial executive secretary and the heads of satellite offices are appointed and, if necessary, relieved of their duties following a decision by the president of the NIEC, which is discussed by the Plenary Assembly.[119]

The NES is mandated to implement the NIEC's decisions. It is composed of technical and administrative directorates set up by the president of the NIEC, after deliberations in the Plenary Assembly. It is headed by a national executive secretary. The latter's mandate is to coordinate the activities of the provincial executive secretariats and the satellite

---

115 Ibid.: section 43(1).
116 Ibid.: section 44(1)(2).
117 Thamba Thamba R (2012) *Le financement des élections en Afrique : Esquisse des enjeux et défis à partir de l'expérience congolaise.* LL.B. dissertation, University of Kinshasa.
118 CENI (2012) *Les élections présidentielle et législatives du 28 novembre en République Démocratique du Congo. Défis, stratégies et résultats.* Kinshasa: CENI. p. 40.
119 Act 13/012 of 19 April 2013, section 35.

offices.[120] The provincial executive secretariat is mandated to manage NIEC activities at provincial level. It provides administrative and technical services, and is also set up by the president of the NIEC, after deliberations in the Plenary Assembly. It is headed by a provincial executive secretary. The satellite office deals with NIEC activities at local level, meaning at the level of each city and provincial or administrative capital. It also provides administrative and technical services and is set up in the same way. It is headed by a head of satellite office. The national executive secretary, the provincial executive secretaries and the heads of satellite offices are all assisted by deputies.[121]

In the current administrative configuration of the DRC, the NIEC has one national executive secretary, 26 provincial executive secretaries and more than 243 heads of satellite offices. This constitutes an effective specialised administration. Its tenure would need to be secure to ensure an electoral administration capable of contributing not only to the regularity of electoral processes, but also to the consolidation of democracy. As permanent civil servants, their mission is to ensure the institutional memory and permanency of electoral knowledge and to protect the NIEC's heritage. The fact that they are civil servants constitutes a mechanism to combat cronyism, which is at the heart of wrongful practices within the NIEC.

Beyond this category of NIEC agents, the national executive secretariat, the provincial executive secretariats and the satellite offices all have administrative and technical staff.[122] They are recruited on the basis of several criteria, namely competency, experience and moral standing, following a call for applications, and taking into consideration national representation, including gender.[123]

Following a request from the NIEC, career civil servants can be made available by the relevant authorities. They are seconded in compliance with their existing rank and their status is governed by the ordinary contractual laws applicable.[124] The technical structures and organisation of the NIEC, and the recruitment of its members and administrative staff, are regulated by its administrative and financial guidelines.[125]

Dispute resolution mechanism

The electoral law provides that all political parties and candidates have the right to challenge any election. The aggrieved party would have to approach the courts after the results had been announced.[126] The NIEC put in place mediation mechanisms in order to reduce

---

120 Act 13/012 of 19 April 2013, section 36.
121 Rules of Procedure of the NIEC, section 38.
122 Ibid.: section 38.
123 Ibid.: section 40.
124 Ibid.: section 43 (3).
125 Ibid.: section 44.
126 The constitutional court is mandated to hear disputes related to presidential and national parliamentary elections. Electoral disputes at provincial level are heard before administrative appeal courts. For urban, municipal and local elections, jurisdiction is granted to the administrative tribunals and peace tribunals. However, the administrative jurisdictions have yet to be set up. In the meantime, electoral disputes are heard by appeal courts and grand instance tribunals.

electoral tensions. In 2011, a national committee for the mediation of the electoral process (NCMEP) was set up, one of its mandates being to 'peacefully resolve electoral disputes and incidents by acting as mediator' and to promote dialogue and recommend consensual measures to resolve potential crises. However, this was an impossible mission to fulfil in the context of an electoral debacle and a widespread and violent dispute of the 2011 elections.

The new NIEC team was set up in 2013 and created the Commission of Integrity and Electoral Mediation (CIEM), composed solely of religious leaders. It has had no impact on the electoral crisis that has unfolded since 2015. Furthermore, the Catholic Church, which has decisive political weight in the DRC, has suspended its participation in the commission because of the lack of visibility of the actions of the NIEC in the electoral process.

Interactions with stakeholders

As its name suggests, the NIEC was conceived as an independent, impartial and permanent institution by the political and social actors who were represented at the ICD.[127] It has legal, administrative and financial independence. Within the institutional framework of the DRC, the NIEC has the status of a body governed by public law.[128]

The organic law uses varying concepts to support the NIEC's independence. However, it is not yet effective. Several factors affect the independence of the commission, including its partisan composition and the politicised recruitment of its staff. To end these practices, political parties need to stop influencing their delegates sitting on the NIEC. However, this appears to be impossible in the current DRC context, since elections are no longer healthy political competition but have become a full-on war waged through other ways to serve the same purpose: take or maintain political power and its socio-economic benefits to the detriment of the people.

The organic law of the NIEC provides that its members 'enjoy full independence from the political forces that have appointed them'. However, the relationship between the NIEC members and their former political parties remains in practice. The outcome is that members of the NIEC follow instructions from their respective political parties. Whoever seeks to take an independent stance is removed from his or her position. The vice-president, André Mpungwe Songo, resigned because of pressure from his political party. Chantal Ngoyi Tshite Wetshi, quaestor of the NIEC, was forced to resign by the ruling party because the political party the Social Movement for Renewal (SMR) was excluded from the ruling coalition. These two examples illustrate the dependence of the NIEC on the political parties to which its members used to belong.

Members of the electoral commission are also recommended to assert their independence in particular towards the political parties to which they used to belong. The question then remains as to how far this request and potential assertion of independence should go. Until they risk their lives?

---

127 Resolution no. DIC/CPJ/09 on the national Independent Electoral Commission. Sun City, 18 April 2002.
128 Act 13/012 of 19 April 2013 (consolidated and updated version), sections 2 and 6.

Because of the nature of its mandate, the NIEC engages with public institutions, international bodies, political parties, civil society organisations and local and international NGOs.

Technical and financial partners (TFP)

The technical and financial partners are primarily international organisations (UN, EU) and the international cooperation agencies from foreign states. Legislation authorises the NIEC, through government, to 'request, from bilateral, multilateral and other funders, the assistance and support necessary for the organisation and the efficient operation of electoral and referendum processes in compliance with relevant legislation'.[129]

The NIEC can request two kinds of support. It can be either financial or technical. In the latter case, the NIEC would require expertise relating to, among others, auditing the electoral or logistical database or transporting electoral material. In the current context of the DRC, organising free, transparent and credible elections, within the constitutional timeframes, can only take place with the financial support of the international community.

Political parties

The primary partners of the NIEC are all the political parties involved in the electoral process. The NIEC organises the elections for them and with them. To this end, the NIEC has created a consultation platform with the political parties to involve them in the electoral process. This consultation platform constitutes a mechanism aimed at instilling trust in the work of the NIEC and a process to access the outcome of the elections. If this framework is not fully functional, there is a high risk of suspicion towards the NIEC.

The role of political parties does not appear to meet the NIEC's expectations. Political parties do not contribute sufficiently to ensuring that electoral processes are transparent, one reason being that they are manifestly absent from electoral processes. The same can be said regarding awareness-raising of their members regarding the role they could play in monitoring elections. The challenges faced by political parties are justified by a lack of public funding of their activities.[130]

Civil society organisations

The credibility of an electoral process largely depends on society's adherence to the said process. The elections were put in place in order to allow the population to elect its leaders. The process that leads to this election must, as far as possible, be understood by voters in order to obtain the desired outcome.[131] Involving society in the electoral process is a difficult task which requires time, and the NIEC is currently alone in carrying out this task.

---

129 Act 13/012 of 19 April 2013, section 48(2).
130 Interview with Flavien Misoni Mbayahe, Kinshasa, 2 October 2015.
131 Cihunda J (2003) Culture électorale. Une formation pour l'observation des élections. *Politikonzoo – Journal des étudiants* November 2003: 4.

The NIEC must therefore create partnerships with civil society organisations. These include NGOs that focus on civic and electoral education, women's organisations, the youth and media workers as well as traditional or customary authorities. Among the most important sectors of civil society are religious groups.[132] The latter are involved in civic and electoral voter education, in popular awareness-raising and rallying, in election monitoring and more recently in mediating electoral disputes. Considering the NIEC's logistical challenges, extensive involvement of civil society in civic and electoral voter education is a much welcomed contribution, which can materialise without requiring extensive formalities.[133] The same can be said about the NIEC's fragile quest for independence from other public institutions.

Overall assessment

The NIEC inherited from the IEC a set of electoral knowledge and skills, including relating to electoral challenges and an electoral culture which was resurfacing after a long one-party period. Additional assets include the rallying capacity of Congolese voters, the strength of civil society and the watchfulness of the international community.[134]

It should be noted that elections in the DRC are influenced by political, economic, social and cultural factors. The legal framework for these elections includes national, regional and international instruments, generally upholding human rights, but with some specific factors relating to elections as well. The NIEC is the institutional framework for the organisation of any electoral process in the country. It is composed of delegates (majority and opposition) and of civil society, but is considered too partisan. This is a legacy of the war that took place between 1996 and 2003. Women are the only social class to be mandatorily represented. The youth and people with disabilities are not expressly represented within the NIEC.

The NIEC is granted the necessary powers to organise elections. Its members are dispatched throughout the country. However, it faces many financial, logistical and political challenges. At the financial level, the executive does not adequately implement the budget allocated to the NIEC by parliament, which causes equipment not to be dispatched according to its pre-determined strategic work plan. Politically, the independence of the members of the NIEC is affected by political pressure put on NIEC commissioners who were former members of political parties.

The relationship between the NIEC and the political parties is structured through a consultation framework. It should be noted that, due to lack of funds, not all the political parties participate in the electoral process in the same manner. Political parties are not funded by the state, which means that only political parties with sufficient financial means

132 Rules of Procedure of the NIEC, section 46.
133 Interview with Flavien Misoni Mbayahe, Kinshasa, 2 October 2015.
134 Cihunda Hengelela J& Mvita Kalubi R (2015) Les Institutions d'Appui à la Démocratie (IAD) en République Démocratique du Congo: cas du CSAC et de la CENI. *Congo-Afrique* January 2015: 36–48.

are able to contest every election. This state of affairs distorts political competitiveness and violates the principle of equality between candidates.

Civil society plays a significant role in the electoral process, including through voter education initiatives, public awareness-raising and election observation. International election observation missions also play an important role in overseeing elections. However, and regrettably, some of these international election observation missions appear to do more of what could be qualified as 'electoral tourism' than a global observation of the entire process, including what happens before and after voting day. But this does not mean that technical and financial partners should play a lesser role. Their role remains essential, especially in the context of an economic recession. Furthermore, the African community should also provide technical and financial support to its member states.

Electoral disputes are heard before the courts. However, the judiciary lacks independence from political and financial powers at play. Attempts at putting in place alternative resolution mechanisms to address electoral disputes have not yet been successful. Together, these factors explain the underperformance of the NIEC since 2011.

Therefore, the NIEC's performance can be assessed against the 2011 elections and against the current electoral process which should result in the presidential and parliamentary elections of November 2016. Performance can be assessed by examining the technical preparations of the elections, how voting operations were managed, how written records of proceedings were collected, how provisional results were compiled and published, and how electoral disputes were handled.

Technical preparations of the elections

Technical preparations of the elections did not take place according to acceptable standards. Updating the voters' roll was hampered by several logistical and technical issues. This is the reason why it was extended in six provinces. Although very advanced technology was used, the updated voters' roll was contested by the opposition on the basis of a lack of transparency. Indeed, the NIEC refused to audit the updated voters' roll, which was requested by those contesting it.[135] The difficulties which characterised the revision of the voters' roll had a negative impact on, among others, the publication of electoral lists and the issue of the lists of the omitted.[136]

The actions of the NIEC in preparing for the 2011 elections was marked by a lack of civic education or information for the voters, despite these being one of its main tasks. Considering the high levels of illiteracy among the Congolese population and the complexity

---

135 MOE-UE (2012) *République Démocratique du Congo. Rapport final des élections présidentielles et législatives du 28 novembre 2011*. Kinshasa: MOE-UE. p. 33. See also http://www.moeue-rdc.eu [accessed 22 September 2013].

136 MOE-UE (2012) République Démocratique du Congo. Rapport final des élections présidentielles et législatives du 28 novembre 2011. Kinshasa, 2012. p. 35. See also Abbel Ngondo Ndjondo (2005) *La révision du fichier électoral par la Commission électorale nationale indépendante dans l'antenne d'Idiofa: Analyse des problèmes techniques et socio-politiques*. LL M thesis, Social, Administrative and Political Sciences Faculty, University of Kinshasa, 2004–2005 academic year. p. 135.

of the electoral process, an awareness-raising campaign on civic and electoral matters was necessary. This task was left to civil society organisations without support from the NIEC.[137]

One of the major problems of the NIEC was the distribution of electoral material of a sensitive and non-sensitive nature. The reasons for this were the size of the country, the choice of providers of this material, the constraints of the electoral calendar and the combination of both elections (presidential and parliamentary). These included non-secure transportation of sensitive material, the distribution of such material on voting day, and the postponement of elections in certain areas.[138] All these challenges were bound to contribute to electoral fraud.[139]

It is bizarre to note that the same mistakes are being committed in the current electoral process. Although the current voters' roll is being audited, there has yet to be an agreement on the registration of new young voters. The NIEC was unable to organise the governors' and vice-governors' elections in those provinces that were the result of the new territorial division, because it lacked two million dollars.

Support to voters on voting day

The lack of technical preparations for the elections inadvertently impact election-related operations on the day of the vote. Of particular concern is the lack of training. As underlined by Daniel Ngoy Mulunda, training on election-related matters is one of the key activities in managing the electoral process. Quality training contributes to adequate performance levels on the part of election officials and to the success of pre-electoral and post-electoral operations.[140]

A lack of quality training on election-related matters can largely explain the irregularities that affected the elections of 28 November 2011. In this regard, it must be noted that the NIEC did not dedicate a large amount of time or resources to train election officials. Therefore, inadequate recruitment choices of local election officials could not be corrected through sufficient training.[141] This resulted in dysfunctions on voting day.

For example, only 70% of voting stations set up by the NIEC were operational on 28 November 2011. The remaining 30% opened on 29 and 30 November 2011, contrary to the regulations to the electoral legislations, which were adopted by the NIEC itself. In any case, the election monitors noted that many voters cast their vote late because of issues relating to technicalities in preparing for voting day. Either they were not on the voters' roll, or they did not know in which voting station they could cast their vote, or voting material had been delivered late.[142]

---

137 MOE-UE (2012) *République Démocratique du Congo. Rapport final des élections présidentielle et législatives du 28 novembre 2011.* Kinshasa: MOE-UE. p. 38.
138 Ibid.: 39.
139 Ngoma-Binda EP (2012) Elections en RD Congo 2006 et 2011. Bref regard comparatif et prospectif. *Congo-Afrique* 462: 119.
140 Ngoy Mulunda D (2011) Avant-propos. *Guide pratique du formateur électoral.* Kinshasa. p. 1.
141 Interview with a former NIEC Head of Antenna who requested anonymity, Kinshasa, 18 August 2015.
142 Ibid.

Collection of written records of proceedings, compilation and publication of provisional results

The performance of the NIEC can also be assessed against the manner in which records of proceedings of coting and counting stations (VCSs) were collected as well as the manner in which election results were compiled and published. Firstly, one must consider the manner in which records of proceedings of VCSs were transported to local result compilation centres (LRCCs). As for sensitive electoral material, the safety of such transportation had not been ensured in several locations around the country.[143]

Since the 2006 elections, many cases of misconduct have been reported within the LRCCs, either because of political influence or of corruption on the part of election officials. Irregularities include the expulsion of party observers and election monitors or the refusal to publish records of proceedings, which were in any case not signed by observers. Some LRCC records of proceedings were sent to Kinshasa and examined by an 'ad hoc committee' mandated to 'consolidate' the election results before these were forwarded to the national processing centre (NPC). At that level, neither the party observers nor the monitors were present. This is clearly in breach of the principle of transparency.[144]

Almost two thousand records of proceedings from VCSs in Kinshasa were lost, although LRCC officials received them. This was a major failure in the oversight structure and appeared furthermore planned, as the city was fully supportive of the opposition. Nobody was prosecuted or criminally sanctioned for the loss, although this is provided for in sections 82, 83 and 89 of the Electoral Act.[145]

The Electoral Act authorises the publication of election results, which must start at the lowest level, meaning at the VCSs, the LRCCs and then the NIEC. It does not provide for the publication of provisional results. The NIEC, however, made provisional results public on national television without indicating the VCS or voting districts from which the results emanated, or the voter turnout. This lasted for days and was in violation of the Electoral Act but also the general principle of transparency which applies to any electoral process.[146] The results of the presidential elections of 9 December 2011 were not comprehensively published. The results were only published on the NIEC's website and there was no detailed breakdown per VCS and LRCC. Scanned copies of the records of proceedings of the VCSs, containing the results, were not made public either.[147]

Without mentioning the material, technical and financial challenges which the NIEC faced in managing election results, it is obvious that the handling of said results was deficient. This is one of reasons explaining the massive protests that followed the publication of the 2011 election results. The NIEC acted in violation of the Electoral Act

---

143 MOE-UE (2012) *République Démocratique du Congo. Rapport final des élections présidentielle et législatives du 28 novembre 2011.* Kinshasa: MOE-UE. p. 20.
144 Ibid.
145 Ibid.
146 Ibid.: 21.
147 Ibid.

and of its regulations, which it had itself adopted. The NIEC's senior management and leaders lacked the necessary diligence to adequately manage election results. This lack of diligence had an impact on the manner in which the NIEC handled electoral disputes.

Electoral disputes

Electoral disputes are heard by the courts, which explains why the NIEC has links with the judiciary, as outlined above. However, the organic law obliges the NIEC to also establish quasi-judicial mechanisms to resolve electoral disputes. In 2011, the NIEC set up the national commission for the mediation of electoral processes. The impact of its work was, however, minimal compared to the extent of the electoral crisis. In 2014, the NIEC established the committee for electoral integrity and mediation (CEIM), composed of various religious leaders. However, before it started operating, the Catholic Church suspended its participation in the committee to condemn the tactics it accuses the executive of using in order to block the current electoral process.

As for the electoral disputes heard before the courts, the NIEC's attitude made the work of the judiciary difficult, resulting in a lack of confidence in the judiciary to handle the said disputes. It is important to note that overall, the Congolese judiciary faces many challenges, including that of a lack of independence from the other branches of power, and that of a lack of resources. Justice is granted to those who offer the most rather than those who are right.

In relation to the presidential and parliamentary elections of 2011, electoral disputes were handled in a climate of denial of justice. The constitutional court was not yet operational in 2011, and its mandate was still exercised by the supreme court of justice (SCJ). However, the executive took several actions which undermined the independence of the SCJ. For example, the bench of the SCJ was changed during the election campaign and 18 new judges were appointed, in violation of the act of the status of magistrates.[148]

Another step that undermined the SCJ was the change, also during the election campaign, in the manner in which electoral disputes were heard. Indeed, it switched from an adversarial system: oral, transparent, in which the court's hearings were public and both parties could present their arguments, to an inquisitorial system which is written, opaque, and in which a judge investigates 'ex officio' and obtains all necessary evidence to resolve the dispute.[149] This amendment was not justified considering the lack of confidence in, and independence of, the judiciary.

In any case, the NIEC and the SCJ did not act in compliance with relevant legislation while dealing with electoral disputes:

---

148 Wetsh'okonda Koso M & Kahombo B (2014) *Le pari du respect de la vérité des urnes en Afrique. Analyse des élections présidentielles et législatives du 28 novembre 2011 en République démocratique du Congo.* Brussels. pp. 68–78; MOE-UE (2012) *République Démocratique du Congo. Rapport final des élections présidentielle et législatives du 28 novembre 2011.* Kinshasa: MOE-EU. p. 21.
149 Ibid.: 22.

- In relation to disputes around party lists, the NIEC validated lists which had more candidates than seats to be filled, although this constitutes a ground for rejection of the list. Although this was challenged in court, the application was rejected on a technicality.[150]
- Violations of the Electoral Act during the election campaign remained unpunished. The NIEC received complaints relating to the buying of voter cards, the use of public resources during the campaign, confrontations between members of different political parties, the posting of campaign material on public buildings, assault of candidates, biased attitudes of law enforcement and security officials, as well as the recruitment of some partisan NIEC staff. None of these complaints was dealt with by the NIEC, and the prosecution services did not take any criminal action against anyone.[151] This created mounting frustration and contributed to escalating violence, fed by a desire for revenge.
- The UNC challenged the provisional results of the presidential elections, a challenge which was declared admissible but unsubstantiated, and eventually denied. The ruling of the SCJ was criticised on two main grounds. Firstly, the judges gave an interpretation of section 74 that contradicted the law, which requires that the application be notified to all parties.[152] The SCJ had not done this. Secondly, the SCJ's ruling did not make any reference to the records of proceedings of the VCS, but to CDs which were provided by the NIEC. Therefore, the court did not investigate whether the results which had been provided by the NIEC were accurate, and hence whether the allegations of the complainant were accurate or not. The SCJ entirely rallied behind the NIEC, thereby becoming a 'simple echo chamber of the NIEC'.[153]

The constitutional court has now been established and will hear potential electoral disputes that will arise following the upcoming presidential and parliamentary elections. However, the constitutional court faces two primary criticisms, which were levelled at it by the now defunct SCJ. Firstly, the majority of judges sitting in the constitutional court are appointed by the president and many are members of the ruling party, which creates a real risk of bias. Some of them are former SCJ judges who heard electoral disputes in 2006 and 2011.

---

150 Ibid.
151 Ibid.
152 Interview with Advocate Symphorien Kapinga Kapinga Nkashama, advisory expert to the EU election observation mission of 2011, Kinshasa, 23 August 2015.
153 MOE-UE (2012) *République Démocratique du Congo. Rapport final des élections présidentielle et législatives du 28 novembre 2011.* Kinshasa: MOE-UE. p. 25.

Secondly, the ruling of the constitutional court following an application of the NIEC was seen as controversial and has affected its credibility towards the public. Indeed, the NIEC requested that the constitutional court interpret section 10 of the act on the planning of setting up of provinces and indicate whether the NIEC could continue with its planned electoral calendar, considering the current context. Although the court found that it did not have jurisdiction to interpret legislation and provide guidance to the NIEC, the constitutional court nevertheless granted itself the power to instruct the government and the NIEC. It requested the latter to independently review its electoral calendar. The NIEC's court application shows the challenges it faces in fulfilling its mandate in a very hostile political environment.

Current debates on electoral reform

The issue around electoral reform was raised after the presidential, parliamentary, senate and provincial elections of 2006 and 2007. Because the electoral cycle was interrupted, the issue was set aside and replaced by the establishment of a new institution, namely the NIEC. At the time, the establishment of the NIEC may have been perceived as electoral reform, but it appeared a year later as being inadequate.

Incremental or institutional electoral reform

The adoption of the organic law on the organisation and functioning of the NIEC gave rise to intense debates on which organisations and institutions should be represented on the bureau of the NIEC. Members of parliament had by and large opposed the idea that members of civil society be represented on the bureau, as their delegates at the IEC had been regarded as subject to the influence of political parties. Because previous civil society representatives had been too unreliable, representatives of both the governing coalition and the opposition refused formal representation of civil society within the NIEC.

Following the presidential and parliamentary elections of 28 November 2011, all stakeholders expressed the need to reform the NIEC. The organic law was amended to change the representation on the bureau of the NIEC, and to create a new representative body. The NIEC is now composed of two bodies: the Plenary Assembly and the bureau. The number of commissioners of the NIEC was increased from 7 to 13, with a mandatory 31% of female commissioners. The other important innovation is that civil society organisations are again represented within the NIEC, with three seats (or 23%) in the bureau, including the presidency.[154]

---

154 For further details, see AETA (2012) *Rapport général sur l'atelier technique sur la réforme électorale en RDC*. Kinshasa: AETA. pp. 12–16.

Legislative reforms

It is important to mention that the NIEC barely contributes to the debate on electoral reform, despite its mission being to contribute to reforming the electoral process. Those driving the reform are politicians, guided by their own interests. Civil society has been doing exceptional work on electoral reform for the past ten years.[155] However, not all its recommendations are taken into consideration. A certain instability results from this, the ultimate outcome being a reform for each new election cycle. It may well be claimed that the situation is close to one in which law is being manipulated for motives that have nothing to do with adjusting the electoral legal framework or the consolidation of democracy.

Debate around the electoral calendar

The NIEC started taking part in the discussions around electoral reform between 2014 and 2015, after the establishment of its entities and a wave of protests against its president.[156] On 26 May 2014, the NIEC published the timeline for urban, municipal and local elections.[157] This timeline was primarily challenged on two grounds. Firstly, it only related to some elections, whereas public opinion was expecting a timeline that would include the presidential and parliamentary elections of 2016. Secondly, it appeared that the local elections could not be organised within the intended timeframe.

In response to the criticism expressed by all stakeholders involved in the electoral process except the party of the president, the NIEC published a comprehensive timeline, containing 23 limitations.[158] However, this new global calendar appeared as unrealistic as the first one, and did not decrease the mounting tension that could be felt at political parties' headquarters. The comprehensive timeline scheduled 11 different polls to be organised within a year and a half. The 23 limitations appeared to be insurmountable to many observers, no matter what their orientation.

Many alternative suggestions were made to adapt this timeline and ensure it could be implemented. These were made by opposition political parties and civil society. The comprehensive timeline was also criticised by some within the governing party.[159] The main thrust of the alternative suggestions to the NIEC's global calendar was to postpone

---

155 Ngoma-Binda P (2002) Quel type de système électoral faudrait-il pour les prochaines échéances électorales en RDC? *Le Scrutin*. Kinshasa. pp. 15–16; CENCO (2004) *Education civique pour la préparation des populations aux élections en République Démocratique du Congo. Programme d'action de l'Eglise catholique pour une transition réussie*. Kinshasa: Secrétariat général.

156 Sumaïli K, Ngoyi Mutamba C & Fayulu M (2014) *Petition: démission de Monsieur l'Abbé Malumalu de la CENI*, Kinshasa, 17 February 2014; Complaint against Mr Mulohongu Malumalu Apollinaire, President of the NIEC, Kinshasa, 25 June 2014.

157 Decision 012/CENI/AP/14 of 26 May 2014 containing publication of the calendar for the urban, municipal and local elections. Available at http://www.ceni-rdc.dc [accessed 21 August 2015].

158 Decision 001/CENI/BUR/15 of 12 February 2015 containing publication of the calendar for the provincial, urban, municipal and local elections of 2015 and for the presidential and parliamentary elections of 2016, Kinshasa, 12 February 2015.

159 Lutundula Apala Pen'Apala C (2015, 2 March) Nécessité et urgence d'un calendrier électoral global réaménagé en République Démocratique du Congo. *Le Potentiel*. Available at http://www.lepotentiel.com [accessed 21 August 2015].

the urban, municipal and local elections to 2017, so as to allow the NIEC to adequately organise the provincial and senate elections in 2015 and the presidential and parliamentary elections in 2016, in accordance with the constitutional timeframe.

The NIEC did not engage much with these alternative suggestions. It rather requested an opinion from the constitutional court, which invited the NIEC to independently reorganise the electoral calendar. However, without the NIEC setting up a consultation platform with all political parties, time passes too quickly to enable the NIEC to comply with all steps of the said electoral calendar. In the meantime, the government submitted a bill to parliament on the boundaries of the voting districts for the urban, municipal and local elections. The bill was adopted by the National Assembly without the representatives of the opposition, who rejected the bill. At senate level, there needed to be a second extraordinary session (which was the third one held by the senate during that year) to adopt the bill. Again, the opposition senators boycotted the said extraordinary session.

These electoral reforms made without consensus from all stakeholders undermine the political climate and will have a negative impact on the entire electoral process, as they did for the 2011 elections. In this context, the NIEC appears to be moving with much scepticism and dubiousness. It appears to face many challenges in effectively contributing to the electoral process or, more broadly, to the young Congolese democracy.[160] This could explain the weak performance of the NIEC.

Conclusion and recommendations

The current electoral process must be successful in order to consolidate peace in the DRC and in the entire Great Lakes region. In order to successfully address the challenges that the NIEC faces, two kinds of solutions must be found before the end of 2015. At a political level, all political forces must commit to strictly complying with the constitution of the republic. More specifically, political leaders must take all the necessary steps to ensure that the presidential and parliamentary elections take place on 27 November 2016. In addition, President Joseph Kabila should publicly state that he will respect the constitution, in order to dispel any uncertainties caused by his claims that he may run for a third mandate, which would be unconstitutional. Such a statement would positively impact on the current tense political climate in the country. The international community must maintain pressure on the Congolese political actors in bringing them to comply with the constitutional framework.

At a technical level, the NIEC must rearrange its calendar and only organise the presidential and parliamentary elections in 2016. The other elections should be moved to 2017, starting with the provincial and senatorial elections, which should be held in January of that year. The local elections would be held between May and August 2017, ending the electoral cycle. The period from January to September 2016 would be dedicated to the

---

160 Interview with Advocate Marcel Wetsh'okonda Koso, Kinshasa, 22 August 2015.

technical preparations for the November 2016 elections. The NIEC will need to recruit officials and Congolese from abroad and conduct other necessary election preparatory work. The international community is urged to provide financial and logistical means to ensure that the NIEC can fully perform its mandate.

Executive

- Stand by its international commitments regarding the holding of elections: the government must implement the international legal instruments on elections and introduce a bill in parliament to ratify the African charter on democracy, elections and good governance;
- Respect the independence and impartiality of the NIEC: the president of the republic and members of the executive must ban any attempt to influence members of the NIEC;
- Facilitate the NIEC's operations by complying with the budget adopted by parliament, including by making funds available that would allow the NIEC to follow its strategic work plan;
- Facilitate access to the public media for all candidates without discrimination, no matter what their political affiliation;
- Ensure the neutrality of security and defence forces, including by ensuring that all candidates are protected during election violence;
- Rehabilitate the infrastructure needed to hold elections, the roads, the NIEC buildings and the units producing election material.

Parliament

- Stabilise the positions of national executive secretary, provincial executive secretaries and the heads of local EMB structures by promoting them to permanent civil servant positions in the employ of the NIEC;
- Stop the practice of adopting inopportune electoral reforms before every electoral process;
- Oversee NIEC spending to ensure it remains within its budgetary allocation;
- Adopt a bill ratifying the African charter on democracy, elections and governance.

NIEC

- Develop the relevant legislation to create a permanent civil servant position for the key stakeholders within the election administration;
- Ensure that all scheduled elections are compliant with the constitution of the republic;
- Appoint local service providers to produce election material;

- Build strong partnerships for civic and electoral awareness-raising and specialised NGOs;
- Recruit and train election officials a long time prior to the elections.

Judiciary and prosecution services

- Establish its independence from all candidates by rejecting corrupt practices and patronage;
- Ensure judges are trained on election-related matters. The high judicial council (*Conseil Supérieur de la Magistrature*) should organise, in collaboration with the NIEC, training seminars for judges on the settlement of electoral disputes;
- Punish all violations of election-related legislation without having regard for the political membership of either party;
- Ensure it receives the records of proceedings from the VCSs and the LRCCs directly and not through the NIEC: the president of the constitutional court, who also sits as chairman of the high judicial council, must develop a mechanism that will allow the courts to directly receive the minutes of the election operations from the VCSs and the LRCCs.

Political parties

- Be involved at all stages of the electoral process, by sending monitors to the VCSs and LRCCs;
- Ensure civic and electoral awareness-raising of all its members by organising awareness raising workshops before each stage of the electoral process;
- Ensure training on election-related matters for all its candidates, including on the content of the Electoral Act, political communication and techniques to run an election campaign;
- Look for alternative funding in the absence of public funding;
- Prevent their current members from influencing their former members who joined the NIEC;
- Approach the courts in case of electoral disputes;
- Prohibit any culture of violence during elections. Candidates will have to challenge election results through the courts and not on the street.

Civil society

- Conduct civic and electoral awareness-raising campaign with the general population by organising awareness-raising workshops, especially during the election campaign;
- Monitor the entire electoral process;

- Be a neutral partner to the NIEC, by avoiding any collusion with political parties and their supporters;
- Conduct studies on alternative funding mechanisms for the NIEC.

Technical and financial partners

- Assist the young Congolese democracy in the interests of its members, without supporting a candidate to the detriment of another and by ensuring that all its actions go towards respecting the will of the Congolese people;
- Use their influence to bring political leaders to respect the constitutional order by organising elections within the timeframe set out in law;
- Contribute to the funding of electoral processes;
- Ensure that international election observation missions monitor the entire electoral process.

4

LESOTHO

Prof. Mafa M Sejanamane

Political developments and electoral history

Lesotho, previously Basutoland, was a British Protectorate which gained independence in October 1966. Independence was preceded by three important developments which have played a critical role in shaping the present political environment and have in one way or another shaped the electoral reforms which have been made.

First, was the formation of the Constitutional Commission, which was to shape the 1966 Lesotho constitution.[1] Discussions and debates on the report did not lead to a national consensus on the way forward. On the contrary, sharp differences began and continued well beyond the constitutional negotiations on independence.

The second factor that poisoned the environment was the elections which were held in 1965 in terms of the Draft Constitution of Lesotho. These were narrowly won by the Basotho National Party (BNP) led by Chief Leabua Jonathan. Most analysts had expected the Basutoland Congress Party (BCP) to win those elections.[2] Following the election setback, the BCP dug in its heels and demanded new elections and amendments to the constitution. Differences around these became so pronounced that both the Paramount Chief, Bereng Seeiso, who later became King Moshoeshoe II, and the BCP delegation walked out of the negotiations in London leaving the BNP to agree on the new constitution and also the date of independence. Jonathan came back from the negotiations and the newly elected parliament approved the new constitution which came into effect on 4 October 1966 when Lesotho gained independence.

The fact that church denominational issues entered the fray was not helpful. Khaketla points out that for most of the period before and after the 1965 elections the Catholic Church, which had the largest followership in the country, openly supported the BNP, while the Protestant Churches supported the BCP.[3] This was very important at the time since an overwhelming majority of Basotho belonged to either of those churches. Lesotho

---

1   Basutoland Constitutional Commission (1963) *Report of the Basutoland Constitutional Commission.* Maseru: Basutoland Council.

2   Khaketla BM (1973) *Lesotho 1970: An African Coup under the Microscope.* Berkeley: University of California Press.

3   Ibid.: 18–25.

thus had a complete breakdown of the national consensus on the way forward, which was also complicated by the church denominational squabbles.

These developments had a huge bearing on the post-independence period up to the present, since acrimony and mistrust began even before the country acquired independence. The struggle for constitutional changes, even after independence, occasionally flared into violence, where several people died in Thaba Bosiu in December 1966.[4] Supporters of King Moshoeshoe II clashed with police in Thaba Bosiu on 27 December 1966, resulting in the deaths of nine people. Prime Minister Leabua Jonathan placed King Moshoeshoe II in 'protective custody' in Maseru on 28 December 1966. A few days later the King's supporters attacked a police station in Leribe on 3 January 1967, resulting in the death of at least one person. As a result of these developments, King Moshoeshoe II agreed to abide by the constitution on 5 January 1967.[5] This meant that the newly independent Lesotho had started its freedom in discord and that has been the foundation of the instability that has characterised the country up to now.

Post-independence

The first post-independence elections in Lesotho were conducted in 1970. Just like the 1965 elections, they were administered by the director of elections in the ministry of interior and chieftainship affairs. The fact that there was no trust amongst the political stakeholders meant that the elections organised directly by the government through the Ministry helped to diminish confidence even before the elections were held. Indeed, voices from the opposition were adamant that they would be rigged.

The elections were held in an atmosphere of tension and were fiercely contested by the two main political parties, the BCP and BNP. The BCP and the Marematlou Freedom Party (MFP) made several allegations of election fraud against the government. The allegations were not sent to the courts of law since the elections were annulled by the government. It is significant that before the elections the government seemed satisfied with whole electoral process. Government only started talking about rigging when it became clear that they were losing the elections. Gill argues that the government was so over-confident that it never attempted to rig the elections.[6]

Early results of the first post-independence elections in January 1970 indicated that the Basotho National Party (BNP) might lose control. Under the leadership of Prime Minister Chief Leabua Jonathan, the ruling BNP refused to cede power to the rival Basutoland Congress Party (BCP), although the BCP was widely believed to have won the elections. Citing election irregularities, Prime Minister Leabua Jonathan declared a state of emergency, suspended the constitution, nullified the elections and dissolved the parliament. Jonathan said that he was making all those moves because of alleged electoral fraud by the opposition. He accused the opposition of intimidation of his supporters, kidnapping of

---

4   Ibid.: 147.
5   Ibid.: chapter X.
6   Gill S & Giessen JAM (1973) *Afrika Museum*. Amsterdam: Netherlands-Lesotho Foundation. p. 220.

electoral officers and grabbing of ballot boxes from polling stations.[7] From then onwards, Lesotho was run at the whim of the BNP government and without a constitution.

1985 'no show' elections and the military coup

After fifteen years of one-party rule, and an intense period of South African destabilisation in Southern Africa,[8] Jonathan sought to legitimise his rule through elections. He, however, wanted to run a one-man-show election, where the opposition was largely in exile and domestically constrained by draconian security legislation. When the date for nominations of candidates came, the opposition did not nominate candidates. As a result, the ruling party's candidates went unopposed and, as such, were declared winners in all constituencies.

The opposition boycott ensured that the legitimacy that Jonathan sought was not provided. Jonathan's victory was a puerile one and was short-lived. Under intense South African pressure, including a blockade meant to force the regime to expel South African refugees, the Jonathan regime was overthrown in January 1986. Between 1986 and 1993 Lesotho was the first and only country under military rule in Southern Africa.

Military rule and transition to democracy

The internal tensions within the military itself soon boiled over as a result of their direct control of state power. The critical issues were the nature of power itself and the direction the country would take. Briefly the junta seemed to have, from the beginning, been split down the middle, with one faction favouring a strong Royalist direction. They argued that power rested with the King, and that the military should support that. This group seemed to have been led by the two Letsie cousins, Sekhobe Letsie and Thaabe Letsie. Another faction was led by the Commander of the army, Major General Lekhanya, who seemed to be leaning towards an independent role for the military.[9] Initially the latter seemed to have triumphed when the Royalist faction was ousted from power and the King dethroned. However, soon thereafter another coup, led by the Captains, ousted Lekhanya and installed Major General Ramaema, who now sought to remove the military from power.[10]

It must have dawned on Ramaema that the military's role in politics was undermining its very survival as a cohesive body. Thus, between 1986 and 1993 when a new constitution was drafted, adopted and elections were held, there were two convulsions within the military caused by factions contesting for power. In 1993, the military handed over power to the first democratically elected government in Lesotho since its independence. The BCP, under the veteran leader Ntsu Mokhehle, won all 65 constituencies under the First-

7   Machobane LBBJ (2001) *Kings Knights: Military Governance in the Kingdom of Lesotho, 1986–1993*. Roma: Institute of Southern African Studies. p. 25.
8   Sejanamane MM (1985) The crisis of apartheid: South African destabilisation in Southern Africa. *Dalhousie African Working Paper No 5*. p. 25.
9   Machobane LBBJ (2001) *Kings Knights: Military Governance in the Kingdom of Lesotho, 1986–1993*. Roma: Institute of Southern African Studies.
10 Sejanamane MM (1988) Lesotho in Southern Africa: From an assertive to a submissive foreign policy. *Lesotho Law Journal* 4(2): 7–31.

Past-the-Post electoral model, which had been in use since independence, with a 74.7% share of the votes.[11]

1993 elections and continued instability

From 1965 until 1998 Lesotho used the first-past-the-post (FPTP) electoral model. This is a model that operates on the basis of constituencies where the candidates contesting the elections come from constituencies. Each constituency has to elect one individual to represent it. Parliament has the number of seats equivalent to the number of constituencies, which means that each member of parliament is responsible for a constituency. The main challenge of this model is that it does not require a candidate to win an election by an absolute majority. The simple plurality of votes qualifies one to be a member of parliament. Theoretically this electoral system could deliver a minority winner to legitimately represent electorates in parliament. This means that a minority government could govern the country. Critics of the system view it as adversarial and not conducive to nation-building, especially in fragile, conflict ridden and polarised societies like Lesotho. More importantly, as the Lesotho case shows, there is a possibility that minority voices can be shut out of parliament and thus express themselves through violent means.

The 1993 elections in Lesotho vividly demonstrated the above. With 74.7% of the national vote, the BCP received 100% of the constituencies in parliament. The next in line in the national vote was the BNP with 22.66%, but they were not rewarded with even one seat.[12] While these elections were, according to all reports, fair and representative, there was a feeling that the views of almost 25% of the electorate had been discarded.

This outcome was rejected outright by the BNP. The party claimed electoral fraud and lodged no fewer than 20 petitions in the High Court on the basis of a tampering with the ballot boxes.[13] Some of the claims raised by the BNP were that the ballot paper used in some constituencies was different from the official one in terms of colour, texture and hardness; and that some ballot papers appeared to have been pre-marked by 'mechanical' means rather than by human hand.[14] The High Court rejected eight of those petitions and the remainder were withdrawn.

Ultimately, though the elections were declared free and fair, the outcome was a familiar one-party system of government with its attendant arrogance. The issue, however, was magnified by the history of antagonism between the victor and the loser of those elections. From 1965 up to then, the contest for power between the BCP and BNP was characterised by acrimony and fear. Indeed, Jonathan's justification of the cancellation of the 1970 elections had a lot to do with fear of retribution by the BCP if they got to power.

---

11 African Elections Database: Elections in Lesotho. Available at *http://africanelections.tripod.com/ls.html* [accessed 20 June 2016].

12 Ibid.

13 Sekatle, PM (1995) Disputing electoral legitimacy: The BNP's challenge to the results. In: R Southall and T Petlane (eds) *Democratisation and Demilitarisation in Lesotho: The General Election of 1993 and its Aftermath*. Pretoria: Africa Institute. p. 114.

14 Ibid.

The problem with the BCP, however, was that, unlike in a classical one-party state, it had no real power.[15] Before leaving office the military had abrogated to itself exclusive power on the management and discipline of its members – the state within a state syndrome.[16] In addition to this, the army had, by dethroning the King, laid a trap for the new government. The matter could not have been resolved without establishing a broad national consensus on the way forward. The one-party syndrome led the new government into a completely divisive direction, by not only maintaining the status quo, but by also establishing a Commission of Inquiry into the monarchy which brought about an immediate confrontation with the King.[17]

It is under these circumstances that King Letsie III, who had been throned by the military, staged a coup in 1994 and set up an alternate government shortly after the newly elected government came into office. The alternate government was, however, short-lived as a result of determined pressure by the Southern African Development Community (SADC).[18] The new government was facing a disgruntled opposition; and the King indicated that there was a need to bring about national reconciliation. The political system clearly needed to be nurtured in order to earn the confidence of both the internal and external stakeholders. It was clear that confidence had to be restored in the political system as a whole. The FPTP electoral model was thus clearly not suitable in a divided country like Lesotho, which had experienced over 20 years of undemocratic rule, followed by over seven years of military rule. Divided societies, as Lijphart has pointed out, require an electoral model which assures all political groupings that they have a stake in maintaining the system as it is.

This grievance, however, was to remain. Some in the opposition continued to feel that elections are not fair and transparent. They felt similarly about the 1998 elections. This was despite the lack of proof that there was anything fraudulent about the 1993 or 1998 elections. Indeed, unlike in previous elections where ballot boxes were physically transferred from the voting stations to the constituency head office for counting, in the 1993 elections counting was done at the voting station in the presence of both election monitors and party agents. Only the numbers of votes were sent to a central place for consolidation. This made it very difficult to rig elections. It is on the basis of this that Kapa has argued that there may have been election malpractices in some constituencies, but that there has not been electoral fraud in recent Lesotho elections.[19]

15 Sejanamane MM (1996) Peace and security in Southern Africa: The Lesotho crisis and regional security. In: I Mandaza (ed.) *Peace and Security in Southern Africa*. Harare: SAPES. p. 66.
16 Ibid.
17 Ibid.
18 Lijpart A (1977) *Democracy in Plural Societies: A Comparative Exploration*. New Haven: Yale University Press.
19 Kapa MA (2015) Fraud or Malpractice in Lesotho Election? Trend Analysis 1965–2015. Conference Paper. Electoral Integrity Conference 2015: Cultural Programme, Cape Town.

1998 elections and post-electoral crisis

The BCP ruled as a de facto one-party state from 1993 until it experienced a split in 1997. The prime minister broke away with a majority of members of parliament to form a splinter party called the Lesotho Congress for Democracy (LCD). The new party continued to rule until the 1998 elections. From 1997, after the BCP split, there was now an opposition party in the Lesotho parliament. That was, however, short-lived since new elections were soon held and they reversed all the gains of the past few months by returning the LCD to government with all but one of the seats in parliament.

The 1998 elections in Lesotho were held under different circumstances to the previous elections. Then, an elections management body named the Independent Electoral Commission (IEC) was established and three commissioners – Messers Sekara Mafisa, Letjeea Qhobela and Morie Khaebana – were appointed. As the commissioners were grappling with the establishment of the new structure, they were immediately faced with organising the 1998 elections – just nine months after their appointment. With the establishment of this seemingly independent elections management body, there was hope that confidence in the elections processes would improve. This, however, was not to be.

Two reasons can be proffered for the failure of the increase in confidence on the process. First, was the alienation of sections of the population arising from the outcome of the 1993 elections where no opposition party was represented in parliament. Throughout the intervening period, no confidence-building mechanisms other than establishing the IEC had been put in place. It was a case of hoping that the situation would repair itself. Inevitably it did not.

Secondly, the IEC inherited a poor voters' roll. Southall and Fox argued that a number of names on the voters' roll for each constituency were at variance with the total number of voters.[20] Prior to the elections, the IEC had published and displayed for public inspection a provisional voters' list. It, however, refused to provide copies of the list to political parties for their own inspection. Three political parties attempted to force its hand through an application to the High Court but failed. The High Court ruled that it had no jurisdiction on the matter.[21] It is within the environment of mistrust that the 1998 elections were held. The mood within the opposition political parties was foul with accusation that the new commission was intent on rigging the elections. The commission's refusal to provide copies of the electoral roll to political parties was viewed as tantamount to waving a red flag. Mafisa, the first chairperson of the IEC, has since conceded that it was an error to refuse to provide the opposition parties with the voters' roll.[22] He, however, argues that there was no malice intended. At the time they thought displaying the names at IEC offices was adequate.

---

20 Southall R & Fox R (1999) Lesotho's general election of 1998: Rigged or de rigeur? *Journal of Modern African Studies* 39(3): 669–696.

21 Ibid.

22 Interview with Mr Sekara Mafisa. 14 November 2014.

The fact that the newly established commission had to defend itself in the courts before the elections did not augur well for the aftermath of the elections. In the end, elections were conducted peacefully and observers agreed that the outcome reflected the will of the people. Thus the Commonwealth Observer Group, led by former Botswana president, Festus Mogae, in the interim report pointed out that:

> Based on our observation and consultations with a broad range of stakeholders, our preliminary conclusion is that the elections were peaceful and well conducted. The shortfalls observed to date by members of the Group are not of a magnitude significant enough to question the credibility of the outcome.[23]

Rigging elections on election day in Lesotho is a difficult proposition because of the transparent way in which voting and counting of the ballots is done. Some observers have pointed out that after the establishment of the IEC each political party not only observed the counting by electoral officers, but they all signed forms indicating how political parties have performed in each polling station, prior to the display of the results outside each polling station. This makes it extremely difficult to rig elections on election day.[24]

During elections, however, the challenge is not whether there was rigging, but the perception of rigging is even more important. The outcome of the 1998 elections was unsettling because the LCD got a disproportionate number of seats in parliament, while the opposition only managed to secure one seat. This matter was pertinently captured by *The Economist* of 8 October 1998. At a general election in May the ruling party, the LCD, won roughly 60% of the vote, but 79 of the 80 seats. The opposition claimed that the poll was rigged. Most observers, however, concluded that although some LCD supporters may have played dirty, the cheating was not on a scale that could have influenced the result.[25] The investigations under Justice Pius Langa on behalf of the Southern African Development Community (SADC) reached the same conclusion.

As a result of the rigging allegations the opposition supporters took to the streets instead of going to challenge the results in the courts of law. Rioting took an uglier turn when rioters paralysed the whole governmental operation. While some set up camp at the Royal Palace, demanding that the King dissolve the LCD government and call for fresh elections, others rioted in Maseru and other areas. The point, however, is that fresh elections would not have resolved the issue since the problem was the operation of the electoral system

23 Commonwealth Observer Group (2015, 2 May) Lesotho Elections Interim Statement. Available at http://thecommonwealth.org/media/news/lesotho-election-commonwealth-observer-group-interim-statement [accessed 15 November 2015].

24 Sekatle, PM (1995) Disputing electoral legitimacy: The BNP's challenge to the results. In: R Southall and T Petlane (eds) *Democratisation and Demilitarisation in Lesotho: The General Election of 1993 and its Aftermath.* Pretoria: Africa Institute.

25 Sad aftermath (8 October 1998) *The Economist.* Available at http://www.economist.com/node/167826?zid=304&ah=e5690753dc78ce91909083042ad12e30 [accessed 21 June 2016].

itself, and not rigging. The 1998 election saw the worst post-election violence in Lesotho characterised by riots and the burning of property.

The rioting and the ensuing lawlessness in the country were made worse by the apparent support that both the police and army gave to the rioters. There was a clear case of mutiny with no security forces obeying instructions by the government to stop the rioters. In the middle of this, several senior military officers were detained by their juniors until they were released after negotiations by SADC military officers. Shortly after that most of the senior military officers fled to South Africa leaving junior officers in control. Though there was no clear move to take over government, there was a concerted effort to render the country ungovernable.

It is in the face of this that SADC intervened to bring about law and order. The South African Defence Force (SANDF) and the Botswana Defence Force (BDF) were the first to arrive. They were later joined by units from Mozambique. This, however, produced unexpected consequences as there was strong resistance by both the mutinous military and civilians in Lesotho. It is immediately after the arrival of the SANDF that most of the looting and burning down of a large number of businesses in Maseru and other neighbouring areas occurred. The chaos spread from Maseru to other towns, noticeably Mafeteng and Teya-Teyaneng. There were casualties on both sides before calm was restored within a week of the SADC military intervention, but the political crisis had now become more internationalised. It was soon recognised by both SADC and the Lesotho political elite that the military action by itself had only helped to stop the violence, but that the roots of the crisis needed political and diplomatic action.

Recognition of the need to find a lasting solution was, however, hampered by the hardened positions of the Lesotho adversaries. The government, which had been brought from the brink of collapse by the SADC military intervention, dug in its heels regarding receiving continued SADC support to rule unimpeded but no other action was necessary in the constitutional and political arena. The argument was that it had won the elections and no fraud had been proven. The opposition, on the other hand, continued to argue that the elections were fraudulent and at the very least, they demanded to be part of a government of national unity until new elections were held. SADC and, particularly the states with forces on the ground, had to find an exit strategy. Such a strategy would eventually have to include both stabilisation mechanisms and political reforms.

Political and electoral reforms

Guided by SADC in general and South Africa in particular, political parties in Lesotho began a process of negotiations on the future of the country. SADC roped in both the Commonwealth and the United Nations Development Programme (UNDP) to support the negotiations amongst the adversaries. After weeks of deadlock, the outline of the solution was reached. The first commitment that had was made was that elections would be held to resolve the contentious issues that had brought about the impasse. Getting over that hurdle was critical since the ruling party was adamant that it had won the elections fairly.

The initial agreements covered three areas. First was the agreement to go back to the polls; second was to ensure that elections would be fair and transparent; and third was the establishment of the Interim Political Authority (IPA) which would facilitate both the constitutional and electoral reforms in order to ensure that future elections would be representative.[26] This agreement was, however, largely a result of intense pressure by South Africa which was leading the political discussions. In a speech in Maseru, while talks were making little progress, Thabo Mbeki had made it clear that electoral reform could not be avoided. He argued that Lesotho's post-elections crisis sprang from its FPTP voting arrangements which gave disproportionate results. 'Thabo Mbeki, South Africa's deputy president has at least offered to give Lesotho a new electoral system.'[27] Mbeki's gift, according to the *Economist,* was about proportionality in election results. He, however, did not prescribe how that would be implemented. It was then up to the IPA, along with Sydney Mufamadi, then South African Minister of Safety and Security, to determine in specific terms which model and how it would operate.

From the beginning therefore, there was recognition of the need to change both the constitution and the Electoral Act in order to defuse the tensions within the country. The instrument chosen for that task was the formation of the IPA.[28] Chaired by Sydney Mufamadi, deliberations on the bill were completed and passed by parliament days after it was approved by the IPA. The Authority was tasked with working in close conjunction with the Lesotho government and parliament, which will be forced to implement its decisions, he said. This condition constituted a victory for the opposition, as the LCD had argued that the Authority should merely be an advisory body to the government. The law made it clear that the decisions of the IPA were final. However, the government later argued that the IPA's decisions were mandatory to it, but not to parliament. This contributed to the delays in holding national elections.

The IPA was made up of two representatives from all the political parties which stood for the 1998 elections. Its objectives were to facilitate and promote, in conjunction with the government, the preparations for the holding of general elections within a period of eighteen months from the date of its commencement in law. Specifically, the law sought to create and promote conditions conducive to the holding of free and fair elections; eliminate any form of intimidation which has a bearing on the elections; and ensure equal treatment of all political parties and candidates by all governmental institutions, and in particular by all government-owned media, prior to and during the elections.

26 Sad aftermath (8 October 1998) *The Economist.* Available at http://www.economist.com/node/167826?zid=304&ah=e5690753dc78ce91909083042ad12e30 [accessed 21 June 2016].
27 Ibid.
28 Lesotho Government (1998) Interim Political Authority Act. *Government Gazette.* Maseru: Government Printer.

The powers of the Authority were spelled out in section 6 of the Interim Political Authority Act. Amongst the powers the following were critical in charting the future of electoral politics in Lesotho:

> 6(d) to review the Independent Electoral Commission and make appropriate recommendations to the relevant public institutions on its structure and functions;
>
> 6(e) to review the Lesotho electoral system with a view to making it more democratic and representative of the people of Lesotho;
>
> 6(f) to recommend changes to existing laws, including the Constitution, to relevant public institutions in order to enable it to attain its objectives;
>
> 6(g) to take such lawful steps as may be necessary to exercise its powers.[29]

This law was important in view of the contestation between the government and the opposition on the way forward. On one hand, the government did not want to lose power soon after winning the elections. The opposition, on the other hand, wanted to move towards constitutional reform and the holding of fresh elections. After the SADC intervention, and with South Africa leaning heavily on all parties to move towards the promised Mbeki solution, passing the law was a substantive forward-movement. The creation of the IPA with power over constitutional and electoral matters, and the government retaining power over other issues, had a potential of creating deadlock on some issues. The IPA was, however, given power to take all necessary means to exercise its mandate. That was important, because a legal mechanism was created to resolve differences whenever they arose.

With support from donors like the UNDP and the Irish government, the IPA workshopped the mixed member proportional (MMP) model to several stakeholders before it was adopted. Key features of this model are to bring in proportionality and compensation to smaller partners. According to this system, votes translate into seats in a manner that when a party has a certain number of votes, it is able to benefit in the same proportion when votes are translated to parliamentary seats. Again smaller parties are able to amass dispersed voters throughout the country rather than in a specific constituency.

Concretely, the first action by the IPA was the development of the law amending the constitution to allow for, among other things: the introduction of an MMP electoral system for; greater independence for the Independent Electoral Commission; and to provide for special provisions for the conduct of elections.[30] Section 3 of the amendment provides, inter alia, that the National Assembly shall be 'constituted by eighty members to be elected in respect of the constituencies', while 'forty members will be elected in accordance with the

---

29 Lesotho Government (1998) Interim Political Authority Act. *Government Gazette*. Maseru: Government Printer.

30 Lesotho Government (2001) Fourth Amendment to the Constitution Act 2001. *Government Gazette*. Maseru: Government Printer. XLVI, 22.

principle of proportional representation applied in respect of the National Assembly as a whole'.[31]

On the IEC, section 4 of the same law stipulates that all registered political parties shall be consulted and requested to make nominations of commissioners under an agreed procedure to the Council of State, which recommends appointments to the King. This means that the key stakeholders were to be part of the decision-making process on the appointment of the commissioners. The arrangement, however, is not entirely flawless. The Council of State, despite the participation of several stakeholders in its make-up, has an automatic majority of members who are either allies or appointees of the prime minister. Section 95 of the Lesotho Constitution establishes the Council of State to advise the King in discharging his duties under the constitution. Amongst the numerous allies and appointees are the speaker of the National Assembly, commander of the Lesotho Defence Force and the commissioner of police. Thus in reality the Council of State expresses the disproportionate interests of the prime minister in the appointment of the IEC.

National Assembly elections in 2002 were thus held under the new constitutional and electoral provisions. The new model was tested in those elections and produced an inclusive parliament with the two main political parties gaining 98 seats (LCD 77, BNP 21), while the smaller parties took the rest of the remaining seats. It was not surprising that those elections were the first to be unconditionally accepted by all political parties. A comparison of the 1998 and 2002 election results below illustrates the inclusivity or otherwise of the two electoral models which were used.

Table 1: 23 May 1998 National Assembly elections

Party	Number of votes	% of votes	Number of seats
Basutoland Congress Party	398 355	74.78%	65
Basotho National Party	120 686	22.66%	0
Marematlou Freedom Party	7 650	1.44%	0
Popular Front for Democracy	947	0.18%	0
Hareeng Basotho Party	646	0.12%	0
United Democratic Party	582	0.11%	0
Kopanang Basotho Party	417	0.08%	0

Source: African Elections Database: Elections in Lesotho. Available at http://africanelections.tripod.com/ls.html [accessed 20 June 2016]

---

31 Lesotho Government (2001) Fourth Amendment to the Constitution Act 2001. Section 3(1)(C)(i). *Government Gazette.* Maseru: Government Printer.

Table 2: 25 May 2002 National Assembly elections

Party	Number of votes	% of votes	Number of seats
Lesotho Congress for Democracy	304 316	54%	77
Basotho National Party	124 234	22.41%	21
Lesotho People's Congress	32 046	5.78%	5
National Independence Party	30 346	5.47%	5
Basutoland African Congress	16 095	2.90%	3
Basutoland Congress Party	14 584	2.63%	3
Lesotho Workers' Party	7 788	1.40%	1
Marematlou Freedom Party	6 890	1.24%	1
National Independence Party	3 985	0.72%	1

Source: African Elections Database: Elections in Lesotho. Available at http://africanelections.tripod.com/ls.html [accessed 20 June 2016]

2007 elections and electoral reforms

The 2007 elections were not very different from the 2002 elections. This was the second time that the MMP model had been used in Lesotho. Shortly before the elections, some political parties formed pre-election alliances, which in reality would subvert or distort their electoral strength within the MMP model. The LCD formed an alliance with a small political party, the National Independence Party (NIP), while the All Basotho Convention (ABC) formed an alliance with the Lesotho Workers Party (LWP). In terms of these alliances, the two major parties contested the elections in the constituencies, while the minor parties did not contest elections in the constituencies, but submitted a list to the IEC which included people from the bigger parties. This was meant to defeat the key feature of the MMP, to be compensatory to those parties which have not been successful in the FPP elections.

Kapa argues that the allocation of seats in Lesotho's 2007 parliament took the form of a mixed member parallel, which does not take into account the compensatory factor, rather than the mixed member proportional. The key elements of inclusivity, reconciliation and compensation were therefore, abandoned.[32] In a similar vein Matlosa points out that, had the model not been subverted, the LCD/NIP alliance could have obtained 62 seats rather than 82 seats out of the 120 parliamentary seats.[33]

After the allocation of seats, it became clear that the spirit of the law had been violated, even if there was no successful challenge of the allocation in the courts. Once again SADC appointed an envoy to mediate between the different political parties. This was of no avail since no common ground was reached. It was left to the Christian Council of Lesotho to attempt to resolve the issues, but with a focus on future elections rather than those of 2007.

32 Kapa MA (2009) The case of Lesotho's mixed member proportional system. *Africa Insight* 39(3). 1–10.
33 Matlosa K (2008) The 2007 General elections in Lesotho: Managing the post-election conflict. *Journal of African Elections* 7(1): 20–49.

A new electoral law was finally agreed upon by representatives of political parties before the 2012 elections.

Legal framework

The Constitution of Lesotho 1993, as amended, provides for elections to the National Assembly. In addition, elections are provided for in the National Assembly Elections Act of 2011, the Local Government Act of 1997 and Local Government Elections Act of 1997.

The objectives of the National Assembly Elections Act of 2011 provided, amongst others, that the law would give effect to the constitutional right of citizens to vote and stand for elections and provide for additional powers, duties and functions of the Independent Electoral Commission.

As a direct result of the 2007 controversies about the allocation of seats in the National Assembly, a new law replacing the National Assembly Elections Order of 1992 by the National Assembly Elections Act of 2011 came into being.[34] Three significant innovations were brought about by the law. First, the law attempted to close some of the gaps which had become apparent in the 2007 elections where some political parties manipulated the model by forming unregistered pre-election alliances. Section 55 of the National Assembly Elections Act eliminated the 'two ballots two votes', which was used in the two previous elections, to a 'one ballot two votes' system. The section stipulates that during general elections, 'constituency votes shall be counted both for the candidate and be converted into party votes'. This ensured that political parties will not find any value in bringing about pre-election pacts which had proved contentious in the 2007 elections.[35]

While this simplified and speeded up the election process, it has often been observed that voter's choices in a system like the one adopted in Lesotho are constrained. This means that a voter who may not like a candidate in a particular constituency does not have the option of choosing an alternate candidate, while at the same time voting for another party. The system essentially strengthens the party bosses and weakens the voter choice. The proportional list remains closed to party members. It is only the party bosses who determine seniority or otherwise. This could at times account for the low voter turnout as we have observed in Lesotho.[36] Data from the Institute for Democracy and Electoral Assistance (IDEA) below shows that voter turnout in Lesotho has been low over time. No study has so far been undertaken to understand why voters are so uninterested in participating in elections.

The second significant change in the 2011 Elections Act is the provision for political party funding. While under the previous law, there was an insignificant allowance provided to political parties which stood for elections; the new law improved the amounts allocated to political parties. It established two categories of political parties which are eligible to get

34 Lesotho Government (2011) National Assembly Elections Act 2011. *Government Gazette.* Supplement No. 1 to Gazette No. 61 of 26 August 2011.
35 Letsie TW (2013) The 2012 general elections in Lesotho: A step towards the consolidation of democracy. *Journal of African Elections* 12(1): 69.
36 Voter turnout data for Lesotho. Strömsborg, Sweden: International IDEA. Available at http://www.idea.int/vt/countryview.cfm?CountryCode=LS [accessed 7 August 2016]

funding. Category one is for the parties which stood in the previous elections. The formula in terms of section 70(5) will be based on the number of votes a political party gained in the previous elections. Category two is for those political parties which did not take part in the previous elections. For the latter, funding will be based on the threshold for registering a political party. It is presently 500 voters.

Table 3: Voter participation in elections

Lesotho voter participation in election years	Voter turnout	Registration
2015	46.61%	563 972
2012	50.04%	564 451
2007	49%	448 953
2002	66.69%	554 386
1998	71.83%	617 738
1993	72.28%	532 678
1970	81.90%	306 529
1965	62.32%	259 844

Source: Voter turnout data for Lesotho. Strömsborg, Sweden: International IDEA. Available at http://www.idea. int/vt/countryview.cfm?CountryCode=LS [accessed 7 August 2016]

The third innovation was gender equity in the party lists for the proportional representation (PR) submission by political parties. Section 47(2) provides that the arrangement of the candidates in the proportional representation shall be arranged 'in order of preference from top to bottom, with a female or male candidate immediately followed by a candidate of the opposite sex'. This was important in view of the concern that female candidates are not increasing in the parties' constituency nominations. The introduction of this element in the election law has had a very big impact on female representation in the National Assembly in Lesotho. Previously, the presence of women candidates was relatively poor, despite them constituting the majority of voters. As a result of the changes, the 2012 elections saw a total of 237 women candidates, against 807 men. This translates into 22.7 % of female candidates against 72.2 % of male candidates. Of those 237 women candidates, only 13 (16.3 %) won in the FPTP. Another 18 women (45 %) got into parliament through the PR.[37]

It's worth reiterating the importance of party funding. It was critical in view of lack of alternative campaign funding in Lesotho. Without that type of funding, the majority of smaller parties would be unable to campaign effectively. The major problem, however, is that the commission itself has capacity constraints in ensuring the accountability for the funds disbursed to political parties.[38] Staffing shortages in the commission has apparently

37 Matlho L (2012) Gender Dimension of the 2012 Lesotho National Assembly Elections Outcome. p. 14. Available at http://www1.uneca.org/Portals/awro/Documents/gender-dimensions-in-2012-elections-study. pdf [accessed 21 July 2016].
38 Interview with Ms Mookho Makhele head of the IEC Finance Section. 22 November 2015.

made it impossible to follow up the disbursements given to political parties. The commission has had to rely solely on the financial statements provided by political parties. Section 71(6) (a–e) provide for impromptu visits and seizure of documents from political parties, but that cannot be done with the current staffing.

Other than the constitution and the National Assembly Elections Act, there seems to be no other laws, domestic or international, which regulate the work of the commission in matters related to elections. In an interview with the Chairman of the IEC, it became clear that there are no treaties or other international bodies that have a direct bearing on the work of the commission. The commission therefore relies on the domestic legislation mentioned above and the good practices of transparency and fairness adopted in the region, and Africa as a whole.

Appointment and powers

The establishment of the elections management body is relatively new development in Lesotho. The IEC was established by section 66 of the constitution, as amended in 1997. The commission is made up of three persons appointed by the King after receiving advice from the Council of State. The appointment is preceded by the nominations by political parties registered with the IEC. The Council of State has to be served with six names from the nominations of the political parties before it advises the King. The IEC is responsible for the management of elections. Three commissioners are appointed for a five-year term.

The present commission is made up of Justice Mahapela Lehohla, chairperson, Advocate 'Mamosebi Pholo and Dr Makase Nyaphisi. The political affiliation of the commissioners is not known even though they were nominated by political parties.

The IEC's main responsibility is to conduct and supervise National Assembly and local government elections and referenda and to ensure that they are free and fair. It is also charged with constituency delimitation, registration and maintenance of the voters' roll and to register political parties. In addition, the commission's powers, duties and functions are spelled out in section 135 of the National Assembly Elections Act 2011. Some of the key responsibilities are:

- Liaison and cooperation with registered political parties and other stakeholders and to establish and enforce a code of conduct by political parties and their agents;
- Promote knowledge of sound electoral practices and processes through the media and other appropriate and effective means;
- Promote research into electoral matters;
- Review legislation and other matters relating to elections and referenda and make appropriate recommendation; and
- Appoint a tribunal to hear and determine complaints concerning the contravention of the code.

Undertaking the above adequately is a big challenge at the moment largely due to resource constraints. There has generally been inadequate financial provision for the work of the commission. That has also had an impact on staffing. Officials have shown that in some departments, the vacancy factor is as high as 50%. However, whenever elections are held, the IEC has resorted to hiring part-time staff in order to ensure that work gets done.[39] Despite the challenges it has faced, the IEC has now come of age. It organised smooth free and fair snap elections in March 2015 in the midst of political turmoil in the country. There were no reports of violence or fraud on election day. The results of the elections were not challenged by any political party, except for a late challenge in the courts by the Basotho National Democratic Party (BDNP) complaining about the use or non-use of votes of independents in the allocation of seats in the National Assembly.[40] The application was dismissed among other reasons, because it had been lodged after the deadline for such challenges. Other than the 2002 and 2012 elections, this was the first time since Lesotho gained independence that election results were not disputed.

It must be noted, however, that in an MMP model as used in Lesotho, allowing independent candidates to stand for election is a misnomer. While political parties are expected to have constituency based candidates and also to submit a list for the proportional side of the elections, independents can just stand, thus distorting the proportionality part of the elections.

There are two main reasons which can be said to have ensured that there were no controversies to the 2015 election results. First, was that the 2011 electoral law had largely improved the regulatory framework and had also closed the loophole that allowed some political parties to form pre-election alliances. The law had created a good environment for people to elect candidates of their choice freely.

The newly appointed commissioners were seen as credible and held political parties by the hand on all matters related to elections. Political parties through several liaison committees fully participated in the procurement of suppliers of election materials; oversaw the transportation of ballots; and were allowed to observe the voting and counting of ballots. Indeed, as some of the leaders of the political parties pointed out after the elections, the IEC did not provide anybody with a reason to challenge the results. Almost everything was done with or in the presence of political party representatives.

In its report, for instance, the Electoral Commissions Forum of SADC countries (ECF-SADC) observes that:

- The Independent Electoral Commission of Lesotho prepared and managed to deliver a credible election given the limited period after the collapse of the coalition government.

---

39 Interview with both Mrs Matete formerly Acting Director of Elections during the 2015 elections and Mrs Mosola head of Human Resources section at IEC. 22 October 2015.
40 Court to hear BDNP poll challenge (2015, May 14) *Lesotho Times*. Available at http://lestimes.com/court-to-hear-bdnp-poll-challenge/ [accessed 21 July 2016].

- Electoral procedures and principles to manage elections were in substantive conformity to Principles on Elections Management Monitoring and Observation (PEMMO).

- The National Assembly elections of Lesotho held on 28 February 2015 were conducted in a peaceful environment.

- The ECF-SADC Mission therefore, affirms that the political and electoral environment was conducive for the elections and the people of the Kingdom of Lesotho were indeed afforded the opportunity to exercise their democratic right to vote.

- The ECF-SADC is satisfied that the 2015 National Assembly Elections were free and fair.

In a similar manner, the Electoral Institute of Sustainable Democracy of Southern Africa, in its preliminary assessment of the context and conduct of the 28 February 2015 legislative elections in Lesotho, 'concluded that the process has been so far peaceful. It was conducted, in a manner that generally allowed the Basotho voters to express freely their will, and in general conformity with the laws of Lesotho and international, continental and sub-regional standards for credible elections'.[41] The commission has been lauded by all for the way it conducted the 2015 elections. The International Centre for Parliamentary Studies (ICPS) awarded the IEC two International Electoral Achievement Awards in recognition of the IEC conducting the 2015 National Assembly Snap Election successfully. The IEC was nominated by the Electoral Stakeholders Network for the Electoral Conflict Management Award and the Minority Participation Award.[42]

While the work of the IEC has become commendable, the role of the media in Lesotho is a major cause of alarm. With some in the media, there was not even a pretence of impartiality. If there is anything that can derail future elections in Lesotho it is the media. Prior to the elections, there were several vitriolic statements arising from some radio stations against some political parties and political leaders. On the other hand, public media was monopolised by the party which controlled the ministry of communications. After the IEC had published the election calendar, all political parties were given access to the public media. The problem, however, is that the presentations which were taken to the media were mechanical. That is, politicians were not grilled on their presentations. It was as if they were addressing political rallies.

Human resources and ICT

Staffing at the IEC is worrying. Almost all heads of sections expressed uneasiness about the staff shortages. In some areas, like finance, the vacancy factor is about 50%. It was

---

41 EISA Lesotho 2015 Election Observer Mission (2015) Preliminary Statement on the Pre-Election Period and Election Day. EISA. Available at http://aceproject.org/ero-en/regions/africa/LS/eisa-election-observer-mission-to-the-28-february/view [accessed 21 July 2016].

42 Independent Election Commission Press Release. 23 November 2015.

revealed that some of the vacancies are due to lack of funding, while others are as a result of the desire to restructure the organisation before filling the positions.[43] While efforts have been made to develop a new organisational structure, such efforts have been stalled by the ministry of public service where IEC staff still belongs. From a staffing point of view, IEC staff may be recruited directly, but structure, salary and benefits are still with the ministry of public service. There is hope, however, that the structure which better represents where the IEC wants to go will be approved by the ministry of public service.

One of the critical sections within the IEC is the information communication technology (ICT) section. Though Lesotho elections are largely manual-based, the ICT is important for voters data management. Registration of voters and the maintenance of an accurate voters' roll are some of the most sensitive activities of the commission. In the past, there was a widespread belief that the IEC, through the ICT section, manipulates voters data and election results. The complaints by the BNP in both the 1993 and 1998 elections tended to be based on this belief even though there was no evidence to support it.

In terms of the hard and software provisions at the IEC, there are very few doubts about the adequacy of what is available. The officer in charge of the section actually feels that, if he had sufficient staff, he would have been totally happy with what he has at the moment. He is confident that the infrastructure is adequate and data is well protected.[44]

Independence

When the IEC was established, there was no concurrent law which provided for its independence. Indeed, the IEC continued to have administrative and financial dependence typical of the public service. The law provides for two ways in which the IEC recruits staff. First, it can recruit directly, but has no independent budget to finance that. IEC staff so recruited are part of the public service as defined in the Public Service Act of No. 1 of 2005.[45] As already pointed out above, remuneration of IEC staff is within the public service and the IEC is treated like any other government department.

The second way in which staff can be recruited for the IEC is to identify people from the public service for deployment to the commission. It is not clear to what extent this practice has been put into operation. Efforts to find information on this aspect have not been successful. The point, however, is that this provision could bring about a lot of suspicion on the part of the political parties, particularly in the context of the tension Lesotho has been going through.

Another challenge is funding. The IEC gets its funding through the ministry of law and constitutional affairs. It does not account directly to parliament for funds it has received since they are allocated through the parent ministry. It is clear therefore, that the IEC is dependent on the government of the day, hence the hint of interference will always be

---

43 Interview with three senior IEC staff. 22 October 2015.
44 Interview with Mr Lebohang Bulane, in charge of IEC data.
45 Lesotho Government (2005) Public Service Act No. 1 2005. *Government Gazette*. Maseru: Government Printer.

there. It is one thing, however, to say that funding goes through a ministry, and another to suspect collusion.

In its present form, and given the constraints it faces, the IEC is not independent. It is, however, operationally independent when it has to deliver on its mandate. This operational autonomy has also been enhanced by international support when it organises elections.[46]

IEC stakeholders

Section 135(a) of the National Assembly Elections Act 2011, in defining the responsibilities of the IEC, appropriately begins by mentioning its liaison role with the political parties and other interested civic groups. It is important to underline that, because there cannot be fair and transparent elections without the active participation of political parties. Thus, the electoral management body (EMB) in Lesotho has over the past few years now ensured participation in almost all registered political parties in all its activities. Several sub-committees have been established where joint work goes on in preparation for elections.

Since 2012, the IEC has largely outsourced voter education. This has freed its hands to focus on strategic organisational issues about elections while trained organisations take on the role of educating voters. The challenge, however, is whether the trainers are sufficiently monitored in order to ensure that voter education is rooted in the communities across the country.

In addition, the IEC has been able to recruit several qualified personnel to oversee its tribunals, which deal with pre-poll conflicts in line with the code of conduct. The success or otherwise of the Tribunals has not been assessed, but they play an important role. A number of concerns, however, have been raised in the reports of the Tribunal for both the 2012 and 2015 elections.

At present there is no direct link between the National Assembly and the IEC, because the IEC presently does not report to parliament, even for funds it has been allocated. That remains the role of the minister responsible for the IEC. Perhaps the only link that parliament has with the IEC is when the latter submits a list of members of parliament to relevant bodies.

The Lesotho media is one of the key stakeholders of the IEC. We, however, have to note the negative role that some media has been playing. It is not clear whether there is sufficient monitoring of what the media does for the IEC.

The IEC and electoral reform

Section 135 of the National Assembly Elections Act, amongst other things, provides that the IEC shall have the following powers:
- To undertake and promote research into electoral matters;
- Continuously review legislation and other matters relating to elections and referenda and to make appropriate recommendations; and

---

46 Interview with the chairperson of the IEC, Justice Lehohla. 22 November 2015.

- To develop and promote the development of electoral expertise and technology in all spheres of government.

Evidence exists that the coming into existence of the improved electoral law in effect now, was the initiative of the IEC. It developed, workshopped and finally had it drafted for submission to parliament. In all those stages, the IEC worked hand in hand with the political parties.

As part of the overall responsibility to continuously review legislation and make recommendations, the IEC has arranged a number of workshops with different stakeholders on election-related issues. A new initiative by the IEC to review the present electoral law has recently been unveiled. The IEC is apparently mooting the eventual abandonment of the MMP model in favour of a fully fledged proportional representation model. One of the commissioners, Dr Nyaphisi, has recently unveiled a proposal to gradually move away from MMP to full proportional representation. Beginning with the next elections, he proposes that the number of seats the constituencies receive should be reduced to 50% of the total number of seats in the National Assembly and then by the next elections the country should have moved to proportional representation.[47] It was largely to advance this reform process that the IEC, working with other stakeholders, arranged a two-day workshop in November 2015 to chart the way forward. This shows that there is a determination to fulfil the mandate about legislative reform and creating a pool of people who are versed in electoral matters. It has however been discovered that the above proposal was not an official IEC position. Dr Nyaphisi was expressing an individual opinion which had not yet been approved by the IEC and its stakeholders.

Conflict resolution and enforcement

Section 135 of the National Assembly Elections Act provides for the appointment of a person who can conciliate a complaint concerning the infringement of the code of conduct. At the same time, section 122 of the same law read with section 123 provide that complaints made against a political party and/or an official of the party shall refer the complaints to the Tribunal set up in terms of section 135. The Tribunal set up in terms of this law can only issue a formal warning; prescribe a fine; bar a political party from accessing media arranged by the commission; and bar the political party for a specified period to hold public meetings. The Tribunal can, however, forward a recommendation to the commission to consider issuing a punishment which could deregister the political party concerned.

It has become common in Lesotho now to precede the elections with the agreement of all political parties to accede to an electoral pledge facilitated by the Christian Council of Lesotho. They all pledge to honour the constitution and laws of Lesotho and to observe the electoral code of conduct. More importantly, they undertake to accept the outcome of the

---

47 Dr Nyaphisi was quoted in several radio stations in Lesotho on 26 November 2014. Attempts to reach him for confirmation were not successful.

elections. This was done prior to the 2012 elections and also the challenging 2015 elections. The Tribunal is the primary organ the IEC uses to enforce the code. Before complaints go to the Tribunal, there is an elaborate system beginning with mediation at local and district levels. However, both the 2013 and 2015 reports[48] by the Tribunal indicate that those structures have tended to be skipped by the complainants.

The IEC puts a lot of effort in recruiting staff to fill the conciliation structures at district level, but they seem to be ignored by the political parties, and also to some extent, by the executive branch of the IEC election management. The idea was that when those interventions fail for whatever reason, the complaints should be passed to the Tribunal. It now seems that one leg of the conflict management system is broken and the Tribunal has had to do things which it ordinarily would not have had to. The fact that the number of cases lodged with the Tribunal have increased over time, but that there is a large number of those cases which have been abandoned, may be an indication that some of the complaints did not need to go so far as the Tribunal.

More pertinently, in its report on the 2012 elections the Tribunal makes serious observations about the way the IEC has mismanaged the decisions of the Tribunal. Amongst the most serious observations made by the Tribunal are the following in observation 4 of its report:[49]

> a. Lack of, or insufficient appreciation of the Code of Conduct and the powers conferred by law to the Tribunal (e.g. Case No. 2), where the Tribunal imposed a sanction to DC suspending them from campaigning for seven days in the constituencies where the DC had impeded the LCD to compete on level ground. The IEC took the responsibility to deliver judgement to DC when it was not required by law. According to evidence (IEC letters addressed to the LCD and to DC dated 20 May 2012) the IEC apologised for delaying conveyance of the Tribunal judgement. This showed lack of appreciation that the Tribunal delivers judgement direct to the affected parties and the IEC has no role to deliver it to them. Also the letter indicated that there was a belief that the IEC has powers to review judgements imposed by the Tribunal.
>
> b. Acted as an impediment to the Tribunal sometimes even sent out confusing signals to the political parties about the Tribunal. For example, the National Assembly Elections Act 2012 Section 122(5)(a) and (b) read with Section 122(6) (a) provides for the Tribunal to impose fines. In the case ET/CASE/12/2012 between Motlatsi 'Mota and two others against Sakaria Kele and DC the Tribunal actually imposed a fine of M 5 000. Since the Tribunal is not mandated

---

48 IEC Tribunal (2013) IEC Tribunal Final Report for the 2012 National Assembly Elections. Unpublished. 7 November 2013; and IEC Tribunal (2015) 2015 National Assembly Report of Complaints Lodged with the Electoral Tribunal. Unpublished. Submitted by the Electoral Tribunal April 2015.
49 IEC Tribunal (2013) IEC Tribunal Final Report for the 2012 National Assembly Elections. Unpublished, pp. 12–14.

with administrative powers it seems logical that the IEC is intended to collect such a fine. The IEC until the time of writing this report has not collected such a fine from the Democratic Congress. It can only be deduced that failure of the IEC to collect this fine reflects negatively on the effectiveness of the Tribunal. The message it sends is that the Tribunal is irrelevant and political parties need not heed its determinations.

The matters above are serious and can break the goodwill which the election management system enjoys unless there is a serious attempt to ensure that the challenges are dealt with. There is no evidence so far that IEC commissioners have ensured that the director of elections is made aware of the consequences of these actions and omissions.

Prior to the 2015 general elections, a large number of complaints were filed, but very few were ultimately handled, because the complainants withdrew them before they could be processed. According to the Tribunal: 'Of the dismissed cases 6 (86) were a direct result of the Complainants abandoning their cases in the middle of the process apparently because they felt that their time would be better spent at the campaign trail as opposed to IEC boardroom making arguments that won't earn the politician votes.'[50] A number of rulings were handed down, particularly against the main political parties. It is not, however, clear whether they were enforced.

Two observations about the powers of the Tribunal to sanction political parties and individuals, and also of the powers of the IEC on serious violations, require further commentary. First, the Tribunal in its mandate to enforce the code of conduct (section 123) is empowered to impose, amongst others, sanctions to prohibit 'the political party for a specified period, from utilizing any media time made available by the Commission to the political party for electoral purposes'. For purposes of clarity, the time provided by the IEC is in the public media which it regulates after announcing the elections time table. In Lesotho the public media has more resources than the private media, but it is largely not as credible as the alternative media. More pertinently, barring a political party from getting involved in public media arranged by the commission is really not a punishment at all. There are simply too many open channels to be bothered with using public media.

The Tribunal may also recommend to the IEC to issue an order 'disqualifying a political party if the contravention involves violence, intimidation or gross or systemic violence of the rights of another political party, a candidate or an elector and consequently its right to participate in the elections'.[51] This is a very serious action which necessarily would have implications for the IEC. For an election management body on its own to bar a political party from elections may be possible, but the perception would always remain

50 IEC Tribunal (2015) 2015 National Assembly Report of Complaints Lodged with the Electoral Tribunal. Unpublished, p. 36.
51 Lesotho Government (2011) National Assembly Elections Act 2011. Section 122(5)(a) – (d). *Government Gazette*. Maseru: Government Printer.

that the body is not neutral. It probably would be better if a matter as serious as that were adjudicated by a court of law rather than the IEC.

Conclusion

Following the enactment of the National Assembly Elections Act in of 2011, which minimised the post-election conflicts of the past, the IEC can only improve on the substantive issues. Two issues need to be highlighted in the law. First, the question of 'one vote two ballots' may be popular with party bosses, but it is limiting the options in an election for voters. There are cases where some people have actually not voted because they may like a candidate for the constituency and not the party, and the other way round.

Second, the MMP is important in broadening representation in parliament. However, lack of a threshold in MMP elections can be detrimental to the system, since even political parties which get votes below the set quota end up being brought into parliament on a compensatory basis. This tends to over-represent smaller political parties and thus complicate the formation of a government after elections. It enhances political instability in the post-election period since they can easily shift alliances even though they did qualify to have seats in parliament in the first place. A good example is provided by both the 2012 and 2015 elections in Lesotho. There was a multiplicity of voices which emerged after the elections, but some of them would not have qualified if there was a 3% or 5% threshold. In 2012 there emerged a three-party coalition. In 2015 the situation was desperate, because the two main parties have almost equal numbers of voters. A coalition of seven political parties was cobbled up. It is a very unstable situation. At least one of the political parties in the present coalition did not manage to get even 2 000 votes while the quota was 4 700. The table below provides a comparison of the votes for the different political parties since 1993.

A major threat to Lesotho's democracy is the unregulated and unprofessional media. Both the public media and the private media in Lesotho have the potential to undermine the work of public institutions like the IEC. During election time, the law must not only regulate the public media, but also the private media. After the announcement of the elections time table, the IEC is empowered to ensure equitable access to the public media and also to ensure that there is adherence to the code of conduct in the public media. The recent practice in Lesotho has been for political parties to buy slots in the private media to campaign. Some have had a privileged association with some anchors in the private media. This is where broadcasts, which can only be described as bordering on promoting disharmony and violence, are aired. The IEC has no control over that. The best that can be done is to monitor individual political party members who work at such radio stations. The IEC has no capacity to do that. This view about the media in Lesotho is also raised by the Electoral Institute for Sustainable Democracy in Africa (EISA) election monitoring team report on the 2015 elections in Lesotho. The report states:

Many stakeholders, including media monitoring institutions, informed the Mission that freedom of the press is guaranteed and practised in Lesotho. However, they expressed concerns over the open partisanship of some media outlets, particularly the private radio stations. According to these reports, these radio stations used inflammatory language, which has the potential to trigger electoral violence.[52]

The situation is made worse by the fact that the body established to regulate the media in Lesotho has not been visible.

Recommendations

It is clear that the IEC in Lesotho is presently held in high esteem and the shortcomings shown above have not diminished the confidence stakeholders have in it. The challenges, however, have to be addressed soon so that the country does not revert to the old habits of disputed elections. Key recommendations are listed below.

- Remove the 'one vote two ballots' system in favour of the 'two votes two ballots' system since the former limits the choices of the voters.
- Introduce a threshold which will determine whether political parties should be allocated any seats in parliament. A 3–5% threshold would ensure representability while eliminating political parties which have not acquired the necessary number of votes.
- Forbid independents from standing in elections because Lesotho operates on the basis of the MMP model. The Lesotho Constitution specifies that votes must be equal. Political parties are forced to contest a minimum number of constituencies and also have a minimum number of people in the proportional list. Allowing independents seems to give them the privilege of standing for elections on a preferential basis.
- Introduce media reforms during elections. The IEC should be able to control the activities of the public media once it has issued an election time table. It must also oversee the private media during that time in order to ensure that inflammatory and biased statements are not made during the election process.

---

52 EISA 2015 Lesotho Election Observer Mission (2015) A preliminary statement by the EISA Election Observer Mission on the 28th February 2015 Legislative Elections in The Kingdom of Lesotho. Available at http://aceproject.org/ero-en/regions/africa/LS/eisa-election-observer-mission-to-the-28-february/view [accessed 21 July 2016].

5

MALAWI

Ms Ann Maganga

Introduction

Having been a colony for 70 years, from 1891 to 1961, Malawi became independent on 6 July 1964. Malawi held its first multiparty elections in August 1961. These were followed by fresh elections in April 1964, three months before independence. These elections were held under the inherited British Westminster Constitution, which provided for a multiparty parliamentary system of government. The first post-independence electoral commission was appointed in 1970 under the chairmanship of Mr JRN Chinyama who was succeeded upon his death in 1971 by Mr ND Kwenje. This commission was appointed to oversee the demarcation of constituencies in readiness for the 1971 elections. Sixty constituencies were demarcated during this period.[1] These elections operated under the terms of the provisions of section 31 of the then Malawi Constitution as amended by Act 25/1969.[2]

This report intends to describe how elections have been managed since post-colonial days in Malawi, and how the political dynamics of the time have continued to shape the current behaviour of the electoral management body. The first part outlines the historical, political and electoral context. We then consider the Malawi Electoral Commission's (MEC) powers and functions, legal framework, operations and funding before concluding with an evaluation and assessment, and some resolutions.

Historical, political and electoral context

Malawi, originally known as Nyasaland, was a British protectorate for 70 years, from 1891 to 1961.[3] In 1922, Europeans requested that they be granted a form of electoral representation and submitted names of European candidates for the legislative council. However, neither Africans nor Asians were represented by members of their own community in the council.[4]

---

1   Khofi LM (1974) *Malawi Parliament – Practice and Procedure.* Malawi: Government printer. pp. 4–5.
2   Ibid.
3   Chijere-Chirwa W (2014) *Malawi Democracy and Political Participation.* Johannesburg: Open Society Initiative for Southern Africa.
4   Khofi LM (1974) *Malawi Parliament – Practice and Procedure.* Malawi: Government printer.

After the constitutional talks at Lancaster House in London in 1960, a new constitution was agreed upon, which provided for a legislative council of 28 members and five officials to be elected on the basis of a qualified franchise. Two voters' rolls were established: the higher roll with eight representatives for Europeans, and a lower roll with 20 representatives for Africans. All voters had to be at least 21 years of age at the time of voting. With this arrangement, Africans had full voting rights and direct representation in the legislative council.

First multiparty elections

Malawi held its first multiparty elections in 1961. During these elections the Malawi Congress Party (MCP) made a clean sweep of all 20 seats allocated to Africans on the lower roll, as well as two more from the higher roll intended for Europeans. By the beginning of 1962, Dr Banda had become the de facto prime minister, a position that was later regularised on 1 February 1963. On 9 May 1963, the legislative council was renamed as the legislative assembly.[5] The last elections under the Monarchical or Westminster Constitution were held in Malawi on 28 April 1964,[6] three months before Malawi attained independence from Britain on 6 July 1964. During these elections the MCP, once again, won all seats unopposed, and the opposition was wiped out through elections.[7] In 1966 Malawi became a republic with a new constitution which abolished all other political parties.[8] Dr Banda became the first president of Malawi with a legislative assembly of 55 members.[9] In 1971 he became president for life. Because of this status, he was spared any electoral contestation;[10] only parliamentary and local councillors' elections were held.

Elections under the one-party rule

During the one-party era, vacancies in the legislative councils were filled through appointments by the president after a selection process by MCP leaders in consultation with traditional leaders, representatives from district and town councils, women's and youth leagues and through party conferences. A maximum of five names from each constituency were proposed for election. Once elections were conducted, and votes were counted, these were submitted to the president for his final decision.[11] The candidate chosen through this process would normally stand unopposed. This explains why there was a very high retention rate of members of parliament (MPs) during the MCP's era, from 1964 to 1994.[12]

---

5   Ibid.
6   Chijere-Chirwa W (2014) *Malawi Democracy and Political Participation*. Johannesburg: Open Society Initiative for Southern Africa.
7   Khofi LM (1974) *Malawi Parliament – Practice and Procedure*. Malawi: Government printer. pp. 7–8.
8   The 1966 republican constitution abolished the multiparty system. The MCP became the sole legal political party to be allowed in the country.
9   Khofi LM (1974) *Malawi Parliament – Practice and Procedure*. Malawi: Government printer. p. 4.
10 Khembo NS (2005) *Elections and Democratization in Malawi: An Uncertain Process*. Johannesburg: EISA. p. 3.
11 Ibid.
12 Chimunthu-Banda H (2014) *Malawi Parliament: Origins, Reforms and Practice*. Lilongwe: Pan African Publishers. p. 33.

Loyalty to Banda was more important than the popularity of a candidate with voters.[13] The president also had the prerogative to appoint members of parliament and ministers.

Transition to multiparty democracy in 1993

Banda's personal rule came to an end in 1994 following international and domestic pressure, especially from three local pressure groups known as the Alliance for Democracy (AFORD), the Public Affairs Committee (PAC), the United Democratic Front (UDF),[14] and from the Catholic bishops through an Episcopal letter in 1992. The principal objective of these pressure groups was to carry out negotiations with the then MCP government to change its policies in the economic, social and political spheres. Banda agreed to hold a referendum and went on to set up a negotiation structure, dubbed the Presidential Committee on Dialogue (PCD), comprising government, representatives of various civil society organisations, and the aforementioned pressure groups.[15] The PCD was established to discuss issues of national interest and concerns that would be raised from time to time. Several meetings were held through the PAC over the modality and management of the transitional period resulting in the establishment by Banda of the first National Referendum Commission on 11 January 1993 comprising 12 members. This number was increased to 20 by 23 March of the same year.[16] Professor Brown Chimphamba was appointed chairperson of the National Referendum Commission.[17]

National Referendum Commission

The National Referendum Commission was established in order to: (i) organise and direct the registration of voters; (ii) devise and establish voters' registers and ballot papers; (iii) print, distribute and control ballot papers; (iv) approve ballot boxes; (v) establish and operate polling stations; (vi) take measures for ensuring that the entire referendum process would be conducted under conditions of complete freedom and fairness; (vii) establish security conditions necessary for the conduct of the referendum in accordance with the referendum regulations; (viii) educate the citizens on the purpose of the referendum; (ix) ensure that there would be no hindrance to free and open discussion of the referendum questions; and (x) ensure compliance with the referendum regulations and adopt measures necessary to guarantee that the referendum would be free and fair. The commission was

---

13 Interview with former clerk of parliament on 2 September 2015 in Lilongwe, Malawi.

14 These pressure groups, except the PAC, eventually evolved into political parties.

15 These were pressure groups because political parties were outlawed under Section 4 of the 1966 Republican Act.

16 Malawi Government (1993) *Report of the National Referendum Commission.* pp. 6–9.

17 Prof. Brown Chimphamba is an eminent person in Malawian society. Before his appointment he was vice-chancellor of the University of Malawi, coordinating five constituent colleges, including the college of medicine. He was an ambassador, and a chairperson of various international and local institutions. He has also written several academic books and journals, and was a commissioner in the MEC. He has been recognised by the president as 'man of the decade' for his contribution to the development of Malawi.

mandated to investigate any complaints submitted to it in writing relating to any aspect of the referendum process.[18]

National Consultative Council (NCC)

After a very peaceful transition where Malawians overwhelmingly voted by 63% to return to multipartyism on 14 June 1993, [19] Banda was left with no choice but to establish a multiparty National Consultative Council (NCC) [20] to act as an interim parliament.[21] The referendum was strong evidence that the one-party system of government had failed to meet the expectations of the majority of the people.[22] One of the first major tasks to be undertaken by the NCC was to repeal section 4 of the 1966 constitution abolishing all other political parties except the MCP. This resulted in a proliferation of political parties. By May 2004, a total of 28 political parties had been registered.[23] A 49-member team comprising international and local experts was set up to draft the new Malawi Constitution to help shape multiparty democracy in the country and oversee the 1994 elections. This team of experts was answerable to the NCC. Parties that came later to join the negotiating block, such as the Second Republic of Malawi led by Kanyama Chiume, were not allowed because negotiations with government were at an advanced stage. There were fears that allowing latecomers would derail gains made up to that point.

Laws governing elections before the referendum

Before the 1993 referendum, three laws governed elections in Malawi. These were: the Presidential and Parliamentary Act; the Elections Act; and the Voter Registrations Act. After the referendum, the forces of change agreed with the government that there should be one law for the presidential and parliamentary elections. It was under that consolidated law that the president appointed the first commission under the chairmanship of Justice Anastazia Msosa in December 1993, after withdrawing the name of Justice Chatsika after it had been rejected by the opposition.[24] The same law also set the precedent that all chairpersons to the commission should be judges and that the commission should be composed of people from diverse backgrounds and political parties.

However, when this first commission was appointed it did not have offices or a secretariat of its own. It relied on parliament, which was then located in Zomba, for its

---

18 Malawi Government (1993) *Report of the National Referendum Commission.* p. 9.

19 Khembo NS (2004) *Overview of Multipartyism in Malawi.* p. 3.

20 The National Consultative Council (NCC) was formed by an Act of Parliament in 1993.

21 There was also the National Executive Council (NEC) which was composed of the heads of all the parties that emerged after the referendum. These were at first pressure groups because the law did not provide for their existence. The NEC acted as the interim executive while the NCC acted as the interim parliament, and was made up of an equal number of representatives of the seven political parties.

22 Khaila S & Chibwana C (2005) Ten years of democracy in Malawi: Are Malawians getting what they voted for? *Afrobarometer Working Paper* No. 46.

23 Khembo NS (2004) *Overview of Multipartyism in Malawi.* pp. 4–5.

24 Interview with the executive director of the National Elections Systems Trust (NEST) on 9 September 2015 in Blantyre, Malawi.

accommodation and secretariat services.[25] The clerk of parliament (COP), served as chief elections officer (CEO) managing elections and by-elections. When he was on electoral duties, he was referred to as supervisor of elections or supervisor of registration of voters.[26] The first commission, therefore, and all who were appointed later, were serviced by parliament.

Although the constitution changed due to the new political dispensation in Malawi in 1994, the COP continued to serve as CEO until an Act of Parliament was passed in 1998 establishing the commission and mandating it to appoint its own CEO and secretariat. Through this act the COP was delinked from the role of the CEO.

Malawi Electoral Commission

Section 75(1) of the Malawi Constitution establishes the Electoral Commission (MEC) when it stipulates that:

> there shall be an Electoral Commission which shall consist of a Chairperson who shall be a judge nominated in that behalf by the Judicial Service Commission and such other members, not being less than six, as may be appointed in accordance with an Act of Parliament.

Section 4(1) of the Electoral Commission Act stipulates that:

> the President shall, subject to the Constitution and in consultation with the leaders of the political parties represented in the National Assembly, appoint suitably qualified persons to be members of the Commission on such terms and conditions as the Public Appointments Committee of parliament shall determine.

Enabling the constitutional provisions are three key Acts of Parliament: the Electoral Commission (EC) Act (11/1998); the Parliamentary and Presidential Elections (PPE) Act (31/1993); and the Local Government Elections Act (24/1996). In addition, there is the Public Financial Management Act – Public Procurement Act, which is used for procurement purposes. Closely related to these is the Political Parties Registration and Regulation Act (15/1993), in the sense that it provides a framework for political parties and their candidates to participate in elections. In 2012, the Malawi parliament unanimously amended the constitution so that the 2014 local government elections could be conducted on the same day as the general elections. The constitution and the related pieces of legislation provide an adequate legal framework for the conduct of democratic elections in

---

25 Ibid.
26 Interview with former clerk of parliament on 2 September 2015 in Lilongwe, Malawi.

137

the country. The High Court has the right of judicial review of the electoral commission to ensure that it acts in accordance with the constitution and Acts of Parliament.

Powers and functions

The MEC's functions and responsibilities are stipulated under section 76 of the constitution and section 8 of the EC Act. It is empowered to undertake the following tasks.

Constituency and ward determination

According to section 76(a) the MEC is mandated to determine constituency boundaries impartially on the basis of ensuring that constituencies contain approximately equal numbers of voters eligible to register. The National Assembly has the power to confirm constituency boundaries, but it is not empowered to alter them, except upon the recommendation of the MEC.[27] In addition, section 8(1) of the EC Act mandates the MEC to undertake and supervise the demarcation of wards for local government elections. However, demarcation of constituencies has not taken place in Malawi since 1998. Delimitation of wards was done in 2011 in preparation for local government elections.

Voter registration

The MEC is mandated to oversee the voter registration process as stipulated in section 77(2b) of the constitution and Section 15 of the PPE Act. The EC Act section 8(d) defines the role of the electoral commission in the process of voter registration. The commission has been using the optimal-mark-recognition (OMR) system during the registration process of voters. This is a manual registration process which is paper-based. This system has two main challenges: (i) the margin of error or room for manipulation of voter registration is high; (ii) it is prone to inefficiencies leading to limited time for voter verification.[28] However, there has been strong resistance from stakeholders on the MEC's proposal to migrate from OMR to a biometric voter registration system. Stakeholders have cited limited time, and lack of capacity and resources as reasons for this resistance.

Voter education

The EC Act (1998), section 8(j), mandates the commission to promote public awareness of electoral matters through the media and other appropriate and effective means, and to conduct civic and voter education. In order to carry out this task effectively, the MEC has invited several civil society organisations, political parties and the media to assist with the delivery of civic and voter education (CVE). The MEC has also developed a code of conduct with some stakeholders to ensure best practice in the Southern Africa Development

27 Lodge T, Kadima D & Pottie D (eds) (2002) *Compendium of Elections in Southern Africa 1989 – 2000.* Johannesburg: EISA. p. 228.
28 MEC (2015) *Malawi Electoral Support Network National Taskforce on Electoral Reform.* pp. 42–43.

Community (SADC) region, and the SADC guidelines on reporting elections were adopted by SADC countries in September 2012.[29]

Candidate nomination

The MEC presides over the nomination of candidates according to section 51 of the constitution which defines the eligibility criteria for a parliamentary candidate, requiring among other things that s/he should be a citizen of Malawi, at least 21 years of age, and able to speak and read English well enough to take part in the proceedings of parliament. S/he must not have been convicted of a crime, must not be a holder of a public office, and must not be in the defence force or the police force. A presidential candidate must be at least 35 years of age and of sound mind; s/he must not have been convicted of a crime in the previous seven years involving dishonesty or moral turpitude; must not owe allegiance to a foreign country; and must not be a holder of a public office as stipulated in the parliamentary candidate above.

Media monitoring

The media in Malawi is governed by the Communications Act (1998).[30] The Communications Act and the PPE Act (1993) provide a framework for political equality in the electoral process. In order to strengthen the relationship between the commission and the media, the commission visited and held meetings during the 2014 elections with 33 media houses, the Media Council of Malawi and Media Institute of Southern Africa (MISA).[31] The commission also reviewed the media code of conduct to ensure best practice in the SADC region. Further, section 63(1–3) of the PPE Act regulates how political parties should campaign. It states how the commission would allocate time on television and radio to political parties. Section 8(1)(j) of the EC Act mandates it to provide civic and voter education through the media and other appropriate and effective means.[32] Another of its duties is to try to ensure a level playing field for all candidates.

Political party registration

Although political parties are the main players during elections, the MEC does not have the power to register them. This responsibility is under the jurisdiction of the registrar of political parties. However, there is no law to regulate or compel the registrar of political parties to monitor the activities of political parties once registered.

Funding of political parties

Section 40(2) of the Constitution of Malawi stipulates that:

29 MEC (2014) *Tripartite Election Report*. p. 67.
30 Khembo NS (2005) *Elections and Democratization in Malawi: An Uncertain Process*. Johannesburg: EISA.
31 MEC (2014) *Tripartite Election Report*. p. 67.
32 MEC (2015) *Malawi Electoral Support Network National Taskforce on Electoral Reform*. p. 47.

the State shall provide funds so as to ensure that during the life of any parliament, any political party which has secured more than one-tenth of the national votes in elections to that parliament has sufficient funds to continue to represent its constituency.

However, there is no electoral law to monitor the funding of political parties in Malawi or a candidate's campaign expenditure. Nor is there any law to compel party candidates to disclose the source of their funding.

Organising elections
Section 67(1) of the Constitution of Malawi stipulates that:

the National Assembly shall stand dissolved on the 20th of March in the fifth year after its elections, and the polling day for the general elections for the next National Assembly shall be the Tuesday in the third week of May that year.[33]

Since the dawn of the new political dispensation in Malawi in 1994, four general elections have been held every five years; one local government election in 2000 and a tripartite election in 2014. All these were administered by the MEC. The first elections, held on 14 May 1994, were judged largely free and fair by observers. The leader of the UDF, Bakili Muluzi, was elected president, his party winning 87 of the 177 seats.[34] The second elections were held in 1999; the third in 2004. The 2009 general elections which took place on 19 May 2009 had a high turnout of about 78% registered voters, and Professor Bingu wa Mutharika won with a majority. On 20 May 2014, Malawi held its first tripartite elections. Professor Peter Mutharika won the presidential election by 36.4%, followed by Dr Lazarus Chakwera with 27.8% of the total votes. These results were disputed, and the High Court ruled for a recount. However, the warehouse where election materials were being stored mysteriously caught fire and burnt to ashes all the materials that were stored there.

Security of data, material and personnel
The MEC oversees the security process throughout the electoral cycle. During each cycle there are different types of security measures required. The cycle consists of: printing of ballot papers; shipment and offloading; polling; counting; and announcement of results. The police force is deployed throughout the electoral cycle to ensure the safety of voters, of personnel conducting elections and even of warehouses where materials are stored. Their deployment continues even after the results of the elections have been announced to ensure a peaceful transition of power to the successor. The army complements police efforts in

---

33 MEC (2014) *Malawi Electoral Laws*.
34 Chijere-Chirwa W (2014) *Malawi Democracy and Political Participation*. Johannesburg: Open Society Initiative for Southern Africa.

ensuring that there is peace and calm throughout the country. The army is also deployed in transporting ballot boxes to remote areas of the country, and back to the tally centre.

Dispute resolution mechanism

There is no distinct electoral law for resolving electoral disputes in Malawi except through the High Court. Disputes arising at the polling centres are referred to the commission. When the MEC is unable to solve the problem, the case is referred to the High Court. However, two structures were established in 2003 to improve the relationship between the MEC, political parties and civil society organisations (CSOs). One is the National Elections Consultative Forum (NECOF), which provides a platform for the MEC, political parties and CSOs to discuss electoral issues at the national level. At a lower level, the MEC established multiparty liaison committees (MPLCs), which bring together different stakeholders at the district level to resolve electoral issues.[35] The MPLCs are composed of the following: leaders of political parties that are in the district; director of the district commissioner's office; director of planning; information officer; police officer in charge of the criminal investigation branch; and traditional and religious leaders in the district. There is a need, however, to cascade these mechanisms to the constituency level as well.

Recently, the Centre for Multiparty Democracy (CMD), a grouping of all political parties represented in the National Assembly, has provided a platform for the secretaries general of political parties to resolve their political and other electoral differences through dialogue. The CMD also acts as a bridge at times between political parties and the MEC to resolve electoral problems and misunderstandings. The Public Affairs Committee (PAC), a grouping of mostly religious leaders, also provides a platform for peace mediation during the electoral cycle, for example, when there has been a stalemate between government and opposition political parties or and between presidential candidates. In the run-up to the 2014 tripartite elections, the PAC was instrumental in ensuring that presidential candidates sign a peace accord before elections.

Legal framework

Elections in Malawi are guided by section 77 of the Malawi Constitution which entitles every eligible voter to cast his or her vote during general and local government elections. Malawi is a signatory and a member of several regional, continental and international treaties governing elections. These include the African Charter on Democracy, Elections and Governance which the African Union (AU) adopted in January 2007. Malawi ratified this convention on 11 October 2012 and adopted the same on 24 October 2012.[36] The country also subscribes to the SADC Principles and Guidelines Governing Democratic Elections, which provide a framework for conducting democratic elections in the region.

35 Lodge T, Kadima D & Pottie D (eds) (2002) *Compendium of Elections in Southern Africa 1989–2000.* Johannesburg: EISA. p. 239.
36 Chijere-Chirwa W (2014) *Malawi Democracy and Political Participation.* Johannesburg: Open Society Initiative for Southern Africa.

Malawi also belongs to the SADC Electoral Commissioners Forum, the Association of African Electoral Authorities, and the Association of World Election Bodies. Because of these affiliations, these international institutions and governments are able to send election observers to Malawi every election year.

Likewise, Malawi is able to send electoral observers to countries that subscribe to the same values. Affiliations to these bodies have assisted the country to build the capacity of the MEC and its personnel in providing technical services in areas such as boundary delimitations, administration and information management.[37] During the tripartite elections, the MEC was able to establish a situation room to help link the voters with the commission, and promote the credibility of election through such regional affiliations. With regard to gender, Malawi ratified the United Nations (UN) Convention on the Elimination of all Forms of Discrimination Against Women on 12 March 1987 and submitted its last report in 2015. Sections 20 and 24 of the Malawi Constitution have been formulated based on these international statutes. Further, Malawi laws are guided by international law on principles of suffrage as well as the underlying factors in Malawian electoral law. All these have international practice as their benchmark.[38] The MEC has also formulated guidelines and codes of conduct for international and local elections observers; traditional chiefs; the media; and political parties. These too have their origins in the international and regional electoral conventions which are validated by parliament. The international human rights clause also assures Malawians of their right to vote for leaders of their choice, and not to be discriminated against. These are enshrined in the Malawi Constitution, sections 32–35.

Operations and implementation of programmes

The commission's secretariat is managed on a day by day basis by the chief elections officer who is supported by two deputies; one responsible for operations, the other for administration and finance. In addition, the commission has three regional election officers responsible for all electoral activities at the regional level. These are assisted by district elections clerks who are based in all councils. Section 12(1) and 13(1) of the EC Act guides the recruitment of MEC staff. The commission also hires temporary staff during elections, such as primary education advisers, who act as constituency returning officers, and district commissioners, who act as district election coordinators.[39]

In order to enhance its performance, the commission has also established four committees chaired by commissioners. These are:
- Finance and admin committee;
- Audit committee;
- Electoral services committee; and
- Civic and media committees.

---

37 Interview with Steven Duwa, Malawi Electoral Support Network (MESN) on 8 September 2015 in Blantyre, Malawi.
38 Interview with commissioner Chinkwita Phiri on 8 September 2015 in Blantyre, Malawi.
39 MEC (2014) *Tripartite Election Report*. pp. 27–28.

The commission also gets technical assistance through the basket funding from the United Nations Development Programme (UNDP) in various areas, such as legal advice, logistics and elections. The chief elections officer is appointed on a five-year contract, while the lower and middle professional staff are on long-term pensionable conditions. In the past the commission relied on seconded staff from government. However, with the passing of the 1998 Act, the commission is able to advertise and recruit appropriate personnel when necessary.

With regard to the implementation of its programmes, the MEC operates according to its strategic plan, which later translates to an operational plan once the commissioners have approved the activities for that particular year. In addition, the commission runs other programmes with government and development partners, such as the UN, the European Union (EU) and the AU. The different programmes are consolidated into an annual work plan.

Funding

Section 15 of the EC Act (articles a, c and f) stipulates that funds for the commission shall be appropriated by parliament, but shall exclusively be under the control of the commission and shall be utilised solely for the purposes of the act in accordance with the written directions of the commission, and for no other purpose. In order for the commission to implement its activities it submits its budget to the treasury through parliament and once they are funded they begin the implementation. Another source of funding for the commission is from development partners. Because Malawi's dependence on donor funding is high, it has been exposed to donor interference in its governance programme and in the government's decisions and policies.[40]

Below is a sample of the MEC's election funding since 1998.

Table 1: Funding of elections: 1998–2014

Year	Approved budget	Total expenditure	Donors' contribution
1998–1999	Not indicated	MWK 1.2 billion	Not indicated
2008–2009	MWK 5 000 000 000 USD 35 714 286	MWK 7 170 613 000 USD 51 218 665	Not indicated
2010–2014	MWK 18 406 020 554 USD 29 687 129.93[42]	MWK 18 595 543 916 USD 29 992 812.77	MWK 6 967 382 539

Source: MEC Elections Report 2009 & 2014

The table above illustrates how expensive elections are getting in Malawi. Also the table highlights the fact that although the budget may be approved, when it comes to actual implementation the figures change due to various factors, including global effects and

---

40 Khembo NS (2005) *Elections and Democratization in Malawi: An Uncertain Process.* Johannesburg: EISA. p. 50.
41 USD 1 = MWK 620 (a rate which varies and fluctuates every day).

increases in local commodities, from the moment the budget is approved to the time elections take place.

Development partners

As the commission begins to look at elections as a cycle, basket funding administered by the UNDP has been established. Bilateral donor partners – such as the Irish, British, Germans and Norwegians – are putting financial resources into that basket for continued electoral activities. There has also been technical support from multilateral institutions such as the UNDP, the EU and lately from UN Women. Funds from the baskets have also been drawn to assist with audits in districts. A technical committee where issues are discussed with bilateral partners has been established. The committee comprises representatives from the government of Malawi, the ministry of justice, the ministry of finance, the MEC, the the United States Agency For International Development (USAID), all the observation missions, and the EU.

Once issues have been discussed they are presented to the steering committee which is co-chaired by the minister of finance and the UN resident coordinator. The steering committee comprises the MEC chair, the minister of finance, the attorney general, all ambassadors, the director of the Malawi Communications Regulatory Authority (MACRA) and the army commander. This is a very high powered delegation symbolising the importance of electoral funding. Using this approach, the UNDP has been able to draw resources from the basket to fund the commission's activities, such as meetings which would otherwise not have been funded before. There is a proposal to put in place more funds for programmes. It is envisaged that these funds would be utilised to develop national IDs to be used during registration which Malawi does not have at the moment. In the 2014 tripartite elections the UNDP undertook to fund electoral activities directly without going through government. They procured and shipped 24 million ballot papers and delivered services and technical assistance.[42]

Evaluation and assessment

The MEC plays a critical role in ensuring that elections are credible, free and fair. An institution that would be able to assess the commission would probably be composed both of international and of local election observers. However, these observers are called to assess elections not the commission per se. Section 110 of the PPE Act provides guidelines for observers. For example, in 2004 the Commonwealth secretariat observer mission noted that the MEC did not fully discharge its obligations even though it had known for five years that it had to organise an election in 2004. The EU mission observer report of 2009 also noted that the MEC's lack of adequate management as well as operational and logistical structures was evident in the handling of the elections. Similar concerns were

---

42 Interview with the UNDP's senior elections adviser on 11 September 2015 in Lilongwe, Malawi.

raised in the 2014 tripartite elections. The MEC seems to get feedback from international observers more than from local election observers. Further, there are observations that need government intervention before the MEC can begin to get involved.

However, there are several issues that need to be highlighted:

Institutional issues

Independence of the electoral commission

Section 76(4) of the constitution guarantees the MEC's independence in its functioning and decision-making process. However, section 6 of the EC Act makes the commission answerable to the president on the overall fulfilment of the functions and powers of the commission.[43] Because of this condition, most stakeholders, such as political parties, civil society organisations, some electoral observers, and the general public, including the MEC themselves, have questioned its independence.[44] The executive appears to interfere with the commission and reinforces the perception that the MEC lacks independence. For example, although commissioners are nominated by political parties, the president has a final say on who should be appointed. The same goes for the appointment of the chairperson. For these positions to be independent there is a need for them to be advertised, for the selection to be made by an independent panel, and for the appointments to be made by parliament. The president, who belongs to the executive arm of government, should not appoint either the chairperson or the commission in order for them to be seen as independent. For as long the chairperson is answerable to the president his independence, as well as that of the institution that he heads, is questionable.

Secondly, although the MEC's budget gets approved by parliament, it is not guaranteed timely funding by the treasury. The MEC has to beg funds from the treasury to be able to fund its activities. As one commissioner indicated, sometimes they have to seek the president's intervention to obtain funding. This situation places the commission in an awkward position, and could easily be influenced by the executive. As the saying goes: 'He who pays the piper calls the tune'.[45] If the MEC is not funded on time, it is not able to implement important activities or follow up on issues raised by international and local election observers. Further, when the MEC is not funded as required by law, it could give the impression that government is deliberately withholding resources as a form of rigging. There is a need for the MEC to be financially independent and not to be seen to be toeing the government line in order to be funded.

Appointment of commissioners from political parties

Section 75(1) of the constitution stipulates that the MEC should be composed of a chairperson and a minimum of six members from political parties appointed in

---

43 MEC (2015) *Malawi Electoral Support Network National Taskforce on Electoral Reform.* p. 32.
44 Ibid.
45 Interview with governance adviser, UN Women, on 11 September 2015 in Lilongwe, Malawi.

accordance with the Act of Parliament. Appointing a commissioner in consultation with political parties discriminates against independent MPs who currently constitute 17% of the total complement in the National Assembly, and also against political parties that may acquire seats during by-elections.[46] Further, the provision stipulates that the appointment of these commissioners should be 'in consultation' with political parties. The concept of consultation lacks clarity of definition and is interpreted differently by each president. For Presidents Bakili Muluzi in 1994 and Joyce Banda in 2012, this was interpreted to mean asking political parties to submit two names to the presidents in order for them to appoint commissioners. For President Bingu wa Mutharikait it meant identifying the people himself, and later submitting their names to the respective political parties for their information. According to him that was consultation. This interpretation culminated in a legal challenge between the state and the state president.[47] The accurate interpretation of the concept of consultation remains unresolved.

Further, while drawing members from different political parties may be advantageous because it promotes acceptance of post-election results, electoral participation of members and buy-in, commissioners tend to be perceived as toeing party lines when there are political disputes. This was the case in the 2014 tripartite elections where the determination and announcement of results faced challenges with respect to court injunctions and interference by the executive arm of the government.[48] Commissioners who belong to different political parties might find it difficult not to be partisan lest they be accused of being sell-outs. Further, the clause is silent on the maximum number of commissioners to be appointed and the necessary qualifications. Having appropriate skills is important for them to carry out their duties effectively. Although Malawi is a signatory to the SADC gender protocol on increasing women representation in decision-making positions, there are no specific gender equality provisions to guide the inclusion of men and women in the commission. Except for the 2009 commission which had gender parity, all the other commissions have had less female representation.[49] The current commission has a complement of only three women out of ten.

Chairmanship of the electoral commission as a judge

Section 75(1) stipulates that the chairperson of the electoral commission should be a judge. However, this clause contradicts the spirit of section 75(2) of the constitution which disqualifies any person holding public office from being a member of the electoral commission.[50] A judge is a public officer; this clause seems to be discriminatory and puts

---

46 Currently there are 32 independent MPs in a house of 193 seats.
47 Miscellaneous Civil Cause Number 99 of 2007 between the state and the president of the Republic of Malawi which the president won. In his ruling, Judge Healy Potani said: 'the obvious fact that has led to the present case is that section 4(1) of the Electoral Commission Act does not prescribe how the consultations by the respondent are to be done'.
48 MEC (2014) *Tripartite Election Report*. p. 88.
49 MEC (2015) *Malawi Electoral Support Network National Taskforce on Electoral Reform*.
50 Ibid.

one profession and discipline above another. Although this is historical, there is a need to revisit this clause to ensure equity and transparency, which are fundamental principles of democracy.

Security of tenure for commissioners

According to section 75(3) of the EC Act, commissioners are appointed for a period of four years with the possibility of a renewal for a further term. However, the four-year term is not in tandem with the five-year term provided for the president, MPs and chief elections officer. After being appointed government spends a lot of resources to build the capacity of the commissioners. When they leave after just one term, there is loss of institutional memory, skills and knowledge which the commission and the public could have benefited from.

Secondly, although the law protects commissioners from arbitrary removal, section 75(4) of the constitution gives power to the public appointments committee to recommend their removal to the president on grounds of incompetence or incapacity in the performance of their duties. However, how does one define incompetence or incapacity without appearing to be partisan or politically motivated? The executive arm of government could be very heavy handed, as witnessed in 1997 when President Muluzi decided to suspend the commission without offering any explanation.

Although the commission contested this in the High Court, they lost. The president went ahead and appointed Justice William Hanjahanja to replace Justice Msosa as chairperson in 1998. Unfortunately, he too was forced to leave before the 1999 elections due to pressure from civil society, because it was alleged that he displayed traits of partisan and biased conduct.[51] He was replaced by Justice Kalaile who after serving his term handed over the reins to Justice Msosa in 2007. In 2010, President Mutharika closed the electoral commission's office over alleged financial irregularities. However, while the case was still being investigated the president appointed the chief elections officer at that time, Mr David Bandawe, High Commissioner of Malawi in Zambia. The MEC's offices were re-opened without an explanation of why they had been closed in the first place. Again, this illustrates how the executive arm of government seems to control the electoral management body in Malawi. Its independence is therefore questionable. Justice Msosa served as chairperson until 2012 when she handed over the reins to Justice Maxon Mbendera who presided over the contentious tripartite elections on 20 May 2014, which were won by Professor Peter Mutharika.

Blurred roles between commission and secretariat

Commissioners are mandated to provide strategic leadership and management of the MEC. The chief elections officer who is appointed by the commission is answerable to the commissioners. However, a key challenge is that there is a lack of clear understanding

---

51 Khembo NS (2004) *Overview of Multipartyism in Malawi.* p. 4.

of distinct roles between the secretariat and the commissioners. This has led to internal governance issues and ineffective work practices, including a culture of mistrust between commissioners and the secretariat.[52] One of the reasons for this problem is that a commissioner's orientation or training focuses mainly on election management without paying attention to corporate governance.[53] This situation has been exacerbated by the fact that management and the secretariat lack adequate capacity to deliver on their mandate, let alone handle electoral operations and logistics effectively. The 2014 tripartite elections are an illustration of how the MEC secretariat failed abysmally to distribute adequate voting materials throughout the country. This contributed to the chaos that ensued on polling day, especially in Blantyre where there was widespread electoral violence.

Voters' roll

A reliable voters' register is critical to the MEC's credibility. However, Malawi does not currently have a system for recording births and deaths resulting in the MEC having to register voters manually every election period. In 1999 the polling day was postponed from 25 May 1999 to 15 June 1999 due to the extension of the voter registration exercise. An extraordinary session of parliament was called to amend section 67(1) of the constitution. In 2004, the general elections took place on 20 May 2004 instead of 18 May 2004. This was caused by the opposition's complaint to the High Court after the MEC had failed to publish the voters' roll on time. The High Court ordered the MEC to postpone the poll to allow for a proper inspection of the voters' roll to take place. The perceived lack of an accurate voters' roll affects the MEC's credibility. The proposed national ID would ease the lack of trust that voters and political parties have in the MEC. An accurate voters' roll would reduce accusations of inflated figures, under-age voters, foreigners being ferried in from neighbouring countries and votes being cast on behalf of dead people.

Disposal of electoral material

Section 119 of the Presidential and Parliament Act stipulates that:

> At the end of its functions, the Commission shall deposit all documents forming the official record of an election (including voters' registers, ballot papers, records from districts and polling stations and summaries thereof and the record and summary of the national result) with the clerk of parliament who shall retain and preserve such documents in safe and secure custody without destruction for a period of twelve months.

This clause appears to contradict the 1998 EC Act (1998) which delinked the COP from electoral processes since he belongs to an arm of government. The lack of a procedure for

---

52 MEC (2015) *Malawi Electoral Support Network National Taskforce on Electoral Reform.*
53 Ibid.

the disposal of electoral materials after elections has contributed to the lack of confidence in the MEC, especially when fire consumed the contested 2014 election materials which were stored in a warehouse in Lilongwe. The opposition, which were contesting the results, have attributed the fire to a lack of transparency and integrity on the part of the MEC.

The first-past-the-post electoral system

Malawi has used the first-past-the-post (FPTP) electoral system in all its general elections, the local government elections in 2000 and the tripartite elections in 2015. Several reasons have been advanced for its adoption and continued use. One of them is its simplicity and its ability to produce a single-party government. Secondly, it has been observed that almost all countries that were once colonised or were protectorates continue to use this electoral system. Its continued use has been attributed to several factors, including colonial legacy, while others have attributed it to the fact that it benefits some individuals, especially where people vote along ethnic and regional lines as is the case in Malawi.

However, recently there have been several complaints about its ineffectiveness and how it contributes to a lack of legitimacy for the winning candidate and disadvantages the majority. The problem of the FPTP system has been compounded by the fact that Malawi uses a hybrid constitutional system that combines elements of presidentialism and parliamentarianism. The seats in parliament do not determine who forms a government but, rather, the winning president. This has led to minority governments. Further, the FPTP system has created negative competitive politics between MPs, even within the same party, due to conflicts over resources for the same district because of the need for re-election. Because of this, legislators become preoccupied with private income instead of focusing on national policy. This issue diverts attention from the role of parliament, which is to have a strategic vision of what is best for the country.[54] Another glaring disadvantage of the FPTP system is its negative effect on the election of women to decision-making positions.

Boundary delimitation

Boundary delimitation is an important activity carried out by the MEC. However, it is very hard to conduct boundary delimitation because of the unequal number of voters in constituencies. Some constituencies in Malawi have more registered voters than others; for example, there are 32 000 registered voters in some and 120 000 in others. Fairness in drawing up constituencies is important because it is about equal power of the vote. Although it is important to delimit constituencies before 2019, it is equally important to know the population using the latest statistics. In the last election the government used the 2008 national statistics. The next census takes place in 2018, a year before the elections. These figures will not be available for use by the MEC. Lack of credible figures to be used in the delimitation of constituencies hinders the functioning of the MEC.

---

54 Interview with senior elections advisor, UNDP, 11 September 2015, Lilongwe.

Funding of elections

Elections are a sovereign activity which should be funded by the state because the democratic process of a nation depends on a successful outcome of an election. In the past Malawi has relied on donors who have provided 40% towards its budget. However, funding from the donors has slowly eased off due to corruption in government. Malawi has not received any supplementary funding from donors since last year when the financial irregularities dubbed 'cashgate'[55] were exposed. The issue of funding and the issue of reporting to the president are tied because there are times when there is delayed funding to the commission and it has to seek the president's intervention for funding to be released. Unfortunately, this is not a healthy situation because it continues to draw the executive into the commission. This has the potential to compromise its independence. If the commission were to have a protected budget it would be more independent, and would not be perceived to be influenced by the executive arm of government. There is a perception that if the incumbent wants to rig an election it starts by withholding funding, or releasing it late so that appropriate systems and mechanisms are not put in place on time to conduct credible elections. Linking funding of the commission to government compromises the MEC's efficiency and trustworthiness during elections.

Vote tabulation and announcement of results

Malawi has had four general elections, one stand-alone local government election, and one tripartite election. Apart from the 1994 elections which have been hailed as free and fair, all subsequent elections since 1999 have had flaws. Election observers of the 1999 elections noted that the transmission of results to returning officers was undermined by delays and errors of documentation. The 2004 parliamentary and presidential elections were also marked by irregularities; to an even greater extent than the 1999 elections. The processing and declaration of results in the 2004 elections highlighted a number of flaws that impacted on the credibility of the results. In the days after the polling closed on 18 May 2004, the electoral commission failed to display all results for verification by stakeholders before announcement, which led to the announcement and gazetting of different sets of election results.

When the MEC finally gazetted the 2004 results on 16 July 2004, these had discrepancies. It took three months for the presidential and parliamentary results to be published in the *Daily Times*. In the 2014 tripartite elections, a good number of presiding officers had challenges. However, Malawi swears in the new government at supersonic speed, and it is difficult for challenges to take effect when the person being challenged has already been sworn into office.

---

55 The 'cashgate' scandal involved billions of Malawi Kwacha embezzled by government officials from government coffers. Donors have stopped providing any budgetary support to government. The country is therefore going through a very difficult economic phase.

Mechanism for resolving electoral disputes

Malawi courts have taken centre stage in resolving electoral disputes. However, some civil society organisations have questioned the fairness of this practice. Firstly, the MEC is chaired by the 'learned' judge, and if he is the one who has adjudicated the case, how do his fellow 'learned' judges overrule his ruling because courts work on precedence. And if the High Court judge is the chairperson, how does an ordinary judge overrule him or her. In the 2014 tripartite elections, there were 343 complaints received across the presidential, parliamentary and local government elections. Of these, all presidential complaints had been processed by the commission at the time of announcement of the results for the presidential election on 30 May 2014.[56] However, other litigations still remain unresolved. There is a need for alternative dispute resolution mechanisms other than courts. The MEC has invested in carrying out conflict management training for some of its stakeholders because it is important in electoral dispute resolution that the rules of the game are very clear so that the constitution, Acts of Parliament, and codes of conduct that are signed, form part and parcel of the MEC's legal framework. The MEC is also moving towards turning all codes of conduct into regulations so that they are all enforceable. The MEC is also considering establishing a tribunal. Also, with the help of UNDP lawyers a legal unit was constituted, but the MEC is gradually moving towards having its own legal department headed by a director.

Relationships with stakeholders

The MEC deals with several stakeholders, including parliament and government, through various committees, such as the legal affairs committee (because the MEC needs to validate their actions through legal instruments); parliament's public appointments committee (MEC staff are employed under public service conditions); and the parliamentary women's caucus (because of the ongoing women's empowerment programme). It is also important for the MEC to communicate with political parties in order to expel suspicion and mistrust. The MEC is able maintain this relationship through the NECOF and CMD. The MEC also ensures periodic announcements during the pre-election period on whatever activity it is undertaking, including a calendar of events so that the MEC and political parties are on the same page. The MEC also interfaces with the electorate through television, radio and print media to educate the populace on how to register and vote. This could not be achieved properly if the MEC did not have accredited civil society organisations committed to disseminating the necessary messages to voters. The MEC has a good relationship with the army, which is well-trusted by Malawians according to the *Afrobarometer* survey. The police, too, play a major role during election periods.

---

56 MEC (2014) *Tripartite Election Report.*

Use of public officers in elections

The MEC uses teachers, and district commissioners who are civil servants as returning officers during elections. The MEC also uses government infrastructure, such as district commissioners' offices and school blocks and classrooms for elections, at times even accommodating regional elections officers in the north, centre and south. Continuous use of these civil servants has created tension and a lack of trust between political parties in the opposition and the MEC during election periods. These civil servants are perceived to be agents or stooges of incumbents and are suspected of altering election results in favour of the incumbent. For example, in the 2014 tripartite elections, it was observed that a good number of presiding officers had problems with arithmetic. In some cases, there were signs of erasures or overwritten figures.[57] Yet, these are supposed to be teachers. Continuous use of these civil servants has undermined the MEC's credibility in the eyes of political parties, and sometimes even the public.

Political issues

Inter-party conflicts

Conflicts between political parties, triggered by various factors including disagreements between the opposition and the incumbent as was witnessed during the 2014 tripartite election, can escalate to violence on polling day. Polling booths were set on fire and vandalised in the 2014 election. Roads leading to polling centres were blocked by stones and burning tyres. There was such immense anger towards the MEC that even the signpost leading its offices was vandalised. This action undermined the MEC's credibility. In the 2009 general elections the relationship among the three main political parties (UDF, MCP and the Democratic Progressive Party [DPP]) was characterised by intense competition before the elections. Sensitive issues, such as the wish of President Muluzi to stand again after being in office for two terms contrary to section 83(2) of the constitution, could have created potential for violence that might have impacted negatively on the MEC and its credibility. These inter-party conflicts have their legacies in post-independence days when the MCP did not tolerate other political parties. According to Tsoka,[58] elections during Banda's era were not competitive, nor was there any direct campaigning. Over time, political apathy set in. When the political landscape is tense, the credibility and trustworthiness of the MEC is questioned because it is perceived as biased against opposition.

Intra-party conflicts

Elections are highly competitive even within political parties and if primary elections are not conducted democratically they can trigger an increase in the number of independents. In Malawi, the number of independents has significantly been rising from four in 1999

---

57 MEC (2014) *Tripartite Election Report.*
58 Tsoka MG (2002) Public opinion and the consolidation of democracy in Malawi. *Afrobarometer Working Paper* No. 46.

to 32 in 2014. This makes the proportion of independent MPs in parliament higher than political party MPs. This undermines political parties and puts a lot of pressure on the MEC because, as already alluded to, commissioners are appointed from political parties that are perceived to be partisan. Secondly, the increased number of independents puts pressure on the MEC when printing ballot papers. The printing of extra ballot papers with many different photos from the independents increases financial pressure on MEC considerably. With a country that depends on donors for 40% of its budget support, every additional expense exerts extra financial pressure on the already meagre resources. In the case of Malawi, because of the infamous cashgate scandal where billions of tax payers' money have been stolen from government coffers, donors have decided to cut financial support until the government puts its house in order. This will affect election funding even more than before.

Political party financing
The MEC does not monitor political party financing because it is not mandated to do so. In other countries, political funding is regulated by the electoral management body. This ensures transparency and accountability of elections which feeds into the credibility of the election management body. In Malawi there is no such regulation. The centre for multiparty democracy is championing the review of the Political Parties (Registration and Regulation) Act of 1993 and to ensure that this is taken on board. This situation when compounded by the FPTP system entrenches the 'monetisation' of politics. In order to lure voters, candidates ensure that they have resources, no matter what the source. If the MEC is not mandated to demand transparency, these actions could have negative consequences.

Participation of women and the fourth ballot
Women in Malawi constitute 52% of the total population. However, these figures do not translate into more women in decision-making positions. For instance, in a house of 193 seats only 32 women (16%) were elected for the 2014 parliament, which is a notable drop of 6% from the 43 elected in the previous elections. In a cabinet of 20, only three are women. In order to increase the number of women, civil society organisations are urging the MEC to introduce a special quota whereby every council should have a woman voted for. This means four votes: one for the MP, a councillor, and president, but a specially designated vote for a woman. This will guarantee at least 35 women MPs from 35 councils which will supplement those that will be elected through the normal voting.

In order to increase the participation of women in elections, in 2014 the MEC introduced a reduction in nomination fees for female parliamentary candidates from MWK 200 000 (equivalent to USD 365.62)[59] to MWK 150 000 (equivalent to USD 274.22); female councillors paid MWK 15 000 (equivalent to USD 27) instead of MWK 20 000 (equivalent to USD 37) for male councillors. However, for all presidential candidates the fee remained

---

59 Approximately USD 1 = MWK 547 as at 5 October 2015.

at MWK 1 million. This gesture could be interpreted in two ways. It reinforces stereotypes about the inferiority of women and their inability to raise nomination fees on the one hand; on the other hand, it could be looked at as a good gesture to encourage women to participate in politics. However, this gesture impacts negatively on the MEC's impartiality because it seems to favour or promote one group over another.

Social issues

Illiteracy and poverty

In terms of literacy, more males aged 15 years and above (74%) are literate than females (57% of the same age group). Urban areas have registered a higher literacy rate (89%) compared to rural areas (61%). The northern region registered a higher literacy rate (77%) followed by the central region (65%) and then the southern region (62%).[60] Children, women in female-headed households, illiterate women and people from large households (more than seven members) are the most strongly affected by poverty and inequality. There are correlations between poverty on the one hand, and social category (social status, social vulnerability, marital status, age and the rural-urban divide), on the other.[61] Illiteracy and poverty go hand in hand. In order to reach this grouping during elections, there is a need for the MEC to carry out intensive civic education. This would have huge resource implications on the MEC's budget, which, as already indicated, operates on a shoestring, waiting for donor support. It means translating voting material into different languages to be understood. If this is not done properly, there is a risk of high null and void votes.

Further, because of poverty this grouping is sometimes forced to sell off their voter ID cards, and is easily manipulated by some politicians who use handouts to buy their votes during elections. The implication of this is that unwarranted people get into parliament using money. Currently, there are no laws to curb this habit of using handouts to buy voters' support. This also discourages people, especially women who may not be able to stand as candidates for fear of being unable to offer handouts.

Ethnicity voting

Malawi is divided into three administrative regions: north, centre and south. The distinguishing feature of Malawi's political scene is the party's regional bases which become more apparent during elections. Except for the 2009 elections when the DPP made inroads in the northern region and in 2014, when the Peoples Party of Joyce Banda also made inroads in the north, Malawians tend to vote along ethnic and regional lines. It is common knowledge among Malawians that the Alliance for Democracy (AFORD) has its stronghold in the northern region, the Malawi Congress Party (MCP) in the central

---

60 National statistical office of Malawi (2012) *Integrated Household socio-economic characteristics report.*
61 Chijere-Chirwa W (2014) *Malawi Democracy and Political Participation.* Johannesburg: Open Society Initiative for Southern Africa.

region, and the United Democratic Party (UDF) is strongest in the heavily populated southern region.

This pattern emerged in Malawi's first democratic elections (1994), and continued in 1999 and 2004. Consequently, Malawi's elections resemble a 'regional' census: where a voter lives (her region) predicts quite strongly how she will vote. Although there are many possible micro-level explanations for census elections, the most prominent remains Horowitz's expressive voting hypothesis, which argues that ethnic voters use their vote to register their identities as members of groups. Voting is therefore an act of identity expression, not a careful weighing of policy positions or performance evaluations. Elections become 'head counts' in which ethnic demographics predetermine outcomes, creating permanent winners and losers and jeopardising the stability of democracy as a whole.[62]

The regional demographic configuration of Malawi gives no chance to AFORD to win a presidential election or have a majority in the National Assembly. The table below confirm the ethnic divides which manifest themselves more during elections.

Table 2: Voting patterns per region, 1994 and 1999

Region	Year	MCP	UDF	AFORD
North	1994	0	0	33
Centre	1994	51	14	3
South	1994	5	71	0
Totals		56	85	36
North	1999	4	1	28
Centre	1999	54	16	1
South	1999	8	77	0
Totals		66	94	29

Source: Electoral Commission Reports of 1994 and 1999

Religious factors

Religion plays a very significant role in Malawi's politics and on election management. Firstly, it was the pastoral letter from the Catholic Bishops in 1992 that triggered a chain of events culminating in the new political dispensation in 1994. In Malawi, the main religious traditions are Islam and Christianity. There are 1 690 087 Muslims and 10 770 229 Christians (13% and 82.7%) respectively.[63] Secondly, there is a perception that some political parties have affiliations to synods such as AFORD, which is perceived to be linked to the Livingstonia Synod in the north; the MCP in the centre which is perceived to be linked to Nkhoma Synod; and the UDF which is perceived to be linked to Islam because its founder and chairperson is Muslim.

---

62 Ferree K & Horowitz J (2007) Identity voting and the regional census in Malawi. *Afrobarometer Working Paper* No. 72.
63 National statistical office of Malawi (2008) *Report.*

During the election period, it is perceived that these church groupings play a significant role in swaying voters' choice along religious lines. In 1999 when the UDF won the presidential elections, mosques in the north were burnt down. In retaliation, Muslims burnt down churches. Religious violence, especially before, during and after elections can impact negatively on election management.

It is the coincidence of these identities and their politicisation that can quickly cascade down to the people at a religious level. It is that conflation of elements that make religion political, and when that happens, election management is in trouble, because instead of managing elections, the MEC has to manage the religious divides. For instance, a candidate perceived to be Christian may not be allowed to hold a rally in a Muslim dominated area, and vice versa. This politicisation of religious identities makes a contentious environment for election management leading to perceived lack of transparency and integrity for the MEC. In order to avoid this situation, the MEC has developed codes of conduct for traditional and religious leaders. These, however, lack mechanisms for enforcement.

Economic issues

Malawi is a landlocked densely populated country in Southern Africa with a total population of 16.4 million in 2013. Gross national income (GNI) per capita stood at USD 320 in 2012 and USD 270 in 2013.[64] It has a relatively larger population in the younger age groups with almost 48% of the population being younger than 15 years. Malawi is therefore considered as a very youthful state. About 85% of people live in rural areas while only 15% live in urban areas. Agriculture remains a priority sector in Malawi's pursuit of economic transformation and poverty reduction.[65] The agricultural sector accounts for 33–40% of gross domestic product, more than 90% of exports and provides employment for more than 70% of the citizens. Agriculture is also a main source of livelihood for more than 90% of the rural population.[66]

Malawi experienced rapid economic development during the first one and a half decades of independence (1964–1979). This was largely due to a development strategy that focused on the promotion of agricultural production with estates producing export crops such as tobacco, tea and coffee. However, despite several episodes of rapid growth over the past five decades, such growth has not translated into poverty reduction, nor has it led to inclusive growth. The 2010/2011 Integrated Household Survey (IHS) recorded a national poverty rate of 50.7%. More than half of Malawi's population is therefore poor. The figure for the ultra-poor has in fact increased over time from 22% to 25%. The high levels of poverty are compounded by the high levels of inequality. The 2010/2011 IHS noted that the richest 10% of Malawi's population has a median per capita income that is eight times

---

64 Republic of Malawi (2014) *National Human Development Draft Report (NHDR)*. Lilongwe, Malawi.
65 Government of Malawi (1971, 1987, 2012).
66 Chirwa E (2014) Smallholder agricultural development in Malawi in the past 50 years: Has public policy resulted in unsuccessful transformations? The 16th Professorial Inaugural Lecture delivered at Chancellor College, University of Malawi on 29 October 2014.

higher (MWK 50 373/USD 119 per person per annum) than the median per capita income of the poor (MWK 6 370/USD 15 per person per annum). Moreover, the richest 10% of the population has a median income that is three times higher than the overall median income in the country.

The fact that the population is youthful and rural means that there is high unemployment and poverty levels among them. Sometimes some unscrupulous politicians have paid these youths to disrupt opponents' political rallies with violence. Violence perpetrated by these groupings affects the management of elections and even the credibility of the election results.

Poor infrastructure and communication

As already alluded to above, 85% of Malawi's population lives in rural areas. There are certain areas where road infrastructures are non-existent during rainy seasons. In the 2014 tripartite elections, the commission experienced transport challenges in delivering some voting materials such as a voters' register for verification because of poor road infrastructure.[67] It was also difficult to transport ballot papers let alone get election results in time. This caused delays in reaching polling centres leading to late opening and closing of polling centres. Some did not even vote because it was getting dark. Further, it was difficult to count the votes with poor or no lighting in some polling stations. Results from these centres could be contested. This put pressure on the MEC's credibility.

Electoral reform

In the aftermath of past elections, a number of organisations, such as the Malawi Electoral Support Network (MESN), the National Initiative for Civic Education (NICE) and the Public Affairs Committee (PAC), among others, have conducted and produced post-election reviews. There has been a consolidation of this initiative after gathering grassroot-level reactions on the conduct of the 2014 tripartite election. In the current post-election reviews, the MEC and the MESN cooperate in the review and consolidation of issues that have been raised in the aftermath of the 2014 elections. In the areas that the MEC feels responsible for, it is ensuring that reviews are taken on board. There are certain areas that are outside of the MEC's jurisdiction. Although changes may be proposed, these could not be implemented because they would require either political parties or government to initiate the process before the MEC can take any action. This goes for election observer reports. Some of the proposed recommendations to enhance future elections hinge on government or other stakeholders' input before the MEC can implement them.[68]

However, below are some of the recommendations which have been made by the national taskforce on electoral reforms, chaired by the MEC and the MESN, to improve elections and election management in Malawi. Some of the issues raised include raising

---

67 MEC (2014) *Tripartite Election Report.* p. 44.
68 Ibid.

the standard for nominations for president from ten to 1 000; having a two-rounder for the presidential race; introducing a quota for women and exploring the possibility of changing the electoral system from first past the post to proportional representation.

People's perceptions

Studies have been conducted since 2002 to assess the MEC's credibility and trustworthiness. This is critical if elections are to be perceived to be free and fair and their results accepted. In an Afrobarometer survey conducted by Tsoka in 2002 to assess how often people felt they could trust governmental or public institutions to do what was right,[69] 30% of respondents felt that they could trust the electoral commission to do what was right. However, by comparison with the army's, the MEC's trust rating was among the lowest. According to the survey, trust in the army was rated at 71%. One possible explanation for the relatively low levels of trust in the MEC could have been the contested election results. A case against the electoral commission was also in the courts at the time this survey was being conducted.[70]

A similar study by Khaila and Chibwana in 2005[71] revealed that the electoral commission as an institution was not trusted much. Again, the army and police received higher ratings than the electoral commission. In 1999, 71% said they trusted the army most of the time or always. The electoral commission fared relatively poorly, with only 38%.

In 2014 another Afrobarometer study was conducted just before the tripartite election to establish people's confidence in the MEC.[72] Key findings revealed that a majority of Malawians were confident in the capabilities and neutrality of the MEC, but a significant minority disagreed. In terms of adequate preparations for the elections, 55% thought that the MEC was 'very well prepared' for the upcoming election; 20% thought it was at least somewhat prepared; while 16% thought it was 'not at all' or 'not very well' prepared. In terms of gaining trust in the MEC, 57% indicated that they trusted the MEC 'somewhat' or 'a lot' in 2014. This was less than the percentage in 2012 when 64% trusted the MEC more; while 38% stated that they trusted the MEC 'not at all' or 'just a little'. In terms of the MEC's performance, nearly two-thirds (63%) believe that 'the MEC performs its duties as a neutral body guided only by law'. This was an increase from 56% in 2012. However, one person in three (32%) in 2014 voiced the concern that 'the MEC made decisions that favoured particular people, parties or interests'. These are illustrated in the Afrobarometer chart below:

---

69 Tsoka MG (2002) Public opinion and the consolidation of democracy in Malawi. *Afrobarometer Working Paper* No. 46.

70 Ibid.

71 Khaila S & Chibwana C (2005) Ten years of democracy in Malawi: Are Malawians getting what they voted for? *Afrobarometer Working Paper* No. 46.

72 Logan C, Bratton M & Dulani B (2014) Malawi's 2014 elections: amid concerns about fairness, outcome is too close to call. *Afrobarometer Dispatch* 1.

Figure 1: How much Malawians trust the MEC (2014)

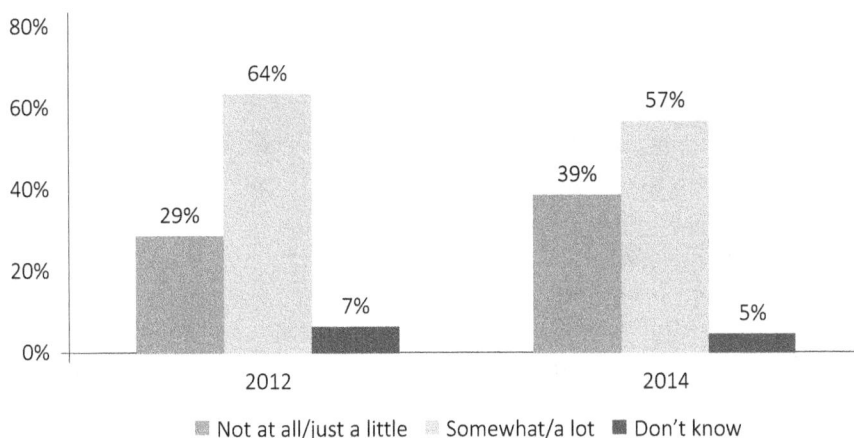

Source: *Afrobarometer Dispatch* 1: How much people trust the MEC

From the Afrobarometer chart above, people's trust in the MEC seems to vary over the years. However, what is consistent is that people do not seem to trust the MEC for various reasons, such as the use of teachers as returning officers, the lack of financial and institutional independence, the lack of a credible voters' roll (which is contentious every electoral year), and the electoral system which ushers in minority governments. There is a need for the MEC to address some of these issues in order to gain voters', politicians' and civil society's trust as a credible and independent institution capable of running a free and fair election.

Conclusion

In conclusion, the MEC in Malawi has evolved since 1971 when the first electoral commission was set up to demarcate constituencies. Between 1971 and 1994 the electoral commission in Malawi did not appear to be very active because elections were controlled by the one-party political system. Candidates for elections were handpicked by the president, while others were nominated or appointed. With the new political dispensation since 1994, the MEC appears to operate legally as an independent institution. There are still many obstacles to be surmounted before it can be described as fully independent. Issues such as the appointment of the commission and its chairperson and the lack of financial independence continue to challenge the effective functioning of the MEC. Although there are normative guidelines on how the commission should work, these are hampered by lack of political will by the party in government. Further, there are no mechanisms to track and enforce some of the practices and conventions derived from international and regional instruments.

Recommendations

The following are some recommendations to enhance the efficiency of the MEC.

Election management

- Appointment of commissioners: In order to enhance the independence of the commission, the chairperson and commission should be appointed by and report to parliament, and tenure for commissioners should be extended to five years in order to enhance institutional memory.
- Voters' roll: In order to defuse tension in the electoral process, the MEC should ensure that every registered voter has an ID card for the next general election.
- Financial independence: To enable the MEC to implement their programmes between the ballots and follow up on elections observers' recommendations, the MEC should have a protected budget.
- Political party spending: The MEC should set up ways to monitor party spending during campaigns.
- Use of civil servants: In order to protect the integrity of election results, the MEC should stop using civil servants as returning or coordinating officers. This will reduce electoral conflicts and disputing of results.
- Storage of used ballot materials: In order to avoid what happened to the 2014 ballot papers and enhance trust in the MEC as an electoral management body, the MEC should strengthen security around the storage of used ballot papers.
- Electoral observer recommendations: The MEC should follow up on observer reports before the next election.
- Conflict resolution mechanism: The MEC should establish its own tribunal for resolving electoral conflicts instead of the traditional courts.
- International and regional instruments: The MEC should evaluate international and regional election management practices.
- Observer reports: The MEC should establish mechanisms for tracking the implementation of electoral observer reports, and for ensuring that these are incorporated into the action plans between elections.

Legislation

- Voter buying: In order to level the playing field, the MEC should revise the electoral law to disqualify candidates or parties who engage in any form of handouts.

- Electoral system: Malawi uses the FPTP system. This electoral system can usher in a minority government while wasting votes. The electoral system should be changed to embrace proportional representation or a mixed electoral system.
- Fourth or special ballot for women: In order to enhance women's political participation and representation, the electoral law should be amended to include a fourth ballot for women.

6

MAURITIUS

Dr Roukaya Kasenally

Introduction

In 2018, Mauritius will be celebrating half a century of independence. Unlike a number of other ex-colonies, the island negotiated its independence from the British and has subsequently developed what is now termed a 'ballot as opposed to a bullet culture'.[1] Since independence the island has run ten general elections (the most recent one in December 2014) and all of them have been deemed as 'free and fair'. In fact, pre-independence Mauritius had already put in place the foundation of multiparty politics through the creation of the Labour Party (1937), the Parti Mauricien Social Democrate (1956), the Comite Action Musulman (1957) and the Independent Forward Block (1958).

This chapter looks at Mauritius' election management body. The idea is to understand the role played by the various commissions in making Mauritius a stable democracy. Note that in Mauritius, electoral work is done by multiple bodies, namely: the Electoral Commission, the Electoral Boundaries Commission and the Electoral Supervisory Commission. To that end, the focus here falls on all three bodies, albeit unevenly.

The focus, however, goes beyond evaluating the performance of the said bodies. Socio-economic conditions and the history of the country also comes under close scrutiny. This chapter will also offer a short overview of what is considered to be some of the specifics of the Mauritian democratic model, namely: its current electoral system, the growing presence of dynastic politics and the advent of ethno-politics in the Mauritian politics.

Before independence

Mauritius lies in the Indian Ocean, 800km west of the island of Madagascar, and occupies a total land area of 2040km². The Republic of Mauritius comprises the islands of Mauritius, Rodrigues, Agalega and the Cargados Shoals. As per the last census carried out in 2011, the total number of inhabitants of Mauritius was 1.24 million.[2]

---

1   Bunwaree S & Kasenally R (2005) Political parties in Mauritius. *EISA Research Report No 19*. Johannesburg: EISA.
2   Statistics Mauritius (2012) *Mauritius in Figures: Year 2012*. Available at http://statsmauritius.govmu.org/English/Publications/Documents/MIF/mif12.pdf [accessed 23 June 2016].

Mauritius is often referred to as the 'key and star of the Indian Ocean'. It was initially colonised by the Dutch (1638–1710), then by the French (1710–1810) and lastly by the British (1810–1968). The Dutch were sporadic in their settlement and were not totally interested in exploiting the full potential of the island. It is interesting to note that it was the Dutch who introduced sugar cane to the island in 1639, but it was the French who developed the island into an important sugar and trading post.[3] The British left their imprint at the administrative and parliamentary level (prevailing Westminster model of democracy). This sequential colonisation is responsible for populating the tiny island.

The need for labour on the sugar cane plantations, during the French presence, saw slaves shipped over from Madagascar and Mozambique.[4] With the official abolition of slavery in 1835, the huge void in labour that this created prompted the 'Great Experiment' on the part of the British to replace slaves with free workers from Asia, specifically India. At the beginning, a trickle and then a flood of labourers landed on the island with the promise of regular wages, housing, and a return passage home (a process known as 'indenture').

The better life promised to workers did not materialise. Instead, they experienced appalling conditions, which, for all intents and purposes, amounted to slavery. The difference was that the 'coolies' had arrived of their own free will, albeit under false pretences, whilst the slaves had not. Unsurprisingly, this experiment proved hugely successful, and between 1834–1912 some 453 063 labourers were brought to Mauritius (of which 97% came from India) under the indenture system.[5] The presence of Indo-Mauritians[6] soared and by the time the island attained independence, people of Indian descent constituted two thirds of the population.[7]

From colonial outpost to politically mobilised island

Mauritius attained independence in 1968. As Mauritius negotiated its independence, the island was split with 44% of the population voting against independence. This split was due to a fear of what was termed the rising of the 'Hindu hegemony' on the island who had become the dominant political elite.

Constitution building and political awareness

The Letters Patent of 16 September 1885 gave Mauritius a new constitution and elections were held for the first time in January 1886. The franchise was based on educational qualifications, ownership of immovable property of a certain value, prescribed licence

---

3 Salverda T (2010) Sugar and power: How Franco-Mauritians balance continuity and creeping decline of their elite position. Unpublished PhD thesis, Vrije University, Netherlands.

4 Allen R (1999) *Slaves, Freedom and Indentured Labourers in Colonial Mauritius.* Cambridge, UK: Cambridge University Press.

5 Mishra AK (2009) Indian indentured labourers in Mauritius: Reassessing the new system of slavery vs. free labour debate. *Studies in History* 25(2): 229–251.

6 From 1846–1952, Hindu and Muslim people were classified as Indo-Mauritians. By 1968, Mauritius had four officially recognised ethnic categories: Hindus, Muslims, General Population and Sino-Mauritians.

7 Allen R (1999) *Slaves, Freedom and Indentured Labourers in Colonial Mauritius.* Cambridge, UK: Cambridge University Press.

fees for trade activities, amongst others. Only males aged 21 and above with the ability to read and/or write were allowed to vote. These requirements resulted in only 1.5% of the population entitled to vote. Two political groups reflecting roughly the reformist tendency and the democratic/liberal wing of the political elite of the time participated in the polls. The campaign was acrimonious and ended up in a hung council.

The exclusion of the majority of the population in decision-making processes could not be ignored for long. The liberal group, made up of moderate whites and the coloured elite, campaigned for representative government and extension of the franchise. They adopted the cause of the indentured labourers and the small planters. Their campaign for free primary education and better care struck the right chord with the Indian labourers. However, such commendable overtures did not yield any political dividend. They lost all successive general elections: 1901, 1906 and 1911.

Politics in the first decade of the 1900s was dominated by the Franco-Mauritians and a group of educated coloureds. Previous electoral defeats triggered new approaches in mobilising the progressive elements of the Mauritian society. They launched the "Action Liberale"[8] in 1907, grouping the liberal Franco-Mauritians, the coloured elite and Indian cadres and businessmen. Action Liberale cut across the racial and communal divide of the country. It called for the extension of the franchise, but was bitterly opposed by the conservatives who defended the existing system.

The end of the First World War stirred a new feeling of French patriotism among the Franco-Mauritians and the coloured elite of the Action Liberale. With the British authorities supporting the conservatives (owners of sugar plantations and factories) an anti-British feeling grew in the coloured community. They believed that Mauritius should be retroceded to France and its link with the British Crown severed. The Retrocession movement roused great anxiety in the Indian community. They felt betrayed by supporters of the movement, to whom they lent total support in the past. In the general elections of 1921, candidates supporting the Retrocession movement were routed. The elections also saw the candidacy of two Indo-Mauritians. Though they were unsuccessful at the polls, their candidacy illustrated the interests of their community in local politics.

Greater mobilisation led to an increase in the number of Indian voters. Five Indo-Mauritian candidates stood in the 1926 elections, and two won. Their election was a landmark in that it indicated the beginning of the involvement of the Indian community in the governance of the country. The Retrocession movement jolted the community, shook them from their political apathy and instilled interest to participate in national affairs. Whilst the restrictive franchise limited their electoral success, it did not discourage them.

Responding to various petitions, appeals from pressure groups and unofficial delegations to London for a more liberal constitution, the British Government only acceded to a cosmetic change of the 1885 constitution in July 1933. The size of the elected

---

8   The Action Liberale (which translates as 'liberal action') was not a party as such, but a collection of anti-oligarchic elements.

corps remained the same and the franchise had not widened. The progressive and liberal element in the country felt disappointed, whilst the conservatives gloated over their success.

Advent of the Mauritian Labour Party

Social agitations and labour unrest in a restrictive political system were fertile ground for the emergence of a structured political party. Maurice Curé, who had been agitating for workers' rights, participated actively in politics since his return to the country at the end of the First World War. His socialist policies incurred the wrath of the plantocrats and local British administrators. In February 1936, Curé launched the Labour Party. The world economic crisis following the crash of 1932 and the onset of the Second World War tempered the aspirations of the Mauritian polity. The country joined the rest of the Empire in its war efforts. Political demands awaited the end of the war. The British economy suffered irreversible damage and the process of decolonisation was set in motion with the advent of a Labour Government in London. It began with the end of the British Raj in 1947. It was only a question of time for the colonies to march towards greater autonomy and complete political independence.

In 1945 the British Secretary of State for the Colonies advised the Governor to draft a new constitution in line with the legitimate aspiration of all sections of the Mauritian society. Two opposing tendencies emerged from the consultations on the draft. The conservatives, mostly Franco-Mauritians, opposed radical reforms. The progressive elements, which included the coloureds and Indo-Mauritians, pressed for the relaxation of the franchise qualifications. A simple literacy test in English/French, or any of the approved oriental languages, was ultimately introduced for registration.

This franchise modification drastically altered the political landscape in the country. A significant number of Mauritians qualified to vote in the ensuing general elections.

Post-war constitution

An Order in Council dated 19 December 1947 was gazetted in Mauritius on 7 January 1948. It formalised the new constitution of the colony, the main features being a widened franchise, a legislature with a higher elective element and an executive body with members appointed from the elected and nominated members of the Legislative Council. The right to vote was granted to any resident aged 21 or above who 'can speak and can read and write simple sentences in, and can sign his name in any of the languages'. The languages referred to a host of oriental languages besides English and French. An aggressive campaign was launched to get the largest possible number of electors among the Indo-Mauritian community. That campaign proved successful, as the electorate expanded from 11 000 to 72 000.

The 1947 constitution represented a modest improvement over the previous one. Two general elections (1948, 1953) were held under that constitution. Participation in the democratic processes could only result in the legitimate demand for wider involvement in the governance of the country. Progressives were also encouraged in the demands of constitutional developments elsewhere in the empire. The Labour Party made responsible government and universal suffrage their electoral platform in the 1953 general elections. The Labour Party won 13 of the 19 elected seats.[9]

Post-1955 saw the beginning of a series of consultative discussions concerning constitutional changes. A new constitution promulgated by an Order in Council of 30 July 1958 removed the last obstacle for genuine democratic representation – universal adult suffrage. Henceforth, any adult in the country was entitled to vote and the existing first-past-the-post (FPTP) voting model was maintained. That same year, the Trustram-Eve Electoral Boundary Commission recommended that elections be held in forty single-member constituencies and the Representation of People's Act (1958)[10] was instituted.

Following the recommendations of the Trustram-Eve Commission in 1958, 'one man one vote' became a reality and was first implemented in the 1959 general election. There was an upsurge in the number of eligible voters that rose from 92 000 (1953 elections) to 208 000[11] and the greater visibility of four political parties, namely: the Labour Party had a national following with strong roots in the rural areas; the Muslim Committee of Action (CAM), an ally of the Labour Party, representing sectarian interests; the Independent Forward Block (IFB), a protest movement in the rural areas competing against the Labour Party; and the Parti Mauricien Social Democrate (PMSD), a party with strong links in the urban areas that based its policy against anything that the Labour Party stood for.

Path to independence

The 1960s were a decisive decade. Following a constitutional review Conference held in 1961, it was decided that two stages would be adopted. Stage one (which was implemented in 1962) proposed that the leader of the majority in the Assembly would be called the 'Chief Minister' and the latter would be 'consulted on the appointment and removal of ministers, on the summoning, proroguing and dissolution of the Legislative Council'.[12] The second stage saw the appellation of 'Chief Minister' change to 'Premier' and that of 'Legislative Council' to 'Legislative Assembly'. These two stages were duly embodied in the Mauritius Constitution Order 1964.

The following year, after a series of consultations with political parties, the British Government announced that 'it was right that Mauritius should be independent and take her place among the sovereign nations of the world'. It decided against referendum, but agreed that if a majority in the new Legislative Assembly voted for independence, Her Majesty's Government would fix a date for that purpose. An Electoral Commission was appointed to devise an electoral system and the method of allocating seats in the Legislature most appropriate for Mauritius.

---

9   Selvon S (2012) *A New Comprehensive History of Mauritius*. Mauritius: MD Selvon Editions.
10 This Act lays out the modus operandi for the registration of electors, election expenses, etc.
11 Mathur H (1991) *Parliament in Mauritius*. Port Louis: Editions de L'Ocean Indien.
12 Ibid.

Sir Harold Banwell chaired the Electoral Commission and held hearings with all political groups and interests in January 1966. His report, submitted in May 1966, comprised two elements: Electoral Boundaries and voting system/allocation of seats. Banwell proposed that the existing 40 constituencies be grouped into pairs of two, giving 20 new enlarged constituencies, which would return three members each. The island of Rodrigues would henceforth elect two members.[13] Whilst welcome, the proposal on the voting system and allocation of seats in the Legislative Assembly was far from being straightforward.

Proposed electoral model

It was proposed that each constituency would elect three candidates and this would be through a multi-member voting based on a FPTP system. Each elector would cast three votes (two for Rodrigues) and the three candidates with the highest number of votes in each constituency would be elected.

In fact, one of the mandates of the Banwell Commission was to ensure 'the system should give the main sections of the population an opportunity of securing fair representation of their interests'. In order to compensate for the possible under-representation of minority communities or inadequate number of elected members (with respect to the percentage of votes polled nationally by certain parties), additional seats would be allocated through constant and variable corrective seats.

Achieving consensus

The Banwell proposal of constant and variable correctives was amended after the Labour Party rejected the original suggestion. A system of 'best losers' was devised by which eight additional seats (to the 62 directly elected members) would be allocated to the communities most under-represented. The result of this new proposal would not alter the overall verdict of the electorate as reflected in the election of the 62 directly elected members. The Legislative Assembly would have 70 members directly or indirectly elected. There was no need for reserved seats for specific communities or interests.

Once the amended version of the Banwell Commission was approved by all parties, an Order in Council gave force of law to the new constitution and the country headed for the general elections which took place in August 1967. The elections were more a referendum on independence. The Labour Party and its allies won with 54% of the popular vote and, as agreed at the September 1965 London Conference, a motion was successfully presented at the New Legislative Assembly requesting Her Majesty's government to take the necessary steps for Mauritius to gain independence within the Commonwealth. Further to the agreements of the London Conference, an Order in Council dated 21 March 1966 allowed the leader of the party that won the general elections of 1967, the Premier, to preside over the Council of Ministers. That order became operative on 12 August 1967 just a week after

---

13 Banwell H (1966) Mauritius: *Report of the Banwell Commission on the Electoral System*. London: HMSO.

the general elections. The articles of the Order in Council of 1966 conferred all powers on the Premier. Mauritius achieved independence on 12 March 1968.

As mentioned in the opening section of the chapter, Mauritius transitioned smoothly towards independence and this despite the fact that 44% of the population voted against independence in the general elections held in 1967. One of the most important tasks of the victorious Labour Party, who had at its helm Sir Seewoosagur Ramgoolam, was to bring together all the communities. In a bid to reconcile and rally all the different ethnic communities (namely the Creoles and Franco-Mauritians), the PMSD was invited to be part of a post-electoral coalition government. Important overtures were also made towards the Franco-Mauritian business elite to reassure them that nothing would be done to put in jeopardy their economic interests.[14] This reassurance was capital in enlisting the support of all and ensuring that the newly independent island focused on charting out its social and economic future.

After independence

Post independent populist slogans such as 'unity in diversity', 'one nation one people' and 'rainbow nation' became the mantra of those in power or vying for power. Ten post-independent general elections have since been organised in Mauritius and in principle they have been held more or less every five years, except in the case of the early dissolution of parliament. In fact, in 1982 an amendment was brought to the Constitution of Mauritius to include the following clause: 'Parliament unless sooner dissolved, shall continue for five years from the date of the first sitting of the Assembly after any general election and shall then stand dissolved' (Section 57: 2). This is considered necessary as the first post-independence election, scheduled for 1972, was delayed to 1976.

The 1982 debacle

The general election of 1982, to a great extent, demonstrated the limitations of the FPTP electoral model. The coalition party headed by the Mauritian Militant Movement (MMM) won all the 62 seats. The latter was formed in 1972, sparked by a clampdown on workers following an eruption of wildcat strikes. It quickly became an advocate of the working class. Despite winning 25.8% of the popular vote, the outgoing ruling party headed by Sir Seewoosagur Ramgoolam retained no seats (except those that were allotted to them following the best-loser-system [BLS]). What is termed the 60–0 phenomenon was reproduced during the general elections of 1995. A number of observers have spoken about such 'disproportionate wins'[15] that produce non-existent or weak oppositions (the case of the 1982, 1991, 1995 and 2014 legislature).

---

14 Salverda T (2015) (Dis)unity in diversity: How common beliefs about ethnicity benefit the white Mauritian elite. *Journal of Modern African Studies* 53(4): 533–555.

15 Sachs A et al. (2002) *Report on Constitutional and Electoral Reform in Mauritius.* Port Louis: Government of Mauritius; Bunwaree S & Kasenally R (2005) Political parties in Mauritius. *EISA Research Report No 19.*

To address the shortcomings generated by the FPTF, the need for electoral reform was proposed following an electoral pledge of the winning coalition party that came to power in 2000. The retired South African Judge Albie Sachs was commissioned to make proposals concerning constitutional and electoral reforms. Sachs' mandate was to make suggestions around 'introducing a dose of proportionality into the current electoral system'.[16] Five models were considered. The 'PR Model C' proved popular. It limited the number of additional proportional representation seats to 30 members, chosen on the basis of lists provided by parties that receiving at least 10% of the national vote.

Unfortunately, the Sachs Report proposal was not implemented. Consensus was not achieved among the key political parties. Keen to demonstrate its political willingness to electoral reform in 2011, the ruling coalition commissioned Professor Carcasonne, a French constitutional expert, to revisit/revive discussions on electoral reform. His report was published but once again there was no consensus among the key political stakeholders.

Discussions on electoral reforms have been ongoing for almost 15 years. Yet, no real outcome has been reached. This speaks to how skewed the discussions have been, reflecting the short-term gains received by those who benefit from the status quo. In fact, no political party or political leader wants to change a process where he or his party have benefited from landslide victories (see general election results of 1982, 1991, 1995 and 2014).

Before this chapter turns to the role played by the electoral commissions in Mauritius, it is important to refer to what are considered to be specifics of the Mauritian democratic model. They have in a significant manner shaped the way in which politics is conducted on the small island.

Party splits and pre-electoral coalitions

Post-independent Mauritius witnessed some spectacular party splits[17] and the brokering of some of the most unexpected pre-election coalition arrangements.[18] It is worth noting that all of the three mainstream parties – the Mauritius Labour Party (MLP) the MMM and the Militant Socialist Movement (MSM) have been in coalition with each other at least once during the 1983–2014 period. When asked for the motivation behind these pre-electoral coalitions,[19] the answer is always 'to ensure national rallying and promote broad-based politics'. However, realpolitik dictates another reality; that of political survival and

Johannesburg: EISA; Sithanen R (2012) Roadmap for a Better Balance between Stability and Fairness in the Voting Formula in Mauritius. Unpublished.

16 Sachs A et al. (2002) *Report on Constitutional and Electoral Reform in Mauritius*. Port Louis: Government of Mauritius.

17 Of all the mainstream political parties, it is the MMM that underwent the most 'spectacular' splits: in 1983, when the Mouvement Socialiste Militant (MSM) was founded, and in 1993, when the Renoveau Militiant Mauricien (RMM) emerged. To date, Paul Berenger remains the enigmatic leader. The MLP also underwent a number of splits.

18 Kadima D and Kasenally R (2006) The formation, collapse and revival of political party coalitions in Mauritius: Ethnic logic and calculation at play. In: D Kadima (ed.) *The Politics of Party Coalitions in Africa*. Johannesburg: EISA & KAS.

19 Nine out ten post-independent elections have been pre-electoral coalitions.

ensuring the inevitability of winning. These pre-electoral coalition agreements have not always lasted; once the ruling coalition wins power, instability and political jockeying for additional power becomes the name of the game. This has been evidenced during the coalition partnership following the 1983, 1987, 1991, 1995, 2005, 2010 elections, where the coalition partnership collapsed well before its five-year mandate. It is interesting to note that the only time that the coalition party lasted was following a historical agreement between Sir Aneerood Jugnauth (leader of the MSM) and Paul Berenger (leader of the MMM) to share the prime ministership following the 2000 general election.

Rise of dynastic politics and ethno-politics

In nearly five decades of independence it is quite disillusioning to note that Mauritius has witnessed only two families bear the mantle of prime minister – Ramgoolam and Jugnauth. Sir Seewoosagur Ramgoolam was prime minister from 1968–1982, his son Navin Ramgoolam from 1995–2000 and 2005–2014. As for Sir Aneerod Jugnauth, he was prime minister for an uninterrupted 13 years from 1982–1995, then from 2000–2003[20] and is currently the incumbent prime minister following the coalition party win of the general election of 2014. Such a state of affairs is quite disheartening as it does not bode well for the quality of Mauritian democracy. Although, Mauritius is celebrated for its culture of political alteration, it seems that a very small set of names continue to dominate the political landscape.

As for the rise of ethnicity,[21] this has become an inevitable feature of Mauritian politics visible in the manner in which candidates are chosen and nominated, coalition partners selected, ministerial portfolios distributed and the ranking within the government determined. Political party leaders defend themselves from being ethnically obsessed and say that they must be sensitive to the realities of Mauritian society.

Is the best-loser system to be blamed?

The need to ensure minority rights has always been a concern and it was the essential condition to enlist the support of the leaders of these minority parties at independence. In fact, the BLS was devised at the time of independence as a mechanism for inclusion. However, the question that should be posed is whether nearly five decades after independence the latter is still relevant? There has been a fair amount of deliberation on the BLS. Certain quarters have termed it as 'unconstitutional and favouring communalism/ethno-politics' whilst others (albeit a small minority) view it as the only mechanism 'to ensure minority representativeness'.

Entrenched in the first schedule of the constitution (see section 31[2]), the BLS was designed for fair and adequate political representation of minorities. In short, it involves

---

20 Jugnauth and Berenger brokered a pre-electoral coalition deal agreeing to share the prime ministership.
21 Eriksen TH (1998) *Common Denominators: Ethnicity, Nation-Building and Compromise in Mauritius*. Oxford & New York: Berg; Bunwaree S & Kasenally R (2005) Political parties in Mauritius. *EISA Research Report* No. 19. Johannesburg: EISA; Kasenally R (2011) Mauritius: Paradise reconsidered. *Journal of Democracy* 22(2): 160–169.

the division of the population into religious groups and the allocation of eight additional seats as best losers.

The third and fifth paragraphs of the first schedule detail it as follows:

> Every candidate for election at any general election of members of the Assembly shall declare in such manner as may be prescribed which community he belongs to and that community shall be stated in a published notice of his community. ... For the purposes of this Schedule, the population of Mauritius shall be regarded as including a Hindu community, a Muslim community and a Sino-Mauritian community; and every person who does not appear, from his way of life, to belong to one or other of those three communities shall be regarded as belonging to the General Population, which shall itself be regarded as a fourth community.

The allocation of the BLS seats are calculated once the 62 seats have been officialised; it is the responsibility of the Electoral Commissioner to allocate and announce these additional seats. Over the years, the method of allocating seats to candidates along ethnic classification has attracted a lot of criticism. In fact, a BLS seat is allocated with reference to a population census that dates back to 1972, which was the last time when the Mauritian citizen was asked to classify him/her according to the official four ethnic classifications: Hindu, Muslim, Sino-Mauritian and general population.

There have been a number of civil society movements that have strongly decried the BLS and the group 'Rezistans Ek Alternativ'[22] brought it to the attention of the UN Human Rights Council. In 2012, the government was summoned to respond to this urgently and in July 2014 (a couple of months prior to the general election), 'The Constitution (Declaration of Community) (Temporary Provisional) Bill' was passed in parliament. The Act gives candidates the option of declaring or not declaring their ethnic community on the nomination form. A number of observers mention that the passing of this Act has not really changed things and this is clearly evidenced by the fact that all the candidates from the mainstream parties opted to declare their ethnic community so as to be eligible for a BLS seat.

Roles and responsibilities

Constitutional and legal framework

The position and the composition of the electoral management bodies are clearly stipulated within the Constitution of Mauritius (see articles 38, 39, 40 and 41). There is provision for

---

22 Rezistans Ek Alternativ is a trade union movement that morphed into a political party. For the last decade it has been fighting against what it terms as the rise of communalism in Mauritian politics. It has systematically refused to field candidates using the required ethnic classification outlined in the first schedule of the Mauritian constitution.

three different entities, namely: the Electoral Commissioner's Office (ECO), the Electoral Supervisory Commission (ESC) and the Electoral Boundaries Commission (EBC).

To guarantee the independence of the ECO, the latter is appointed by the president upon advice from the 'Judicial and Legal Service Commission[23] (article 40 [i]) and 'shall not be subject to the direction or control of any other person or authority in the exercise of his powers and functions'. As for the commissioners of the ESC and EBC, their appointment is done by the president after consultation with the prime minister and leader of the opposition. It must be noted that the chair and members of the ESC and EBC are the same, and that the two commissions function on a part-time basis. There have been suggestions to merge the two commissions and to make the position of the chair full-time but to date no changes have been initiated.[24] There is a relatively good gender balance across the three commissions – nine out of 16 staff members from the ECO are women while two out of eight staff members of the ESC and EBC are women. However, the Electoral Commissioner and the chair of the ESC and EBC are both male. There is no current legal requirement to ensure gender parity in any of the public institutions in Mauritius. However, appointments are at times sensitive to this notion and try to strike a balance.

The functions of both the ESC and ECO are clearly stipulated in article 41 where, the ESC 'shall be responsible and supervise the registration of electors, and the conduct of elections' (subsection 1); whilst the ECO 'shall have functions and powers relating to the process of registration and the elections' (subsection 2).

As for the EBC, article 39 of the constitution, stipulates that 'there shall be the 21 constituencies' (including Rodrigues) and that the commission shall review the boundaries that must be conducted every ten years (subsections 1 and 2).

The other legislation that details out the role and responsibilities of the EMBs are the Representation of the People Act (1958) and the National Assembly Elections Regulations (2014). In the case of the first one, it sets the requirements concerning (i) the registration of electors; (ii) elections in terms of the issuing of the writs and election petitions; (iii) election expenses; and (iv) election offences. As for the National Assembly Elections Regulations (2014) it outlines all the necessary procedures related to the organisation and running of an election, namely: appointment of returning officers and their deputies, registration of parties (single party or coalition parties), nominations and withdrawals of candidates, polling and counting agents, allocation of symbols, mode of voting and counting, declaration of polls and allocation of additional seats (under the BLS). These different regulations are clearly outlined in the twelve different forms that need to be duly filled and signed by candidates, political parties/coalition parties and their agents.

---

23 This commission is chaired by the Chief Justice and enshrined in the Constitution of Mauritius (see Chapter VIII).
24 Sachs A et al. (2002) *Report on Constitutional and Electoral Reform in Mauritius.* Port Louis: Government of Mauritius.

Voter registration and election preparedness

The organisation and management of elections are no doubt the most important task of electoral commissions. All attention is usually focused on polling day, but the process starts well before with the registration of voters, recruitment and training of staff, ballot-related material, etc.

Section 57(2) of the Constitution of Mauritius caters for the holding of general elections every five years. An important feature of any election is to ensure that it is as inclusive as possible – allowing citizens who are eligible to vote to be duly registered. The voter registration process starts with a house-to-house electoral enquiry that is usually undertaken at the beginning of each year and lasts between 3–4 weeks, following which a provisional voters list is produced. The Representation of People's Act (1958) clearly outlines the role and responsibilities of the registration officer (see part II, section 5). Representations from interested parties regarding their claims/objections are considered and decided upon 15 days prior to the publication of the final list, which is called the register of electors. The Register of electors then comes into force on 16 August in that year and remains in force until the next register compiled comes into force.

For the general elections of 10 December 2014, 936 975 voters were registered (compared with 879 897 for the May 2010 general elections). Although voting is not compulsory, voter turnout has usually been high, hovering between 80–85%. At the last general election, a turnout of 74.41% was recorded.[25]

Voter information

In accordance with the electoral laws, the Electoral Commissioner's office keeps the electorate informed of the administrative arrangements for voter registration and elections through publication of notices in the *Government Gazette*. Notices are also published in the local media and there is an awareness campaign that is aired on national television and on the various local radio stations. The small size of the island allows voters to be amply informed about their eligibility to vote at a forthcoming election. The Electoral Commission's office is consistent in its engagement with the public and, as expected, this exchange is increased during electoral campaigns.

Staff recruitment and training

Professionalism, rigour and high standards are required from those who will be responsible for the administration of an election. Staff working for an election are sourced and selected through the public sector and a database is created. Usually, seniority and prior experience are considered. Over the different elections, it is interesting to note that a gender sensitivity in selection and nomination of electoral staff (at all levels) has been factored in.

Once the selection and nomination process has been completed, the designated staff undergo an intensive training programme between their time of appointment and polling

---

25 See http://electoral.govmu.org/English/Overview/Pages/The-Office.aspx [accessed 29 July 2016].

day. To ensure the smooth running of an election, the appointment of a returning officer (for each of the 21 constituency) is done and this process is dictated by the National Assembly Elections Regulations (1968). The returning officer prior to his/her appointment must sign the Writ of Elections and must at all times demonstrate a sense of impartiality when disbursing their respective duties. Returning officers hold senior positions at the State Law Office. There is no legal requirement to appoint women as returning officers. However, the ESC in consultation with the ECO, are usually sensitive to a gender balance. At the last general election held in December 2014, seven out of 21 returning officers were female.

Election materials and ballots

This is the most sensitive and important part of election management and it is imperative that any possible tempering of ballot paper is eliminated. Ballot forms are printed by the government's printing office and are guarded by the Mauritian police force. Ballot forms are printed according to the number of registered voters per voting room and usually an allowance of 1% is made for any spoilt ballot. All ballot forms are numbered serially.

All movement of ballot forms are done under tight police escorts and to date there has been no case of ballot tempering or stuffing.

In 2000, translucent ballot boxes were introduced for elections that were held that year. The aim was to ensure greater transparency and be in line with international standards.

Election security

Maintaining law and order is key to the running of a peaceful election. The Mauritian police force, together with members of the Special Mobile Force (SMF),[26] is responsible for the security during election time. Both entities fall under the home affairs division of the prime minister's office. The police force has demonstrated both rigour and professionalism during the election campaign and during polling day.

Vote counting

Unlike many parts of the world, counting is not done just after the closing of poll. Instead, the process of counting begins on the next day at 8am. The process is continuous and done in the presence of candidates and their duly appointment agents. Once the counting is done to the satisfaction of all concerned parties, the results can be proclaimed and this falls under the responsibility of the returning officer. The National Assembly Elections Regulations (2014) makes provision for a recount process (see Section 51).

International election observation

In 2005, the Representation of People's Act (1958) was amended to include a new section, Section 77, that allows for the following clauses:

---

26 The SMF is a paramilitary force that falls under the Mauritian police force.

(1) The Electoral Commissioner may, with the approval of the commission, invite any international or regional organisation to deploy a mission comprising of International Election Observers to Mauritius for the purpose of observing, subject to any regulations made under this section, the conduct of any election process in Mauritius.

(2) Every International Election Observer forming part of an election observation mission deployed by an international or regional organisation pursuant to an invitation made under Subsection (1), shall, within such delay as may be prescribed, apply to the Electoral Commissioner for accreditation in such form and manner as may be determined by the Electoral Commissioner.

(3) The Electoral Commissioner may, with the approval of the commission, grant the application for the accreditation where he is satisfied that the applicant is a fit and proper person.

(4) The Electoral Commissioner may, with the approval of the commission, withdraw the accreditation granted to an International Election Observer where he is satisfied that the International Election Observer has failed to comply with the laws of Mauritius relating to elections or with such Code of Conduct for international election observers as may be prescribed.

The first set of international observers were invited to observe the 3 July 2005 general elections and have subsequently observed the 2010 and 2014 general elections.

Election code of conduct
Political parties in Mauritius add their own folklore to elections. There is no harm in adding a distinct local touch. However, this must be done with respect to the adversary and to ensure that the playing field for all contenders remains levelled. To that effect, the Electoral Supervisory Commission has devised a code of conduct. Following recommendations from the Sachs Report (2002), the code was put into effect for the 2010 general elections. One of the key objectives of the code is as follows:

> ... to ensure the integrity of the electoral process and to enable the election to take place freely and fairly, in an atmosphere of tolerance, conducive to free campaigning, unrestricted but responsible public debate so that the electorate may make an informed choice.[27]

There is no doubt that the code is laudable, however, it remains a voluntary code that to a great extent depends on the good will of political parties, their candidates and their agents.

---

27 Electoral Supervisory Commission (2010) Code of Conduct for the National Assembly Elections 2010. Port Louis, Mauritius: Government Printer.

In fact, one of the major concerns issuing from electoral campaigns is the impact of money. We shall speak to this in detail when dealing with the key challenges faced by the EMBs.

Information and communication systems

The use of new forms of communication is becoming popular and institutions that deal with matters of public importance and interest (such as elections) need to explore and invest in these new communication tools. It is interesting to note that in a number of African countries such as Kenya, Malawi, Ghana and Zambia, the electoral commissions have used technology through the GotToVote platform[28] to facilitate the registration of electors, voters' education and interactive exchanges between candidates and voters.

In the case of Mauritius, social media platforms such as Facebook and YouTube were extensively used by leaders of political parties and individual candidates in the 2014 general elections. As for the EMBs in Mauritius, they have a common website.[29] Unfortunately, the website is not very user friendly or dynamic. It essentially acts as a repository of classified data (past election results, core legislations and statistics on registers) and does not offer any live or interactive link.

Legislative, financial and operational independence

As mentioned earlier, the Constitution of Mauritius clearly guarantees the independence and autonomy of the EMBs. The legislature in any country is an important body as it is responsible for the passing of laws. As mentioned earlier, there has been protracted discussions on electoral reform in Mauritius. To that effect, the National Assembly set up three select committees[30] on 'Electoral and Constitutional Reforms' (2002), 'Public Funding of Political Parties' (2002) and 'The Proposed Introduction of Electronic Voting Machines in our Electoral System' (2004). However, none of the recommendations have been put into practice. Another area where the Mauritian legislature has vetoing power is the 'Electoral Boundaries Commission Report' (this is discussed in greater details in a later section).

The ECO, ESC and EBC receive an annual fund that is provided under the budget head of the prime minister's office. It should be noted that the ESC and the EBC were allocated a budget voted by the National Assembly for the first time for the financial years 1996–1997. The Electoral Commission is a public office and the Commissioner enjoys security of tenure under the constitution. The salary scales of the employees of the Electoral Commission is established by the Pay Research Bureau.[31] The salary of the Electoral Commissioner was revised in 2013 and stands at par with that of a judge in the Mauritian Court.

Sachs (2002) believed that the manner in which the allocation of funds to the EMBs is done slightly compromises their autonomy and suggested that

---

28 See http://electoral.govmu.org/English/Pages/default.aspx [accessed 29 july 2016]
29 See www.electoral.govmu.org
30 Whenever the need arises, the National Assembly, by resolution, appoints ad hoc (committees known as select committees) to enquire and report on designated matters to the House.
31 The Pay Research Bureau was set up in 1977 as a permanent and independent institution to keep under continuous review the pay and grading structures and conditions of service in the public sector.

... the budgetary requirements of the Commission should be a charged expenditure, and not voted by the Assembly, and it should be provided under a separate budget head. After the budget has been provided for, the Commission should be fully competent to operate it without any approval/clearance from any other authority.[32]

Key stakeholder relationships

The EMBs, especially the ECO and the ESC, are mostly visible once the dissolution of parliament is announced. It is the Prime Minister's prerogative to announce the date of the general elections. This has been decried by a number of observers who believe that it gives the incumbent prime minister undue advantage in choosing a time that is most convenient to him and his party.[33] Once the election writs are announced, the ECO and ESC come into full operation as per National Assembly Elections Regulations (2014) and Representation of People's Act (1958).

Political parties

There is very little interaction between the EMBs and political parties outside an election period. However, during elections, all political parties are required to register with the ESC as stipulated by the Mauritian Constitution. The National Assembly Elections Regulations (2014) lay out the modus operandi which according to section 7(2) should be recorded in:

> Form 3 and shall be made and signed in the presence of the Electoral Commissioner, by the president, chairman or secretary of the party duly authorised to do so by a resolution passed by the executive committee of such party and such application shall be supported by a certified extract of the minutes of proceedings of the meeting at which the executive committee of such a party passed such resolution. The relationship between the different political parties and the EMBs are deemed to be cordial and respectful. There have been no major recorded incidents between the EMBs and any political parties in any of the ten post-independent general elections. In fact, this ascertains to the fact, the two commissioners (ECO and ESC/EBC) are considered to be apolitical and independent in the conduct of their respective tasks.

Civil society

Civil society is quite an eclectic group as it is made up of different segments of society and often has a quite diverse set of interests. Civil society in Mauritius operates in a rather siloed approach and there has not been much interaction between the EMBs and the different civil society-based organisations. However, a number of potential areas can be

---

32 Sachs A et al. (2002) *Report on Constitutional and Electoral Reform in Mauritius.* Port Louis: Government of Mauritius. Section 88.
33 Ibid.

identified where collaboration could be beneficial to all parties, namely: voter education, electoral reform, tracking party political expenses, incumbency abuses, etc. In fact, this collaboration should be nurtured outside election periods, which would go a long way in strengthening the quality of democracy in Mauritius.

The media

Considered as the fourth estate, a free and independent media is crucial to any democracy. Mauritius has a well-established culture of a free press and private radios. There is only one national television station, which has been the cause of a lot of criticism for its biased and partial treatment of news, especially during election time. The written media is essentially self-regulated and remains sensitive to the manner in which election-related news items are covered/reported. In the case of broadcast media, the Independent Broadcasting Authority (IBA) as per the second schedule of IBA Act (2000), issues guidelines for private and public media concerning political broadcasts and party election broadcasts. One should note that so far the Mauritian news columns or airwaves have not carried any hate speech or enticement to violence during election time.

As for the national television station, the Mauritius Broadcasting Corporation, formal political electoral broadcasts (PEBs) are accessible through a well-codified time allocation scheme that is worked out in consultation with stakeholders (for the purpose of election campaigns). Time allocation is based on two criteria, namely the number of seats held in the outgoing parliament and the number of candidates fielded. However, what is urgently required is that the national television station abides by the MBC Act (1982) section 4(a) when it comes to 'providing impartial and independent services'.

Here it is worth noting (as detailed in an earlier section) the ESC is the highest constitutional body vested with general responsibility for the registration of electors, conduct of elections and the supervision of the entire electoral process. Unfortunately, it has not had the required impact to deal with the case of partial and imbalanced treatment of news during election periods.

Evaluation and assessment

The organisation and management of elections in Mauritius have always received kudos from the various election observation missions.[34] This was reiterated in the Electoral Integrity in Africa 2015 Report, where the Mauritian EMB scored the highest score – 87 out of 100. The Electoral Commissioner of Mauritius is often invited to share the Mauritian experience in managing elections with his peers.

---

34 African Union Observation Statement (2014) *Parliamentary Elections in the Republic of Mauritius*. Port Louis, Mauritius: African Union; Southern African Development Community (2014) *Electoral Observation Mission Statement on the 2014 National Assembly Elections*. Available at http://www.dirco.gov.za/docs/speeches/2014/mash1211.html [accessed 23 June 2016].

At a national level, there has never been any major complaints against the different EMBs. In fact, both the current Electoral Commissioner and the chair of the ESC and EBC are viewed as professionals exercising their duties as defined by the Constitution of Mauritius. In 2014, the leader of the opposition, Paul Berenger declared at the National Assembly that he has 'every respect for the Electoral Commissioner and the present members of the Electoral Commission'. This was reaffirmed by the then prime minister, Navin Ramgoolam, when he mentioned that 'party politics has nothing to do with the Electoral Commission Office and the Electoral Supervisory Commission'.[35]

The quality of elections is deemed important to the Mauritian citizen. This was reflected in the results of Afrobarometer's Round 6[36] survey on Mauritius. Nine in ten respondents surveyed 'agreed very strongly' or 'agreed' that leaders should be chosen through 'regular, open and honest elections'. The credibility of elections conducted on the island was confirmed when two thirds of the respondents said that 'votes are always fairly counted'. Unfortunately, the credibility of well-managed elections does not seem to translate in the manner that respondents view the Electoral Commission as a stand-alone body. Only one in five of those interviewed said that they 'trusted it a lot' and 46% said that they 'somewhat trusted' the Electoral Commission. In fact, the trust generated in the Electoral Commission is on par with other public bodies such as the Mauritian courts of law or the Mauritius Revenue Authority.

Maybe, it is important that the EMBs develop a more aggressive public awareness campaign among the Mauritian public on the crucial role they play in delivering safe and competitive elections. In fact, most citizens hear or see the EMBs only during elections.

Key Challenges

Strengthening the EMBs

It was mentioned that the EMBs are mostly visible during elections and their roles and responsibilities are clearly outlined in the different legislations mentioned in earlier sections. However, one of the key challenges faced by the EMBs is to turn them into enforcement bodies. One of the terms of reference of the Sachs Committee on electoral and constitutional reform was to:

> review the role of the Electoral Supervisory Commission and make recommendations on how it can be strengthened and its responsibilities extended to uphold the democratic fundamentals of the Mauritian society in particular to ensure really free and fair elections.[37]

---

35 National Assembly of Mauritius (25 March 2014) Parliamentary Debates: Second Session. Available at http://mauritiusassembly.govmu.org/English/hansard/Documents/2014/hansard0114.pdf [accessed 23 June 2016].

36 Round 6 was conducted in June/July 2014 and included 1 200 Mauritian adults.

37 Sachs A et al. (2002) *Report on Constitutional and Electoral Reform in Mauritius.* Port Louis: Government of Mauritius. Section 3.

This was also a concern that was raised by political parties, namely the Mouvement Militant Mauricien (MMM). In a position paper it published for its 40-year anniversary entitled 'The Reform of Institutions for a Democratic Mauritius', it mentions 'the Electoral Supervisory Commission is independent and has functioned in a neutral manner in the past, yet there is still need to consolidate its practices and vest it with more powers'.[38]

Making enforcement bodies effective

Despite the well-established regulations concerning the organisation and management of elections,[39] there are a number of important loopholes that exist and that give undue advantage to the incumbents.

Therefore, the ESC must be given the necessary power to ensure that once parliament is dissolved and the writs are announced that the incumbent government assumes the status of a caretaker government. This will legally limit the abuse of state apparatus from undue advantage. In fact, previous incumbent governments have abused the system to their advantage – favouring and recruiting political agents in public sector jobs, allocating funds for important infrastructure projects in key constituencies and systematically abusing national television for government propaganda. In 2005, following the 3 July general elections, a defeated candidate (Raj Ringadoo) filed an election petition (as provided in the Representation of People's Act 1958, Part 3, section 45) against the victory of a candidate (Ashock Jugnauth) who was from the outgoing incumbent government, on the following case:

> ever since the dissolution of the National Assembly on 24 April, and at any rate since the issue of the Writ of Election on 9 May 2005, the respondent and his agents and persons acting on his behalf with his consent and knowledge have indulged in bribery, contrary to sections 45(1) (a)(ii) and 64(1) of the Representation of the People Act, in order to procure, promote and/or influence the election of the respondent in constituency no. 8.[40]

Ashock Jugnauth lost his case in the Supreme Court of Mauritius, as well as his appeal to the Privy Council. Unfortunately, this has not totally fixed the situation and state apparatus is still very much abused. Also it might be worthwhile giving statutory power to the code of conduct devised by the ESC, which remains essentially a voluntary one.

Political parties' registration remains an important bone of contention. As mentioned earlier, political parties in Mauritius are only required to register once the election writs

---

38 Mouvement Militant Mauricien (2009) *Reform of Institutions for a Democratic Mauritius, 40th Anniversary.* Port Louis: MMM.

39 Government of Mauritius (1958) *Representation of People's Act.* Government of Mauritius; Government of Mauritius (2014) *National Assembly Elections Regulations.* Available at http://electoral.govmu.org/English/Documents/National%20Assembly%20Elections%20Regulations.pdf [accessed 23 June].

40 See *Jugnauth Ashock vs. Ringadoo Raj.* Available at http://www.saflii.org/mu/cases/UKPC/2008/50.html [accessed 22 July 2016].

are announced.[41] Otherwise they remain unregulated and out of the purview of any legislation. It is quite difficult to maintain a collaborative rapport between the EMBs and political parties. Therefore, it might be worthwhile considering that the ESC extends the registration of political parties between electoral periods.

Currently the ESC and EBC operate on a part-time basis and, as mentioned earlier, the two commissions have the same chairperson and committee members, but neither of them have a full-fledged staff, nor a building or dedicated space. According to Sachs[42] this seriously affects their autonomy and ability to invest in any permanent outreach programmes. Unfortunately, Sachs' recommendations of merging the two commissions into a 'one high-level constitutional body', nor that of appointing a full-time chairperson to the two commissions, have been implemented. In recent times, there has been discussion in parliament concerning the period of appointment of the ESC and EBC. As per the Constitution of Mauritius, the chair and members of these two commissions 'shall vacate his office at the expiration of five years from the date of his appointment' (see section 38: 4[a]). The discussion was brought about as one of the members of the two commissions was re-appointed by the then prime minister, Navin Ramgoolam, and this despite the fact that the Constitution of Mauritius is explicit about the re-appointment of existing members. Another element worth highlighting is that the appointment of the current chair of the ESC and EBC expired on 29 July 2014.[43] To date no new chair has been appointed.

Boundaries and delimitations

It is incumbent on the EBC 'to review the boundaries of the constituencies every ten years and to present a report to the National Assembly'.[44] As mentioned earlier, the current delimitations of boundaries date back to the Banwell Commission in 1966 where the existing 40 constituencies (under the Trustram-Eve Commission) were merely joined together to create the existing 20+1 constituencies (Mauritius and Rodrigues).

The major problem with the current constituencies is that they do not reflect the guiding principle, which is to ensure 'that the number of inhabitants of each constituency should be as nearly equal as is reasonably practicable to the population quota'.[45]

Unfortunately, over the decades there has been wide variation in the number of electors in each of the 21 constituencies. Those that pose the biggest concern are constituencies 3 and 14. Constituency 3 is the smallest of the 20 constituencies in Mauritius covering 6.10km², whilst Constituency 14 is the largest covering some 320.3km². As per the current

41 Government of Mauritius (1958) *Representation of People's Act*. Section 8. Port Louis: Government of Mauritius.

42 Sachs A et al. (2002) *Report on Constitutional and Electoral Reform in Mauritius*. Port Louis: Government of Mauritius.

43 National Assembly of Mauritius (25 March 2014) Parliamentary Debates: Second Session. Available at http://mauritiusassembly.govmu.org/English/hansard/Documents/2014/hansard0114.pdf [accessed 23 June 2016].

44 Constitution of Mauritius (1968) Government of Mauritius Publications. Section 39(2).

45 Ibid.: Section 39(3).

electoral system of three-past-the-post, all constituencies return at least three elected members (depending on the BLS). This has been decried by a number of observers[46] as this frustrates the process of democratic consolidation.

Since the first boundaries exercise that was carried out in 1966, the Constitution of Mauritius requires that every ten years the EBC conducts an exercise to that effect and submits a report. So far there have been four reports submitted (1976, 1986, 1999 and 2009). The 1976 report was rejected whilst the 1986 and 1999 reports were accepted. As for the 2009 report, it was tabled at the National Assembly on 10 November 2009. There have been a number of private notice questions from the leader of the opposition (20 November 2009 and 24 March 2014) as to the implementation of the 2009 EBC report. In his latest response, the then prime minister, Navin Ramgoolam, was extremely cautionary:

> Mr Speaker Sir, I have indicated in my proposals that although there is quite a variation between Constituency size and the number of voters per Constituency, we believe that adjusting the number of electors per Constituency will create more problems than it solves. That is why I unambiguously stated that Government is minded not to accept any changes in the electoral boundaries.[47]

To date debates concerning the EBC 2009 report have not resumed and its recommendations are yet to be accepted or rejected. The next electoral boundaries report is due in 2019.

Money and politics

Across the world money, and for that matter big money, has significantly changed the manner in which politics is conducted. The issue of political party funding in Mauritius has been a matter for debate for some time now.

In 2002, the Sachs Report recommended the creation of a 'public fund' for political parties, to be administered by the Electoral Supervisory Commission. Subsequently, a parliamentary select committee was set in the same year to assess Sachs' recommendation and make further recommendations with 'a view to promoting sound, dynamic and lively democracy and eliminating the risks of corruption and influence peddling'. Unfortunately, there has not yet been any further traction in the discussions.

What does the law say? According to the Representation of People's Act (1958), a ceiling is imposed in terms of electoral expenses incurred by candidates and is detailed as follows (in respect to a legislative election):

---

46 Mathur H (1991) *Parliament in Mauritius*. Port Louis: Editions de L'Ocean Indien; Sachs A et al. (2002) *Report on Constitutional and Electoral Reform in Mauritius*. Port Louis: Government of Mauritius; Bunwaree S & Kasenally R (2005) Political parties in Mauritius. *EISA Research Report* No 19. Johannesburg: EISA; Sithanen R (2012) Roadmap for a Better Balance between Stability and Fairness in the Voting Formula in Mauritius. Unpublished.

47 National Assembly of Mauritius (25 March 2014) Parliamentary Debates: Second Session. Available at http://mauritiusassembly.govmu.org/English/hansard/Documents/2014/hansard0114.pdf [accessed 23 June 2016].

Where the candidate does not belong to any party, or there is no other candidate belonging to the same party at the election in a constituency, 250 000 rupees.[48]

Where the candidate is not the only candidate belonging to a party at the election in a constituency, 150 000 rupees (section 51).[49]

The above ceilings imposed by the law have been systematically violated at every general election where party candidates and their election agents 'cook the books' to submit their respective election returns to the Electoral Commission of which the veracity is sworn in the presence of a magistrate (see section 56).

Commenting on the expense ceiling imposed by the law, the current Electoral Commissioner[50] believes that 'the amount is unrealistic'. According to him when the Representation of People's Act came into force in 1958, the ceiling for a party candidate was 10 000 rupees. This amount was reviewed to 20 000 rupees in 1985 and to 150 000 rupees in 1989. Since 1989, there has been no further review.

Concerning the obligation election returns, once they are duly received by the Electoral Commission, the latter is required to make a public notice in a daily newspaper that the election returns can be inspected by any member of the public. Once this process is completed, matters pertaining to electoral expenses are filed and deemed closed.

The major problem is that there is a massive mismatch between what the political parties and their candidates spend and what is actually prescribed by the law. This problem stems from the fact that (i) political parties are only required to register during the official election and (ii) the EMBs have no power of sanction.

Under the present legislation and the provisions of the National Assembly Elections Regulations, a political party's registration with the Electoral Commission may be done a few days before a general election and serves only for the purpose of the first schedule to the constitution (namely the allocation of seats under the BLS). According, to Sachs[51] such a situation can be addressed through public funding. However, such a concept does not seem to echo well with the Mauritian public as evidenced in the findings of Round 6 of the Afrobarometer survey. Nine in ten respondents agreed that 'political parties are private entities and they should raise their own funds' with eight in ten disagreeing with the following statement: 'the state should provide funding to registered political parties based on how they perform in elections'.

The second issue is to give the power of sanction to EMBs (and in this case the Electoral Supervisory Commission). More than eight in ten of the respondents to Round 6 of the

---

48 Approximately USD 7 000.
49 Approximately USD 4 000.
50 Financement des parties politiques: Voyage dans un trou noir (15 December 2015) *ION News-Mauritius.* Available at https://www.youtube.com/watch?v=299osdJxWuk [accessed 23 June 2016].
51 Sachs A et al. (2002) *Report on Constitutional and Electoral Reform in Mauritius.* Port Louis: Government of Mauritius.

Afrobarometer survey agreed that the ESC should be 'mandated to scrutinise the finances of political parties'.

What does the private sector think? The private sector is an important source of funding for political parties in Mauritius. A fair majority of the established Top 100 Mauritian companies are thought to contribute regularly to electoral campaigns of the mainstream political parties. Over the years, the veil of opacity that has clad the private sector's financing of political parties has slowly started to lift. In 2005, the Joint Economic Council (that acts as the coordinating body for the Mauritian private sector) requested that its members, in line with good governance and transparency practices, declare the amount given to political parties in their annual reports. Today a growing number of private companies are adhering to this practice.

As for the political actors, and more specifically the party leaders, they remain extremely elusive on this issue and prefer to use the generic term of well-wishers when it comes to party donations. Campaign managers often refer to a long list of electoral expenses ranging from the organisation of public meetings, printing and distribution of electoral pamphlets, banners, transport, public rallies, the payroll of political agents, website and social media platforms. In a newspaper article[52] a politician, and once leader of a small political party, detailed the core electoral expenses and their breakdown costs to be estimated at some 330 million rupees[53] for a 30-day campaign for one political party. This, in fact, correlates with what the leader of the Labour Party, Navin Ramgoolam, mentioned in an interview in December 2015.[54] In principle, all the political leaders of the mainstream parties have publicly declared that there is an urgent need to tackle the issue of political party financing. Paul Berenger even refers to how 'money in politics has denatured the democratic game'.[55]

In December 2015, the government set up a ministerial committee to make recommendations on electoral reforms. These reforms include the introduction of a dose of proportional representation in the National Assembly, and guarantee better women representation; the mandatory declaration of community; anti-defection measures; and the widening of the powers of the Electoral Supervisory Commission and the Financing of Political Parties Bill.

Reigning in the executive

Mauritius follows the separation of power doctrine where the role and responsibilities of the executive, legislative and judiciary are clearly defined. However, it is clear that the executive retains the upper hand when it comes to the decision-making process. The Constitution of Mauritius presently provides for 'the president, acting in accordance with the advice of the prime minister may at any time prorogue or dissolve parliament'

---

52 Valayden R (2014, 14 May) An insight into the expenses incurred during our electoral campaigns in Mauritius. *Le Mauricien.*

53 Approximately USD 9 million.

54 Financement des parties politiques: Voyage dans un trou noir (15 December 2015) ION News-Mauritius. Available at https://www.youtube.com/watch?v=299osdJxWuk [accessed 23 June 2016].

55 Ibid.

(Section 57[1]). This has been source of debate and was one of the terms of reference of the Sachs Commission on 'Constitutional and Electoral Reform in Mauritius'. The aim was to enhance the role and responsibilities of the President of the Republic, but the latter was not taken on board. It is interesting to note that in the UK parliament the Fixed-term Parliaments Act (2011)[56] was passed automatically, dissolving parliament every five years and setting into motion the 'pre-election period'[57] as defined in the Political Parties, Elections and Referendums Act (2000).[58]

Another issue that has seen the clear domination of the executive is the manner in which electoral reform has been dealt with. Although there seems to be a clear understanding among all political leaders that electoral reform is key to enhancing the quality of Mauritian democracy, no concrete action has been taken yet.

Recommendations

Enforcement
The fact that the different EMBs (namely: the Electoral Commission Office, the Electoral Supervisory Commission and the Electoral Boundaries Commission) are enshrined in the Constitution of Mauritius guarantees the independence and autonomy of these bodies. However, the current weakness of these bodies (especially the ESC) is that they have no power to enforce. The Sachs Report,[59] political commentators and even leaders of certain political parties have demanded a review of the powers of the ESC during and after elections.

Electoral expenses
The current ceiling of expenses prescribed by the law is both outdated and unrealistic. The latter must be reviewed to reflect in a reasonable manner the costs of taking part in an election. Perhaps more importantly, the ESC must be given the power to sanction those candidates who have obviously breached the authorised limit.

Dealing with incumbency abuses
Earlier, it was mentioned that the power is vested in the prime minister as per the Constitution of Mauritius to determine the time to prorogue or dissolve parliament. This is believed to give undue advantage to incumbent governments that in the past have systematically abused public resources. Sachs[60] is quite forceful in his suggestion of

---

56 Government of the United Kingdom (2011) Fixed Term Parliament Act 2011. London: HMSO. Available at http://www.legislation.gov.uk/ukpga/2011/14/pdfs/ukpga_20110014_en.pdf [accessed 23 June 2016]; Government of the United Kingdom (2000) Political Parties, Elections and Referendums Act. London: HMSO.
57 Specific restrictions on the use of public resources.
58 Government of the United Kingdom (2000) Political Parties, Elections and Referendums Act. London: HMSO
59 Sachs A et al. (2002) *Report on Constitutional and Electoral Reform in Mauritius*. Port Louis: Government of Mauritius.
60 Sachs A et al. (2002) *Report on Constitutional and Electoral Reform in Mauritius*. Port Louis: Government of Mauritius. p. 48.

conferring the authority on 'the Electoral Supervisory Commission in consultation with the Electoral Commissioner to fix the date of an election'. This will allow the ESC to set the rules of engagement for a caretaker government.

Registration of political parties

Political parties in Mauritius are the only entities that are not formally required to be registered outside the timeframe of an election. Also, the period of required registration is very short – between 45 to a maximum of 100 days after which they return to their unregistered status. Numerous suggestions have been made for political parties to become legal entities and submit regularly audited accounts.[61] In fact, this might act as the first step in helping to cull the influence of big money on politics in Mauritius.

Code of conduct

One of the major weakness of this instrument is that it remains voluntary. It would perhaps better serve its cause if it had statutory power.

Modernise the voting system

Voting in Mauritius is conducted in the traditional manner using ballot papers and boxes. In 2004, a Parliamentary Select Committee was set to look into the 'Proposed Introduction of Electronic Voting Machines in our Electoral System'. Unfortunately, the subsequent debate has been skewered, at times bordering on scaremongering, where the dangers of possible manipulation of technology have been highlighted. Maybe it is high time that the discussion be re-initiated, and no doubt the most appropriate body to lead the discussions is the Electoral Commission Office.

Electoral boundaries

It is inconceivable for a modern democratic nation like Mauritius to have such wide discrepancies between constituencies that are expected to return an equal number of parliamentarians. Earlier on, details were given of the current discrepancies that exist and how the Constitution of Mauritius requires that the basic guiding principle 'is that the number of inhabitants of each constituency should be as nearly equal as is reasonably practicable to the population quota' (section 39:3). The current boundaries report (submitted in 2009) is still being deliberated upon in parliament and no discussion has been taken concerning the recommendations of the report. The question that must be addressed is how to develop greater political synergy and commitment across political parties on such an important issue.

---

61 Ibid.; Joint Economic Council (2005) *A Road for Achieving Meaningful Competitiveness*. Port Louis: Mauritius; Transparency Mauritius (2013) *A Code for Free and Fair Elections*. Port Louis: Transparency Mauritius; Parlement Populaire de la République de Maurice (2015) *For Free and Fair Elections*, available at http://www.maurice-info.mu/wp-content/uploads/2015/10/For-clean-and-fair-elections-petition.pdf [accessed 23 June 2016].

Greater visibility

The EMBs become visible and vocal once the election writs are proclaimed. Unfortunately, outside elections they are off the public radar. The EMBs, and especially the Electoral Commission Office, is a public institution that enjoys the same profile as the Mauritian courts, the Mauritius Revenue Authority or the Mauritian police. Also it seems that the public is not sufficiently aware of the different functions of the EMBs in ensuring clean and credible elections. Therefore, it would be to the advantage of the different commissions to engage in a less technical and more user-friendly manner with the public. Here the use of technology can be enlisted to that effect. It is also imperative that this public outreach extends beyond election time frames.

Electoral reform

Electoral reform has been a subject of debate for the last 15 years and has generated numerous reports. Unfortunately, political consensus and commitment has been lacking. In fact, electoral reform is the solution that will help bring about some of the key changes that will strengthen the role and responsibilities of the EMBs.

Conclusion

Governance, the rule of the law and relevant institutions are crucial for the functioning of a democracy. Democracy is also synonymous with the ability to organise and manage elections that reflect the will of the people. To that effect, the presence of legitimate and credible EMBs are fundamental.

Mauritius offers a good case where its EMBs have played a key role in delivering 'free and fair elections'. However, as outlined earlier, a number of key challenges inhibit the EMBs' ability to play its full role as a democracy watchdog. These challenges are not impossible to tackle and can be done in an incremental and inclusive manner where all stakeholders are duly consulted and made aware of the implications.

As an endnote, it would be important to stress the fact the quality of democracy does not solely depend on the how well organised and managed elections are – what I call the end product – but more importantly on the electoral process which takes into account the whole ecosystem in which democracy thrives and is consolidated.

7

MOZAMBIQUE

Dr Domingos M do Rosário

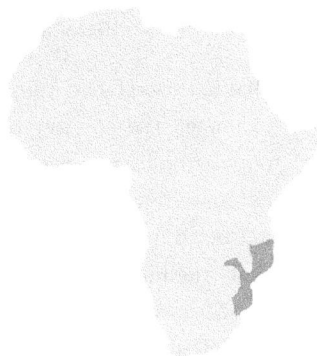

Introduction

The approval of the new multiparty constitution in 1990 and the signing of the Rome general peace agreement in October 1992 were important turning points in Mozambique's political history. Following a civil war which devastated the social, political and economic fabric of the country, five presidential and legislative election processes took place in Mozambique (1994, 1999, 2004, 2009, 2014); four local election processes (1998, 2003, 2008 and 2013) and two elections for members of the provincial assemblies (2009, 2014), all won by Frelimo and its candidates. All the general elections have been contested by the opposition.

This chapter evaluates the performance of the country's election management body. It starts with the discussion of the socio-historical and political factors that had an impact on the functioning of the electoral organ. It then provides a review of the existing legal framework. It examines different aspects of institutional design and performance of the electoral bodies, and shows that the instability of the electoral body and the strong control which is exercised by political parties interferes with its performance and undermines its credibility in managing elections. The chapter then concludes with an assessment and recommendations that can assist the election management body (EMB) and other key actors to promote changes that can help to improve electoral integrity.

Socio-historical and political context

Mozambique is a former Portuguese colony. The Front for the Liberation of Mozambique (Frelimo) waged the fight against Portuguese colonialism. The armed struggle led to Mozambique's independence in 1975, granting Frelimo the reins of government. Two years later and now a 'Marxist-Leninist' party, Frelimo declared the country a one-party state. A civil war consequently ensued, principally against the Mozambican National Resistance (Renamo), and ended only 16 years later in 1992. The country was in ruins. Mozambique is amongst the five poorest countries in the world, with one of the lowest ratings in the Human Development Index (ranked 178 out of 187 countries). It is only recently that the country has been considered a successful example of economic growth, characterised by an annual GDP growth rate of 8%. Despite being considered a successful example,[1] the country remains part of the least developed with more than 90% of its population living on less than USD 2 per day.[2] High levels of corruption,[3] low funding and excessive bureaucracy also hinder development.[4] The potential for recurrence of conflict has not diminished either.[5] The Mozambican Information Agency, for instance, recently said: 'the high poverty of the northern provinces will bring serious political problems to any Mozambican government'. [6]

Political stability was interrupted in 2012. Security forces squared up against the forces of Renamo. To put an end to these confrontations, on 5 September 2013 an agreement for the cessation of hostilities was signed which resulted in the approval of a consensual electoral reform between the country's two main political forces. However, Mozambique now experiences a post elections conflict as a result of the opposition's refusal of the 2014 general, presidential, legislative and provincial election results. The Mozambican political life is dominated by the two main actors of the civil war, Frelimo and Renamo. This bipartisanship overrides the development of other political or social movements. Nevertheless, in 2009 a small political party, the Democratic Movement of Mozambique (MDM) managed to be represented in parliament. However, in terms of discourse and policy, MDM does not represent an alternative as it does not distinguish itself from the two dominant parties.

Constitutional and legal framework

The Constitution of the Republic of Mozambique establishes a multiparty democracy well founded on periodic elections, by means of universal, direct, secret and equal suffrage. The president and the deputies of the National Assembly as well as the members of the Provincial Assemblies are elected for a five-year term. The 1990 constitution sets the duration of the term of the assembly and the mandate of the president of the republic as five years. The president of the republic may be re-elected, but cannot accumulate more than two consecutive mandates.[7] The deputies of the assembly are allowed to be re-elected

---

1   World Bank (2010) *World Development Report: Development and Climate Change*. Washington DC: The World Bank.
2   Alkire S & Santos M (2010) Acute multidimensional poverty: A new index for developing countries. *Oxford Poverty & Human Development Initiative (OPHI) Working Paper* No. 38. Available at http://www.ophi.org. uk/wp-content/uploads/ophi-wp38.pdf [accessed on 7 July 2016].
3   Mozambique is ranked 119 amongst the 183 most corrupt countries of the world. International Transparency (2013) Índice de Percepção de Corrupção de 2013: Os níveis percebidos de corrupção no sector público em 183 países e territórios em todo o mundo, 2014. Available at http://cpi.transparency.org/ cpi2013/results/ [accessed 27 September 2015].
4   http://www.sapo.pt/noticias/economia-mocambicana-travada-por-burocracia-e_560b0d59c410b7d224a87 adf [accessed 3 October 2015].
5   Hofmann K (2013) *Transformação económica em Moçambique –implicações para a segurança humana*. Maputo: FES. p. 11.
6   Mozambiquefile (2000) *AIM Information Bulletin* No. 289. p.20.
7   Article 147 of the Constitution of the Republic of Mozambique of 2004.

for indefinite consecutive terms.[8] The president of the republic is elected through a system of absolute majority.

The constitution of 1990, approved during the period of single-party governance, provided for a system of majority voting.[9] However, in 1992 a law[10] was passed that defines the articles of the constitution of 1990 amended according to the compromises made in Rome between the government and Renamo. A proportional system was adopted.[11] Its characteristics allow a better inclusion of political forces, according to their actual votes. However, despite removing the 5% obstacle, which was in force until the 2004 elections, the electoral formula (Hond't method) which is used for transforming votes into mandates still represents an important obstacle for small parties.

One of the characteristics of the Mozambican electoral and political system is the instability of the electoral legislation. Since the institutionalisation of the multiparty democracy, for each electoral cycle, a new electoral legislation is approved with different amendments both in terms of the constitution of electoral structures (the Mozambique Electoral Commission [CNE] and the Technical Secretariat for Election Management [STAE]) and in terms of rules for electoral competition. The majority of these changes are based on the recommendations of the international observation missions.[12] The interest of the two main parties, Frelimo and Renamo, determines the amendments made to the electoral legislation. The difficulty of the two main parties in making lasting compromises for the functioning of the Mozambican electoral system puts constraints on the process.

Electoral history and political parties

Since the adoption of the first multiparty constitution in 1990, five general presidential and legislative elections (1994, 1999, 2004, 2009 and 2014), four local elections (1998, 2003, 2008 and 2013) and two provincial elections (2009 and 2014) have taken place. All the general elections were won by Frelimo and were characterised by accusations of fraud and followed by tension and, sometimes, localised violence (1999). Opposition parties, in turn, managed isolated victories in local elections. Electoral administration bodies are considered partisan by opposition parties in favour of Frelimo.

1994 multiparty presidential and legislative elections

The 1994 elections were won by Frelimo (44.33%) and its presidential candidate Joaquim Chissano (53.3%), against 37.78% for Afonso Dhlakama and 33.7% for Renamo. At a distant third was the Democratic Union alliance with 5.44% of the votes. Voting patterns

---

8 Article 185 of the Constitution of the Republic of Mozambique of 2004.
9 Article 107 of the Constitution of the Republic of Mozambique of 1990.
10 Law 12/92 of 9 October.
11 Article 107(3) of the Constitution of the Republic of Mozambique of 1990.
12 EU-EOM (2015) *General Elections of 15 October 2014. Final Report*. Maputo: EU-EOM.

showed a historical[13] rural/urban split, and an ethnic-regional split. Urbanites voted mainly for Frelimo (59%) over Renamo (29%), while rural-based voters, especially in the centre and north regions, voted for Renamo. Regions that are associated with the intellectuals and military brass – Changana and Maconde; and Cabo Delgado respectively – voted Frelimo, whilst Renamo was stronger in the areas of Ndau-Sena, Chona and Macua influence. The vote structure created during the 1994 elections[14] remains almost unchanged to this day.

1999 multiparty elections

These were the second elections taking place in Mozambique since the end of the civil war, and the first in which Renamo participated with 'institutionalised' political strength across the national territory. With an abstention rate of 30.49% (presidential) and 32.9% (legislative), Renamo took part in these elections in alliance with a coalition of small parties,[15] forming the *Renamo-União Eleitoral* block (RU-E).[16] Even with the coalition formed, Renamo obtained 38.81% of the votes against 48.54% for Frelimo. Joaquim Chissano obtained 52.29% of the votes against 47.71% for Afonso Dhlakama. Renamo improved in its strongholds. Whilst registering marginal growth nationally (1.03%), RU-E managed an upset: they won the province of Niassa, which previously fell to Frelimo. Afonso Dhlakama's support grew by 14.81%.[17] But Renamo still contested election results, accusing the electoral administration bodies of fraud. It demanded a recount, which was rejected by the Supreme Court.[18] The Carter Center, one of the organisations that observed elections in Mozambique qualified their evaluation as doubtfully 'free and fair'.[19] Violent clashes ensued, resulting, among other things, in the death of 93 prisoners (at Montepuez), who had participated in anti-government demonstrations.

---

13 Historical factors linked to the Portuguese colonisation and the authoritarian modernisation policies implemented by Frelimo during the single-party regime, had a considerable influence on the economy and society. See De Brito L (1995) O comportamento eleitoral nas eleições gerais de 1994. In: B Mazula (ed.) *Moçambique, Eleições, Democracia e Desenvolvimento*. Maputo: Embassy of the Kingdom of Netherlands.

14 Ibid.: 473–479. Frelimo obtained significant results from 2009 in Zambézia and the MDM in the urban areas including Maputo. This tendency was confirmed in the last elections of 2014.

15 1994 data showed that of the votes obtained by this party, about 5% were arbitrary, caused by errors committed by electors.

16 The RUE coalition, constituted in 1999, was composed of the following political parties: Frente Democrática Unida (UDF), Movimento Nacional de Moçambique (MONAMO); Partido de Convenção Nacional (PCN); Frente de Aliança Patriótica (FAP); Partido do Progresso do Povo de Moçambique (PPM), Frente Unida de Moçambique (FUMO); Aliança Democrática de Moçambique (ALIMO), Partido de Renovação Democrática de Moçambique (PRD) and União Nacional de Moçambique (UNAMO).

17 Grande subida de Dhlakama (1999, 23 December). *Notícias*. p.4.

18 When one looks closely at the aggregated data published by the STAE, one can see that null votes and abstention strongly penalised the areas under Renamo's influence. In absolute terms, only 224 678 votes separated Chissano and Dhlakama. However about 550 notices, which amounted to 377 773 electors were not counted by CNE. If these votes favoured Dhlakama , this could have changed the election results in favour of Dhlakama. See Secretariado Técnico de Administração Eleitoral (STAE) *Eleições Gerais 1999* (CD Rom). Maputo: Pandora Box Lda; Cahen M (2000) Mozambique: l'instabilité comme gouvernance? *Politique africaine*. 80: 113.

19 Carter Center (2000) *Observing 1999 elections in Mozambique. Final Report*. Atlanta: Carter Centre.

2004 presidential and legislative elections

Renamo's rise caused a dent in Frelimo's political fortunes. The 2004 election pitted Dhlakama against Frelimo's new leader, Armando Guebuza.[20] With an abstention rate higher than 50%, Frelimo got 63% and Guebuza 62%, against 32% for Dhlakama and 30% for Renamo. The victory of Guebuza and Frelimo expressed the hegemony of the party within Mozambican society, but this legitimacy did not have a social basis.[21] These elections were contested due to irregularities, not only during voter registration but also during voting.[22]

2009 presidential, legislative and provincial elections

Frelimo improved its victory margin in the 2009 elections. Guebuza got 75.01% against 16.4% for Dhlakama. The presidential candidate of the third largest party, Davis Simango, received 8.9%. In the legislative elections, Frelimo obtained 74.66% of the votes (winning them 191 seats in the National Assembly), against 17.69% for Renamo and 3.39% for MDM. The abstention rate − over 50% − is worrying. These eligible voters are opting out of the electoral system.[23] Most affected were the provinces of Nampula and Zambézia, areas under Renamo's influence. In these areas the voters travelled more than 25km to vote.[24] The bias of the institutions of electoral administration (CNE/STAE) in these elections was again notorious.

2014 presidential, legislative and provincial elections

The 2014 elections took place within a tense environment. They were preceded by military confrontation between the armed forces and Renamo. Frelimo fielded a new presidential candidate, Filipe Nyusi-Maconde (of Frelimo's military elite), who represented the transition between the generation of the 'old combatants' from the anti-colonial fight and the new generation. Renamo still had Dhlakama and the MDM Davis Simango, whose constituency was younger and more urban. Frelimo's Nyusi won the election by 57% of the votes, against Dhlakama's 36.6% and 6.4% for Simango. Their parties got 57.03%;

---

20 Elected general secretary of Frelimo in 2002, Guebuza started an internal offensive to reorganise the party giving special attention to the party cells at the base and to the district administrators, who historically constituted an essential control link for territory and population. Guebuza developed a nationalist deliberate speech breaking away from the old leadership of Joaquim Chissano. He promised to fight poverty, bureaucracy and the *laissez faire* attitude. In 2014 Frelimo's political commission organised a march to bring Armando Guebuza to power and presented Armando Guebuza as a promoter of peace and development, at a time when the country was experiencing armed conflict and a steep decrease in the Human Development Index.

21 Cahen M (2009) Resistência Nacional Moçambicana, de la victoire à la déroute? Pluripartisme sans pluralisme et hégémonie sans stabilité *Sociétés politiques comparées* 17. p. 13.

22 The electoral universe set by CNE (9 142 151 voters) didn't correspond to the universe of people with active electoral capacity (7.6 million). Association of European Parliamentarians with Africa (*AWEPA*) (2005, 3 January) 2004 Election Special Issue. *Mozambique Political Process Bulletin* No. 33. Amsterdam: AWEPA. p. 6.

23 Hyden G (1980) *Beyond Ujammaa in Tanzania: Underdevelopment and An uncaptured Peasantry.* London: Heinemann. p. 127.

24 De Brito L (2009) Uma análise preliminar das eleições de 2009. *Ideias* 22: 1. Maputo: IESE.

36.61% and 6.36% respectively. Admittedly these elections were conducted within a markedly improved legislative framework. Yet Frelimo's victory was clouded by the bias and misconduct of the bodies of electoral administration. At the CNE[25] the electoral results were approved by a majority of ten votes against seven; a marked division.[26]

Domestication of international conventions

Mozambique has signed a number of United Nations treaties on human rights as well as regional conventions and declarations on human rights with implications for the electoral process, namely: the international covenant on civil and political rights (1993); the African Charter on Human and Peoples' Rights (1990); the Protocol on the Rights of Women in Africa (2003) and the Declaration of the African Union on the Principles for Democratic Elections in Africa (2002). As a member of the Southern African Development Community (SADC), Mozambique is bound to SADC's principles and guidelines for democratic elections (2004) and to the principles for electoral management, monitoring and observation in the SADC region (2003).

In accordance with article 18 of the Constitution of the Republic of Mozambique (2004), international treaties and agreements legally approved and ratified by Mozambican competent bodies are parts of its legal framework, once they have been officially published, and are internationally binding for the state of Mozambique. Internally, international norms are considered law. In the internal legal order, the rules of international law have the same value as normative acts emanating from the National Assembly and the government. Mozambique signed, but hasn't yet ratified, the African Charter on Democracy, Elections and Governance (2007), which doesn't oblige electoral institutions to comply with the fundamental principles of election management.

Electoral management body composition

The CNE is defined as an independent and impartial state body, responsible for the supervision[27] of voter registration and electoral acts.[28] The STAE is a public service, customised for electoral administration and subordinated[29] to the National Elections Commission, which is held accountable for the accomplishment of its tasks at all levels.[30] In the electoral period, which runs from the census until the validation of results by the

---

25 Ibid.: 5.
26 CNE (2014) *Acta da centralização Nacional e Apuramento Geral dos resultados das eleições Presidenciais, Legislativas e das Assembleias Provinciais de 15 de Outubro de 2014*. Maputo: CNE.
27 Supervision is defined by the same law, in its article 6 number 2, as being the function of guiding, overseeing and supervising the electoral process.
28 Article 2 of Law 6/2013 of 22 February.
29 'Subordinate' means to submit oneself and depend on the guidelines and decisions of the National Elections Commission.
30 Articles 48 and 49 of Law 6/2013.

constitutional council, the STAE staff integrate elements from the political parties[31]. At a local level, the CNE is represented by the Provincial Electoral Commission (CPE) and at the district level, by District Electoral Commission (CDE). The composition of the CPE and CDE and the appointment of their members are governed by the law establishing the CNE at central level. The CPE and the CDE cease their activities after the announcement of the final results of the electoral process. The STAE is a permanent organ of public administration in Mozambique. Although, it is formally meant to operate all-year round at the provincial and district levels, it actually only operates in electoral periods.

Formally and in accordance with the law, the STAE is subordinate to the CNE.[32] In spite of this, there are in fact two parallel structures of electoral administration. One, the STAE, is linked to the hierarchy of the Mozambican public administration and the other, the CNE, is independent but exercises the same functions. The strong politicisation of the public administration and the influence exercised by the Frelimo party in public institutions (STAE) partly explains the insubordination of the STAE in relation to the CNE. Although the CNE is considered independent, the strong influence of the political parties means that the members of the commission represent the interests of its parties more than institutional interests.

CNE functions and responsibilities

The CNE exists to:

- Ensure that voter registrations and electoral processes are organised and developed ethically and with obeisance to the conditions of full freedom, justice and transparency;
- Register political parties, party coalitions, or groups of voter groups;
- Promote, through the bodies of social communication and other means of mass broadcasting, civic education and clarification for voting citizens on matters of electoral interest;
- Formally distribute copies of the edict and original letter for the centralisation of general tabulation (duly signed and stamped) to the representatives of each application, to observers and journalists, and when disclosing electoral results;
- Ensure that funding assigned to political parties or party coalitions and candidates of the opposition is distributed before the date planned for the start of the electoral campaign;
- Determine the locations for the registration and polling stations, in accordance with the proposals of the lower level electoral bodies; and
- Tabulate presidential, legislative, provincial and local elections results.[33]

---

31 Article 51 of Law 8/2014 of 12 March.
32 Article 17 of Law 4/1997 of 1 July.
33 Article 9 of Law 6/2013.

STAE functions

The STAE exists to:

- Perform the electoral registration;
- Ensure the production, transport and distribution of all registration and voting material on schedule;
- Enrol and train electoral agents;
- Organise, follow, execute and control electoral processes; and
- Organise electoral statistics and perform studies on electoral processes and ensure their publication, once approved by the National Elections Commission.[34]

Looking for an electoral administration model

Each cycle of elections in Mozambique is an opportunity for electoral reform. So different electoral law reforms were implemented. However, their results remain modest. In this section we shall show how the different reforms operated over time, but failed to stabilise the electoral governance model in Mozambique.

Electoral bodies for the 1994 electoral process

Despite the inclusion of the members of civil society in the electoral structures in 2009, the bodies of electoral administration remain highly partisan. This partisanship undermines their credibility and transparency. For the first general elections, the CNE[35] was created, which had, as a result of the compromise made in Rome (1992), equal party representation in its composition: Frelimo, the ruling party, and the opposition parties. Of the 21 members of this commission, ten were selected by the governing party (Frelimo), seven by Renamo and three by other political parties, excluding Frelimo and Renamo.[36] The president of the commission was appointed by the president of the republic, following a selection by the members of the commission.

This CNE operated with two vice presidents, one chosen by Frelimo and the other by Renamo. In the exercise of its functions, CNE was backed by a permanent body, CNE and STAE have been introduced twice now already[37]), whose operation was regulated by a decree of the council of ministers.[38] According to the law, the STAE was subordinate and answerable to the CNE. This decree defined that the STAE would be constituted, centrally, by 25 technicians from the government, 13 from Renamo and the other parties and 12 from the United Nations.[39] The mandate of this commission ended 120 days after

---

34 Article 52 of Law 6/2013.
35 Law 4/1993 of 12 January.
36 Ibid.: Article 15.
37 Ibid.: Article 19.
38 Decree 6/1994 of 9 March.
39 Ibid.: Article 8.

the publication of the official elections map.[40] This meant that both the principles adopted for its creation and the commission itself terminate at the end of this first electoral process. A new electoral legislation was to be adopted for the following electoral processes.

1997 electoral reform for local elections

The aim of 'balance, objectivity and independence' in terms of the composition of the CNE was abandoned in subsequent legislation.[41] Thus, the new commission created to run the 1998 local elections[42] was composed of nine members. The president of the CNE was nominated by the president of the republic; seven members were indicated by Frelimo and Renamo in accordance with their parliamentary representation, and subsequently confirmed by the parliament. The ninth member of the electoral commission was nominated by the council of ministers.[43]

With these arrangements, the principles of parity (between Frelimo and the opposition) and consensus in the decision-making process which prevailed in the 1994 electoral administration body (CNE) were abandoned in favour of the principle of majority voting.[44] This principle consecrated (theoretically) the control of electoral bodies by the government's party, Frelimo, as a result of the parliamentary majority which it had obtained in the 1994 elections. Decision-making based on CNE consensus had delayed the process in 1994 but created legitimacy for the electoral process.[45]

1999 electoral reform

The composition of the EMB changed for the 1999 elections. The CNE comprised 17 members, appointed by parliamentary parties based on their representation,[46] and the other members were chosen by the government. The work undertaken by these electoral bodies was contested. Renamo accused the CNE/STAE of partiality. The poor performance of the electoral bodies during the presidential and legislative elections of 1999 led organisations like the Carter Center to consider the elections not 'free and fair'.[47] Donor pressure and the international observation missions' recommendations resulted in a deep reformulation of the electoral legislation and electoral bodies' composition. In this context, the electoral law changed once again in 2004.[48]

---

40 Ibid.: Article 18.
41 De Brito L (2012) Revisão da legislação eleitoral. Algumas propostas para o debate. In: L de Brito et al. (eds) *Desafios para Moçambique 2011*. Maputo: IESE. pp 94–95.
42 Law 4/1997 of 1 July.
43 Article 5.
44 Article 15.
45 Van den Bergh L (2011) *Porque prevaleceu a paz. Moçambicanos respondem*. Maputo/Amsterdam: Annick Osthoff Editora.
46 Article 5 of Law 4/99 of 2 February 1999.
47 Carter Center- Election Observation Mission (EOM) (2000) *Observing 1999 Elections in Mozambique*. Final Report. Atlanta: Carter Center-EOM. p. 14.
48 Law 7/2004 of 17 June.

2002 electoral reform

The reforms resulted in a CNE with 19 elements, one being the president, two vice-presidents and 16 commissioners.[49] The 18 members were appointed by the political parties based on parliamentary representation, and the president was proposed by members of civil society.[50] The inclusion of representatives of the political parties led to excessive politicisation of tasks, which, despite possessing political implications, have a purely technical character. The CNE's mandate changed to five years[51] and the STAE was permanently subordinated to the National Elections Commission. It was during the mandate of these bodies of electoral administration that the opposition managed, for the first time in the history of Mozambique since independence, to win local elections in five municipalities.[52]

2007 electoral reform

The work done by the electoral body created by Law 7/2004 for the general presidential and legislative elections has been considered positive, because of the relative impartiality with which it conducted the 2004 election process. However, reforms continued to be introduced. In February 2007 a new law[53] was approved with the aim of 'improving the organisation, coordination, execution of voter registrations and electoral processes'. Besides its composition, with 13 elements (one president and 12 commissioners),[54] the majority of the members (eight) were proposed by civil society organisations and only five by political parties in accordance with parliamentary representation. The president of the CNE was nominated by the members of civil society, and elected by his/her colleagues in the commission by consensus or secret ballot.[55]

The inclusion of civil society members as commissioners in the CNE structure (with the same tasks and responsibilities as the members from political parties) was the first step toward the transformation of this body into an independent institution of political parties. The STAE was permanently subordinated to the National Elections Commission. The permanent subordination of the STAE to the CNE was the solution found to lessen the level of conflict registered between these two bodies during the 2003 and 2004 elections. During this process, the STAE often defied the CNE decisions and regulations.[56]

---

49 Article 4.
50 Article 6.
51 Article 11.
52 In the 2003 local elections, Renamo (the opposition) managed, for the first time, to win the elections in five municipalities of the centre (Beira and Marromeu) and north (Angoche, Ilha de Moçambique and Nacala Porto) of Mozambique.
53 Law 8/2007 of 26 February.
54 Article 4.
55 Article 5.
56 Mazula B (2005) Reflectir as eleições a partir da teoria da elipse política. In: B Mazula (ed.) *Moçambique: Eleições Gerais de 2004. Um Olhar do Observatório Eleitoral*. Maputo: UEM University Press. p. 17.

Inclusion of civil society

The performance of the bodies of electoral administration in the general presidential and legislative and provincial elections of 2009 was criticised by almost all the segments of Mozambican society, and by donors. The main criticism directed at the electoral structures was linked not only to the restrictive and abusive interpretation of legal norms to the disadvantage of the opposition, but also to the absence of transparency and impartiality.[57] One of the reasons which explain the lack of transparency and credibility of the CNE is related to the fact that the appointment of the civil society members is linked to proportionality in parliamentary representation, which continues to give preference to the main political parties and puts the involvement of civil society in the process in secondary position.[58] Given that the decision-making process follows the majority rule, this architecture reinforces Frelimo's position, for it appoints most civil society members that are loyal to it.[59] This is why candidates submitted by a group of NGOs, following a long process of consultation, dialogue and public debates in all the provinces, were omitted in favour of candidates simply presented by civil society organisations close to the Frelimo party.[60]

2013 and 2014 electoral reform: Same pattern as 1994?

For the 2013 electoral process, a new electoral legislation was approved and a new CNE institutionalised. The refusal of the parliament, dominated by Frelimo, to review article 85 of the electoral law,[61] essential in the opposition's opinion for the 'transparency of the electoral process' resulted in the withdrawal of Renamo and a group of 12 small opposition parties. They accused the STAE of deliberately disorganising the voter registration and the counting process.[62] According to article 85, 'in the case of a discrepancy between the number of ballot papers in the ballot boxes and the number of voters, if the number of ballot papers in the ballot box is not greater than the number of registered voters the vote will be considered valid … in case of the number of ballot papers in the ballot box being higher than the number of registered voters, the vote will be considered null'. For Renamo, this article of law introduces the possibility of fraud, because it allows people (the

57 CIP/AWEPA (2009) Três contagens rápidas e exactas. *Boletim Sobre Processo Político em Moçambique* No. 32. Amsterdam: AWEPA.

58 MOE-UE (2009) *Relatório Final. Eleições Presidenciais, Legislativas e das Assembleias Provinciais de Outubro de 2009.* p. 15.

59 De Brito L (2012) Revisão da legislação eleitoral. Algumas propostas para o debate. In: L de Brito et al. (eds) *Desafios para Moçambique 2011.* Maputo: IESE. p. 97.

60 Ibid.

61 Sousa G (2013, 6 August) Renamo está fora das eleições autárquicas. *DW.* Available at http://www.dw.com/pt/renamo-est%C3%A1-fora-das-lei%C3%A7%C3%B5es-aut%C3%A1rquicas/a-17002492 [accessed 8 July 2016].

62 Da Silva R (2013, 30 July) Coligação de partidos moçambicanos fazem boicote às eleições. *DW.* Available at http://www.dw.com/pt/coligação-de-partidos-moçambicanos-faz-boicote-às-eleições/a-16987144 [accessed on 8 July 2016].

presidents of polling stations) to illegally stuff ballot boxes in favour of Frelimo candidates, thus disregarding the popular will.[63]

Renamo abandoned the electoral process and began armed attacks in the central region of Mozambique. In response to these armed attacks and criticism of civil society organisations, an agreement was reached in September 2013 to end hostilities. Then Frelimo agreed to a set of electoral reforms presented by Renamo and enforced by Law 9/2014.[64] According to this law, the CNE would be composed of 17 members, five being indicated by Frelimo; four by Renamo and one by MDM. The remaining seven members would be drawn from civil society organisations duly constituted and legalised within the national legal framework and nominated by political parties.[65]

Two of the main characteristics of the 2014 legislation were: (i) the (re)inclusion of representatives from the three political parties (Frelimo, Renamo and MDM) with parliamentary representation in the electoral administration body (STAE) at the province, district and city levels; and (ii) the indication of a member of each party for each one of the polling stations constituted for the 2014 elections. This legal arrangement aimed to ensure the credibility and transparency of the electoral process.[66] The new legislation includes a mechanism for the submission of electoral claims through district courts. Despite the underlying political foundation of these reforms, the politicisation of the electoral infrastructure contradicts international norms for the constitution of independent, neutral and professional bodies of electoral administration.[67] In reality, despite the integration of elements from civil society, the structure of the bodies of electoral administration, created by Law 9/2014, is similar to the model of the first electoral structures, created for the 1994 elections.

63 EISA (2015) *Relatório da equipa técnica de Avaliação do Eisa. Eleições autárquicas moçambicanas de 20 de Novembro de 2013*. Maputo: EISA.
64 Parlamento aprova revisão da lei eleitoral para silenciar armas (2014, 24 de Fevereiro) *O Pais*. p. 3.
65 Law 9/2014 of 12 March.
66 The provincial electoral commissions are now composed of 15 elements, compared to the previous 11. Of those 15, nine will be chosen by civil society and six chosen by political parties with parliamentary seats. Of those, three will be chosen by Frelimo, two by Renamo and one by MDM. With regards to the technical secretariat for electoral administration, parliament decided to reintroduce two assistant general-directors, one chosen by Frelimo and the other by Renamo. Besides the assistant directors, each national directorate of the STAE, namely the finance, operations and suffrage, and civic education and training directorates will have three assistant directors, one chosen by Frelimo, the other by Renamo and the third by MDM. Besides these directorate elements, STAE will have, centrally, the collaboration of 18 technicians from the political parties with parliamentary seats, in a proportion of nine chosen by Frelimo, eight by Renamo and one by MDM. At the provincial level, STAE directors also now have two assistants, presented by Frelimo and Renamo. This configuration will be replicated at the district and city levels. Besides the 'assistants', Frelimo, Renamo and MDM will appoint technicians to work with the STAE at district and city level. For these levels, Frelimo will choose three elements, Renamo two and MDM one.
67 Carter Center- Election Observation Mission (EOM) (2014) *Mozambique Presidential, Legislative, and Provincial Assembly Elections, October 2014*. Preliminary Statement. Maputo: Carter Center-EOM. p. 34.

Operational and institutional independence

According to legislation, the members of the CNE are independent, impartial and irremovable, and their functions cannot cease before the end of their appointed term.[68] The members of the CNE also have their own status, through which, during the respective term, they have the right to: (i) protection and security for themselves, their spouses and property; (ii) protocol vehicle, apart from vehicles with the option to purchase that were allocated individually; (iii) state housing or house rental subsidy; (iv) medical and pharmaceutical assistance for themselves, their wives and dependents under their responsibility; (v) business class travel.[69] The state also guarantees the members of the CNE a basic salary, subsidies and allowances, subsidies for water, lights, telephone, domestic employees, representation expenses, cell phone subsidy, fuel, maintenance and periodic repair of vehicles allocated individually.[70] Upon attaining five, ten, 15 and 20 years of effective service with the commission, the member receives special seniority payments corresponding to 15% of the basic payment, which should be successively incorporated into their payments.[71]

Apart from this, the members of the CNE do not lose seniority in their respective employment and cannot be prejudiced in promotions that they have in the meantime acquired or may acquire during the course of time.[72] They furthermore benefit from the most favourable social welfare regime applicable to members of state bodies[73] and, whatever may be their age, they may ask for voluntary retirement from any position, regardless of the ruling of the medical board, within 180 days following the cessation of functions, so long as they have completed two successive or interpolated terms.[74]

The mandates of the CNE members end when the new members take office. This means that there are no term limits for the members of the CNE. But they could cease their functions before the term of office when there are some of the following situations: (i) death or permanent disability; (ii) resignation and (iii) illegal acts inconsistent with the exercise of the function. It is the responsibility of the CNE to verify the occurrence of those situations outlined above. The cessation of the functions of a member is announced by the president of the CNE and published in the *National Gazette*.[75]

In a country where about 90% of the population lives on not more than USD 2 a day, with high unemployment levels, very low salaries for the civil service, and completely non-existent social welfare mechanisms, allocating this set of benefits to the members of the CNE, who carry out activities only during the electoral period, has an impact on their independence in the exercise of their duties. Despite being a state agency, independent and

68 Article 19 of Law 6/2013 of 22 February.
69 Article 26 of Act 6/2013.
70 Article 28 of Act 6/2013.
71 Article 30 of Act 6/2013.
72 Article 32 of Act 6/2013.
73 Article 33 of Act 6/2013.
74 Article 34 of Act 6/2013.
75 Article 22 of Law 6/2013 of 22 February.

impartial, the members of the CNE are selected by political parties; they thus do their best to please their parties' leadership in order to retain their employment in the commission.

Technical operations

Normally the technical operations of elections are poor in Mozambique. Next we will discuss the execution of some of these activities. We focus on those that affect the transparency and credibility of the electoral process during the different reforms operated in the electoral bodies, namely: voter registration, registration of candidates, the voting process and results tabulation.

Voter registration

Voter registration in Mozambique follows the same logic as the electoral process. Due to the poor reliability of the processes of voter registration and the opposition parties' high distrust of the bodies of electoral administration, a new registration and/or update of the registration is undertaken for each electoral act. The law that governs voter registration[76] ordains that 'all citizens resident in the country or overseas, over eighteen years old on the date of the elections register and update their registration every elections'.[77] This involves sending out staff to register eligible voters.[78] Parties supervise the registration process. The preliminary voters' roll is verified and then published by the CNE in the official gazette. This contains the total number of registered voters, code, location of the registration book and respective number of voters.[79] The CNE/STAE are the only bodies responsible for voter registration.

Registration was done manually for the 1994, 1998 and 2004 elections. It was updated before the elections of 1999, 2003 and 2004 based on the barcode reading. The updates of 1998 and 2004 were highly contested by Renamo, which accused the STAE of bias.[80] Renamo's grievances centred around: (i) errors resulting from the transcriptions of the books in 1998/99 and the lack of a unified source of data; (ii) inaccuracies and inconsistencies of the data recorded in the voter registration books in 2004;[81] (iii) refusal of the CNE and STAE to supply political parties with a detailed list of polling stations and their respective electoral book numbers;[82] (iv) discrepancies between registration staff operating in the southern urban areas, on the one hand, and those working in the centre and northern rural areas, on the other hand. According to the reports of the international observation missions, brigades in the urban areas registered four times more voters than the brigades in the rural areas of the centre and north, where Renamo was politically

76 Law 8/2014 of 12 March.

77 Article 7.

78 Article 10.

79 Article 38.

80 Association of European Parliamentarians with Africa (*AWEPA*) (1998, 18 March) Local elections delayed one month. *Mozambique Peace Process Bulletin* No. 20. Amsterdam: AWEPA. pp. 6–7.

81 Wall A (2010) *Recenseamento Eleitoral em África. Uma Análise Comparativa.* Johannesburg: Electoral Institute for Sustainable Democracy in Africa (EISA). p. 226.

82 Carter Center- Election Observation Mission (EOM) (2005) *Observação das Eleições de Moçambique.* Final Report. Atlanta: Carter Center-EOM. p. 12.

strong.[83] This implied that the basic principle of registration, according to which enrolment must be easily accessible to all, was systematically violated.[84] At fault here was the lack of administrative capacity.[85] The EMB was consequently forced to create a new system for voter registration.

In 2007, a new registration law was approved.[86] This led to computerisation of voter registration. Despite this innovation, registration for the 2009 elections was marked by significant problems. Besides the late delivery of the equipment which affected the possibility of testing it and using it while training the staff involved, the equipment also broke down[87] and was not sufficiently robust to work in rural areas.[88] These problems – insufficient material and lack of staff – tended to affect opposition strongholds, and resulted in poor voter enrolment.[89] Renamo and MDM argued that, on the contrary, Frelimo's strongholds were not affected by similar problems.[90] Observers also noticed that, for the 2008 elections in general, the CNE lacked transparency, which could have improved trust in the process.[91]

For example, for the 2013/14 electoral process, despite the amendments made to the legislation, discrepancies in the final number of voters announced by the CNE in Gaza, Nampula, Sofala and Zambézia provinces were strongly criticised by opposition parties,[92] because they affected negatively their electoral results in legislative and provincial elections. Parties that had finalised their applications could not amend them.[93] As a result of all these problems, the EMB is not trusted by the public. This has meant that the opposition and the citizenry in general are prone to accusing the governing party of electoral fraud, even for genuine problems.

Candidacy processes

The constitution and electoral law[94] set out the process of registration of candidates. Candidacies should be presented by political parties, coalitions of legally established parties,

83 Ibid.: 15

84 Office of the United Nations High Commissioner for Human Rights (1966) International Covenant on Civil and Political Rights. Available at http://www.ohchr.org/Documents/ProfessionalInterest/ccpr.pdf [accessed 7 July 2016].

85 Rosário DM (2013) Uma reflexão sobre o calendário e o recenseamento eleitoral para as eleições autárquicas de 2013. *Ideias* 50.

86 Law 9/2007 of 26 February.

87 MOE-UE (2009) *Relatório Final, Moçambique 2009, Eleições Presidenciais, Legislativas e das Assembleias provinciais*. Maputo: MOE-UE. p. 7.

88 Wall A (2010) *Recenseamento Eleitoral em África. Uma Análise Comparativa*. Johannesburg: Electoral Institute for Sustainable Democracy in Africa (EISA).

89 Ibid.: 231.

90 Observatório Eleitoral (2010) *Relatório do projecto 'Observatório Eleitoral' 2009–2010*. Maputo: Observatório Eleitoral. p. 5.

91 MOE-UE (2009) *Relatório Final, Moçambique 2009, Eleições Presidenciais, Legislativas e das Assembleias provinciais*. Maputo: MOE-UE. p. 4.

92 CIP/AWEPA (2013) Recenseamento atinge 85% no meio de problemas técnicos. *Boletim Sobre o Processo Político em Moçambique* No. 54. Amsterdam: AWEPA. p. 7.

93 Carter Center- Election Observation Mission (EOM) (2014) *Mozambique Presidential, Legislative, and Provincial Assembly Elections, October 2014*. Preliminary Statement. Maputo: Carter Center-EOM. p. 11.

94 Law 8/2013 of 22 February.

or by groups of citizens, supported by 10 000 signatures[95] of citizens who are registered voters,[96] and must be recognised by a notary. The submission of candidacies for the post of president of the republic is made to the Constitutional Council (CC), up to 120 days before the anticipated date of the elections.[97] The CC is also responsible for the analysis and validation of candidacies, and its decision is final. The presentation of candidacies for legislative elections is done at the initiative of the relevant bodies of political parties or coalitions of political parties. All citizens who are registered voters may participate in these elections and present their candidacy to the CNE up to 120 days before the elections.[98]

Appeals against the rejection of candidates must be submitted to the CNE within a deadline of five days. The CNE makes a declaration and submits complaints to the CC, together with the supporting documents and electoral materials.[99] This has largely ensured inclusivity and greater level of electoral participation. The one complaint that arose in the 2009 elections, where six candidates were declined registration for presidential election, was due to ignorance of regulations.[100]

The process of candidacies for the legislative and provincial assembly elections was marked by controversy. It was governed by various legal documents[101] which created confusion both among electoral administration bodies and political parties. The main law that governed the process (Act 15/2009) was inconsistent with the other laws of 2007. The main problems related to the distinction between the various phases of the process of submission of candidacies and on the stipulated period for verification of documents and eligibility of candidates.[102] The CNE did not respect its own schedule and applied the majority of the provisions of Act 15/2009 and Deliberation 10/CNE/2009 in relation to the procedures for the presentation of candidacies. Thus, from a total of 24 parties and five coalitions that submitted their lists, the CNE rejected the full lists submitted by ten political parties or coalitions and rejected some of the lists submitted by 17 political parties or coalitions. Only two political parties had all of their lists approved. Of these 19 parties, five were accepted in more than seven electoral constituencies.

For the provincial assembly elections, the lists of four political parties were approved. However, in 64 of the 141 electoral constituencies, only one party ran: Frelimo and this constituted a significant limitation to the right of choice of the electorate.[103] Such exclusion exacerbated the lack of trust by the political parties on the impartiality of the electoral

---

95 Article 135.
96 Article 137.
97 Article 136.
98 Article 117.
99 Article 184.
100 Conselho Constitucional (2009) *Acórdão n.° 30/CC/2Q09:Valida e proclama os resultados das eleições Presidenciais, Legislativas e das Assembleias Provinciais, de 28 de Outubro de 2009*. Repeated names, voter registration numbers that did not correspond with the names and falsified signatures.
101 Law 7/2007 of 26 February; Law 10/2007 of 5 June; Law 15/2009 of 9 April Deliberation 10/CNE/2009 of 14 May 2009.
102 Article 131 and subsequent articles of Act 10/2007 of 5 June.
103 MOE-UE (2009) *Relatório-Final, Eleições Presidenciais, Legislativas e das Assembleias provinciais de 2009*. Maputo: MOE-UE. p. 18.

administration bodies, even more so because the arguments behind the exclusion of these political parties[104] were never clear. For the 2014 electoral process, 11 candidates submitted their candidacies and three were selected; Filipe Nyusi of Frelimo, Afonso Dhlakama of Renamo and Daviz Simango of the MDM. No women submitted their candidacy. For the legislative and provincial assembly elections, 30 parties and coalitions of parties were selected; only four were excluded from the process.

Voting, counting and verification

Despite different constraints faced in the Mozambican electoral process, it is agreed that there is transparency and respect for the procedures in the voting process. However, the same cannot be said regarding the procedures for the verification of results. It is considered unduly long, complex and not transparent.[105] In the 1999 presidential and legislative elections, for instance, observers and the media were denied access to the venue where verification took place.[106]

Despite reforms in legislation having introduced more than one level of verification (district/city), this legislative operation did not bring about improvements to the transparency of the verification process. However, according to interviews with political parties, the CNE did not take into account the results obtained at district level, but gave greater priority to the data on general verification resulting from a new counting process conducted in secret by the STAE.[107]

This was the case in the 2009 elections. In these elections, for example, while the average participation in most districts of the country varied between 30–40%, in various districts of Gaza, Tete and Niassa provinces, the average participation was 90 or 100%,[108]

---

104 Observatório Eleitoral (2010) *Relatório do projecto 'Observatório Eleitoral' 2009–2010.* Maputo: Observatório Eleitoral. p. 13.

105 The reform of electoral legislation in 2007 introduced district or city verification, with verification taking place at four levels, as opposed to the previous three which were in force until the 2004 elections. See: Act 3/1999 of 22 February, Act 7/2004 of 17 June. In the 1994, 1999 and 2004 elections, the verification of results occurred at three levels: partial verification at the polling station; intermediate verification at provincial level; and national verification at central level. Provincial verification falls under the responsibility of the CPE, which must centralise the results of the respective polling stations for each of the districts. Counting is carried out based on the acts and polling station notices and on all the documents submitted to the electoral commissions. Regarding national verification, national centralisation and general verification of the election results, as well as the distribution of mandates, this falls under the responsibility of the CNE. The CNE should decide in the first place on the contested votes and verify the votes classified as null.

106 Carter Center- Election Observation Mission (EOM) (2000) *Observing 1999 Elections in Mozambique.* Final Report. Atlanta: Carter Center-EOM. In reality, many notices originating from the rural areas were excluded from the national centralisation process, because the deadline for dissemination of the legally established election results had passed.

107 Interviews with Salomão Moiana – CNE commissioner (civil society), 16 September 2015, and António Namburete, Deputy in the Assembly of the Republic for Renamo. 18 September 2015; CIP/AWEPA (2013) *Recenseamento atinge 85% no meio de problemas técnicos. Boletim sobre o processo político em Moçambique* 54. p. 4

108 Carter Center- Election Observation Mission (EOM) (2005) *Observação das Eleições de Moçambique.* Final Report. Atlanta: Carter Center-EOM. p. 52.

and Frelimo obtained 100% of votes. This had a great impact on the distribution of seats in provincial assemblies. The CNE has been reluctant to investigate allegations of electoral fraud.[109] For example, in the municipal elections of 2008, when more than 10 000 additional votes for Frelimo were discovered in the city of Beira, the chairman of the CNE declared that 'they were votes resulting from technical faults, not the result of a deliberate act of fraud'.[110] However, in 2013, the CC annulled the municipal elections of Gurué due to fraud committed at the district and provincial verifications. This led to Renamo insisting that the CC be allocated an investigative role to probe allegations, which was effected in 2013/14.

However, despite these and other reforms, the process of verification did not improve. Now the process was even characterised by chaos and disorder.[111] There were no guidelines from the STAE, which led to each district electoral commission creating its own verification system.[112] In the 2014 presidential and legislative election, for example, district verification in the city of Pemba was carried out covertly by the STAE for the province.[113] Renamo and the MDM rejected the results of these elections and expressed their discontent with the lack of transparency. They pointed out various irregularities and suspicious acts of manipulation and fabrication of results, both at district and provincial level, by electoral officials at these levels.[114] Electoral officials filled ballot boxes to inflate the vote count for the governing party.

Dispute resolution mechanism

Efficient, transparent and fair procedures for the resolution of election disputes are an essential part of the proper operation of electoral processes. The Mozambican election act indicates a set of mechanisms for the resolution of electoral disputes. According to the law, the irregularities occurring during voting and verification can be submitted for appeals, so long as complaints or objections have been presented at the time of verification.[115] In the 2009 elections, the mechanism for the resolution of electoral conflicts did not offer solutions for opposition political parties. There have been cases of chairs of polling stations refusing to receive complaints about voting, counting, etc.[116] which made

109 MOE-UE (2009) *Relatório Final. Eleições Presidenciais, Legislativas e das Assembleias Provinciais de Outubro de 2009.* Maputo: MOE-UE. p. 15.
110 Da Costa L (2015, 5 December) Situação dos votos a mais na beira. *CanalMozambique.*
111 CIP/AWEPA (2014) Apuramento distrital aberto e caótico. *Boletim Sobre Processo Político em Moçambique* 56: 7.
112 MOE-UE (2014) *Eleições Gerais de 15 de Outubro de 2014. Relatório Final.* Maputo: MOE-UE. p. 38.
113 Interview with Salomão Moiana - CNE commissioner (civil society), 16 September 2015 The city of Pemba is the point of imbalance between a pro-Frelimo north and a pro-Renamo south. Thus it was necessary for this verification to be carried out properly. Counting was carried out at the provincial STAE and the minutes were handed over on the next day, with the results of the city verification completed. Despite the complaint, the CNE did not do anything to correct this situation.
114 MOE-UE (2014) *Eleições Gerais de 15 de Outubro de 2014. Relatório Final.* Maputo: MOE-UE. p. 38.
115 Article 183 of Act 7/2007 of 26 February 2007.
116 Cistac G, Marquez T & Chiziane E (2012) *Contribuições a revisão da legislação eleitoral moçambicana.* Maputo: KAS, CEDE e CEPKA.

many complaints unfounded. The difficulty of bringing an appeal and objection which needs to pass through a set of three electoral commissions (CDE, DPE and CNE) and is generally rejected for procedural reasons, also constitutes a problem. Therefore, one of the recommendations of the international observation teams for the electoral administration bodies was: 'they received complaints from political parties on irregularities occurring during voting, counting and verification, which were rejected at the polling station, and which prevented an adequate and timely response by the election authorities with regard to any complaint'.[117]

Therefore the 2013 and 2014 amendments to electoral legislation introduced measures against the members of polling stations who unjustifiably refused to receive written complaints by the delegates.[118] It also transferred the system of disputes of the electoral administration body to the judiciary, giving district judges, in the first instance, the authority to deal with all types of illegal electoral acts and irregularities.[119] This legislation introduced three levels for the resolution of electoral litigation and conflicts in the legal framework. The first one was the principle of prior complaint – where the election complaint should be submitted to the electoral authority where the irregularity occurred; the second was the involvement of district judges and the third was the intervention of the CC, which, apart from constituting the last instance of appeal,[120] also became an investigative body.[121]

There were a number of criticisms levelled at the new electoral dispute resolution system. First of these was, the introduction of the principle of prior complaint, which one of the judge counsellors of the CC described in the following terms:

> I understand that the principle of prior complaint, a fundamental presupposition of the electoral dispute, in the form in which it is designed, is complex, unachievable and unfair and only serves to support the irregularities and some of them, due to their profile, were brought about intentionally.[122]

---

117 MOE-UE (2009) *Relatório final das eleições Presidenciais, Legislativas e das Assembleias Provinciais de 2009*. Maputo: MOE-UE. p. 40.

118 Article 232 of Act 8/2013 of 22 February.

119 Carter Center- Election Observation Mission (EOM) (2014) *Mozambique Presidential, Legislative, and Provincial Assembly Elections, October 2014*. Preliminary Statement. Maputo: Carter Center-EOM. p. 16.

120 Article 192, 193 of Act 12/2014 of 23 April.

121 This prerogative was used in the 2013 municipal elections when the constitutional council, after allegedly failing because this party did not respect the 'principle of prior complaint', having decided that 'irregular facts occurring during voting and partial, district or general verification which are of an administrative or procedural nature can be appreciated by the CNE, so long as it has previously been a matter of complaint or objection presented at the polling station where the fact was verified, immediately they became aware of it', but proceeded to annul the elections for Gurué district.

122 Frank M (2012) *Validation and Declaration of the Results of Presidential, Legislative and Provincial Assembly Elections of 15 October 2014* Avaialble at http://www.cconstitucional.org.mz/content/download/1043/5926/file/Acordao%2021%20CC%202014.pdf [accessed 30 September 2015].

Second, it does not make reference to the procedures and deadlines for complaints related to irregularities during provincial verification. Third, it does not make reference to how to deal with irregularities not related to the verification process involving CDEs and CPEs. Fourth, it does not stipulate deadlines for the CC to announce decisions validating the final results of the elections.[123] Fifth, it presents deadlines which represent restrictions for district tribunals, due to the fact that the judges do not have sufficient time to collect independent evidence in order to make decisions.[124] And lastly, the district judges' have insufficient experience with electoral law and lack the time or tools to implement the new system of electoral disputes.[125]

Despite these criticisms, a new form of prevention of electoral disputes was introduced, albeit in an incipient form, consisting of the 'committees for the resolution of electoral conflicts'.[126] This new mechanism was introduced to implement techniques for the prevention, mitigation and management of electoral conflicts and to improve the mechanisms of contact, exchange of information and experiences in the resolution of problems, that would give credibility to the electoral process. These forms should be institutionalised through their incorporation into electoral legislation.

Stakeholders

The success of elections is largely determined by the relationship between the different stakeholders in the electoral process. Inclusiveness, transparency and taking responsibility are essential for creating public trust in the elections. The European Union observer mission, for instance, recommended, at the end of the 2009 electoral process, that the EMBs establish 'a genuine dialogue with all the stakeholders of the electoral process, including civil society, with the objective of improving the electoral system and meeting the expectations of a better administration of future elections'.[127] This recommendation was in response to the criticism levelled by political parties against the electoral administration bodies, who were accused of not having efficient dialogue, information-sharing and communication mechanisms at crucial points in the electoral process. When the review of electoral legislation in 2014[128] granted the commission panel the authority to generally meet with the coordinators of the working committees (the STAE, leaders of political parties,

123 EU-EOM (2014) Final Report of the General Elections of 15 October 2014. Maputo: EU-EOM.
124 Pereira J & Nhanale E (2014) The 2014 General Elections in Mozambique. Analysis of Fundamental Questions. Johannesburg: OSISA. p. 16
125 Interview with Tomas Timbane, President of the Lawyers Association of Mozambique, Maputo, 15 September 2015. De Noronha N (2014, 4 September) CNE de Moçambique propõe comités para resolução de conflitos eleitorais. DW. http://www.dw.com/pt/cne-de-mo%C3%A7ambique-prop%C3%B5e-comit%C3%A9s-para-resolu%C3%A7%C3%A3o-de-conflitos-eleitorais/a-17902805 [accessed on 8 July 2016]
126 Ibid.
127 MOE-UE (2010) Missão de Observação eleitoral da União Europeia. Relatório Final, Eleições presidenciais, legislativas e das assembleias provinciais. Outubro de 2009. Maputo: MOE-UE.
128 Act 30/2014 of 26 September.

the media and other bodies),[129] the door was opened for the strengthening of relationships between the electoral administration bodies and other stakeholders.

In this context, during the last elections of 2014, the electoral administration bodies held regular meetings with political parties, civil society organisations, media bodies, and chairs of national electoral commissions in Southern African countries, ambassadors accredited to Mozambique, religious institutions and national and international observation missions, in order to discuss and update the various stages of the electoral process.[130] In addition, electoral administration bodies participated in round tables on electoral justice and on the participation of civil society in electoral processes, which were organised by civil society platforms.[131] This was a marked improvement.[132] However, there were still some questions relating to accreditation of observers and inspectors of political parties, and operation of the press centre.

ICT infrastructure

Utilisation of information and communication technology (ICT) improves access and participation in electoral processes. Mozambique was one of the first countries in Africa to have a policy on ICT in 2002. The first experience of the use of ICT in the electoral process was during voter registration for the municipal elections of 2008.[133] However, the late delivery of the equipment (which affected the possibility of testing and capacity-building of the staff involved in voter registration), the lack of robust structures enabling it to operate in the rural areas, and frequent breakdowns,[134] caused a wave of mistrust by society and particularly by Renamo in relation to the reliability of this process.[135] In fact, the opposition considered these problems to be evidence of manipulation of the CNE/STAE. Despite the problems described, and their imperfections, ICT plays a fundamental role in the production of voter registration cards and data collection, which enables the verification of records and detection of duplicate entries.[136] This is a major advance in the prevention of inflation of voter registration data.

Mistrust of the ICT, however, remains strong. During the 2009 elections, the EMBs were asked to disseminate the details of the computerised processes used in voter registration, so that an independent audit of the verification software could be carried out, and they refused. This reinforced mistrust. Even the chairperson of the CNE, Sheikh Abdul

---

129 Article 11/B of Act 30/2014 of 26 September.

130 Resolution no. 2/CNE/2015 of 14 May.

131 Organizações da sociedade civil: melhorar articulação com os órgãos eleitorais (2014, Janeiro) *Notícias Online*. www.jornalnoticias.co.mz/index.php/politica/10429-organizacoes-da-sociedade-civil-melhorar-articulacao-com-os-orgaos-eleitorais [accessed 7 July 2016].

132 Carter Center-Election Observation Mission (EOM) (2014) *Mozambique Presidential, Legislative, and Provincial Assembly Elections, October 2014*. Preliminary Statement. Maputo: Carter Center-EOM.

133 This new system was financed directly by funding from the government of Mozambique and cost about USD 15 million; the general costs of establishment of the new records in 2007/2008 cost about USD 41 million.

134 Panos London (2010) *O desafio da inclusão digital em Moçambique*. p. 3.

135 Avaria sistemática de 'Mobiles' fragiliza censo eleitoral (2009, 19 June) *Nampula Fax*.

136 Wall A (2010) *Recenseamento eleitoral em África. O caso de Moçambique*. Johannesburg: EISA p. 207.

Carimo, admitted that 'it was necessary to improve the dynamics and open the doors of the CNE more'.[137] Despite this admission, however, the ICT operations remain closed to public scrutiny. This has even stalled any meaningful discussion on the introduction of, for example, electronic voting – a tool that could play a decisive role in the verification of results and speeding up of electoral process, making them more transparent and credible.

Gender representation

The increased participation of women in politics, as well as their influence in governance processes, has been widely debated by various spheres of society. The Mozambican state regards the participation of women as a way of developing the country. In 2006, the government of Mozambique approved the national gender policy and its implementation strategy, with the objective of promoting gender equality, respect for human rights and strengthening the participation of women in the development of the country. The chart below shows the changes in the composition of the CNE from 1994 to 2014.

Figure 1: Composition of the CNE by gender

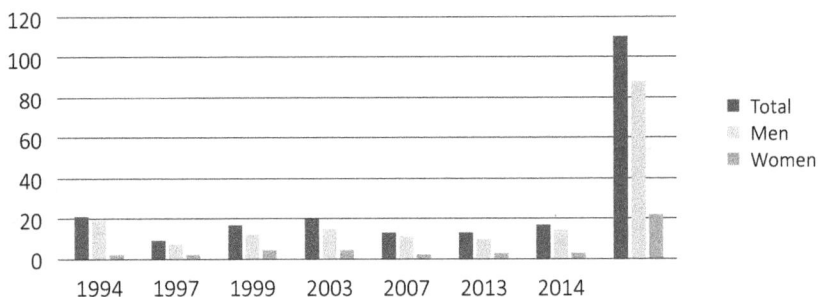

Source: Data culled from editions of the government's official gazette, 1994 to 2014.

The under-representation of women in this body is evident. The highest average of women in the CNE was attained in 1999. Women represented 29% of the members of the CNE, that is, five out of 17. Only in 2003 did a woman occupy the post of deputy chair of the commission for the first time. At the lower level, (provincial and district commissions), this scenario is worse. No woman leads the 11 provincial election commissions[138] and only five out of 22 women occupy the position of deputy chair;[139] and of the 444 chairs and deputy chairs of the commissions at the district level, seven women occupy the position of chairs and only 21 women occupy the position of deputy chair. Only the provinces of Inhambane (seven) and Gaza (four) have a higher number of female deputy chairs.[140] This

---

137 Presidente da CNE promete nova dinâmica e mais abertura nos processos eleitorais (2013, 27 May)
     O País. p. 3.
138 Resolution 4/CNE/2013 of 9 April.
139 Resolution 5/CNE/2014 of 28 March.
140 Resolution 11/CNE/2014 of 17 April.

shows that, despite the advances recorded in Mozambique in terms of gender policies and implementation by civil society of programmes[141] that support and provide incentives for the participation of female politicians, there is a perception that 'politics' is the domain of men. Cultural and economic factors which, for example, affect the school attendance of females place women in a weaker educational situation compared to men.

Electoral funding of political parties

Mozambique is one of the few countries of the southern region of Africa in which legislation covers the financing of the electoral campaigns of candidates and political parties for the general elections (presidential and legislative). The financing of campaigns is governed by Act 7/2007,[142] which grants authority to the CNE to define the criteria for the distribution of funds.[143] Other articles in this act[144] govern the criteria for accountability and prohibition of the use of public assets in the election campaign. One-third of this amount is granted to three presidential candidates in equal parts. Another third is distributed to parties that are running for the assembly of the republic in accordance with the number of electoral constituencies in which they are running. The final portion is allocated to parties whose candidates were selected for provincial assemblies. Each tranche is granted by means of an accounting process, with the supporting documents of amounts received attached, containing details of expenses and the respective invoices corresponding to the receipts for original purchase and sale.[145]

The CNE is responsible for following up on and supervising electoral accounts, and the STAE is responsible for the corresponding execution, and may entrust its technical responsibility to a company that is specialised in financial auditing to verify that the accounts are regular.[146] All those running for election should account for funds they accessed within 60 days after the declaration of the results of the elections[147] and the CNE has a deadline of 60 days to verify compliance and publication of the results of the accounts.[148]

According to the CNE, in the 2014 elections, most of the parties justified their use of the funds, with the exception of some small parties which did not provide proper justification on the third tranche that had been allocated. Political parties, mainly those outside of parliament, have the perception that the CNE does not adequately implement the law, because the CNE is more demanding when it comes to the smallest parties, making them follow all the painful procedures for the justification of expenses, leaving the large parties unpunished, even without having to justify the amounts.[149]

---

141 Programme for women in politics and women in democracy implemented by IBIS/Fórum Mulher in some regions of the country.
142 Article 36 of Act 7/2007 of 26 February.
143 Deliberation 54/CNE/2014 of 12 June.
144 Articles 39 and 40 of Act 7/2007 of 26 February.
145 Number 10, sub-paragraph b.
146 Number 10, sub-paragraph g.
147 Number 11, sub-paragraph a.
148 Number 11, sub-paragraph d.
149 Magolowondo A, Falguera E & Matsimbe Z (2012) *Regulating Political Party Financing: Some Insights from*

Despite the CNE having legal authority to manage election campaign funds granted under Act 7/2007, it does not have any administrative structure. It also lacks material authority, since it does not have the staff (number and technical quality) to verify if the supporting documents provided are valid; nor does it have the mechanisms, or the authority to apply measures against political parties that do not provide proper accounting of funds received.[150] Upon making a retrospective analysis of the allocation of public funds, we noted that, despite the CNE having an important role granted by the law for the funding of political parties, only in 2010 did it publish a detailed report on the funds allocated[151] and used by political parties during the campaign. Most of the time, the CNE limits itself to describing the parties which benefit from the funds and their level of justification. Even worse is the fact that the parties that have not received other tranches (due to a lack of supporting documents) are not subject to any penalty, which makes it possible for them to benefit again from public funds in subsequent elections.

Due to the lack of enforcement the party in power, Frelimo, uses and abuses state resources to finance its election campaign, which gives them the advantage over the other competing political parties.

Challenges

The constant change of members for each electoral process prevents the conservation of an institutional memory. This results in repetition of errors and irregularities observed in previous elections.[152] While it's true that the continuity of members in the different commissions would guarantee organisational and institutional continuity[153] and the implementation of the lessons learnt in previous processes, the clientelist way in which these members are chosen does not contribute to institutional consolidation. The continuity of the members indicated by the parties to perform their tasks in the commission depends on their loyalty to the mandate granted by the party.[154] The absence of accountability and

the Praxis. Strömsberg, Sweden: International IDEA & Netherlands Institute for Multiparty Democracy (NIMD). Available at http://www.idea.int/publications/regulating-political-party-financing/loader. cfm?csModule=security/getfile&pageid=57052 [accessed on 7 July 2016]. p. 14.

150 António Namburete, deputy in the Assembly of the Republic for Renamo, interview held in Maputo, 18 September 2015.

151 Deliberation no. 1/CNE/2010 of 28 April. A matter that should be discussed with regards to the public funding of the elections in Mozambique is respect for compliance with the dates for the allocation of amounts to the political parties, because it causes very significant imbalances amongst the parties. The other issue is related to the fact that the law does not indicate the maximum limit of the funds to be used by the parties and candidates for the campaign and does not determine any type of measure for political parties when using state assets, which in a way helps parties in power, (municipal and country) regarding the use of public resources for electoral purposes.

152 Interview with Sheik Abdul Carimo and António Chipanga, president and vice-president of CNE. Maputo, 31 August 2015.

153 ECF/EISA (2003) Princípios para a gestão, Monitorização e Observação Eleitoral na região da SADC. Johannesburg: ECT/EISA.

154 We refer to professionalism in the Weber sense. Members with competency, professional merit and knowledge of electoral matters.

reporting mechanisms for the performance of members within the commission further worsens the problem. In a patronage system,[155] as is the case in Mozambique, ensuring permanence in the national elections commission represents a set of material, professional and administrative advantages[156] which must be taken into account.

Although the law provides for the permanent subordination of the STAE to the CNE, and the direct nomination of the director of the STAE by the president of the CNE,[157] the cooperation between these two bodies of electoral administration, especially at the base (province, district and city) is often deficient. The CNE is incapable of exercising a hierarchic control and leadership to ensure the implementation of the law.[158] For example, during the 2003 and 2004 elections serious conflicts between these two bodies were recorded, with the STAE often imposing itself as a parallel body to the CNE, challenging it with decisions and regulations.[159] In the 2013 local elections, observers were not authorised in time to follow the electoral process in the city of Beira[160] and delegates on the MDM list were excluded from the polling stations by the STAE. Although the president of the CNE instructed the local elections commission to issue authorisation, this instruction was ignored.[161]

In the last electoral process of 2014, the technical secretariat for electoral administration continued to issue parallel guidelines at the central level, sometimes in contradiction to those issued by the CNE. An example of this is the STAE's infringement of the CNE guideline regarding the polling station, in terms of its composition, functions, members and role of members indicated by political parties with parliamentary seats'. This guideline indicated that: 'of the seven members which compose the polling station, the members indicated by political parties have the noble function of ensuring the representativeness of opposition candidates and parties and assume the function of first, second and third scrutiniser in the polling station where they are posted'.[162] However, the STAE issued a different guideline, assigning the position of first scrutiniser to the members proposed by Frelimo, with no legal basis. Let's recall that the 'first scrutiniser' besides being responsible for the electoral roll during voting, is also responsible for certification and qualification of the ballot papers announced by the president of the polling station.[163] These are the most

---

155 Chabal P & Daloz J-P (1999) *Disorder as Political Instrument*. Oxford: James Currey & Indiana University Press.

156 This question must also be linked to the problem of the numerical composition of the National Elections Commission itself. The Mozambican CNE is composed of many elements.

157 Article 50 of Law 6/2013 of 22 February.

158 MOE-UE (2009) *Relatório Final. Eleições Presidenciais, Legislativas e das Assembleias Provinciais de Outubro de 2009*. Maputo: MOE-UE. p. 24.

159 Mazula B (2005) Reflectir as eleições a partir da teoria da elipse política. In: B Mazula (ed.) *Moçambique: Eleições Gerais de 2004 . Um Olhar do Observatório Eleitoral*. Maputo: UEM University Press. p. 17.

160 Observatório Eleitoral (2014) *Relatório de Observação do Processo Eleitoral de 2013*. Maputo: Observatório Eleitoral. p. 13.

161 CIP/AWEPA (2013) Frelimo ganha 50 municípios e MDM se impõe. *Boletim Sobre Processo Político em Moçambique* No. 54. Amsterdam: AWEPA. p. 3.

162 Article 8 of Guideline no. 1/CNE/2014 of 8 August. Maputo: CNE.

163 CNE/STAE (2014) *Manual Eleitoral. Eleições Gerais Presidenciais, Legislativas e das Assembleias Provinciais*.

relevant functions, which created a situation in contradiction to the principle of equality between political parties.[164] This problem persists despite the recommendations drafted by the international observation missions and observers.

Need for better funding

Governments should adequately finance electoral administration bodies so that they can organise credible, legitimate and transparent elections. The CNE of Mozambique has the status, staffing and budget for this.[165] However, this budget is not approved by the legislature, but is covered under the General State Budget,[166] which hinders the CNE from exercising effective independence in relation to the government of the day. In the 2014 electoral process, a large part of the budget used to fund expenses on staffing, goods and services, communication and training of the bodies and electoral agents was provided by the state and a few partners.[167] In accordance with electoral structures, these funds were insufficient, because they only covered 80% of the needs, which stopped the electoral administration bodies from implementing some activities programmed for the 2014 electoral process.[168] This created problems such as, lack of voting material and adequate polling stations, as well as blocking others voters from voting, especially predominantly Renamo areas.[169]

Evaluation and assessment

Although not considered official, one of the mechanisms for the assessment of the performance of the Mozambican electoral bodies is implemented through reports by national and international observation missions[170] and public opinion surveys such as Afrobarometer and Comparative National Electoral Project (CNEP). Since the 1994 electoral process, different international observation missions have prepared reports that analyse the electoral process and produce recommendations on the performance of the EMBs. Despite enumerating various irregularities – some of them serious – and criticism mainly related to the final settlement stage, the reports of the missions of international observation state that 'despite the irregularities having negative effects, they do not

Maputo: CNE/STAE.

164 EU-EOM (2014) *General elections of 15 October 2014. Final Report*. Maputo: EU-EOM. p. 40.

165 Article 2, Number 3 of Act 6/2013 of 22 February.

166 Article 61 of Act 6/2013 of 22 February.

167 About USD 121.8 million was allocated by the state and the rest, USD 110 827 000, was to be used exclusively for training, was allocated by the cooperation partners. See Resolution no. 2/CNE/2015. The conversion of meticais into dollars was done using the average exchange rate of 2014, obtained from data from the Bank of Mozambique.

168 Joint interview with the president and vice-president of the CNE, Maputo, 31 October 2015; interview with the director-general of the STAE, Maputo, 2 September 2015.

169 Ainda as queixas da renamo: CNE recomenda ao cc para chumbar recurso (2014) *Noticias Online*. Available at http://www.jornalnoticias.co.mz/index.php/politica/26653-ainda-as-queixas-da-renamo-cne-recomenda-ao-cc-para-chumbar-recurso [accessed 23 September 2015].

170 United Nations, European Union, Carter Center, African Union, Commonwealth, CPLP, SADC, EISA and national electoral observation that became prevalent as of 2004.

change the final result of the election'. These irregularities lead Mozambican society to distrust electoral institutions. According to the last Afrobarometer survey, Mozambicans say that 'the CNE does not guarantee impartiality and independence in the supervision of elections'.[171] Therefore, only 48% of the Mozambicans say that the CNE performs its function with neutrality and independence and based on the law.[172]

Apart from presenting important recommendations to improve the performance of the EMBs, the incorporation of these recommendations in electoral reform is not binding. Generally they are missions of short duration,[173] with the observation focused on large urban centres, voting and verification. There is little attention paid to the voter registration phase, which is fundamental for electoral credibility and transparency. It is necessary to empower civil society organisations and create permanent networks with international electoral institutions in order to exercise this role of supervision of voter registration without high costs. This will allow the missions of electoral observations to draw the recommendations and make judgements based on overall electoral process and not based only on the vote. This procedure can help to make the elections more credible in many countries within the region, including Mozambique.

Within the country, the 2013 and 2014 electoral legislation lays out conditions for evaluating the performance of the EMBs. Evaluation is undertaken by individual parties, not by any independent statutory body. For example, the performance of some commissioners during the general legislative, presidential and provincial assembly elections of 2015 was evaluated by the last National Council held in the city of Beira.[174] In this meeting, the delegates to the meeting accused the Renamo members in the CNE of incompetence, lack of zeal and failure to comply with its obligations, which resulted in the occurrence of fraud. At the end of the conference, they demanded their resignation from the commission.[175] This shows that the members of the CNE provide more accountability to their political parties than to society.

Conclusion and recommendations

Legislation and electoral administrative bodies in Mozambique are unstable. For each electoral process, new legislation which reflects the interests of the two major parties, Frelimo and Renamo, is approved. In a system of institutional fragility, mistrust amongst

---

171 CPGD/Afrobarometer (2013) Qualidade da Democracia e Governação em Moçambique. Maputo: CPDG. p. 42.

172 Ibid.

173 The European Union and Carter Center observation missions are the only ones that carry out long-term observation from the voter registration process until the voting phase. However, for the 2014 elections, the European Union mission focused on the observation of the voting process.

174 Janeiro A (2015, 10 June) Dhlakama no Conselho Nacional da Renamo: Paz é melhor que guerra. *Notícias online*. Available at http://www.jornalnoticias.co.mz/index.php/politica/37851-dhlakama-no-conselho-nacional-da-renamo-paz-e-melhor-que-a-guerra [accessed 24 September 2015].

175 Interview with Salomão Moiana – CNE commissioner (civil society), 16 September 2015.

the stakeholders of the electoral process, lack of mechanisms for accountability, and the selection process of the electoral administration body members did not in any way contribute to the credibility and transparency of the electoral processes. Weak professional structures, the existence of two parallel electoral administration structures and the lack of real administrative autonomy and financial independence affect the exercise of the main responsibilities of the electoral administration bodies, thus undermining their credibility to society. Should it prove too challenging, at this stage of Mozambique's democratisation, for political parties to retain their place in electoral administrations, a more passive role could be established, allowing these parties to observe and discuss matters of electoral process even if they've lost their voting rights.

Based on the problems noted above, the following recommendations should be considered.

Electoral structures

- At a basic level, the electoral structures need to increase professionalism, construct appropriate operational facilities and make use of materials from previous electoral processes (electric generators, mobiles, ballot boxes, voting booths, etc.)
- An acceptable solution for the sustainability of the elections would be to reduce electoral administrators (at all levels) and replaced them with select qualified, competent and recognised professionals, appointed by public tender.
- The newly appointed administrative bodies could then, during non-election periods, establish partnerships with research institutions (universities, private institutions) to carry out studies on abstention, voting behaviour and/or provide services with the installed capacity in terms of ICT for other state and/or private institutions.
- It is important to then establish electoral administration bodies at the provincial and district level and provide them with adequate facilities, not only for their operations but also for storage of electoral material.
- The authority of electoral administration bodies should be extended so that, during non-election periods, they can carry out studies and research (in partnership with universities, private institutes, etc.) on an electoral system which is consistent with the actual political, economic and social phase Mozambique is going through;
- Appropriate institutional channels should be created to enable good practices for the electoral process produced by electoral administration bodies to be incorporated in the review of electoral legislation.
- Forms and mechanisms for accountability in electoral administration structures on electoral processes before the assembly of the republic should be established.

- Recommendations should be given to the assembly of the republic regarding the cost of elections so that they ensure sustainability of the electoral process.

Registration and voting

- A sustainable system for the registration and updating of voter registration compatible with the Mozambican reality should be established.
- The electoral administration bodies should consider simplifying results processing and reduce the levels of verification of election results.
- The electoral administration structures should propose the sustainable use of ICTs in the electoral process to parliament and government. These proposals should be on the best system for computerisation of voter registration and on the possibility of the use of the electronic vote in the elections. The utilisation of these instruments can make the registration, voting and verification processes more credible and more transparent.

Electoral financing

- Regarding the lack of material and human capacity and the means to exercise coercion against political parties, the CNE should only take responsibility for issuing credentials to confirmed political parties, indicating the number of constituencies in which they are running, and leaving the responsibility for allocation of the funds to the ministry of economy and finance and the responsibility for the implementation of the law for non-compliant accounting to the general inspection of finances and the administrative court.
- Budget limits to be used by political parties during the election campaign should be defined and the use of public assets during the election campaign should be penalised, as a way of reducing the imbalance between competing party forces.

Electoral litigation and disputes

- Electoral legislation should be revised so as to eliminate the principle of 'prior claim' and give time to the district courts to investigate and judge illegal election acts.
- Prevention and resolution of electoral conflicts in Mozambican electoral legislation committees should be institutionalised, 'in order to put into practice techniques for prevention, mitigation and management of electoral conflicts and improve the mechanisms of

contact, exchange of information and experience in the resolution of problems, thus adding credibility to the electoral process'.

Political parties in the National Assembly

- The participation of women in the electoral management process should be increased at all levels of Mozambican electoral administration.
- More lasting consensus with other political parties should be sought out in order to ensure stability of electoral legislation and electoral administration bodies.
- A single electoral administration body should be established, composed of a reduced number of personnel, selected on merit and professional competency and outside of the influence of political parties; political parties may indicate their members with the right to speak and without voting rights.

8

NAMIBIA

Mr Moses Ndjarakana

Historical background

Colonialism and apartheid

South West Africa, as Namibia was colonially known, is one of the victims of the General Act of the Berlin Conference of 1885, which cemented the scramble for Africa. As a result of the scramble for Africa, Namibia was colonised by Germany under Kaiser Wilhelm II. The German occupation of Namibia was one of unmatched brutality on the African continent, particularly among the Ovambanderu, Ovaherero and Nama ethnic groups. It started in 1883 with the German merchant Adolf Luderitz purchasing a series of plots and culminated in the German authorities' occupation of South West Africa (SWA).[1] On 24 April 1884, by way of a telegram, Chancellor Otto von Bismarck established a colony by placing Angra Pequena under German protection. This political and colonial action was followed by a series of land deals with native leaders who had no authority, while those with *de facto* authority resisted.[2]

The nature of German imperialism soon assumed an approach of state sovereignty (as understood from the European system of states). This approach, which was one of the major causes of conflict between the settler colonialist farmers and the indigenous pastoral communities, was in turn fuelled by settler farmers' and traders' insecurity in South West Africa. Colonial boundaries were drawn to the disadvantage of indigenous pastoral communities as these boundaries reserved the best land for the whites.[3] Many of the settlers favoured military conflict against the pastoralists over peaceful means to settle boundary disputes, disregarding the concerns of established traders who feared that a military confrontation would create economic instability. In 1904 the war of genocide broke out which had devastating effects on the populations of the indigenous people that

---

1   Wallace M (2011) *A History of Namibia*. London: Hurst. pp. 115–116.
2   Ibid.: 117.
3   Emmett T (1999) *Popular Resistance and the Roots of Nationalism in Namibia*. Switzerland: Schlettwin Publishing. p. 57.

participated in it. According to Drechsler, an estimated 80% of the Hereros, 50% of the Namas and 30% of the Damaras perished.[4]

Land dispossession was followed, among other things, by regulations to restrict the movement of the natives. Africans above the age of 14 years were forced to carry passes. Failure to obey these regulations resulted in the denial of food, lodging or any other social assistance, and often resulted in the arrest of Africans by any white person. Africans were further required to carry pass books in which their labour contracts were entered, otherwise they were subject to accusations of vagrancy.[5]

Namibia under South African occupation

The 30 years of German brutal occupation of South West Africa ended on 9 July 1915 when the German troops surrendered to the numerically superior South African forces at Khorab during the First World War.[6] This was the beginning of a new phase in the colonisation of Namibia which eventually had internal and international repercussions. The original intention of South Africa was to annex Namibia. This policy was frustrated by the decision of the League of Nations to implement a mandate system in all colonies at the end of the First World War.[7] The allied powers, through the permanent mandates commission of the League of Nations, divided the former German colonies among themselves according to a tiered system of mandates designated A, B and C. South West Africa was placed under a C mandate, a category assigned to those colonies considered to be incapable of governing themselves. The mandate was formally granted to South Africa to 'promote to the utmost the material and moral well-being and social progress of the inhabitants'.[8]

However, it took two and a half years for the mandate to come into force. South Africa was formally granted mandate over SWA by the Treaty of Versailles on 7 May 1919. The Treaty was not signed until 28 June 1919. The South African parliament passed the Treaty of Peace and South West Africa Mandate Act (49/1919) whereby delegated authority over SWA was bestowed on the Governor-General of South Africa (Lord Buxton at the time) who in turn delegated to the South African appointed Administrator General of SWA. On 17 December 1920 the League of Nations formally confirmed the mandate and defined its terms.[9] In 1946 after the dissolution of the League of Nations, the mandates in existence at the time were placed under the UN trusteeship system. However, South Africa refused to place South West Africa under the trusteeship system contending that the mandate lapsed with the dissolution of the League of Nations.

The United Nations considered South Africa's refusal to place the territory under the trusteeship system as amounting to annexation. This action by South Africa led the United

---

4   Drechsler H (1980) *Let Us Die Fighting*. London: Zed Press. p. 214.
5   Bley H (1971) *South West Africa Under German Rule*. London: Heinemann. p. 173.
6   Emmett T (1999) *Popular Resistance and the Roots of Nationalism in Namibia*. Switzerland: Schlettwin Publishing. p. 65.
7   Ibid.
8   Wallace M (2011) *A History of Namibia*. London: Hurst. p. 217.
9   Ibid.: 217–218.

Nations general assembly to seek an advisory opinion from the International Court of Justice (ICJ) requesting that the court determine the international status of the SWA and South Africa's obligation towards the territory. The ICJ dismissed the South African claim of sovereignty of SWA and held that South Africa remained bound under the mandate system regardless of the dissolution of the League of Nations. The court opined further that the United Nations had assumed the League of Nations' supervisory powers.[10] South Africa was held to be in violation of the UN charter specifically when it related to violation of human rights through the policy of racial discrimination. The court further held that the principle of self-determination was applicable to Namibia.

The liberation movement

The insistence of South Africa on governing Namibia as its fifth province ushered in the foundation of nationalist movements in the late 1950s. The apartheid system that was implemented in South Africa under the Odendaal Plan was being applied to Namibia and faced resistance from the oppressed populations of both countries. In addition, the increasing migrant labour system that brought northern populations to central Namibia and further into South Africa and the ability of Namibians (especially under Paramount Chief Hosea Kutako's Chief Council) to lobby the international community such as the United Nations, intensified resistance against the South African oppressive regime.[11]

South African Prime Minister Jan Smuts, in an attempt to persuade the UN to allow South Africa to incorporate Namibia as a fifth province of South Africa, held a 'referendum' between December 1945 and April 1946. The referendum was conducted only among some Africans in Namibia and resulted in a 'vote' of 207 310 for incorporation and 33 520 against incorporation. The San, some Namas, Damaras and other ethnic groups were not consulted. The Herero leaders demanded that America, Britain, China, France and Russia (as superpowers) be present to witness their response to the referendum and this was turned down resulting in Hosea Kutako sending a cable to the UN in which he declared the opposition of 'the whole Herero nation' to incorporation.[12] Eventually in May 1946, the South West Africa legislative assembly unanimously adopted a resolution in favour of incorporation.[13]

Resistance to apartheid rule saw the formation of national liberation movements. The first of these was the Ovamboland People's Congress (OPC) formed in 1957 by migrant workers. This movement was mainly Oshiwambo speaking, and led by Herman Andimba Toivo ya Toivo, who was working on the railways in Cape Town. These migrant workers were mainly influenced by the politics of resistance in South Africa. After the expulsion of ya Toivo from Cape Town in 1958, the rest of the group in South Africa formed the

---

10 Nisot J (1951) The advisory opinion of the International Court of Justice on the international status of South West Africa. *South African Law Journal* 68: 274.
11 Wallace M (2011) *A History of Namibia*. London: Hurst. p. 243.
12 Emmett T (1999) *Popular Resistance and the Roots of Nationalism in Namibia*. Switzerland: Schlettwin Publishing. p. 252.
13 Cockram GM (1976) *South West Africa Mandate*. Cape Town: Juta. p. 122.

Ovamboland People's Organisation (OPO) which later became South West Africa Peoples Organisation (SWAPO) under the leadership of Sam Nujoma.[14]

However, prior to the establishment of the OPC and the OPO, there had been a mushrooming of indigenous intellectuals, under the name African Improvement Society (AIS), who mainly served as the secretariat of the Herero Chief's Council under the leadership of Chief Hosea Kutako. The Chief's Council included Chief David Witbooi of the Nama people. This society, the leadership of which consisted of almost all Herero intellectuals, assisted the council with the drafting of petitions, interpretations and translations, analyses of newspaper articles for the illiterates and the politicisation of the population.[15]

At the end of 1958 ya Toivo and Kozonguizi teamed up and persuaded the Chief's Council to form a national movement with the understanding that the latter would be the patrons of the new national movement.[16] It was agreed that ya Toivo was to head for northern Namibia (Ovamboland) to take control there while Kozonguizi was to concentrate on Windhoek. As fate would have it, ya Toivo never made it to Ovamboland as he was arrested by the South African security forces in Tsumeb on his way there. In the meantime, the Chief's Council decided to send Kozonguizi to New York to help Mburumba Kerina and Reverend Michael Scott petition the United Nations on the liberation of Namibia. Thus ya Toivo's arrest and the departure of Kozonguizi for New York delayed the planned launching of the liberation movement, the South West Africa National Union (SWANU).[17]

SWANU was eventually launched in 1959. In the same year, OPO under the leadership of Sam Nujoma decided to reconstitute itself as a nationalist movement offering an alternative to SWANU. The result of this decision was the formation of the South West Africa People's Organisation (SWAPO) led by Nujoma. Some of the leadership of both SWAPO and SWANU went into exile in the early 1960s firstly due to increased oppression by the South African regime and secondly in an effort to garner international material and diplomatic support for the liberation movement.

Transition to independence

In the 1970s international pressure on South Africa to relinquish its hold on Namibia intensified, particularly with the adoption of United Nations Security Council Resolution 385 in 1976. The resolution reaffirmed the United Nations' legal responsibility for Namibia and required that South Africa withdraw from Namibia to be replaced by a UN administration, which would prepare and oversee free and fair elections. South Africa not only rejected the resolution but instituted an abortive attempt in 1977 to impose an internal settlement through the formation of the Democratic Turnhalle Alliance (DTA)

---

14 Ibid.
15 Ngavirue Z (1973) Political parties and interest groups in South West Africa: A study of a plural society. PhD thesis, Oxford University. pp. 286–287.
16 Ibid.: 295–296.
17 Emmett T (1999) *Popular Resistance and the Roots of Nationalism in Namibia.* Switzerland: Schlettwin Publishing. pp. 298–299 (citing Kozonguizi Documents).

which proposed a three tier ethnically based constitutional system excluding SWAPO and SWANU.[18]

This move by South Africa was not only rejected by the liberation movement and the international community but by the right-wing whites who were opposed to any form of self-determination for Namibia. In 1978 the UN Security Council adopted UN Security Council Resolution 435. In terms of this resolution, all South African troops in Namibia were to withdraw under the supervision of a United Nations Transitional Assistant Group (UNTAG) in time for the Namibian national elections scheduled for November 1989. The office of the UN special representative for Namibia under Matti Attisari and UNTAG were created to oversee the implementation of Resolution 435. The key objectives of UNTAG were to supervise the cease-fire and to monitor the return to barracks of the South African forces, to transfer SWAPO guerillas to designated demilitarised areas and monitor their demobilisation, to prevent the infiltration by SWAPO guerillas into other areas and to supervise the maintenance of law and order by the security forces.[19]

Elections under UN supervision

In 1989, after 105 years of colonial rule by various colonial powers, Namibia conducted its first national elections under the supervision of the United Nations from 7–11 November 1989. The United Nationals acted as the election management body in terms of United Nations Security Council Resolution 435.

The basic rules governing the conduct of elections were drawn from paragraph A.1 of the 1982 Constitutional Principles which were taken verbatim from paragraph 6 of the 1978 Contact Group. These included the following:

- Every adult Namibian will be eligible to vote, campaign and stand for election to the Constituent Assembly;
- Voting will be by secret ballot, with provisions made for those who cannot read or write;
- Guaranteed full freedom of speech, assembly, movement and press;
- The electoral system will seek to ensure fair representation in the Constituent Assembly to different political parties which gain substantial support in the election.

The arrangements for the election were conducted under the auspices of the Administrator General of Namibia.[20] However, the Administrator General was to carry out this task 'subject to the satisfaction of the UN Secretary General's Special Representative'.[21]

---

18 Naldi GJ (1995) *Constitutional Rights in Namibia*. Cape Town: Juta. p. 6.
19 Ibid.: 7–8.
20 The position of Administrator General has been created and appointed by the South African government over the years of occupation.
21 Weiland H & Braham M (1994) *The Namibian Peace Process: Implications and Lessons for the Future*. Freiburg: Arnold Bergstraesser Institut. pp. 141–142.

Using the proportional representation electoral system, a Constituent Assembly consisting of 72 members was elected to draft the country's constitution. At independence on 21 March 1990 the Constituent Assembly was transformed into the National Assembly.

Election management

The Electoral Commission of Namibia (1992–2015)

On 31 August 1992, the National Assembly simultaneously passed three critical pieces of electoral legislation namely, the Regional Council Act (22/1992), the Local Authorities Act (23/1992) and the Electoral Act (24/1992). The Electoral Act established the Namibian electoral process and paved the way for the first regional and local authorities elections. These pieces of legislation set the legal framework for elections in Namibia. Thus the Electoral Commission of Namibia, established in terms of the Electoral Act of 1992, put in place the machinery that led to the implementation of the constitutional provisions relating to the second and third tier governments in Namibia.

The legislative framework of the Electoral Commission of Namibia (ECN) has been a subject of controversy among politicians and other stakeholders for a considerable time until recent amendments to the Electoral Act and the Namibian constitution. The bone of contention has been its lack of legal independence or autonomy both physically and administratively. Initially, after its establishment in 1992, the commission was physically accommodated in the office of the prime minister. To make matters worse for the critics of this arrangement, the prime minister tabled and defended the budget allocations of the commission in the National Assembly thus creating a storm of objections, particularly from the opposition benches who felt strongly that the institution was being manipulated to favour the ruling party, SWAPO.[22] Commissioners and management staff were perceived to be either card carrying members of the ruling party or sympathisers, as reported in various media outlets.

In 1994, parliament passed a series of electoral amendments addressing both administrative and substantive shortcomings in the election management body's (EMB) legislative framework, for example the introduction of tendered votes to franchise those who could not meet residency requirements in constituencies where they were temporarily resident. The amendments also empowered the CEO to amend the voters' register during the time of elections.[23]

Prior to 1999, commissioners were directly appointed by the president. Opposition parties and some stakeholders objected, arguing that the process lacked transparency and smacked of partisan political manipulation and influence. In an effort to address this anomaly in the appointment of commissioners, parliament passed an amendment to the Electoral Act in

---

22 These heated debates took place during the discussion of the ECN vote on the Appropriation Bill in both Houses of Parliament. See Parliamentary *Hansards*.

23 Electoral Amendment Act (23/1994).

1999 which established a selection committee, the main functions of which were to drive the recruitment process for commissioners and to make recommendations to the president.[24]

In the mid-2000s, the prime minister declined to move the vote of the ECN citing accusations of bias from the opposition benches. The prime minister categorically distanced his office from being the administrative custodian of the ECN and the institution had to find rental space for its offices. In 2008, after frequent relocations, the ECN moved into its own building, Election House.

Franchising Namibians in the diaspora

In 2009 in response to growing concerns by Namibian citizens living outside the country, the legislature passed a welcome amendment to the Electoral Act which provided for the establishment of temporary registration points outside Namibia.[25] Staff from Namibia and others from Namibian embassies were recruited, in terms of the law, to run the voting process in the diaspora. The same legislation empowered the commission to accredit voter education providers, election observers and for the first time to authorise the counting of votes at polling stations. The latter provision was intended to speed up the counting process and increase its transparency and credibility. The use of electronic voting machines in Namibia was introduced for the first time by the same legislation. These provisions have been retained in the new act.

In 2012 the EMB, in collaboration with the Law Reform and Development Commission of Namibia, engaged in country-wide stakeholder consultations to review the existing act and produce a new electoral legislative instrument. In October 2014, the parliament of Namibia passed the Electoral Act 2014, which inter alia provides for the establishment and constitution of the Electoral Commission of Namibia and its powers and functions.[26] The commission was established as 'a juristic person which is capable, in its own name, of suing and of being sued ... of exercising powers and performing all the acts that a juristic person may lawfully perform'.[27]

Shortly after the promulgation of the Electoral Act (5/2014), parliament passed the Namibian Constitution Third Amendment Act,[28] providing for the establishment of the Electoral Commission of Namibia 'which shall be the exclusive body to direct, supervise, manage and control the conduct of elections and referenda'.[29]

In terms of the Electoral Act, the objectives of the commission are to:

> organise, direct, supervise, manage and control the conduct of elections and referenda in a free, fair, independent, credible, transparent and impartial manner

---

24 Electoral Amendment Act (11/1999).
25 Electoral Amendment Act (7/2009).
26 Sections 2 and 4 of the Electoral Act (5/2014).
27 Ibid.: section 2(4).
28 Act 8/2014.
29 Article 94B.

as well as to strengthen democracy and to promote democratic electoral and referenda processes.[30]

Composition of the commission

The secretary of the National Assembly invites candidates through the public media and the *Government Gazette* to apply for positions of commissioners.[31] Section 5 of the Electoral Act establishes a selection committee. The selection committee is tasked with the recruitment of the commissioners. The committee is composed of the heads of the Public Service Commission (as chairperson of the committee), the council of the Law Society of Namibia, the public accounts' and auditors' board, the Namibia Qualifications Authority and the registrar of the high court.[32] In addition to applicants being Namibian citizens they must possess minimum qualifications of at least a three-year tertiary qualification and be at least 21 years of age, except that the chairperson of the commission must be at least 35 years of age.[33]

The commission is composed of five members, at least two of whom must be women. Only the chairperson is statutorily required to serve on a full time basis. The rest of the commissioners serve on a part-time basis. The commissioners are appointed by the president, with the approval of the National Assembly,[34] for a term of five years and are eligible for reappointment for no more than two terms.[35] The act provides for the security of tenure of the commissioners to the extent that they may only be removed by the president on the recommendation of the selection committee, after an investigation and an opportunity to be heard, and with the approval of the National Assembly.[36]

However, critics argue that members of the selection committee tend to be partisans of the ruling party.[37] Equally, given the majorities of the ruling party in the National Assembly, the legislature will probably serve to rubber stamp the choice of the president. According to the critics, it is hard to escape the view that the president's choice of commissioners and especially the chairperson is likely to be those that will be sympathetic to the ruling party.

The commission is empowered to appoint a chief electoral and referenda officer[38] and other staff of the commission subject to the Public Service Act.[39] However, the EMB argues that provisions in the act and the constitution relating to the appointment of staff place a limitation on their autonomy to make appointments. For instance, appointments have to be approved by the executive, for the prime minister is the ultimate political and administrative head of the public service. Therefore, in terms of creating its operational

---

30 Electoral Act (5/2014) section 3.
31 Ibid.: section 6.
32 Ibid.: section 5.
33 Ibid.: section 7.
34 Ibid.: section 6.
35 Ibid.: section 10(2).
36 Ibid.: section 11.
37 Interview with Graham Hopwood, Director of the Institute for Public Policy Research (IPPR).
38 Electoral Act (5/2014) section 17.
39 Ibid.: section 18.

structure, appointment and dismissal of staff, apart from the chief electoral and referenda officer (CEO), the commission's appointment of staff is subject to the approval of the public service commission.[40] This legislative arrangement compromises the independence of the EMB.

The other permanent staff in the commission are public servants who are recruited and selected in terms of the Public Service Act. The public service conditions of service are applicable to commission staff. However, the Electoral Act empowers the commission to appoint staff on a contractual or part time basis. The latter staff members are usually recruited prior to peak election periods in order to supplement the capacity of the permanent members of the secretariat.[41]

The recently promulgated Electoral Act (5/2014) made the commission responsible for the administration and monitoring of political party funding. However the commission is currently without adequate capacity to perform this task. Since the commission is statutorily vested with this responsibility, it will have to recruit additional personnel to handle this issue.[42]

Powers and functions of the commission

The commission:

> is the exclusive authority to direct, supervise, manage and control in a fair and impartial and without fear, favour or prejudice any elections and referenda … and must exercise and perform its powers and functions … *independent of any direction or interference by any other authority or any person* [emphasis mine].[43]

In terms of the Electoral Act, other powers and functions of the commission include:[44]

- Supervision of and control over the registration of voters;
- Supervision, preparation, publication and maintenance of the voters' registers;
- Registration of political parties and other political organisations, such as associations;
- Supervision of the conduct of elections and referenda;
- Promotion of voter education;
- Supervision of election observers;
- Issuing and enforcing codes of conduct for the electoral process;
- Creating its own organisational structure;

---

40 Interview with Advocate Notemba Tjipueja, Chairperson of the Electoral Commission of Namibia.
41 Ibid.
42 Ibid.
43 Electoral Act (5/2014), section 4(a) and (b).
44 Ibid.: section 4.

- Regulating the domestic financing of political parties and organisations;[45] and
- Receiving political party nominations and publishing names of political party candidates for elections.

Financing

The ECN is financed solely through appropriations from the treasury. The commission prepares its electoral and capital budgets, then motivates and defends its proposal before the ministry of finance. Thereafter, the speaker of the National Assembly tables it to parliament. The EMB does not fall under any cabinet portfolio.

Electoral dispute resolution mechanism

In addition to the semi-formal political parties liaison committee, section 162 of the Electoral Act (5/2014) empowers the magistrate's commission to establish a regional magistrate to act as an electoral tribunal for a particular geographical area to decide on matters arising before polling day. These matters include:

- The inclusion or non-inclusion of any name in a provisional voters' register;
- Conduct attributable to a registered political party or office-bearer thereof;
- Conduct attributable to a registration officer or election official; and
- Matters relating to any election application or any other election irregularity.

The presiding officer at an election tribunal is not strictly bound by any law relating to the admissibility of evidence.[46] This provision is meant to enable a speedy resolution of issues. The presiding officer at an electoral tribunal is mandated to dispose of any matter before her or him in writing or orally before the polling day concerned.[47] The tribunal is enjoined from awarding any costs as part of its decision.

The second leg of the conflict resolution mechanism required by the act is the establishment of an electoral court,[48] which is vested with the powers of the high court. This court consists of the judge president of the high court and two other judges of the high court assigned by the judge president. The court is vested with powers, inter alia, to:

- Hear and determine appeals against the decisions of the electoral tribunals;
- Review decisions of electoral tribunals; and

---

45 Ibid.: sections 141–142.
46 Ibid.: section 164(1)(b).
47 Ibid.: section 165(2).
48 Ibid.: section 167.

- Hear and determine appeals against a decision of the commission in so far as that decision relates to the interpretation of any law or other matter for which an appeal is provided for in the Electoral Act.

The electoral court must give a written or oral decision and finalise any matter before it, seven days before the swearing in of the office bearer concerned. The court has a duty to give reasons for its findings. The court is prohibited from making an order awarding any costs against any party unless a party has acted in a frivolous or vexatious manner.[49]

Stakeholders

The ECN has several stakeholders. The commission interacts with political parties registered with the ECN through the political parties liaison committee (PLC). The interaction with the PLC takes the form of regular consultative meetings on issues relating to the programme of the electoral process such as voter education and registration, management and maintenance of the voters' register and the conduct of elections. Political parties are included in all ECN training programmes for voter education officials, registration and polling officials, as well as workshops conducted jointly with civil society organisations and the media.

The commission maintains a close relationship with relevant government ministries especially the ministry of urban and rural development,[50] which is responsible for tabling all the commission's legislative proposals in cabinet and parliament. The ministry of works, transport and communications is a key stakeholder in providing all transport and other logistical requirements to the commission. The police have sole responsibility for the security of ECN personnel, election materials, polling stations, counting centres and other properties of the commission. The commission conducts regular consultative meetings with the police to share operational plans and updates on the electoral process. Police personnel are also included in the training of ECN electoral officials in order to ensure that they have a common understanding of the registration, polling and counting processes.

The commission considers election observers to be key stakeholders in that they add credibility and integrity to the electoral process through their observation and the provision of useful feedback by way of their reports. The commission is statutorily mandated to accredit observers. During election periods, the ECN conducts pre- and post-election observer briefings to share information on the commission's preparedness for the conduct of elections. The commission maintains a media relations strategy that promotes regular contact with the media and ensures that the media have constant and accurate information on the EMB's programme of activities.[51]

---

49 Ibid.: section 171.
50 The ministry is responsible for regional and local authorities' structures.
51 Interview with Advocate Notemba Tjipueja, Chairperson of the Electoral Commission of Namibia.

Benchmarking

With regard to benchmarking and interface with regional electoral bodies or international treaties and protocols, Namibia is a founding member state of the Southern African Development Community (SADC) parliamentary forum. The founding speaker of the Namibian parliament was not only instrumental in the creation of the forum but also its first chairperson. Further, the headquarters of the forum are in Windhoek, thus making it convenient for the EMB to consult and benchmark with activities of the forum. The EMB is equally a founding member of the Electoral Commissions Forum of SADC Countries (ECF-SADC). The ECF-SADC is an independent organisation in which each country in the SADC region is represented by its electoral management body.[52]

Namibia is a signatory to the SADC protocol on politics, defence and security, which was signed on 14 August 2001 and ratified on 8 November 2002. The African Charter on Democracy, Elections and Governance was signed on 10 May 2007 but is yet to be ratified. The country acceded to the statute of the International Institute for Democracy and Electoral Assistance (International IDEA) on 9 July 2008, which entered into force on 21 November 2008. There has been no domestic law passed to internalise these international instruments. However, some general applications are discernible in the Electoral Act, 2014.

Assessment and evaluation

In terms of the Electoral Act, immediately after the results of any election have been published in the Government Gazette the commission is required to conduct a performance assessment in respect of the electoral processes followed and publish a post-election report thereof in respect of the election concerned.[53] The performance assessment and the post-election report must cover, among others, the following issues:

- Constitutional and electoral issues;
- Systems and logistics, including infrastructure;
- Training of staff members;
- Voter and civic education;
- Voting process and analysis of results; and
- Recommendations for amendments to any electoral legislation.

The chairperson of the commission is required to submit to the speaker the post-election report within six months of the conclusion of the election concerned. The speaker is in turn required to cause consideration of the report by the National Assembly and distribute the same to the president, the chief justice, the chairperson of the electoral court, the chairperson of the magistrate commission and the chairperson of the law reform and development commission. The speaker is equally required to make the report available for

---

52 The ECF-SADC members include the electoral management bodies of 14 SADC countries, namely: Angola, Botswana, DRC, Lesotho, Malawi, Mauritius, Mozambique, Namibia, South Africa, Seychelles, Swaziland, Tanzania, Zambia, Zanzibar and Zimbabwe.
53 Electoral Act (5/2014), section 116.

public inspection. Finally, the commission's financial records, like those of any other entity of the state are subject to scrutiny by the auditor general.[54]

In addition to the statutory assessment measures, the EMB is assessed by local and international observers through their reports, which are made available to the commission. Prior to the electoral reforms, international observers had made recommendations for the strengthening of the independence of the EMB as well as the cleaning and security of the voters' roll. The reforms have eventually addressed these issues in the Act.

There is no doubt that there is tremendous improvement among the EMB and the stakeholders as a result of the reform process. As indicated above, Namibia has had no electoral court cases since the 2009 presidential and parliamentary elections.

Electoral reform

The commission has been proactive on electoral reforms. It prepared a white paper for cabinet and a concept note for stakeholders on recommending amendments to the electoral law as well as the facilitation of stakeholder workshops to discuss proposed reforms. The commission similarly provided technical support to the Law Reform and Development Commission during the electoral law reform process.[55]

The commission has revolutionised the Namibian electoral process through the introduction of the biometric voter registration process and the introduction of the first ever electronic voting machines on the African continent. The credibility of the voters' register has for years haunted all electoral stakeholders and has led to several controversies.[56] The voters' register had been inundated with duplicate names, names of the deceased, registration of voters in the wrong constituencies as well as misspellings and a host of other technical errors. The introduction of the biometric voter registration system has gone a long way in removing the errors and thus improving the credibility of the voters' register.

Protection of electoral materials

There is recognisable improvement regarding protection of ECN election materials as evidenced by local and international election observers who factually witnessed the two above elections. Their observation of the two elections resulted in tangible and useful recommendations most of which the EMB implemented, as evidenced by the reform process.

The manual voter registration and the polling processes utilised by the ECN were hotly contested in the courts in the case dubbed, *Rally for Democracy and Progress and others vs. Electoral Commission of Namibia and Others*.[57] The applicants (eight political parties) sought an order

54 Ibid.
55 Interview with Advocate Notemba Tjipueja, Chairperson of the Electoral Commission of Namibia.
56 See for example: *August and Another vs. Electoral Commission of Namibia*, 1993 (3) SA (CC) para. 17; *Republican Party of Namibia and Another vs. Electoral Commission of Namibia and 7 Others* (unreported High Court judgment in Case No. A 387/2005 delivered on 26 April 2005); *Rally for Democracy and Progress and Others vs. Electoral Commission of Namibia and Others* 2010 (2) NR 487 (SC).
57 *Rally for Democracy and Progress and Others vs. Electoral Commission of Namibia and Others* 2010 (2) NR 487 (SC).

setting aside the November 2009 general election for members of the National Assembly on account of numerous alleged corrupt, illegal, and unprocedural election practices. The respondents, ECN joined by five political parties who took part in the same election, denied the allegations. The case attracted a lot of public interest particularly because the Rally for Democracy and Progress (RDP) campaigned on a ticket of exposing corruption and claiming that their leadership, having been members of the ruling party, knew how that party rigged elections. The applicants were unsuccessful in both the high court and the supreme court, but managed to put the electoral system under intense scrutiny. The ECN, which for years has been looking to introduce technology both in voter registration and polling processes, moved with deliberate speed to engage the government, political parties and other stakeholders with a view to procuring the technology needed to enhance the credibility of the electoral process, particularly the voters' register and the election results.

However, the introduction of the Indian manufactured electronic voting machines (EVMs) were not without controversy among stakeholders, especially political parties, even though they had initially approved of the idea. Initially there were objections from political parties due to the mistrust and the fear occasioned by unfamiliarity with the proposed technology. In 2008, the commission organised, at the commission's expense, an observation mission for all political parties registered with the ECN, to India to observe elections and the use of the EVMs. Thereafter, consensus was reached between ECN and the political parties to procure the EVMs and there was relief among opposition political parties.

Allegations of electoral fraud, however, did not disappear completely. During the process of the procurement of the EVMs and on the eve of the 2009 parliamentary and presidential elections, mistrust on the use of this technology resurfaced strongly, particularly from opposition parties. Allegations were made that the machines contained a computer chip that could be manipulated or hacked and therefore could be used to rig elections in favour of the ruling party. However, these allegations were never proven and only contributed to the delay of the procurement of the machines.

It must be noted that the allegations were made within the context of the volatile political environment that prevailed at the time. Several members of the ruling party SWAPO had resigned and formed a new party led by former minister of foreign affairs, Hidipo Hamutenya. Some members of the new party claimed that, having been members of the ruling party, they knew what methods the EMB and ruling party used to rig elections. Thus the 2009 elections turned out to be one of the most hotly contested and controversial elections in Namibian electoral history except perhaps for the 1989 independence elections conducted under the auspices of the United Nations. Because of the allegations, EMVs were not used in the 2009 elections.

It was only in 2013 that the EVMs were used for the first time. The use of this technology brought much needed credibility to the Namibian electoral process. The voting time taken by the voter was greatly reduced from three to five minutes previously to two to three minutes voting time per voter with the use of the EVM. The tabulation and announcement of results was equally greatly reduced from hours and sometimes days of manual counting to one hour at collation center with the use of the EVM control box and tabulator.[58]

It was the first time since the 1995 elections that there were no court cases challenging election results or the voting process. However there is still dissatisfaction from some political parties regarding the use of the EVMs. The major objection is the lack of a paper trail produced by the machines that can be used to verify the votes cast in the event of a court challenge. The ECN is in negotiations with Bharat Electronics, the Indian company that manufactured the EVMs, to modify the machines in order to produce the controversial paper trail.[59]

Conclusion and recommendations

The ECN has made tremendous improvements since its inception in 1992. The EMB was initially established as an office in the office of the prime minister. This arrangement compromised the independence, credibility and integrity of the institution resulting in numerous court cases that challenged its processes after every general election. Several amendments to the legal framework that sought to remedy the situation proved to be cosmetic measures until the realisation of the 2014 reforms. The reforms have placed the EMB on an improved path that requires fine-tuning as indicated in these recommendations.

- The latest reform process undertaken by the EMB was comprehensive and exemplary in the SADC region. However the reform process could have addressed the issue of autonomy of the EMB more comprehensively with regard to the recruitment and retention of its staff complement. Currently the ECN can recruit staff subject to rules pertaining to the public service. It is therefore recommended that staff of the ECN should not be subjected to the legal requirement pertaining to staff of the public service but should have their own set of conditions of service conducive to the electoral environment.
- Funding of political parties should be monitored and regulated by the National Assembly, which is the custodian of that budget.
- The reform process identified that every time there is an election there is a lack of transport for the electoral process. Consequently, the EMB ultimately has to rely on the executive for its logistical needs. It is recommended the EMB be empowered legislatively to have its own fleet.
- In terms of the Electoral Act 2014, the ECN is empowered to recruit and appoint the CEO through a transparent and participatory process that allows for any registered voter to observe the interview processes

---

58 Interview with Advocate Notemba Tjipueja, Chairperson of the Electoral Commission of Namibia.
59 Ibid.

and, at the stipulated time, lodge an objection against any candidate. This is commendable. However, the Act does not provide for a procedure and circumstances under which the CEO may be removed from office. It is therefore recommended that provision should be made in the Act for a removal procedure for the CEO so as not to unduly compromise that position or to put the EMB in an untenable situation at one point or another.

- The political party liaison as it currently exists is not a formal institution. It is advisable to legalise the committee so as to assist the dispute resolution mechanism process.

9

SEYCHELLES

Dr Nandini Patel

Introduction

Seychelles' 2015 presidential elections took place at a time when the country had gone through an electoral reform process with wide participation and intensive deliberation. The reform initiative, one of the outcomes of which was the establishment of the independent Electoral Commission (EC), had instilled hope and confidence in the system. For the first time there were as many as eight contenders for the presidency, out of which one was a woman. Civil society fully participated in the reform process and has been accredited to observe the presidential elections for the first time. Whilst some reform measures have been implemented there are many still to be taken up. The reform measures came at a time when the political climate after the 2011 elections was heating up and the pressure on the government mounting. The country is seeking to tap into technical support and collaboration from regional and international bodies to strengthen its democratic pillars, specifically elections.

The electoral reform agenda should be read in line with the 2008 balance of payments and debt crisis for which the International Monetary Fund (IMF) authorities have successfully enacted a comprehensive programme of reforms. The authorities floated the exchange rate, eliminated all exchange restrictions, turned fiscal deficits into surpluses and cut public debt in half with the help of a restructuring agreement with external creditors. They also initiated a comprehensive programme of economic reforms to foster long-term growth, which included simplifying the tax system and promoting the private sector. These reforms have supported a strong and sustained recovery: real GDP growth averaged at 5% during 2010 to 2013; unemployment returned to low levels (around 4%); the exchange rate stabilised after briefly overshooting; and reserves rebounded from half a month of imports to nearly four.[1] Sustainability of these programmes required a robust and inclusive political environment.

This chapter presents the historical context of elections and the political-economy setting of Seychelles today. It examines the constitutional and legal framework of elections

---

1 International Monetary Fund (2014) Seychelles: Request for an arrangement under the extended fund facility – staff report; press release; and statement by the executive director for Seychelles.

with particular focus on electoral reforms, the election management body (EMB) and some discussion on critical issues pertaining to elections in the country.

Setting the scene

Political and economic context

Of great scenic beauty, this small Indian Ocean country, with its ethnic and cultural diversity, has had a turbulent political history since its independence in 1976. It is an archipelago of 115 islands scattered over the Indian Ocean, northeast of Madagascar and about 1 600km east of Kenya. Mahé is the largest island and is the site of Victoria, the capital. About 90% of the Seychellois people live on Mahé Island. Most Seychellois are descendants of early French settlers and African slaves brought to Seychelles by the British who, throughout the 19th century, freed them from slave-ships on the East African coast. Seychellois culture is thus a mixture of French and African influences. There is also the influence of the Chinese, Indian and British. Creole (or Seselwa) is the mother tongue of 94% of the population. English and French are commonly used and English is the language of government and commerce. The estimated population of Seychelles is 91 650,[2] making it the smallest population in the Southern African Development Community (SADC) region.

From a coup to mercenary attacks, the country was politically unstable for some years until one-party rule in 1979 under France-Albert René, which consolidated its position and lasted for over 15 years. The Cold War ideological contestation had its spill over with socialist countries supporting René's government and western democracies supporting James Mancham.

Under René, Seychelles had a socialist-oriented economic policy based on a centrally planned economic model. The economy was characterised by price, trade and foreign exchange controls, a prominent role for parastatal companies and robust debt-funded development spending. These policies led to the national development plans (which were rolling and shifted annually) and policy priorities which squarely reflected the long-standing concerns of the Seychelles People's Progressive Front (SPPF) with improving social development for all.[3] Seychelles has shown consistency since 1980 in high per-capita income, good healthcare and education. Thus, Seychelles offers an interesting case study of social development as it has one of the most extensive social policy programmes in the developing world. In the United Nations Development Programme's (UNDP) Human Development Index (HDI) Seychelles ranks highest in sub-Saharan Africa.

The human rights record of Seychelles since its return to multiparty democracy has been less impressive, especially in terms of media freedom and the right to assemble and demonstrate. Seychelles boasts one of the world's highest percentages of women in

---

2   Index Mundi (2014) *Seychelles Demographic Profile: 2014.*
3   Campling L, Confiance H & Purvis M-T (2011) *Social Policies in Seychelles.* London: Commonwealth Secretariat & United Nations Institute for Social Development (UNRISD).

parliament, reaching 45% in 2011. Inheritance laws do not discriminate against women. In general, however, women enjoy fewer educational opportunities. While nearly all adult females are classified as 'economically active', most are engaged in subsistence agriculture. Rape and domestic violence remain widespread.[4] The government adopted a National Strategy on Domestic Violence in 2008, but it has had little success.

The global economic meltdown of 2008 and the subsequent sweeping economic reforms of 2008–2010 led to serious economic imbalances and to the near-depletion of official foreign exchange reserves in October 2008. Seychelles defaulted on interest payments which severely damaged its credibility as a borrower. The government sought support from the IMF, and in an attempt to meet the conditions for a standby loan, began implementing a programme of radical reforms. This economic reform process also brought corresponding political reforms. The ruling party had to soften its socialist stance and embrace economic and political liberalisation.

The democratic wave of the 1990s also embraced this island nation and paved the way for multiparty elections and ushered in a role for opposition parties in the democratic process. In 1991, the Constitution of Seychelles was amended to allow for the registration of political parties and allow those in exile to return to Seychelles. Eight political parties registered to contest the first stage of the transition with the election of constitutional commissioners to draft a new constitution and get the democratisation process going.

Pre-independence and independence phase

The country came under French control in 1768. It was annexed by Britain in 1794 and became a British colony in 1903. The first elections for the legislative council took place in 1948. Regular elections, based on universal suffrage, followed in the 1960s. In 1964 political parties were granted the right to register, opening up space for the formation of two ideologically divergent parties – the Seychelles People's Unity Party (SPUP) under the leadership of France-Albert René, which demanded social reforms with full independence; and the Seychelles Democratic Party (SDP) of James Mancham, representing the interests of the landowners and businessmen with close ties to Britain. The country had three pre-independence elections. The 1967 elections were for the governing council, which was an organ with limited executive and legislative functions. The 1970 and 1974 elections were for the legislative assembly and for 15 elected seats.

Table 1: November 1970 legislative assembly election

Parties	% of votes	Number of seats (15)
Seychelles Democratic Party (SDP)	53.8%	10
Seychelles People's United Party (SPUP)	44.2%	5

4   Freedom House (2012) *Freedom in the World 2012: Seychelles.*

Table 2: 25 April 1974 legislative assembly election

Parties	Number of votes	% of votes	Number of seats (15)
Seychelles Democratic Party (SDP)	21 902	52.37%	13
Seychelles People's United Party (SPUP)	19 920	47.63%	2

Source: African Election Database (n.d.) Elections in Seychelles. Available at http//africanelections.tripod.com/sc. html [accessed 13 August 2016].

The votes/seats discrepancy, a contentious issue in the first-past-the-post (FPTP) electoral system, confirms the yawning disparity in seats between the two contenders. Going by the percentage of votes, the two parties should have received eight and seven seats respectively.

The two parties agreed to soften the imbalance in the representation by adding ten members by appointment; five nominated by Chief Minister Mancham and five nominated by the leader of the opposition. In 1976, Seychelles attained its independence from Britain. The two parties agreed to form a coalition government, with Mancham as the president, René as the prime minister, and members from both the Democratic Party (DP) and the SPUP in the government. Thus, it was a model of compromise politics, which unfortunately did not last long. Soon after forming the government, and whilst President James Mancham was abroad, his government was overthrown in a rebellious attack on 4–5 June 1977 by supporters of the SPUP. Prime Minister France-Albert René was sworn in as president on 5 June 1977. Six individuals were killed during the rebellion. President René dissolved the legislative assembly and suspended the constitution on 6 June 1977. In 1978, the SPUP was renamed the Seychelles People's Progressive Front (SPPF).

Britain, United States, Tanzania and Mauritius extended diplomatic recognition to the René government. Tanzania also provided military assistance to Seychelles. The Soviet Union provided military assistance in the form of supplying weapons to the government from 1978 to 1986. It also received assistance from Algeria, Libya and East Germany. The SPPF was declared the country's only legal political party in 1978. A new constitution was approved in a referendum on 26 March 1979 and the constitution went into effect on 5 June 1979. The new constitution proclaimed the state to be 'a one-party state with all political activity other than that of the organs of government, authorities by statute and local government authorities to be conducted under the auspices of the Seychelles People's Progressive Front'.[5] The subsequent legislative elections were held on 23–26 June 1979, and the SPPF won 23 out of 23 elected seats in the legislative assembly. The parliamentary elections of 1979, 1983 and 1987 were not competitive as the SPPF was the only political party allowed to field candidates.

The René government faced a mercenary raid led by Colonel Thomas Michael ('Mad Mike') Hoare, who gained notoriety as a mercenary in the Congo during the 1960s.

---

5 Constitution of Seychelles (1979) *Commonwealth Law Bulletin* 5(4): 1329–1332.

Hoare's objective was to return ex-President James Mancham to power. The Hoare operation failed. The South African government was suspected of being behind the raid, as it opposed René's socialist regime and was already active in destabilising other leftist governments in Southern Africa. These suspicions were substantiated by the casual manner in which the South African government dealt with the hijackers. Instead of extraditing them to Seychelles where they would be tried for treason, or charging them with hijacking, the South African government opted to unconditionally free 39 of the 44 mercenaries and charge the leaders, including Hoare, with lesser crimes.[6]

The United Nations (UN) security council condemned the mercenary rebellion against the government and so did other international and continental bodies, such as the non-aligned movement and a number of governments across the globe. From 1981 through to the late 1980s, several more coup attempts were suppressed and eventually, after almost 16 years of one-party rule, President René finally announced a return to the multiparty system of government in December 1991.

Election management under one-party rule

In May 1978 the SPPF was declared the only legal party after the independence constitution had been abrogated subsequent to the 1977 coup. René then ruled by presidential proclamation and ordinance for two years, while a six-person constitutional commission drafted a constitution that formalised René's dictatorial powers and left his subjects with effectively no legal protection of their rights. The constitution came into effect on 5 June 1979. The authoritarian rule justified the limitation of fundamental rights on the grounds of avoiding factional conflict and securing political stability and the general welfare of society. Members of the legislature, the so-called People's Assembly, were to be selected by the SPPF, to which they had to belong.

Presidential elections were held in 1979, 1984 and 1989 respectively, with President Albert René as the sole candidate, standing unopposed. The vote was yes/for or no/against the candidate and René won with 97%, 92% and 96% of 'yes' votes. Legislative elections held in 1979, 1983 and 1987 were open solely to members of the SPPF, the country's only legal political organisation. Thirty candidates stood for election, 17 of them unopposed. Two other members were appointed by president of the republic, France-Albert René, to represent the migrant people of the outer islands. President René headed the seven-member council of ministers.[7]

The elections for the establishment of the constitutional commission in 1992 was guided by the Constitutional Act of 1992, which provided for the appointment of an independent director of elections. The duties of the director were to supervise the election of the constitutional commission, the registration of votes and holding of the referendum.

---

6   South Africa History online (nd) South Africa: 1981.
7   Inter-Parliamentary Union (1983) Seychelles.

The Act provided for 'the independence of the director's office by stating that the office will not be subject to the direction or control of any person or authority'.[8]

Democratic wave of the 1990s

The Registration of Political Parties Act was passed in 1991 to enable parties to function. This paved the way for multiparty elections in 1992 – the first since 1977. Eight political parties registered to contest in the elections, which were essentially intended to constitute a constitutional commission. The latter would then draft a new constitution that would define the type of government – a presidential system or some sort of a mixed system.

Table 3: 1992 legislative assembly election

Parties	Number of votes	% of votes	Number of seats (22)
Seychelles People's Progressive Front (SPPF)	24 538	58.39%	14
Democratic Party (DP)	14 150	33.67%	8
Seychelles Party (PS)	1 829	4.35%	-
National Alliance Party (NAP)	672	1.60%	-
Seychelles Movement for Democracy (MSD)	322	0.77%	-
Seychelles National Party (SNP)	259	0.62%	-
Seychelles Liberal Party (SLP)	201	0.48%	-
Seychelles Christian Democratic Party (SCDP)	54	0.13%	-

Source: African Election Database (n.d.) Elections in Seychelles. Available at http//africanelections.tripod.com/sc.html [accessed 13 August 2016].

The SPPF and the DP had existed before 1992 and the rest were new. The commission was elected by proportional representation (PR), with a threshold of 5% to win one of the 22 seats. The former ruling party, the SPPF, emerged as the largest party with 14 of the representatives, whilst the remaining eight went to the SDP.[9] The voter turnout was 85%. The constitutional commission drafted a new constitution providing for a presidential system with presidents limited to three terms of five years. Half of the National Assembly were to be elected proportionally based on the results of presidential elections. The question for approval from the referendum was 'Do you approve the draft constitution'?

A referendum was then held in November 1992. Although the 'for' votes that favoured the adoption of the draft constitution reached 54%, it did not get the required majority of 60% of the national vote. Another attempt was made in 1993. The constitutional commission again worked through a series of consultations, which paved the way for

8   Commonwealth Observer Group (1992) *Elections to the Constitutional Commission in Seychelles, 23–26 July 1992: The Report of the Commonwealth Observer Group.*
9   Nohlen D, Krennerich M & Thibaut B (1999) *Elections in Africa: A Data Handbook.* Oxford: Oxford University Press.

reconciliation between the two major parties and brought some consensus towards establishing a constitutional democracy. With 75% 'for' votes in the referendum, a new constitution was adopted establishing a presidential system of government, and a mixed electoral system for parliamentary elections – 25 seats contested on FPTP and nine seats contested on PR.

The first multiparty presidential and legislative elections were held in July of 1993. These elections were won by President René and the SPPF. James Mancham and the DP came second in both. The Parti Seselwa joined forces with the Seychelles National Movement (SNM) and the National Alliance Party (NAP) to form the United Opposition (UO). Led by Wavel Ramkalawan, the UO obtained one seat in the National Assembly. The 1998 elections were governed by the Seychelles Constitution of 1993, as amended in 1994, 1995 and 1996, as well as by the Elections Act of 1995 (as amended in 1996). The Electoral Act of 1996 (Section 37[1]) provides for a two-round system for the presidency to secure an absolute majority, and in the case of a tie between two candidates for the National Assembly, there is provision for a second ballot (1996: 37[2]).

The second multiparty elections again resulted in a clear win for President René and the SPPF, but brought a change in the leader of the opposition as UO candidate, Wavel Ramkalawan, replaced James Mancham. After these elections, the UO changed its name to the Seychelles National Party (SNP). In the presidential elections of 1993, 1998 and 2001, René won with 59.5%, 66.67% and 54.19% of votes respectively. The SPPF won 21 out of 27 National Assembly seats in 1993, 24 out of 30 in 1998 and 23 out of 34 in 2001.[10] Thus, the SPPF retained its grip on presidential power and the National Assembly.

After 27 years in office, René stepped down on 14 April 2004. Vice-President James Michel became president. This marked a change in the Seychellois political landscape, as President René had ruled Seychelles for the previous 27 years. James Michel won the 2006 presidential election with 54% of the vote, while the opposition candidate for the SNP, Wavel Ramkalawan, supported by the DP, attained 46%. Parliamentary elections in May 2007 saw no change in the structure of the National Assembly: the SPPF retained its 23 seats; the SNP (in alliance with the DP) retained 11 seats.

Legal framework

The key legal instruments for elections were:

- The Constitution of the Third Republic of Seychelles of 18 June 1993 with amendments until August 1996;
- The Electoral Act of 1995 and Elections Amendment Act of 1996; and
- The Political Parties Registration Act of 1991.

10 African Election Database (n.d.) Elections in Seychelles. Available at http//africanelections.tripod.com/ sc.html [accessed 13 August 2016].

There were also some regulations made pursuant to the Elections Act, such as the Election Advisory Board Regulations Act (2010) and the Elections Regulation Act (2006) dealing with signage and the use of government vehicles to transport voters to the polls.[11] Chapter VII of the Republican Constitution stipulates the public offices for which national elections are to be held, namely, for the Office of President, at an election of the members of the National Assembly, or in a referendum held under the constitution. The president is elected for a five-year term and cannot hold office for more than three terms. Members of the National Assembly are also elected for a five-year term. According to the Elections Act, the Electoral Commissioner announces, by notice in the Government Gazette, the date or dates on which the presidential or a National Assembly election should be held.

Articles 115 and 116 of the Constitution of 1993 provided for the establishment of an Electoral Commissioner, who was to be appointed by the president for a period of seven years and eligible for reappointment. The Electoral Commissioner was also the registrar of political parties, whose responsibilities included the disbursement of funds to political parties based on their eligibility to secure state funding.

Institutional framework

Composition and tenure

The Electoral Commission (EC), constituted after the adoption of the Sixth Amendment of the Constitution in 2011, comprises of five members (one woman and four men) who are independent professional persons and not aligned with the interests of any political party or government. They are appointed for seven years, with the possibility of renewing their appointments after that period. The positions are advertised by the Constitutional Appointments Authority (CAA) in accordance with article 115a of the constitution. The CAA is a body composed of three persons – one chosen by the president, one by the leader of the opposition and the third member is a consensus candidate of the latter two. The CAA makes recommendations to the president, who appoints the five members of the commission, including a chairperson who is the only full-time member of the commission. The chairperson of the EC heads the secretariat comprising of four other permanent staff. During election periods, or for specific exercises like voter registration, temporary staff are recruited as per requirement.

The EC's independence is guarded by the constitution (section 115 [2]), which states that the EC shall not, in the performance of its functions, be subject to the direction or control of any person or authority. The salary, allowances and gratuity payable to the chairperson and members of the EC will be prescribed by or under an Act and be charged to the government's consolidated fund.

---

11 Campling L, Confiance H & Purvis M-T (2011) *Social Policies in Seychelles*. London: Commonwealth Secretariat & United Nations Institute for Social Development (UNRISD).

An Elections Advisory Board was set up in December 2010 under the 2010 Amendment of the Elections Act. The Elections Advisory Board consisted of (i) the Electoral Commissioner; (ii) the chief registration officer; (iii) the person who last functioned as the chief electoral officer; and (iv) three other persons with knowledge and experience in the conduct of elections and the delimitation of electoral boundaries, nominated by the EC. During the period between the nomination day and the polling day of an election, a representative of each presidential candidate shall be appointed to the Elections Advisory Board in the case of a presidential election, and a representative of each political party shall be appointed in the case of a National Assembly election. At any election, an aforesaid representative, in respect of one or more independent candidates, shall be appointed to the Board. The Electoral Advisory Board was stipulated to meet at such times and placse as selected by the EC, provided that it meet at least three times a year.

Duties and responsibilities

Since the Seychelles electorate is small, the chairperson and members of the EC undertake the responsibility for policy decisions relating to the electoral process, as well as overseeing the implementation of the electoral process. There is a chief registration officer to supervise the voter registration and a chief elections officer to supervise the elections. There are also registration and elections officers. Other election officials are recruited as and when required during election time. As mandated by the constitution, the Elections Act and the Political Parties Act, the EC is responsible for ensuring that all eligible persons can contest in the elections as candidates and all eligible voters can cast their votes. This is by:

- Maintaining the national register of voters;
- Informing voters about the electoral system and elections;
- Maintaining a register of political parties;
- Ensuring the registration of candidates for elections;
- Overseeing the conduct of election campaigns;
- Administering access to the public media for campaign purposes;
- Reviewing and adjusting electoral boundaries;
- Training electoral staff;
- Conducting presidential and National Assembly elections and referendums, in accordance with the legal framework;
- Reporting to the National Assembly on the administration of elections and referendums;
- Registering political parties; and
- Periodically making recommendations to the government for further reforms.

The function of the Elections Advisory Board was to advise and assist the EC in the performance of its functions generally, and in relation to (i) the registration of voters; (ii) the delimitation of boundaries; (iii) organisation of elections and the setting of election date; (iv) the consultation of members of the public in respect of election matters; (v) liaising with relevant public authorities and stakeholders in the delimitation of boundaries; (vi) reviewing electoral laws as and when necessary; and (vii) other measures to ensure good governance and transparency in the management of elections.[12]

Autonomy and independence

A refreshing departure is the financial autonomy of the EC. It is accountable only to the ministry of finance and the auditor general. The EC reports annually to the National Assembly on the conduct of all elections and it is responsible for the public funding of political parties. The EC is financed through public funds.

Each year the chairperson submits a budget to the ministry of finance, following the same procedure as other government ministries or departments. All expected costs are normally covered. The budgets for elections are prepared separately and all election expenses are covered under the consolidated revenue fund. The EC is well-equipped in terms of new technologies. However, it faces challenges in attracting competent and qualified staff, perhaps due to some fear of working within a politically sensitive institution.

Access to public media for campaign purposes is regulated by the Elections Act and the EC ensures that all candidates and parties have equal access to airtime on national radio and television. The Electoral Commissioner (section 97 of the Act), in consultation with the Seychelles Broadcasting Corporation (SBC), allocates free broadcasting time to each registered political party and each candidate. The Act further guarantees equal broadcasting time for each party and each candidate, and the order of such time slots is drawn by lots. The Act is detailed and explicit on this. While this seems to be quite fair, opposition parties complain that the campaign by the incumbent starts before the official campaigning time, and that there are limitations to opposition parties' free expression. However, the EC has no control over campaign opportunities through privately owned media, although political parties and candidates generally agree to abide by a voluntary code of conduct for elections. The EC collaborates with the Seychelles Media Commission (SMC), which is a relatively new organisation and is still in the process of finalising a code of ethics for the local media. Under the one-party system, the media was completely controlled by the government and this legacy is only gradually being challenged.

The EC works closely with a number of government ministries and departments, including the statistics department, the civil status office, immigration, and information and communications technology departments. It is relatively easy for the EC to communicate with the executive, legislature and judiciary on matters related to elections and electoral reforms. The EC presents annual reports to the National Assembly. The EC is a member of the Electoral Commissions Forum of the SADC (ECF-SADC), and its members participate actively in the ECF's professional development programmes. Close ties are

---

12 Government of Seychelles (2015) Elections Act: Chapter 68A.

maintained with the Commonwealth secretariat, and the EC has welcomed observers from these organisations as well as from local observer groups.

Contentious issues

Several problematic issues emerge clearly from the democratic electoral history of Seychelles, namely, the voters' roll, party finance, campaign expenses, restrictions on public gatherings, equal access to the media and independent electoral observation.

Voters' roll

The voters' roll has been one persistently critical electoral issue. In the run up to 2006 elections, out of an estimated total population of some 70 000, the authorities had come up with an electorate of 49 975 voters. Some opposition parties considered this a gross exaggeration. Based on an update of the 1987 census, which put the population of Seychelles at the time at 68 598, they argued that the voting population should have been closer to 43 000 and not 49 975, even allowing for births and deaths in the intervening period. Allegations were made that the voters' registration list contained names of dead people and foreigners who had either impersonated their way onto the list, or who had been registered as voters against the provisions of the law. This was seen by some stakeholders as a deliberate ploy to serve the interest of the ruling party. The transfer of votes was also a concern, where voters who had registered in one electoral district were transferred to another, apparently without their prior knowledge and consent, thus effectively threatening to disenfranchise them.

The EC admitted that there is a possibility that the voters' roll is bloated. The admission came out of the realisation that the roll included those in the diaspora, who were in possession of national identity numbers or ID cards. Such persons were excluded from official population estimates, which were based on (current) residence in the country. Thus, the official estimate of 43 276 Seychellois over the age of 18 in mid-1991 did not include those living overseas, but that were still on the voters' registration list. The new law provides Seychellois residing abroad the right to vote, provided they hold a national identity card.

In order to settle the controversy over voter registration, the EC recommended to the National Assembly that:

> The Elections Act proposes that a voters' census be carried out in order to update the present voters' list which the Electoral Commission feels lacks credibility. The Commission is also in favour of a continuous voters' registration system whereby the register remains open all year round for consultation and registration and changes to it can be made at any time.[13]

---

13 Electoral Commission of Seychelles (2013) *Report and Recommendations on Electoral Reform in Seychelles.*

Despite the ongoing discussions and some corrective measures, the opposition parties again contested the credibility of the voters' register in the run up to 2015 elections. The main claim being that there is a discrepancy in the number of voters and the statistics on population. Responding to the issue, the EC chairman, Hendrick Gappy, stated that the EC had given the public the opportunity to present their objections, which he said is the mode by which the register can be updated. He further confirmed that they have not had many objections and that 'is one of the only ways we can update the register, it's not a question of just removing people on the register' as currently the law does not allow the EC to just remove a voter's name from the list.[14]

Access to voters' registers by opposition political parties was another area of conflict which was taken to court by political parties. The matter was rectified by the Elections Amendment Act (27 of 2014), which directed the EC to provide the registered political parties with a copy of the registers of voters and amended registers of voters, which should only contain the name, address, national identity number and electoral area of the voter. During the 2015 elections, all the registered political parties could only access the voters' registry after persistent demand.

Party finances

Article 118 of the constitution states that 'an Act shall provide for the provision of financial support from public funds to political parties'. Thus, the Political Party Registration Act as amended established a political parties financial support fund, which is supplied by the National Assembly and administered by a registrar of political parties, who is also the Electoral Commissioner. The amount of the funding was to be determined annually and allocated to all registered parties on 1 January.

Funding was allocated according to the representation of the parties in the National Assembly and allocated to each party as per the proportion of votes received in the previous National Assembly elections. Parties that did not participate in the election but who have registered candidates for the next general election of the National Assembly are also entitled to funding; they are paid a proportion of the lowest sum allocated, determined by the length of time between the close of nominations and the end of the year. Thus, if the lowest amount paid out is 4% of the total payout and nominations close on 31 March, they will receive three-quarters of that year's payout: three-quarters of 4% is 3% of total payouts for the year. The Electoral Commissioner is required to keep an account of the support fund and to submit an annual statement of accounts to the National Assembly. The total amount of the political parties financial support fund was substantially reduced over the last years. Since 2001, the sum appropriated has dropped to RS 0.5 million (USD 41 318) compared to RS 2 million (USD 165 275) prior to that.[15] Although this affects all parties in the National Assembly equally, the perception exists that the ruling party,

---

14 Interview with Hendrik Gappy, Electoral Commissioner, in 2015.
15 Electoral Institute for Sustainable Democracy in Africa (EISA) (2011) *Technical Assessment Team Report of 2011 Elections of Seychelles.*

through incumbency, still has access to other state resources and has a clear advantage over the opposition parties.

In the electoral reform process the rules on party funding were substantially revised. The reforms do not limit spending, but political parties are now required to disclose all expenditure and any donations over SR 5 000 (around USD 355) to the EC.[16]

Campaign expenses

The Elections Act (section 94) dealt with campaigning by stipulating activities such as holding public meetings or organising any public display, and issuing of bills, placards, posters, pamphlet, circulars or advertisements, for which campaign expenses can be incurred. The candidates appointed an agent for this purpose and had to notify the Electoral Commissioner as soon as possible of the appointment. The candidate, or an agent of the candidate, was required to keep proper accounts of all funds received. The Act further required that an agent of the candidate, or a registered political party, who received any funds or incurs any expenditure in connection with an election, should deliver to the Electoral Commissioner a certified statement within 60 days after the declaration of the results.

The legislation, however, did not require the candidates or the agents to disclose the source of the funds or the identity of the person in respect of whom the expenditure was incurred. Thus, while a legal requirement for parties to report on election expenditure existed, there was no legal requirement for the sources of such funds to be disclosed. Furthermore, there was no legal limit set on the level of such expenditure. Stakeholder views demonstrate a discernible need for legislation in these areas and the EC agrees with this as well.

There were several accusations that the ruling party organised its rallies using state resources, including buses, boats, the use of the army and the national flag. Some of these practices were observed by international and local observers.

Right to free assembly

The prevalence of certain laws restricting a number of fundamental civil rights was observed and demands were made for rectification. The electoral reform process brought up the issue of amending the Public Order Act of 1959. Thus, in 2013 the National Assembly passed the Public Order Act (POA) with the objective of correcting the 1959 law. However, the POA was seen by civil society and opposition parties as a way to control public order. For others it was 'a way of criminalising the exercise of the fundamental human rights of the Seychellois, such as to hold private or public gatherings, and use social media to disseminate information or the freedom to carry a poster addressing an issue'.[17] The most contested parts of the law were those that had given the police, the National

---

16 Main opposition group welcomes electoral reforms (2015, 16 March) *The Economist*.
17 New Public Assembly Bill to go before Seychelles MPs soon (2015, 30 July). *Seychelles News Agency*. Available at http://www.seychellesnewsagency.com/articles/3423/New+Public+Assembly+Bill+to+go+before+Seychelles+MP%27s+soon [accessed 12 December 2016].

Drugs Enforcement Agency (NDEA), and immigration and customs officers the right to confiscate any recording device and prevent information from being disseminated on the internet. Thus, freedom of assembly and freedom of expression, which are the essence of democracy, were the two most threatened freedoms.

Access to state media

All party broadcasts in the media during the official campaign period came under provisions in the Election Act of 1995 (amended in 1996), which guarantees all parties and candidates the right to have their views broadcast. It also requires the Electoral Commissioner, in consultation with the Seychelles Broadcasting Corporation (SBC), to allocate free and equal broadcasting time to parties and candidates. The extent of the incumbent's coverage and time has, however, been one of the contentious issues. The establishment of the Seychelles Media Commission (SMC), approved by the National Assembly in 2011, was intended to rectify the incumbency issue, among other things.

Some of the key functions of the SMC were to:

- Provide an independent arbitration medium between different types of media organisations and between members of the public and media organisations;
- Promote the independence of the print and electronic media;
- Formulate in consultation with the Seychelles Media Association, a code of conduct for publishers of newspapers, radio and television broadcasters, news agencies, publishers of online publications, including blogs, particularly those emanating from servers hosted in Seychelles, and journalists, and to publish the code of conduct as prescribed;
- Monitor adherence to the code of conduct and require compliance by all concerned;
- Monitor compliance by all media of constitutional and legal obligations in force in Seychelles in respect of media freedom and expression;
- Monitor any development likely to restrict the dissemination of information, including the expression of opinions on matters of public interest and importance, and to assist in resolving them;
- Defend the constitutional rights of all citizens to accurate, truthful and timely information;
- Assist journalists and broadcasters in developing and maintaining high standards of integrity in the collection and dissemination of news and information in and about Seychelles;
- Assist and encourage the interaction between local media organisations and foreign media organisations, receive complaints from members of the public relating to any infringement of the

individual's right to privacy by journalists or agents of media organisations and to sanction journalists or media organisations according to the law;

- Promote a proper functional relationship among all classes of persons engaged in print and electronic media in Seychelles; and
- Promote the development of privately owned print and broadcasting media.

In the 2011 elections, opposition parties complained about the partiality of state media, arguing that the incumbent was given more airtime than they were. In a joint statement released by all the opposition parties after the election results were announced, opposition parties noted that

> the state-funded media, Seychelles Nation and the SBC, were monopolised throughout the campaign by the government, giving a clear advantage to the incumbent candidate. Both media showed a clear reluctance to be fair and missed no opportunity to give coverage to the president and government initiatives in clear breach of their constitutional and legal obligations. Reporting calculated to influence the outcome of elections continued up to polling day.[18]

This raised concerns regarding the efficiency of the SMC, as it seemed ineffective to ensure impartiality. It was perhaps too much to expect from a newly constituted body. The 2015 elections' assessment will be able to highlight the SMC's performance better.

Domestic election observation

Domestic observers also play a critical role in ensuring a transparent electoral process. The Liaison Unit for Non-governmental Organisations (LUNGOS), a network of all non-governmental organisations in Seychelles, applied to the EC for domestic observation accreditation for the 2011 presidential elections, but was turned down. A similar request was rejected in 2006, when the Centre for Rights and Development (CEFRAD), also a non-governmental organisation (NGO), applied for accreditation as domestic observers. The rejection was based on the basis that CEFRAD had political affiliations. When LUNGOS applied for observation accreditation for the 2105 presidential elections, the EC in turn tabled the request before the Election Advisory Board. While recognising the importance of having domestic observers, the Electoral Advisory Board rejected the application, arguing that LUNGOS was not adequately constituted to run an observer mission. The Board believed that some members of LUNGOS had initially run for political office, and

---

18 Electoral Institute for Sustainable Democracy in Africa (EISA) (2011) *Technical Assessment Team Report of 2011 Elections of Seychelles.* p. 19.

that this would compromise their independence and impartiality as a domestic observer mission.

The Board recommended that immediately after the presidential election, LUNGOS should incorporate into its network an NGO with the specific object of observing elections and conducting civic education programmes. LUNGOS was permitted to observe the 2015 National Assembly elections. LUNGOS has subsequently also participated in election observation in other SADC countries and gained experience and exposure. In the electoral reform process, as a member of the Reform Forum, LUNGOS was accredited without any hesitation for the 2015 presidential elections.

Electoral reforms

Build up to the electoral reform process

The demand for electoral reform has been growing from both within the country from key stakeholders, and from the international community, as can be discerned through election observer reports. Concerns like inaccurate voter registration, use of state resources and government apparatus for ruling party campaigns, the voting rights of overseas Seychellois, among other things, have been raised persistently since the 1992 elections.

In the 1998 Joint Commonwealth/La Francophonie Observer Group report, recommendations were made for measures to be taken towards the 'further improvement of the effective separation of state and party political functions'.[19] This was reiterated once again in the 2006 presidential elections report of the Commonwealth team for the establishment of an independent public service commission to address, inter alia, appointments and promotion of employees which would help to allay current fears and suspicion focused on the tenure of contracts and the issue of security clearance for employment, as well as build sustainable capacity in a permanent civil service.[20] The government was encouraged to consider the establishment of an electoral management body based on international good practice.

The need for a mechanism to facilitate dialogue between stakeholders to promote open discussion on issues of common concern so as to cultivate a climate of greater trust and mutual respect, was realised. Limits on campaign financing was another issue requiring attention, with the legal requirement to declare campaign expenditure needing to be enforced. Recommendations for reform were long and complex, but nothing was done until 2011.

The reform was triggered by the events that unfolded after the May 2011 presidential elections when the incumbent, President James Michel of the Parti Lepep (PL) (formerly

---

19 Commonwealth Observer Group (1998) *The Presidential and National Assembly Elections in Seychelles, 20–22 March 1998*. London: Commonwealth Secretariat.
20 Commonwealth Observer Group (2006) *2006 Presidential Elections in Seychelles: Commonwealth Election Observers Report*. London: Commonwealth Secretariat.

SPPF and SPUP), was re-elected after winning 55% of the votes. The Seychelles National Party (SNP) won 41.43%. The opposition candidates decided to jointly reject the election results on the grounds of massive irregularities in the electoral process, with a particular focus on the role of money in directly influencing how a significant number of voters cast their ballot: 'The refusal of all opposition candidates to accept the results of the election is indeed a serious matter; the opposition was considering how to take forward their allegations and next steps, which may include a possible boycott of future elections.'[21] The leading opposition party, the SNP, stated that 'they would not attend the session of the National Assembly unless a new election law would be proposed' thus giving a strong push for change.[22] Following the boycott, the National Assembly was dissolved in July 2011 and early National Assembly elections were announced.

The National Assembly elections were held in September 2011. The SNP had decided to boycott the election in protest against the government's failure to revise electoral laws concerning the amount of money parties can spend on campaigning. According to Sir James Mancham, former president of Seychelles, 'by not participating in the National Assembly elections, Mr Ramkalawan and his party showed a high level of political irresponsibility and lack of vision in the game of chess that today characterises the democratic process'.[23] The legislative elections witnessed one of the island's lowest voter turnouts in its electoral history at 74.3%. This represented an 11% decrease from the presidential elections held earlier in the year. Further, the count showed that a total of 16 447 voters – almost 32% – spoilt their ballots. This number was indeed large in a country where spoilt ballots historically stood at 1–3%.[24] Indications were clear that electoral reforms were urgently needed. The Commonwealth observer mission report recommended that a 'thorough review of the Elections Act and other relevant legislation and procedures should be undertaken, so as to address key gaps and ambiguities in the legal framework related to elections'. The previous election reports had also recommended several amendments that would directly affect the electoral framework.

Owing to local pressures and international concern on the above issues, Seychelles undertook an impressive reform process. It has been widely acknowledged as inclusive, participatory and satisfactory. The issues were wide-ranging and the process included many suggestions for reforms. The EC spearheaded the process as it is mandated under article 116 of the Constitution of the Republic of Seychelles (Sixth Amendment) Act of 2011 to undertake electoral reforms. The process commenced in October 2011. An electoral reform forum was set up in consultation with all registered political parties and other key stakeholders. The process started in late 2011 and lasted for 14 months.

21 Campling L, Confiance H & Purvis M-T (2011) *Social Policies in Seychelles*. London: Commonwealth Secretariat & United Nations Institute for Social Development (UNRISD).
22 Electoral Institute for Sustainable Democracy in Africa (EISA) (2011) *Technical Assessment Team Report of 2011 Elections of Seychelles*.
23 Mancham J (2014) *Seychelles: The Saga of a Small Nation Navigating the Cross – Currents of a Big World*.
24 Dubbleman B (2011) Seycelles Parliamentary Election Report. *Polity.*

The main purpose of the reform process was 'to enable consensus on the most appropriate changes necessary to enhance the principles and practices of democracy in the country's electoral system'.[25] The forum agreed to review three pieces of legislation, namely the Elections Act of 1991 (as amended in 1996), the Registration of Political Parties Act of 1991 (as revised in 1996), and the Public Order Act of 1959 as it relates to public gatherings and the right to assemble peacefully.

The most fundamental reform issue was the formation of an independent electoral commission. Thus, an important legal reform was the Constitution of the Republic of Seychelles (Sixth Amendment) Act of 2011, which made provision for the establishment of an electoral commission as the Office of the Electoral Commissioner. Thus, article 115 was amended to read as:

(1) There shall be an Electoral Commission which shall perform the functions conferred upon it by this constitution or any other law.
(2) Subject to this constitution the Electoral Commission shall not, in the performance of its functions, be subject to the direction or control of any person or authority.

Table 4: Key reform issues and proposed changes

Issue	Concern	Key suggestion
Voters' registration process	Credibility of the voters' list. Period for voter verification being too short.	Clean up the voters' register. Issue new IDs. Introduce continuous registration process.
Right to vote for Seychellois diaspora	The widespread nature of the diasporic community and the high cost involved	Issue to be taken up as a part of the ongoing electoral reform process.
Determination of election dates	Election dates are announced suddenly.	Fixed dates. Announcement to be made well in advance.
Nomination procedure	The Electoral Act provides for nomination day but does not provide for procedures for nomination.	The Act to specify the opening and closing of nomination centres, verification of candidates' application forms, payment of deposits and issuing of receipts, examination of nomination papers, confirmation of candidates and issuing of certificates.
Election day	The power to call for elections by the president needs to be abolished as it gives too much power to the executive.	The constitution needs to be amended to state categorically that presidential elections shall be every five years.

25 Electoral Commission of Seychelles (2013) *Report and Recommendations on Electoral Reform in Seychelles.*

Issue	Concern	Key suggestion
Electoral constituency boundaries	Boundaries have been adjusted to suit the specific party in power.	Need for review of boundaries.
Election campaigning	Placing and removal of billboards. Inducements to voters, use of public servants and facilities for campaign.	Regulations on where and how to place bill boards. Adherence by all parties to the code of conduct.
Public gatherings	Outdated Public Order Act.	Need to review the Public Order Act. Need to secure the right to assemble peacefully in public places without excessive restrictions.
Campaign financing	Lack of transparency by political parties pertaining to sources of contributions/ donations. Lack of mechanisms for monitoring and enforcement	EC recommends that section 94 of the Elections Act be repealed and replaced by a new stand-alone Act in line with article 117 of the constitution which comprehensively covers all the issues involved in campaign financing.
Role of media	SBC giving extensive coverage to the ruling party.	Code of conduct for the state media to ensure independence.
Vote counting and announcement of results	Long hours of waiting after vote cast and results announcements. Lack of clarity on votes, valid votes and spoilt votes.	Reinforce security measure during vote counting. Access to observers – local and international.
Political party funding	The issue was whether parties should be state funded?	Legalise party funding without having to disclose the source. All sources of funding to be declared.
Electoral justice system	Issues of infringement of electoral rights – allegations not often proven. Adequate time for filing election petitions.	Section 44(4) of the Elections Act to be amended for the petitioner to have 14 days (instead of ten that is currently provided) to file his/her election petition before the Constitutional Court.
Role of the EC	The newly constituted EC to show it is reliable and can deliver credible elections.	EC to improve communication. Allow SBC to broadcast the counting process. EC members and staff to perform their duties without fear or favour.

As can be deduced from the above table, some recommendations were immediate and others long-term. The EC took up the critical issue of reforming the Public Order Act of 1959. The Act has been repealed and replaced by the Public Assembly Act of 2012, 'to make the provision for the protection and promotion of the right to freedom of assembly, the preservation of public safety and order and to provide for connected matters'.[26]

At the end of the reform process the EC released its report in 2013. The most important reforms cover three main components: The Elections Act, the Campaign and Financing Act and the Party Registration Act. Some of these were approved by the National Assembly in December 2014.

Assessment and evaluation

Though Seychelles underwent the transition to multiparty democracy and started holding competitive elections after 1993, measures towards setting up an independent electoral commission in conformity with international norms and practices were undertaken only towards the end of 2000s, culminating in the 2011 electoral reform process. Thus, the EC has conducted only one election since then, the 2015 presidential elections. Seychelles, however, incorporated features like (i) the requirement of an absolute majority of votes with 50%+1 for a presidential candidate to be declared winner, and (ii) a mixed system of representation in the National Assembly – features that some other countries in the region like Malawi, Zambia and Mozambique are struggling to adopt.

A big challenge before the EC pertains to levelling the playing field. The existence of public funding for registered parties has been adopted by Seychelles and most SADC countries, but does not completely resolve inequality in access to state resources. In a situation where public funding of parties is proportional to the number of seats a party occupies in parliament, as is the case in Seychelles, the smaller parties are disadvantaged. Several electoral stakeholders raised concerns about the fact that the total amount of the Political Parties Financial Support Fund was substantially reduced over the last few years. Since 2001, 'the sum appropriated has dropped to RS 0.5 million (USD 41 318) compared to RS 2 million (USD 165 275) prior to that'.[27] Although this affects all parties in the National Assembly equally, the perception exists that the ruling party, through incumbency, still has access to other state resources and has a clear advantage over opposition parties. Thus, despite the fact that there are provisions in the Electoral Act for a level playing field among political contests, there remain serious concerns relating to: the provision of public funding for parties represented in parliament; the requirement that political parties account to the EC for the use of campaign resources; and the prohibition against using state resources in campaign activities.

---

26 Electoral Commission of Seychelles (2012) *Electoral Reform 2012: Recommendations on Reform of Public Order Act (1959)*.
27 Electoral Institute for Sustainable Democracy in Africa (EISA) (2011) *Technical Assessment Team Report of 2011 Elections of Seychelles*.

There is also a visible blurring of lines between the government and the ruling party. The two are considered synonymous, and as a consequence, what is considered a government resource is similarly taken as a resource at the disposal of the ruling party for party political purposes by design or by default. This has been one of the opposition parties' major complaints about the 2011 presidential election because they were prevented from organising public campaigns. They also used this as a reason not to accept the results of the election, along with complaints about the incompetence of the Electoral Commissioner and the police to act against these infractions.

There is no limit in law to either a party's or an individual candidate's campaign expenditure. There is also no restriction on donations from external sources for political campaigns. Clause 94 of the Election Act of 1995 stipulates that within 60 days after the election results are declared, a candidate, party or party agent has to submit to the Electoral Commissioner a statement of funds received and expenditure incurred. The legislation on campaign expenses required teeth and therefore the EC repealed section 94 of the Elections Act and replaced it with a new standalone Act in line with article 117 of the constitution. The new Act also included the issue of external sources of campaign funding: 'In the interests of reducing outside influence on the electoral affairs of Seychelles, the Assembly should consider restricting the source of political contributions to persons eligible to vote in Seychelles elections.'[28]

The Electoral Regulations Act of 2006 clearly bars the use of government vehicles for campaign purposes during election time by stipulating that this constitutes a breach of the Act.

The EC is currently also considering the introduction of biometric identification cards and the use of barcode scanners and existing GIS databases to carry out a voter census that should improve the accuracy of the voters' register considerably. The EC reckons that there is a need to conduct a census of voters.

Whilst a range of stakeholders carry out voter education, during the 2011 presidential elections it was not clear whether voter education had been conducted by any of these groups. Observer groups like the Commonwealth suggested that the EC should have a mandated responsibility to provide voter education on an ongoing basis, and not only at the time of an election.

While the establishment of an independent electoral commission has indeed been a significant step, the EC's capacity needs to be addressed. For almost two decades the Election Commissioner has been in charge of policy issues and administration. It is time to clearly demarcate the two, and delegate them respective authorities.

28 Campling L, Confiance H & Purvis M-T (2011) *Social Policies in Seychelles*. London: Commonwealth
   Secretariat & United Nations Institute for Social Development (UNRISD). p. 9.

Conclusion

The legacy of an entrenched one-party system rendered the democratisation process slow and staggered. A positive sign, however, is that the government seems to take cognisance of this fact and is willing to face the challenge. Reforms induced by the IMF in 2008 brought a wave of economic and political reforms. The inclusive and participatory electoral reform process has instilled a lot of hope in key actors for improvements to the quality of elections and the extension of democracy in general. The challenge is to maintain this momentum. There is a need for concerted efforts to build trust between the EC and political parties. There is also a need for regular forums on issues of democracy and governance.

Addressing contentious electoral issues by the EC is commendable. Much emphasis has been placed on key legal electoral reforms pertaining to levelling the playing field, with reference to campaign financing and the use of state resources for campaigns. As regards the access to state media, a marked improvement was noted in the 2015 presidential elections. This was attributed to the new provision in section 97 of the Electoral Act, which grants equal and free political broadcasting time of up to 134 minutes for television and 149 minutes for radio to each candidate in the presidential election.[29]

Setting fixed election dates for holding the presidential and parliamentary elections concurrently will further enhance the effectiveness and credibility of the process. Calling parliamentary elections could arguably give the party in power an upper hand and tilt the balance in their favour. The power of the president to call elections needs to be abolished as it gives too much power to the executive.

The SADC Observation Mission commends Seychelles for enacting this provision, which went a long way in levelling the playing field and ensuring that citizens are informed about the entire spectrum of political opinions and choices.

Social media was also widely used by citizens, especially youths, political parties and local observer groups. Incidents of insults between supporters of rival political parties on social media were reported.

What becomes apparent whilst wading through the literature on elections in Seychelles is the focus on presidential elections, which relegates the National Assembly elections to the background. There is a need for political parties to focus on the role of the National Assembly and to strive to make those elections competitive, with more parties securing the required threshold. The National Assembly seems to have been reduced to a secondary role. Perhaps the boycott of the 2011 National Assembly elections by the main opposition has weakened it, as well as the opposition's role in governance. There are lessons to be learnt from this experience.

Although Seychelles does not require financial support to hold regular elections, like other countries in the SADC region, it does however need technical support and for regional and international bodies to share their knowledge and experience. It is important

---

29 SADC Parliamentary Forum Election Observation Mission (2015) Interim Mission Statement on the 2015 Presidential Elections.

for Seychelles to retain its membership in forums like SADC. And the emerging civil society needs external support in terms of training.

Recommendations

- The ongoing reform process must be kept on track: the post-election political climate should not dilute the commitment and momentum of reforms. The 2015 presidential elections, which for the first time went to a second round to secure an absolute majority for the winner, and the small margin in which it was won, has created a sense of uncertainty. Political parties have to get to grips with situation and move forward.
- The EC needs competent staff for the effective discharge of its duties and responsibilities.
- There needs to be a greater adherence to electoral laws, especially regarding campaigning and campaign funding, with the disclosure of sources and the amounts of donations.
- The date of elections needs to be set by legislation, and the current practice of the president setting and announcing the date should be discontinued.
- Presidential and parliamentary elections should be held concurrently: this will not only give equal attention and importance to both elections, but it will also be cost effective.
- Civil society observation of elections should be enhanced in the region. The emerging civil society in Seychelles should be given support locally, regionally and internationally so that it can play a viable role in the electoral process.
- Political parties should receive training. Political parties in Seychelles are, like in most parts of the region, personality-driven and they lack ideological and structural capacity.

10

SOUTH AFRICA

Dr Collette Schulz-Herzenberg

Introduction

The ordinariness of South Africa's past few elections, and the general decline in political violence since 1994, signifies a shift away from conflict-based to ballot-based politics and a general maturing of electoral politics. This achievement is due partly to the sterling work of South Africa's Independent Electoral Commission (IEC). Set up in 1993 as an interim body to preside over the historic 1994 elections, the IEC has since become a permanent institutional pillar of the new democratic state, overseeing the administration and management of five credible national and provincial elections and three municipal elections. The IEC is widely regarded as an efficient and independent body, and remains one of the most trusted national institutions. It also provides a role model for similar bodies in post-conflict societies and is often invited to share its expertise with other electoral management bodies (EMBs) and to assist with election processes.

Building a functioning election commission entails a number of institutional, organisational and technical details. There are, however, several key aspects which are critical. An electoral commission should preferably be a permanent body; it should not be part of government, nor should appointments of its senior members be the sole prerogative of government; the body should also have sufficient funding, staff and technology.[1] The South African electoral commission surpasses all these criteria. More than that, however, electoral integrity depends on the character of governance leading up to an election, the quality of the process on the day, and mediated efforts to manage conflicts over contested outcomes. Electoral integrity also presupposes a degree of political competition and a level playing field during the campaign period so that political parties can freely contest an election. While the IEC has been widely credited with the implementation of free and fair elections, the institution is central to several major debates to level the electoral playing field, including party funding, electoral reform and the misuse of state resources during election campaigns.

---

1   Kuhne W (2010) *The Role of Elections in Emerging Democracies and Post-Conflict Countries: Key Issues, Lessons Learned and Dilemmas.* Berlin: Friedrich Ebert Stiftung. Available at http://library.fes.de/pdf-files/iez/07416.pdf [accessed 30 June 2016].

This chapter probes the afore-mentioned issues. It starts with the political imperatives that gave way to South Africa's particular electoral regime and institutions. Thereafter, the chapter provides a review of the existing legal framework. The third section examines different aspects of institutional design and performance and concludes with insights and recommendations that can assist the IEC and other key actors to institute changes to improve electoral integrity and public confidence in election outcomes.

Historical, socioeconomic and political context

South Africa is a divided and pluralistic society. Its social and political divisions are attributed to the legacy of colonialism and later, apartheid, which was institutionalised in 1948 under the National Party (NP). While colonialism reinforced ethnic identity, the apartheid system continued its legacy by building on racial divisions.[2] Today, the diversity of the society is captured in the constitution which recognises 11 official languages. Moreover, prominent social cleavages, such as class and race, reinforce each other, producing a highly polarised citizenry. It was against this backdrop that the move towards democracy commenced in the early 1990s.[3] Negotiations paved the way for the historic 1994 elections and the establishment of a democratic constitutional state. The democratisation process opted for a highly representative electoral system to ensure free and fair elections. South Africa's interim constitution required that the electoral system must be based on a system of proportional representation (PR) at the national and provincial-levels.[4]

The PR voting system is well-suited to South African politics due to its inherent qualities of representivity and inclusivity, fairness and simplicity.[5] The low threshold (0.25%) produces near perfect proportionality and ensures a highly representative outcome that can appease minority interests in the context of majority rule. The closed-list PR system obliges voters to elect parties by voting for the entire list shown by each political party, and not individual candidates. Parties are allocated a proportion of seats in the National Assembly and provincial legislatures according to the percentage of votes won during the elections. The simplicity of the closed-list system maximises voter participation, ensuring the highest level of inclusiveness.[6] These features have bestowed a degree of credibility and legitimacy on the new democratic government since 1994.

The choice of PR has allowed for the emergence of multiparty politics within the context of

---

2   Mamdani M (1996) *Citizen and Subject: Contemporary Africa and the Legacy of Late Colonialism*. New Jersey: Princeton University Press. pp. 109-137.

3   Lodge T (2002) South Africa. In: T Lodge, D Kadima & D Pottie (eds) *Compendium of Elections in Southern Africa*. Johannesburg: Electoral Institute of Southern Africa (EISA). p. 72.

4   Constitution of the Republic of South Africa, 108/1996. Section 46 (1)(d).

5   Lijphart A (1994) *Electoral Systems and Party Systems*. New York: Oxford University Press.

6   Faure M (1996) The electoral system. In: M Faure and J-E Lane (eds) *South Africa: Designing New Political Institutions*. London: Sage. p. 97; De Ville J & Steytler N (eds) (1996) Voting in 1999: Choosing an Electoral System. *Human Rights and Constitutional Law Series* of the Community Law Centre, University of the Western Cape. Durban: Butterworths. p. 67.

a dominant party system by producing a strong majority government with an abundance of minority party representation.

A highly representative system was critical to alleviating further conflict. The African National Congress (ANC), the majority party in South Africa, had maintained a principled objective of the inclusion and representation of all racial and other political groups.[7] The PR system was also a pragmatic choice made by political actors whose electoral fortunes remained uncertain following an inaugural democratic election which was likely to result in dramatic political changes.

Constitutional and legal framework

The inception of the inaugural IEC in December 1993 was preceded by the passing of the Interim Constitution of the Republic of South Africa, 20/1993; the Electoral Act, 202/1993; and the Independent Electoral Commission Act, 150/1993. These provided a regulatory framework for setting up the IEC as well as running the subsequent independence elections.[8] During the Convention for a Democratic South Africa (CODESA) negotiations, there was initial disagreement about the role of an electoral commission, with the apartheid-era National Party calling for the election to be run by the Department of Home Affairs, while the ANC and others called for an impartial, independent body. Ultimately, parties decided upon a well-established international model for the commission: one that was independent from government, that would oversee the electoral process and administer, adjudicate and monitor elections.[9] It was hoped that this model would infuse impartiality and credibility in the final results, vital ingredients for a society with low levels of trust.[10]

The subsequent permanent constitution, adopted in 1996, reaffirmed the primacy of electoral democracy. The founding provisions state that South Africa is founded on a set of basic values, including 'universal adult suffrage, a national common voter's roll, regular elections and a multiparty system of democratic government, to ensure accountability, responsiveness and openness'.[11] Section 19 in the Bill of Rights states that every citizen is free to make political choices, including the right to form a political party, to participate in the activities of, or recruit members for, a political party, and to campaign for a political party. Every citizen has the right to free, fair and regular elections. Every adult citizen has the right to vote in elections for any of the official legislative bodies. Citizens also have the right to stand for public office and to hold office. Sections 46 and 47 stipulate that the electoral system has to be determined by national legislation and it must be based on

7   Lodge T (2003) How the South African electoral system was negotiated. *Journal of African Elections* 2(1): 2.
8   Kabemba C (2005) Electoral administration: Achievements and continuing challenges. In: J Piombo & L Nijzink (eds) *Electoral Politics in South Africa: Assessing the First Democratic Decade*. New York: Palgrave Macmillan. p. 88.
9   Ibid.
10 Lodge T (2003) How the South African electoral system was negotiated. *Journal of African Elections* 2(1): 73.
11 Constitution of the Republic of South Africa, 108/1996. Section 1(d).

a common voters' roll, a minimum voting age of 18 years, and a system that results, in general, in proportional representation.

Elections must be overseen by an electoral commission whose independence is guaranteed by section 181 of the constitution. It lists the electoral commission as one of six state institutions that strengthen constitutional democracy, and specifies that these institutions are independent, and subject only to the constitution and the law. They must be impartial and must exercise their powers and perform their functions without fear, favour or prejudice. The 'Chapter 9' institutions should ensure the accountability of government, and should contribute to the formation of a society 'based on democratic values, social justice and fundamental human rights'.[12]

The responsibilities of the IEC, as defined in the constitution (section 190), are to:

(a) Manage elections of national, provincial and municipal legislative bodies in accordance with national legislation;
(b) Ensure that those elections are free and fair; and
(c) Declare the results of those elections within a period that must be prescribed by national legislation and that is as short as reasonably possible.

A number of pieces of legislation have since followed giving specific expression to constitutional provisions. The IEC manages national, provincial and municipal elections in accordance with national legislation. The relevant statues governing elections are set out in Table 1. They regulate a series of election related issues, including: the composition and operation of the IEC; logistical arrangements for elections; the registration of parties and voters; funding of political parties and their code of conduct; and the resolution of electoral disputes.

Table 1: Constitutional and legal framework

Source	Law
Constitutional provisions	Section 1
	Section 2
	Section 19
	Section 42(3)
	Section 181
	Sections 190 – 194
The 1994 elections	The Constitution of the Republic of South Africa, 200/1993
	The Electoral Act, 202/1993
	The Independent Electoral Commission Act, 150/1993

---

12 Constitution of the Republic of South Africa, 108/1996. Chapter 9.

Source	Law
Legislation for the 1999 and subsequent elections	Electoral Commission Act, 51/1996 (amendments in 1998, 2000, 2003 and 2004)
	Electoral Act, 73/1998 (amendments in 2000 and 2003)
	Public Funding of Represented Political Parties Act, 103/1997 (amended in 2005)
	Electoral Laws Amendment Act, 34/2003
	Electoral Laws Second Amendment Act, 40/2003
	Electoral Commission Amendment Act, 14/2004
	Electoral Amendment Act, 18/2013
	Public Finance Management Act, 1/1999
	Independent Broadcasting Authority Act, 153/1993
	Determination of Remuneration of Members of Constitutional Institutions Matters Amendment Act, 22/2014
Local government elections	Local Government Municipal Structures Act, 117/1998
	Local Government Municipal Structures Amendment Act, 20/2002
	Local Government Municipal Electoral Act, 27/2000
	Local Government Municipal Electoral Amendment Act, 14/2010
	Local Government Municipal Demarcation Act, 27/1998 (amended in 2002)
Regulations contained in legislation	
Electoral Act, 73/1998	Electoral Code of Conduct Regulations on the Accreditation of Voter Education Providers Voter Registration Regulations, 1998 Regulations on the Accreditation of Observers, 1999 Election Regulations, 2004 Regulations Concerning the Submission of Candidate Lists, 2004
Electoral Commission Act, 51/1996	Regulations on Party Liaison Committees, 1998 Regulations for the Registration of Political Parties, 2004 Regulations relating to activities permissible outside voting stations on voting day
Local Government Municipal Electoral Act, 27/2000	Local government: Municipal Electoral Regulations Local government: Municipal Electoral Regulations, 2011 amendment
Public Funding of Represented Political Parties Act, 103/1997	Public Funding of Represented Political Parties Regulations Notice to Deregister Political Parties

Compliance with treaties and conventions

South Africa's legislative framework conforms to international continental and regional treaties and conventions on elections. The country itself is a signatory to a number of these documents.

The International Covenant on Civil and Political Rights 1976 was signed by South Africa in 1994 and ratified in 1998. The optional protocol to the covenant was ratified in 2002.[13]

The 1981 African [Banjul] Charter on Human and Peoples' Rights was signed and ratified by South Africa in 1996.[14] The Constitutive Act of the African Union was later signed by South Africa in 2000 and ratified in 2001.[15] This Act promotes popular participation and good governance, non-interference in internal affairs and respect for democratic principles, human rights, the rule of law and good governance.[16] In 2002, the Assembly of Heads of State and Government of the Organisation of African Unity and the African Union (OAU/AU), which includes South Africa, adopted the Declaration on the Principles Governing Democratic Elections in Africa.[17] Its principles state that, 'Democratic elections are the basis of the authority of any representative government', and that 'regular elections constitute a key element of the democratisation process and therefore, are essential ingredients for good governance, the rule of law, the maintenance and promotion of peace, security, stability and development'; and that 'the holding of democratic elections is an important dimension in conflict prevention, management and resolution'.[18] The declaration includes the African Union (AU) Guidelines for African Union Electoral Observation and Monitoring.[19]

---

13 See the Status of Ratification Interactive Dashboard. Available at http://indicators.ohchr.org/ [accessed 4 August 2016].

14 African Charter on Human and Peoples' Rights, available at http://www.achpr.org/instruments/achpr [accessed 4 August; Institute for Democracy and Electoral Assistance (International IDEA) (2002) International Electoral Standards: Guidelines for Reviewing the Legal Framework of Elections. Stockholm: International IDEA. p. 104. Available at http://www.idea.int/publications/ies/upload/electoral_guidelines. pdf [accessed 29 June 2016].

15 Constitutive Act of the African Union, available at http://www.achpr.org/instruments/au-constitutive-act and http://www.achpr.org/states/south-africa/ratifications/ [accessed 4 August 2016].

16 Goodwin-Gill G (2006) *Free and Fair Elections*. Geneva: Inter-Parliamentary Union. p. 38. Available at: http://www.ipu.org/pdf/publications/free&fair06-e.pdf [accessed 29 June 2016].

17 Thirty-Eighth Ordinary Session of the Organisation of African Unity, 8 July 2002, Durban, South Africa, AHG/ Decisions 171–184 (XXXVIII), AHG/Decl. 1–2 (XXXVIII), Decisions and Declarations. Available at http://www. achpr.org/instruments/guide-elections/ [accessed 4 August 2016].

18 OAU/AU (2002) Declaration on the Principles Governing Democratic Elections in Africa 2002, II.4.; Goodwin-Gill G (2006) *Free and Fair Elections*. Geneva: Inter-Parliamentary Union. pp. 38–41. Available at http:// www.ipu.org/pdf/publications/free&fair06-e.pdf [accessed 29 June 2016}.

19 OAU/AU (2004) Declaration on the Principles Governing Democratic Elections in Africa 2002, Annex II. 2004; Guidelines for African Union Electoral Observation and Monitoring Missions, available at http:// www.achpr.org/files/instruments/guide-elctions/au_instr_guide_elections_eng.pdf [accessed 4 August 2016].

At the sub-regional level, the Southern African Development Community (SADC) adopted the Principles and Guidelines Governing Democratic Election in September 2004.[20] This document emphasises citizen participation in the political process, as well as the impartiality of the electoral institutions, voter education, and acceptance and respect of the election results. Guidelines also include the rights and obligations of SADC observers, and the responsibilities of the state to ensure the civil and political rights of individuals and parties and to implement logistical operations essential to a successful election. This SADC initiative formed the basis of the African Charter on Democracy, Elections, and Governance, adopted by member states on 30 June 2007 in Addis Ababa and ratified by South Africa in 2010.[21] The charter entered into force in February 2012. Its key objective is to promote democracy, human rights and good governance on the African continent. It seeks to: establish the shared values, standards and norms of the African Union and its member states within democracy, elections and governance; promote adherence to democratic principles, rule of law and human rights; reject unconstitutional change of governments; and encourage the strengthening of a culture of democracy and peace in member countries. The IEC was instrumental in the development of both the two above-mentioned doctrines.[22]

The IEC participates as a member of the International Institute for Democracy and Electoral Assistance (International IDEA), the Commonwealth Electoral Network, the International Centre for Parliamentary Studies (ICPS), the Electoral Commissions Forum of SADC countries (EFC-SADC), the Association of African Election Authorities, the Association of European Electoral Officials, and the Association of World Election Management Bodies (A-WEB).[23] The IEC also has strong ties with electoral management bodies in other African countries and beyond, regularly sending delegations to observe elections and staff to provide assistance with, and learn about, the management of elections. The IEC also receives delegations from other countries to observe elections, and share best practice.[24] The IEC has signed memoranda of understanding with counterparts in India, Mexico, Palestine and Russia to benchmark against international best practice.[25]

20 SADC Principles and Guidelines Governing Democratic Elections, available at http://www2.ohchr.org/english/law/compilation_democracy/sadcprinc.htm [accessed 4 August; Gill G (2006) *Free and Fair Elections*. Geneva: Inter-Parliamentary Union. p. 38. Available at: http://www.ipu.org/pdf/publications/free&fair06-e.pdf [accessed 29 June 2016].

21 Ratification Table: African Charter on Democracy, Elections and Governance. Available at http://www.achpr.org/instruments/charter-democracy/ratification/ [accessed 4 August 2016].

22 Interview (telephonic/email) Mr Mlungisi Kelembe, Manager: Commission Services, IEC, 29 October 2015.

23 Interview (telephonic) with Ms Ilona Tip, Operations Director, EISA, 12 October 2015; Interview (telephonic/email) Mr Mlungisi Kelembe, Manager: Commission Services, IEC, 29 October 2015.

24 Independent Electoral Commission (2015) *Annual Report 2015*. p. 3. Available at http://www.elections.org.za/content/About-Us/IEC-Annual-Reports/ [accessed 29 June 2016].

25 Interview (telephonic/email) Mr Mlungisi Kelembe, Manager: Commission Services, IEC, 29 October 2015.

Institutional framework

The Electoral Commission Act, 51/1996, provides for the establishment of a permanent five-member electoral commission, of whom one must be a judge. Commissioners must not have a high political profile, may serve for seven years, and may only serve two terms.[26] The president may extend tenure only on recommendation of the National Assembly (Electoral Commission Act, 51/1996, 7[1]). The president appoints commissioners on recommendation of parliament. At least eight commissioners are nominated and interviewed by a panel consisting of the chief justice of the Constitutional Court, representatives of the Human Rights Commission, the Commission on Gender Equality, and the Public Protector, as required by the Electoral Commission Act 51/1996, 6(2). The interview panel recommends eight candidates to an inter-party committee of the National Assembly. The parliamentary committee submits preferred candidates to the National Assembly for approval. A candidate is only confirmed by a majority resolution of the National Assembly. Names of successful candidates are submitted to the president for appointment.[27] The appointment process is regarded as highly inclusive, non-partisan and transparent, and promotes the impartiality of the commission and the confidence of all actors.[28]

Commissioners embody the institution's mandate to support and promote constitutional democracy, and play a pivotal role in ensuring its independence. They are bound by the constitution and the Electoral Act to act impartially, to show no bias, and perform duties and functions without any favour. Commissioners are not allowed to hold political office or outside positions; they can only be removed by 'the president on the grounds of misconduct, incapacity or incompetence, after a finding to that effect by a committee of the National Assembly on the recommendations of the Electoral Court and the majority vote of the National Assembly on a resolution for removal'.[29] Moreover, the judge whilst employed as a commissioner does not receive remuneration from the IEC so that s/he can offer critical commentary without fear of reprisal or dismissal.[30]

Only the Electoral Court can preside over a dispute concerning a commissioner and recommend a penalty to the president. A recent case involving allegations of unethical conduct by former IEC chief electoral officer (CEO), Pansy Tlakula (see later section) presented a quandary for the jurisdiction of the court. Parliamentary hearings raised

26 Electoral Commission Act, 51/1996, A7.

27 Lodge T (2003) How the South African electoral system was negotiated. *Journal of African Elections* 2(1): 71.

28 Kabemba C (2005) Electoral administration: Achievements and continuing challenges. In: J Piombo & L Nijzink (eds) *Electoral Politics in South Africa: Assessing the First Democratic Decade.* New York: Palgrave Macmillan. p. 89; Fakir E & Holland W (2014) Legal framework. In: *Elections Update South Africa 2014.* Johannesburg: EISA. p. 25. Available at https://www.eisa.org.za/eu/pdf/electionupdate2014.pdf [accessed 29 June 2016].

29 Lodge T (2004) *Handbook of South African Electoral Laws and Regulations 2004.* Johannesburg: Electoral Institute of Southern Africa (EISA). p. 12.

30 Kabemba C (2005) Electoral administration: Achievements and continuing challenges. In: Piombo J & Nijzink L (eds) *Electoral Politics in South Africa: Assessing the First Democratic Decade.* New York: Palgrave Macmillan. p. 90.

the issue of whether the Electoral Court had jurisdiction over a commissioner whilst employed as CEO of the electoral body.[31] However, the court set a precedent by finding that commissioners are not only held accountable for their behaviour while they act as commissioners, their prior conduct is also taken into account.[32] In other words, as Ndletyana asserts, 'the Electoral Court has raised the moral standards to which commissioners are held. This will go a long way towards ensuring that the commission is staffed with individuals of unquestionable moral standing and will thus enhance the integrity of the IEC.'[33]

Commissioners

In terms of the constitution (section 193.3), the composition of the electoral commission should 'reflect broadly the race and gender composition of South Africa'. The IEC has made laudable efforts to prioritise gender and racial representivity in the selection of commissioners and senior staff. The permanent IEC was chaired by a woman, Brigalia Bam, a year after it was set up. In 2004 Bam was joined at the helm by Pansy Tlakula, as CEO.[34] Racial representivity has also been a prominent feature of the commission since inception, until recently.[35] Following the resignation of Raenette Taljaard, who has still not been replaced, the IEC is without a non-African.

Executive officers

Commissioners appoint the chief electoral officer (CEO), who heads the IEC'S administration and serves as its accounting officer (Electoral Commission Act, 51/1996, section 12). The current CEO is Mosotho Moeypa, preceded by Pansy Tlakula. The CEO, in turn, appoints other officers and employees, in consultation with commissioners.[36] The IEC has three deputy chief executive officers who manage the divisions of Corporate Services, Outreach and Electoral Operations. Their race and gender profiles are highly representative.

31 Ndletyana M (2015) The IEC and the 2014 elections: A mark of institutional maturity? *Journal of African Elections, Special Issue, South Africa's 2014 Elections* 14(1): 176-177.

32 Ndletyana M (2015) The IEC and the 2014 elections: A mark of institutional maturity? *Journal of African Elections, Special Issue, South Africa's 2014 Elections* 14(1): 186.

33 Ndletyana M (2015) The IEC and the 2014 elections: A mark of institutional maturity? *Journal of African Elections, Special Issue, South Africa's 2014 Elections* 14(1): 186.

34 Kabemba C (2005) Electoral administration: Achievements and continuing challenges. In: J Piombo & L Nijzink (eds) *Electoral Politics in South Africa: Assessing the First Democratic Decade.* New York: Palgrave Macmillan. p. 89.

35 Quintal G (2015, 15 June) IEC interviews: No women commissioners at moment. *News24.* Available at http://www.news24.com/SouthAfrica/News/IEC-interviews-no-women-commissioners-at-the-moment-20150615; http://www.news24.com/SouthAfrica/News/Search-back-on-for-IEC-commissioner-20150922 [accessed 5 August 2016].

36 Kabemba C (2005) Electoral administration: Achievements and continuing challenges. In: J Piombo & L Nijzink (eds) *Electoral Politics in South Africa: Assessing the First Democratic Decade.* New York: Palgrave Macmillan. p. 89.

Powers, functions and responsibilities

Compared to other regional EMBs, the IEC has a broad mandate.[37] Section 5(1) of the Electoral Commission Act outlines the IEC's functions, which are to:

- Manage any election;
- Ensure that any election is free and fair;
- Promote conditions for free and fair elections;
- Promote knowledge of sound and democratic electoral processes;
- Register eligible voters and compile a voters' roll;
- Compile and maintain a register of political parties;
- Establish and maintain liaison and cooperation with political parties;
- Undertake and promote electoral research;
- Develop electoral expertise and technology in all spheres of government;
- Review electoral legislation and make recommendations;
- Promote voter education;
- Promote cooperation with and between persons, institutions, governments and administrations for the achievement of its objectives;
- Declare election results for national, provincial and municipal legislative bodies within seven days;
- Adjudicate disputes which may arise from the organisation, administration or conducting of elections, which are of an administrative nature; and
- Appoint appropriate public administrations in any sphere of government to conduct elections when necessary.

Programmes

The IEC has three programmes, headed by three deputy chief executive officers, through which it implements its mandate. These programmes are:

- Administration and Corporate Services;
- Electoral Operations; and
- Outreach.

Each programme develops and defines strategic objectives, performance indicators and targets. These are linked to a financial year and the respective budget allocation. In addition, during the election period the IEC develops a project plan with milestones. The plan provides details of activities, start and end dates, and progress.[38]

---

37 Interview (telephonic) with Ilona Tip, Operations Director, EISA, 12 October 2015.
38 Interview (telephonic/email) Mr Mlungisi Kelembe, Manager: Commission Services, IEC, 29 October 2015.

The division functions are as follows:[39]

- Administration and Corporate Services manages the support functions of the IEC, including human resources, skills development and training, support services, financial management, legal services, and information communication technology (ICT).
- Electoral Operations houses the core of the IEC's operations. This division deals with voting district delimitation; the registration and deregistration of political parties; the registration of voters; the compilation and administration of the voters' roll; political party liaison; candidate nomination and the management of proportional representation lists; election day operation; and results compilation. It is also responsible for the IEC's logistics and infrastructure.
- Outreach informs and educates the public on democracy and electoral processes with a view to strengthening participation; conducts research on the latest developments in elections and democracy; actively supports efforts to strengthen electoral democracy and ensure free and fair elections, and works to enhance the image of the IEC through strategic communication with stakeholders, including political parties.

Under the stewardship of the CEO are nine provincial offices and their respective provincial electoral officers (PEOs) and support staff responsible for election-related activities of each province. The IEC's national headquarters in Pretoria functions as a policy making and management unit, while the supporting provincial offices and 441 municipal offices attend to core activities such as voter registration, polling stations and liaison with security and political parties. Thus, the delivery of elections is largely through provincial and local IEC structures.[40]

Information technology operations

Technology forms a dominant part of IEC operations. The IEC provides equipment for its entire operation (e.g. networks, servers, workstations, printers, licenses) at the national office, nine provincial offices and 300 municipal centres. The IEC's data centre is hosted internally and managed and monitored from its national office. All electoral systems are

---

39 Independent Electoral Commission (2014) Roles, Mandates and Challenges. IEC presentation to the Portfolio Committee on Home Affairs, National Parliament, Cape Town, 19 August 2014. Available at https://pmg.org.za/committee-meeting/17384/ [accessed 29 June 2016]; Independent Electoral Commission (2015) Annual Report 2015. p. 9. Available at http://www.elections.org.za/content/About-Us/IEC-Annual-Reports/ [accessed 29 June 2016].

40 Kabemba C (2005) Electoral administration: Achievements and continuing challenges. In: J Piombo & L Nijzink (eds) Electoral Politics in South Africa: Assessing the First Democratic Decade. New York: Palgrave Macmillan. p. 89.

web-based, 'thin-client' applications which are custom-built and supported by internal teams.[41] ICT innovations continue to support various processes and are discussed below.[42]

Programmable barcode scanner unit fleet

Procured in 2008, for the 2009 election, the IEC enhanced their information technology (IT) infrastructure with the roll-out of handheld programmable barcode scanners units (PBSUs) with modern technology and now boasts a fleet of 32 130 PBSUs, also known as 'zip-zips'. Their primary function is the capture of voter registration information. PBSUs are updated with the names of all registered voters allowing officials to more efficiently locate names on the voters' roll during the voting procedure to capture and record voter participation. While the scanners are innovative, user-friendly machines which help to speed up registration and voting processes, several voting stations experienced past challenges due to malfunctioning equipment.[43] To ensure sustained operational effectiveness, the IEC has entered into a maintenance contract with a specialised technical service provider to ensure regular testing, servicing and maintenance. However, the fleet of zip-zips will soon need replacement.

Results operations centres

During elections the ICT team provides and supports results operations centres (ROCs) at national, provincial and municipal-level. Each election has a national ROC and nine provincial ROCs, which are commissioned prior to elections. Each ROC has its own data centre and networks, and provides visual information on results and seat allocation. Additional infrastructure is installed to accommodate the needs of political parties and the media. The national results centre is a model adopted by other countries on the continent.[44]

Voting station infrastructure

Voting stations provide an essential platform for the delivery of elections. For the 2014 national and provincial elections, the voting station network consisted of 22 263 voting stations, an overall 6.5% increase compared to the 20 895 stations available in the 2011 election. Population growth, new settlement patterns, the requirement of improving voter accessibility, as well as the revised municipal demarcation data, continue to be the primary contributing factors to the increased voting station footprint. One voting station is located in each voting district and operational details are recorded and regularly updated. The voting station monitoring system reports on the status of voting stations (open or closed) and the estimated throughput of voters at specified times during election day.

---

41 Interview (telephonic/email) Mr Mlungisi Kelembe, Manager: Commission Services, IEC, 29 October 2015; Ongoing correspondence with Ms Melanie du Plessis.

42 Independent Electoral Commission (2015) *Annual Report 2015*. p. 19. Available at http://www.elections. org.za/content/About-Us/IEC-Annual-Reports/ [accessed 29 June 2016].

43 Maphunye KJ (2009) Evaluating election management in South Africa's 2009 elections. *Journal of African Elections: South Africa, Elections 2009, Special Issue* 9(2): 69.

44 Interview (telephonic) with Ilona Tip, Operations Director, EISA, 12 October 2015.

Additional ICT features

- Voting station finder: This is used on the website, and at the IEC call centre to provide support to voters.
- Results website: This provides the public with a dashboard of pertinent results information.
- Mobile application: This disseminates data to the media and voters in an easily accessible format. The mobile application was developed shortly before the 2014 elections and provides features such as real-time voter registration, voting station information (including mapping), election results data and other generic information. It was very well-received by voters, the media and political parties, with 90 000 downloads and 12 million hits recorded over the five days of the 2014 elections.
- Atlas of Results – 2014 National and Provincial Elections: since 1999, an Atlas of Results has been compiled following national and provincial elections. This condenses election data in a clear, concise, visual format with geospatial referencing. Comparisons are provided with elections held since 1999, making the atlas a valuable planning and analysis tool for political parties and political scientists. Various themes are included, such as delimitation, voter registration, leading party maps, party support, voter participation and party support variance across the two latest elections.
- The IEC also provides other platforms to manage the elections, including the ability of voters to log onto its website (www.elections.org.za) and to visit its call centre (0800 11 8000) or send a short text message to verify their registration details.

A number of measures are in place to ensure the security of data, such as firewalls, network segmentation, patch management and anti-virus software solutions. Stringent backup procedures are in place and data is replicated to a disaster recovery site. Ahead of general elections, external audits are commissioned by the IEC to perform penetration and other security tests. The results system is also externally audited to ensure data and architectural integrity.[45] Safeguards are also implemented to ensure fraud and tampering cannot occur with ballots. Following the closure of voting stations, ballots are counted and results announced on site. The party agents present sign the results slip. The results are also posted outside the venue, so that people can view the outcome. The results slip is photocopied and keyed into the electronic system so that those present at voting stations

45 Ongoing email correspondence with IEC staff Melanie du Plessis, Simon Boyle, and Jake Pretorius, 3 November 2015.

can view the slip, and ensure that the figures tally with system figures. The IEC stated that it continued to improve these systems in the lead up to the 2016 elections.[46]

Financial and legislative independence

The commission is an independent, autonomous body and subject only to the constitution and the law. Several aspects of the IEC's structure and operating principles facilitate its independence and deepen trust. First, the institution's independence is guaranteed by the constitution (Article 190–191) and the Electoral Commission Act, 51/1996, 3 (1–2). This obliges government and any other actor to refrain from interference. Where interference is suspected, the IEC has recourse to the courts.[47] Second, while it remains accountable to parliament it has sole discretion over its expenditure. This allows the IEC to discharge its duties with impartiality, separate from government. Third, the profile of the commissioners is pivotal to the IEC's independence, expressly the stipulations that they must possess high moral standing, and may not have a prominent political profile. Moreover, with at least one commissioner being a judge, they bring to the IEC the non-partisan values associated with an independent judiciary.[48] Finally, their selection process by an independent panel, chaired by the chief justice, and made up of the six independent state institutions tasked with supporting constitutional democracy further strengthens the body's independence.[49]

The IEC's funding process is managed in an effective and transparent manner. The commission drafts its own budget, and then presents it to parliament for consideration and approval. The IEC, in turn, reports annually to parliament by submitting audited financial reports for each financial year (Electoral Commission Act 51/1996, 14[1]). The Auditor-General (AG) audits all the IEC's financial records (Electoral Commission Act 51/1996, 12[2][b], 13). However, neither parliament nor the executive controls the nature of the expenditure, allowing the IEC to act independently in terms of managing its funds.[50] The budget of the IEC for the period 2014 to 2017 was approximately ZAR 1.6 billion.[51]

In addition to financial reports, the president may require reports on the IEC's activities. The IEC must also publish a report after each election and may also, on its own initiative,

46 Independent Electoral Commission (2014) Roles, Mandates and Challenges. IEC presentation to the Portfolio Committee on Home Affairs, National Parliament, Cape Town, 19 August 2014. Available at https://pmg.org.za/committee-meeting/17384/ [accessed 29 June 2016].

47 Ndletyana M (2015) The IEC and the 2014 elections: A mark of institutional maturity? *Journal of African Elections, Special Issue, South Africa's 2014 Elections* 14(1): 181.

48 Kabemba C (2005) Electoral administration: Achievements and continuing challenges. In: J Piombo & L Nijzink (eds) *Electoral Politics in South Africa: Assessing the First Democratic Decade*. New York: Palgrave Macmillan. p. 90.

49 Ndletyana M (2015) The IEC and the 2014 elections: A mark of institutional maturity? *Journal of African Elections, Special Issue, South Africa's 2014 Elections* 14(1): 181.

50 Electoral Commission Act, 51/1996, section 13; Kabemba C (2005) Electoral administration: Achievements and continuing challenges. In: J Piombo & L Nijzink (eds) *Electoral Politics in South Africa: Assessing the First Democratic Decade*. New York: Palgrave Macmillan. p. 90.

51 Independent Electoral Commission (2014) Roles, Mandates and Challenges. IEC presentation to the Portfolio Committee on Home Affairs, National Parliament, Cape Town, 19 August 2014. Available at https://pmg.org.za/committee-meeting/17384/ [accessed 29 June 2016].

publish a report on the likelihood or otherwise that it will be able to ensure that any pending election will be free and fair (Electoral Commission Act, 51/1996, 14[2]–[4]). The IEC also reports to the portfolio committee on home affairs on a regular basis on numerous other matters, including its annual performance plans, and annual reports, which detail past activities, and the budgetary review and recommendations report (BRRR), where an evaluation of the IEC's work is presented to the committee.[52]

Providing an electoral commission with sufficient funds can be a challenge, particularly in developing countries where public funds are limited.[53] Moreover, the running of elections are expensive undertakings. In recent elections, costs especially relating to the procurement of resources such as ballot papers, ballot boxes, electronic equipment, stationery and so on, had a tremendous influence on the management of the elections.[54] Overall, the IEC has succeeded in maintaining its spending within budget. The body received an unqualified audit in 2013/2014 with no matters of emphasis and is expected to do so again in the 2014/2015 financial year.[55]

Besides its own expenditure, the commission also accounts for the use of funds by political parties. According to the Public Funding of Represented Political Parties Act, 103/1997, parties receive funding from a represented political parties fund (RPPF). Payments are made to parties that are represented in parliament on a quarterly basis, commencing within four weeks of the start of each financial year. Funding may be used for any purpose compatible with the functioning of a political party in a modern democracy, for example, civic education, voter registration or ensuring continued contact between government and citizens.[56]

In terms of Section 4(1) of the Public Funding Act the chief electoral officer is responsible for the management and administration of the fund. In effect, the fund is administered through the IEC, which keeps parties informed of the relevant rules and regulations. The administration of the fund forms an integral part of the electoral commission's systems, policies, procedures and internal controls. The IEC must keep accurate financial records of all funds received by or accruing to the RPPF, all payments made from the fund, all expenditures arising from allocating the fund, and all assets and liabilities pertaining to the fund. At the end of the financial year, the audit committee of the IEC must report to parliament's portfolio committee on home affairs on: income and expenditure, disbursements to political parties, the amounts spent by political parties, how the funds are spent, and the balance of the fund. The accounts are audited by the auditor general

52 Ibid.
53 Kuhne W (2010) *The Role of Elections in Emerging Democracies and Post-Conflict Countries: Key issues, Lessons Learned and Dilemmas.* Berlin: Friedrich Ebert Stiftung. Available at http://library.fes.de/pdf-files/iez/07416.pdf; http://www.fes-globalization.org/dog_publications/human_rights.htm [accessed 30 June 2016].
54 Independent Electoral Commission (2015) *Annual Report 2015.* p. 5. Available at http://www.elections.org.za/content/About-Us/IEC-Annual-Reports/ [accessed 29 June 2016].
55 Ibid.
56 See Party Funding. Available at http://www.elections.org.za/content/Parties/Party-funding/ [accessed 5 August 2016].

and the AG's report and related documentation must be submitted to parliament (Public Funding of Represented Political Parties Act, 103/1997, 8[2][3]).

The IEC may suspend allocations to a political party if it is satisfied, on reasonable grounds, that the party has not complied with the Act. Prior to doing so it must inform the party of the intended suspension and give it thirty days to motivate why its funding should not be stopped. The IEC may terminate the suspension once it is satisfied that it is no longer justified.

Political parties must account for their public funding. The Act requires that political parties hold the funds in a separate bank account. An accounting officer must be appointed by each political party to manage and account for the fund, and ensure compliance with the spending requirements as set out by the Funding Act. The accounting officer must also prepare a statement within two months of the fiscal year on amounts received and used, the purposes for which the funds were used, and audit the accounts to evaluate whether the funds were used for purposes other than those allowed by the Act. The auditor's report and audited statement must be submitted to the IEC within three months after the end of the financial year. If money from the fund is spent irregularly, the accounting officer may be liable for the misspent funds. The IEC can recover the funds through a civil claim against the accounting officer or by setting it off against future payments to the party.

The IEC publishes an annual report on the RPPF that includes extracts from the audited statements political parties submit to the IEC.[57] These reports contain basic information about the number of parties that complied with the rules governing the administration and use of public funding for political parties, and contain an overview of the number of parties that violate specific rules. The IEC's report on the fund includes a report by the Auditor-General of South Africa on his audit of the fund. The report is tabled in parliament in September each year, and is made available on the IEC's website. However, these reports do not necessarily contain information about why parties violate the rules or how violations are sanctioned. Moreover, there is little comprehensive information on specific political parties' use of public funding. Political parties have shown reluctance to disclose their financial statements of how they spent their public funds.[58]

Recruitment and staff

Staff are recruited and appointed in terms of a Recruitment and Selection Policy approved by the commission. Commissioners are appointed in terms of Section 7(2) of the Electoral Commission Act, 51/1996, and the IEC have drafted regulations based on this clause for the terms and conditions of service of staff, which are published in the Government Gazette from time to time. Electoral staff is recruited in terms of the Electoral Act, 73/1998, for all national and provincial elections and in terms of the Local Government: Municipal Electoral Act, 27/2000.

---

57 Ibid.

58 Merton M (2011, 11 July) MPs coy on party allowances. *IOL News.* Available at http://www.iol.co.za/news/politics/mps-coy-on-party-allowances-1.1096590?%20ot=inmsa [accessed 5 August 2016].

During election periods, the IEC employs some 211 000 temporary staff members in various capacities to assist at voting stations in the election period, supplemented by 4 656 area managers. Legal safeguards in the Electoral Act, 73/1998 underwrite the vetting and verification processes used by the IEC to recruit staff. Chapter 6, part 4 ss. 72–83 sets out criteria concerning the temporary appointments of presiding officers, voting officers and counting officers for each voting station. These officers must exclude candidates contesting the election, party agents, as well as individuals holding political office in a registered political party. The Act also obliges officials to take a declaration of secrecy as well as a prescribed oath. Thus, the oversight, transparency and accountability mechanisms within both the law and regulatory frameworks appear to be sufficiently robust to ensure the credible management and administration of the elections.[59]

However, repeated concerns have been raised about the impartiality of temporary election staff, many of whom are teachers that belong to the South African Democratic Teachers Union (SADTU), an affiliate of the Congress of SA Trade Unions (COSATU) which has previously urged its affiliates to vote for the governing African National Congress.[60] Moreover, concerns were raised during the 2014 elections about declining standards, particularly with regard to staff training, some of whose decisions on occasion appeared in conflict with legislation or regulations, especially at voting stations.[61] However, Fakir and Holland have pointed out that the number of complaints made against electoral officials, as a proportion of the number of actual electoral officials, is miniscule. In addition, the fact that all parties are entitled to place party agents in every voting station should allay fears of widespread irregular behaviour among IEC officials.[62] Also, election observers have not noted excessive problems with IEC staff, finding them to be generally well-trained.[63]

Public interactions and stakeholders

The IEC has a number of stakeholders. In addition to the obvious state institutions, they include the media, civil society organisations, political parties and traditional leaders; and are managed primarily through the IEC's Administration and Corporate Services Division. For ease of interactions, stakeholders are organised into issues-based target

59 Fakir E & Holland W (2014) Legal framework. In: *Elections Update South Africa 2014*. Johannesburg: EISA. p. 26. Available at https://www.eisa.org.za/eu/pdf/electionupdate2014.pdf [accessed 29 June 2016].

60 Maphunye KJ (2009) Evaluating election management in South Africa's 2009 elections. *Journal of African Elections: South Africa, Elections 2009, Special Issue* 9(2): 56–78; Independent Electoral Commission (2014) Roles, Mandates and Challenges. IEC presentation to the Portfolio Committee on Home Affairs, National Parliament, Cape Town, 19 August 2014. Available at https://pmg.org.za/committee-meeting/17384/ [accessed 29 June 2016].

61 Interview (Skype/email) Professor Jørgen Elklit, Department of Political Science, Aarhus University, Denmark, 26 October 2015; Kotze D (2014) Elections in 2014: A barometer of South African politics and society?' In: *Elections Update South Africa 2014*. Johannesburg: EISA. p. 11. Available at https://www.eisa.org.za/eu/pdf/electionupdate2014.pdf [accessed 29 June 2016].

62 Fakir E & Holland W (2014) Legal framework. In: *Elections Update South Africa 2014*. Johannesburg: EISA. p. 26. https://www.eisa.org.za/eu/pdf/electionupdate2014.pdf [accessed 29 June 2016].

63 Interview (telephonic) with Ilona Tip, Operations Director, EISA, 12 October 2015.

audiences, and are managed through programmes located in the Outreach Division, as follows: [64]

- Youth;
- Women;
- Disabled persons;
- Minority groups; and
- Farming communities.

Arguably, political parties, the media and voters comprise the most important of all IEC stakeholders. Political parties are key stakeholders in an election. A political party that intends to contest an election for a legislative body must be registered with the IEC in terms of section 15 of the Electoral Commission Act (51/1996). During the 2014 national and provincial elections, 45 political parties registered to take part in the elections, compared to 40 in the 2009 national and provincial elections. The IEC has established party liaison committees to conduct communications and relationship building with political parties (see later section on dispute resolution).

The communications division actively works to protect and enhance the image of the commission through strategic communication with the commission's stakeholders, including political parties. In addition, the stakeholder engagement and liaison unit liaises with national and international stakeholders to promote knowledge of and adherence to democratic electoral principles and promote collaboration.[65] On a regular basis, the IEC produces publications as part of its knowledge management, communication and education activities. A key publication is an election guide, aimed primarily at members of the media, political parties and interested stakeholders attending ROCs during elections. Its purpose is to ensure accurate and regular reporting by the media on election results, and to empower political parties with the necessary election information. The publication provides a detailed overview of the commission's mandate, structure and operational procedures; a detailed overview of the commission's preparations for the respective elections, including logistics and infrastructure, civic and voter education, the national voters' roll and political party liaison, among others; an overview of past election results.[66]

Dispute resolution mechanisms

The vibrancy of the foregoing interactions with stakeholders has made it possible to create an elaborate and effective dispute resolution mechanism. Section 103(a) of the Electoral Act empowers the commission to resolve electoral disputes or complaints through conciliation. Provincial coordinators for conflict management are appointed to coordinate initiatives

---

64 Ongoing email correspondence with Dr Nomsa Masuku, 3 November 2015.
65 Independent Electoral Commission (2014) Roles, Mandates and Challenges. IEC presentation to the Portfolio Committee on Home Affairs, National Parliament, Cape Town, 19 August 2014. Available at https://pmg.org.za/committee-meeting/17384/ [accessed 29 June 2016].
66 Independent Electoral Commission (2015) Annual Report 2015. p. 42. Available at http://www.elections.org.za/content/About-Us/IEC-Annual-Reports/ [accessed 29 June 2016].

for the creation of conditions for free and fair elections, intervene in disputes and ensure stakeholders adhere to the electoral code of conduct. The role of the provincial coordinator is to:

- Coordinate the conflict management programme in the province;
- Recruit conflict management panellists;
- Monitor, evaluate and report on existing or potential conflict situations in the province;
- Liaise with provincial stakeholders;
- Facilitate access to legal recourse; and
- Mediate and resolve conflicts by deploying a conflict panellist to affected areas.

In addition to the IEC's provincial coordinator conflict management programme, there are two other important dispute resolution mechanisms.

Party liaison committees
Political parties are key stakeholders in an election. The Electoral Commission Act determines that one of the IEC's functions is to 'establish and maintain liaison and cooperation with parties' (section 5.1[g]). To achieve this objective, the IEC has established party liaison committees (PLCs) with parties represented at national, provincial and municipal levels of government. A strategic objective of the electoral operations unit is to 'provide consultative and cooperative liaison platforms between the IEC and political parties to facilitate free and fair elections'.[67] Political parties have free access to the voters' rolls, and can have no more than two representatives on the committees, which are chaired by IEC representatives.[68] Annual performance indicators for 2013/2014 (an election year) show regular political parties meetings to prepare for the 2014 general elections with a total of 2 060 liaison sessions held (12 national; 77 provincial and 1971 local). PLCs were consulted on the following aspects of the 2014 electoral programme:[69]

- Amendments to the Electoral Act;
- The delimitation of voting districts and establishment of voting stations;
- The vetting of electoral staff;
- The appointment of municipal electoral officers;
- The roll-out of targeted communication and registration;
- The identification of potential hot spots and conflict resolution;
- Ballot paper sign-off; and
- Candidate nomination processes, etc.

---

67 Ibid.: 25.
68 Lodge T (2004) *Handbook of South African Electoral Laws and Regulations 2004*. Johannesburg: Electoral Institute of Southern Africa (EISA). p. 17.
69 Independent Electoral Commission (2015) *Annual Report 2015*. p. 25. Available at http://www.elections. org.za/content/About-Us/IEC-Annual-Reports/ [accessed 29 June 2016].

During the 2014/2015 year, in preparation for the forthcoming 2016 local elections, the number of PLC meetings held at national, provincial and municipal-levels totalled 1 748 meetings (17 national; 69 provincial; and 1662 local). This exceeded the IECs own target of 1 400 sessions.[70]

In past elections the IEC's dealings were restricted to represented parties in the PLCs. The institution has since realised that unrepresented parties and, increasingly, independent candidates often contest elections, sometimes at the last moment, which results in a situation where they are deprived of the consultative and informative processes that take place with represented parties. As a result, the IEC has resolved to strengthen liaison with unrepresented political parties.[71] As such, PLC meetings held before the 2014 national and provincial elections were extended to allow new and unrepresented parties (including the Economic Freedom Fighters and Agang) the opportunity to participate.[72] The IEC believes that their working relationship with parties is largely constructive.[73] Where serious legal differences are experienced with political parties, legal and constitutional means are used to resolve them. The PLCs are widely recognised as one of the most important mechanisms for political conflict management in the post-apartheid era and their success has meant that the PLC model has been exported to other countries for application elsewhere.

Electoral Court
The Electoral Court is established by the Electoral Commission Act, 51/1996 (sections 18–20). Under section 20 the Electoral Court may review any IEC decision concerning an electoral matter; consider an appeal against a decision by the commission; investigate any allegation of misconduct, incapacity or incompetence of a member of the commission. Section 96 of the Electoral Act gives the court final jurisdiction in respect of all electoral disputes and complaints about infringements of the code of conduct. Appeals against commission decisions may only be heard with the prior approval of the Electoral Court chair. Verdicts by the Electoral Court can be appealed at the Constitutional Court. The chief electoral officer may institute or intervene in civil proceedings before a court to enforce the Electoral Act and its codes of conduct. Penalties are broad and includes fines, and in some instances, imprisonment (Electoral Act, sections 97–98). Its members are appointed by the president on the recommendation of the Judicial Service Commission. They must include a chairperson, who should be a judge of the Supreme Court, two

70 Independent Electoral Commission (2015) *Annual Report 2015*. p. 25. Available at http://www.elections.org.za/content/About-Us/IEC-Annual-Reports/ [accessed 29 June 2016].
71 Independent Electoral Commission (2014) Roles, Mandates and Challenges. IEC presentation to the Portfolio Committee on Home Affairs, National Parliament, Cape Town, 19 August 2014. Available at https://pmg.org.za/committee-meeting/17384/ [accessed 29 June 2016].
72 Independent Electoral Commission (2015) *Annual Report 2015*. p. 11. Available at http://www.elections.org.za/content/About-Us/IEC-Annual-Reports/ [accessed 29 June 2016].
73 Ibid.: 2.

additional judges, and two other South African citizens. The court is supported financially by the Department of Justice.[74]

Only the Electoral Court can preside over a dispute concerning a commissioner and recommend penalties. The recent Tlakula case revealed a quandary and a litmus test for the jurisdiction of the court. Parliamentary hearings raised the issue of whether the Electoral Court had jurisdiction over a commissioner whilst employed as CEO of the electoral body.[75] However, the court set a precedent by finding that commissioners are not only held accountable for their behaviour whilst they act as commissioners; their prior conduct is also taken into account.[76]

Generally, objections and disputes have been minimal in recent elections. The IEC received 22 objections relating to the 2014 national and provincial elections. Three of these were withdrawn by the objectors and the remaining 19 were dismissed by the IEC. Most of the submissions were rejected for non-compliance with the provisions of section 55 of the Electoral Act. None of the IEC's decisions were appealed.[77]

Assessment and evaluation

Relationship with the governing party

The IEC has been called on to do more to realise its legislated mandate in section 5(1) of the Electoral Commission Act to 'ensure that elections are free and fair', and to 'promote conditions for free and fair elections'. Several behaviours that violate the international standards of the pre-election environment include: the improper use of public funds and unfair use of government resources; restrictions to freedom of association and political expression, in particular disruption and obstruction of party meetings; and various forms of intimidation and manipulation, especially of poorer voters. The ANC has been accused of extensive targeting of state resources, including public infrastructure, budgets and state goods for campaigning purposes to support its campaign, creating an undue advantage over opposition parties.[78]

---

74 Lodge T (2002) South Africa. In: T Lodge, D Kadima & D Pottie (eds) *Compendium of Elections in Southern Africa*. Johannesburg: Electoral Institute of Southern Africa (EISA). p. 15.

75 Ndletyana M (2015) The IEC and the 2014 elections: A mark of institutional maturity? *Journal of African Elections, Special Issue, South Africa's 2014 Elections* 14(1): 176-177.

76 Ndletyana M (2015) The IEC and the 2014 elections: A mark of institutional maturity? *Journal of African Elections, Special Issue, South Africa's 2014 Elections* 14(1): 186.

77 Independent Electoral Commission (2014) National and Provincial Elections 2014. Ensuring Free and Fair Elections: Celebrating 20 Years of Democracy. Pretoria: Independent Electoral Commission. p. 49. Available at file:///C:/Users/User/Downloads/2014%20National%20and%20Provincial%20Elections%20Report.pdf [accessed 29 June 2016].

78 Schulz-Herzenberg C (2014) The South African 2014 national and provincial elections: The Integrity of the electoral process. *Institute for Security Studies Policy Brief 62*, August 2014. pp. 4–5. Available at https://www.issafrica.org/publications/policy-brief/the-south-african-2014-elections-the-integrity-of-the-electoral-process [accessed 29 June 2016].

Opposition parties have called up the IEC to take a strong stance on these transgressions during election campaigns, arguing that they pose a threat to free and fair elections and that the IEC cannot, in principle, confine the checks on free and fair elections to the process at the voting stations alone.[79] The IEC has responded by arguing that these are political issues to be resolved through judicial courts. Opposition parties believe the IEC is 'passing the buck' and that the misuse of state resources undermines the commission's work by directly affecting the integrity of the electoral process. As political competition increases policy-makers, including the IEC, will need to explore new regulatory mechanisms to manage new forms of manipulation and intimidation that curb freedom of political association and expression in the campaign period.

The IEC's ability to conduct impartial and transparent elections also came under scrutiny during two separate incidents. The first controversy involved the IEC's former chief electoral officer, Advocate Pansy Tlakula. She was found to have unfairly influenced the awarding of a lease contract, for IEC offices, to a company that is partially owned by her business partner, Thaba Mufamadi. Mufamadi also happened to be an ANC member of parliament.[80] This raised concerns that the CEO could have used her influence over the commission to the benefit of the ANC and caused smaller opposition parties to call for Tlakula's immediate resignation.[81] In fact, some opposition party leaders went further and warned of the ANC's potential for rigging the elections through 'rogue elements' within the IEC.[82] In June 2014, following the election, the Electoral Court recommended that Pansy Tlakula be removed from her post. The Constitutional Court rejected her plea, and she was eventually dismissed from the IEC.

The second incident involved by-elections in 2013 in the Tlokwe Municipality (North West Province) that involved candidates that had been expelled by the ANC. The IEC disqualified six independent candidates (all former ANC councillors) on the grounds that they did not meet the required threshold of nominations. Upon appeal, the Electoral

79 Independent Electoral Commission (2014) Roles, Mandates and Challenges. IEC presentation to the Portfolio Committee on Home Affairs, National Parliament, Cape Town, 19 August 2014. Available at https://pmg.org.za/committee-meeting/17384/ [accessed 29 June 2016]

80 Schulz-Herzenberg C (2014) The South African 2014 national and provincial elections: The Integrity of the electoral process. *Institute for Security Studies Policy Brief 62*, August 2014. p. 2. Available at https://www.issafrica.org/publications/policy-brief/the-south-african-2014-elections-the-integrity-of-the-electoral-process [accessed 29 June 2016]; Fakir E & Holland W (2014) Legal framework. In: *Elections Update South Africa 2014*. Johannesburg: EISA. p. 26. https://www.eisa.org.za/eu/pdf/electionupdate2014.pdf [accessed 29 June 2016]; Tlakula and IEC committee guilty of gross maladministration (2013, 26 August) *SABC News*. Available at http://www.sabc.co.za/news/a/2a78fc8040dd8ae49ebfbf434f2981a1/Tlakula-and-IEC-committee-guilty-of-grossmaladministration—20130826 [accessed 6 January 2017]; Pillay V (2014, 18 March) Treasury report slams IEC deal, confirms Madonsela's findings. *Mail & Guardian*. Available at http://mg.co.za/article/2014-03-18-treasury-report-slams-iec-deal-confirms-madonselas-findings [accessed 6 January 2017].

81 Ndletyana M (2015) The IEC and the 2014 elections: A mark of institutional maturity? *Journal of African Elections, Special Issue, South Africa's 2014 Elections* 14(1): 172.

82 Forde F (2014) ANC plotting to rig elections: Holomisa. *The Sunday Independent*. p. 8. Available at http://www.bdlive.co.za/national/politics/2014/04/01/opposition-parties-say-iec-chief-must-resign-within-seven-days [accessed 26 July 216].

Court overturned the qualification. ANC candidates won the subsequent by-elections held in December 2013, but independent candidates alleged that they were rigged. The Constitutional Court is currently hearing the matter.[83]

Both incidents raise the question of whether pressure from the governing party can act to undermine the IEC's impartial conduct. These events also threatened the public's trust in the institution. As such, the IEC must give greater consideration to protecting the institution's credibility by prioritising non-partisan and impartial behaviour among its staff, introducing greater transparency and accountability through and ethics framework, and managing conflicts of interests among senior officials.

Registration process

Voter registration is the cornerstone of an electoral democracy. An inclusive and transparent registration process allows for the broad participation of all eligible voters, which lends credibility to the electoral process and election results. The IEC makes a concerted effort to ensure that information about the voting process is sufficiently accessible to everyone. It runs a series of voter education campaigns using radio, television and print media. Voters can check whether they are registered online or via text message, and can find the location of their voting station online. Voter registration statistics for the 2014 national and provincial elections indicated that the IEC had registered a total of 25 390 150 voters out of a voting age population of about 32.7 million people. This was an increase in registered voters of 2.2 million from the 2009 elections which then had registered 23 181 997 voters.

The increasing gap between the size of the eligible population and registered voters turns our attention to the legal setting and the impact of registration processes. The introduction of an automatic registration process, where the state takes the initiative to register eligible citizens, may lessen the costs of registration for some groups. The current use of voluntary registration procedures might reduce voter participation among those who lack the relevant identification documents to register, voters who are migrant workers, or those based in rural areas and lack the means to complete the registration process.[84] Comparative studies suggest turnout is higher in countries with automatic registration.[85]

Party funding

Finally, the concerns over whether political parties have equitable access to public funds have led to calls for the IEC to revisit the 90:10 allocation formula of public funds to ensure

---

83 Fakir E & Holland W (2014) Legal framework. In: *Elections Update South Africa 2014.* Johannesburg: EISA. p. 26. Available at https://www.eisa.org.za/eu/pdf/electionupdate2014.pdf [accessed 29 June 2016]; Khuthala N (2015) IEC credibility in question after Tlokwe judgment. *Mail and Guardian Online.* Available at http://mg.co.za/article/2013-09-18-00-ieccredibility-questioned-aftertlokwe-judgment [accessed 26 July 2016].

84 Schulz-Herzenberg C (2014) Trends in electoral participation, 1994–2014. In: C Schulz-Herzenberg & R Southall (eds) *Election 2014 South Africa: The Campaigns, Results and Future Prospects.* Johannesburg: Jacana Media & Konrad Adenauer Stiftung. p. 24.

85 Norris P (2000) *A Virtuous Circle: Political Communications in Postindustrial Societies.* New York: Cambridge University Press. p. 255.

more equitable distribution. The IEC is tasked with dispensing public funds to political parties that have representation in provincial legislatures or the national legislature.[86] The bulk of public funding (90%) is allocated on the basis of the proportion of seats a party already has in the legislatures, while 10% is allocated equitably among parties. Thus, larger parties receive a larger proportion of public funding, and have more resources with which to shape political discourse and contest elections. Smaller parties argue that it undermines the capacity of new and local-level political parties to participate in the electoral process and unfairly favours the ruling ANC by supporting incumbency rather than 'multiparty democracy', which is the stated objective of the constitution.

A more equitable distribution of public monies would afford smaller parties an opportunity to utilise more expensive but effective media-based adverts to reach a national audience, better inform voters and thereby strengthen competition at elections. In 2007 the IEC noted that 'the formula used in the funding of political parties was identified as allegedly limiting the capacity of smaller parties to mobilise membership and sustain themselves'.[87] Indeed, some analysts question whether the dominant proportionality principle in public funding is unconstitutional.[88] Arguably, section 236 of the constitution, which states that funding must be provided 'on an equitable and proportional basis', may have intended more weight to equity over proportionality.

The private funding of political parties remains entirely unregulated in South Africa. Public funding comprises a fraction of the total funding to political parties. The rest, which amounts to hundreds of millions of rand per year, comes in undisclosed amounts from private sources.[89] However, given the absence of regulation of private funding for political parties, or any transparency or reporting requirements, definitive figures from private sources are unknown. The lack of party funding regulation and disclosure, combined with parties' increasing demand for funds, has created an unhealthy alliance between government and private interests that is ripe for increased corruption.[90] Several civil society groups – including the Institute for Democracy in Africa (Idasa), which brought a court challenge case in 2004 aimed at compelling political parties to disclose their sources of funds in the absence of disclosure legislation – have long campaigned for both disclosure and regulation of private funding.[91] More recently, in 2015 the *My Vote Counts* (MVC) campaign launched a constitutional court case to compel parliament to pass legislation to

---

86 Public Funding of Represented Political Parties Act, 103/1997.

87 IEC Multi-Stakeholder Conference (2007) *Reflections on Democracy in South Africa*. Pretoria: Electoral Commission. p. 5; Maphunye KJ (2009) Evaluating election management in South Africa's 2009 elections. *Journal of African Elections: South Africa, Elections 2009, Special Issue* 9(2): 62.

88 February J (2015) My Vote Counts Conference. University of Cape Town, Friday 28 August 2015.

89 Money and Politics Project (2011) Money and politics in South Africa: Meeting our next democratic challenge. *Policy Paper October 2011*. Funded by the OSF-SA with Wallace Global Fund.

90 Ibid; and see http://www.bdlive.co.za/national/politics/2014/03/18/secret-party-funding-fuels-electorates-suspicion [accessed 26 July 2016].

91 Money and Politics Project (2011) Money and politics in South Africa: Meeting our next democratic challenge. *Policy Paper October 2011*. Funded by the OSF-SA with Wallace Global Fund. p. 7.

regulate private funding to political parties and called on the IEC to support calls for a new regulatory system.[92]

Although a majority of the Constitutional Court dismissed the MVC's application, the case invited attention towards possible institutional mechanisms for the enforcement of future regulations. The IEC has been identified as a potential regulatory body for private donations, based on the view that the electoral body has a critical role to play not only in terms of advocacy and shaping future legislation, but also as a key institution to implement and manage the regulation of private donations. This model would see the IEC receive private donations at a central point and would then reallocate funds to parties. The Open Society Foundation's (OSF) Money in Politics Project argued that the Public Funding of Represented Political Parties Act, 103/1997, already makes allowance for 'contributions and donations to the Fund originating from any sources, whether within or outside the Republic' and can therefore be logically extended to private sources of funds which could be administered by the IEC to ensure ethical management of public and private funds alike.[93]

However, the IEC has refused to take a position on the regulation of private funds.[94] Moreover, election specialists caution that the regulation of private funding is not within the ambit of the IEC and would create an unnecessary burden. Many believe it wiser to introduce a separate independent institution to regulate and manage private funding to political parties.[95] This will help to insulate the IEC from inevitable conflicts with political parties, a key stakeholder, should it become a regulatory body obliged to act punitively towards parties if they transgress funding regulations. The ANC's response to the Constitutional Court's dismissal of the MVC case suggests it is likely that a new body will implement the regulations of private funds. The ANC issued a statement immediately after the ruling stating that its own party resolutions called for the introduction of 'an effective regulatory architecture for private funding of political parties and civil society groups to enhance accountability and transparency to the citizenry'.[96]

92 Evans S (2015, 9 September) Sources of party funding to remain private. *Mail & Guardian Online*, available at http://mg.co.za/article/2015-09-30-sources-of-party-funding-to-remain-private [accessed 12 October 2015]; Vuka Z (2013, 16 January) MVC Letter to the Chief electoral Officer of the IEC, available at http://www.myvotecounts.org.za/wp-content/uploads/2013/02/Letter-to-IEC-16-January-2013.pdf [accessed 5 August 2016].

93 Money and Politics Project (2011) Money and politics in South Africa: Meeting our next democratic challenge. *Policy Paper MVC*. Available October 2011. Funded by the OSF-SA with Wallace Global Fund. p. 7.

94 Moepya MS (2013, 4 February) Letter from the Chief electoral Officer of the IEC to MVC, available at http://www.myvotecounts.org.za/wp-content/uploads/2013/02/Letter-from-IEC-4-February-2013.pdf [accessed 5 August 2016].

95 Interview (telephonic), Ilona Tip, Operations Director, EISA, 12 October 2015; Interview (telephonic) Mr Gregory Solik, Board of Directors, My Vote Counts, 21 October 2015.

96 ANC Press Release (2015, 30 September) Concourt ruling regarding private party funding, Issued by the Office of the Chief Whip. Available at http://www.anc.org.za/caucus/show.php?ID=4224 [accessed 29 October 2015].

Expert and observer evaluations

Since the inaugural election of 1994, commentators including political parties, observer missions, non-governmental organisations (NGOs), and the media laud the administration of elections in South Africa.[97] The IEC is considered a well-functioning and capable election management body that delivers elections at global standards.[98] The IEC is praised for its logistical preparedness, its management of elections and the counting process. Generally, observers conclude that South Africa's elections are free, fair, transparent and credible. A recent Perceptions of Electoral Integrity (PEI) report rated South Africa's elections as some of the best in Africa (ranked fourth among African countries and 40th globally), with high integrity across most dimensions of the electoral cycle.[99] The African Union's Election Observation Mission (AU EOM) to South Africa to observe the 7 May 2014 national and provincial elections reported that the political and electoral environment was generally peaceful across the country with voters being able to exercise their right to vote. Its 2014 election report found that the institution and legal framework of election in South Africa largely complied with international best practices and standards for the conduct of democratic elections, and based on its overall assessment of the elections, concluded that 'the general elections held in South Africa on 7 May 2014 were conducted in a transparent, peaceful and credible manner and, in general, reflected the will of South African voters'.[100]

South Africa has a well-established culture of allowing independent observers access to polls. The accreditation of international observers is regulated by a code of conduct issued by the IEC.[101] The presence of international observers in recent elections has decreased based on the premise that South Africa's elections are largely peaceful, free and fair events. Yet, the most recent 2014 election still attracted approximately 90 international observer organisations. The IEC has also launched an initiative with the National Democratic Institute (NDI), a US-based institute that will help the IEC to coordinate observer missions in South Africa, showcasing the country as a best-practice model.[102] The South African Civil Society Election Coalition (SACSEC), a national initiative of over 40 non-

97 Piper L (ed.) (2005) *South Africa 10 years later: A consolidated electoral system but not democracy.* EISA *Research Report* No. 11. Johannesburg: EISA; February J (2009) The electoral system and electoral administration, 1994–2009 In: R Southall & J Daniel (eds) *Zunami! The 2009 South African Elections.* Johannesburg: Jacana Media and Konrad-Adenauer-Stiftung. p. 63.

98 Interview (Skype/email) Professor Jørgen Elklit, Department of Political Science, Aarhus University, Denmark, 26 October 2015.

99 Gromping M & Martinez i Coma F (2015) *Electoral Integrity in Africa.* Johannesburg: The Electoral Integrity Project and Hanns Seidel Foundation. p. 24, 26. Available at https://www.dropbox.com/s/ix56hatvgwyk1lc/Electoral%20Integrity%20in%20Africa%20-%20uniofsyd_v5.1.pdf?dl=0 [accessed 29 June 2016].

100 African Union Election Observation Mission (2014) *7 May 2014 National and Provincial Elections in the Republic of South Africa. Final Report.* p. 2. Available at http://pa.au.int/en/sites/default/files/FINAL%20AUEOM%20SOUTH%20AFRICA%202014.pdf [accessed 9 September 2015].

101 Regulations on the Accreditation of Observers, 1999. Available at http://www.elections.org.za/content/WorkArea/linkit.aspx?LinkIdentifier=id&ItemID=1395 [accessed 26 July 2016].

102 Independent Electoral Commission (2014) Roles, Mandates and Challenges. IEC presentation to the Portfolio Committee on Home Affairs, National Parliament, Cape Town, 19 August 2014. Available at https://pmg.org.za/committee-meeting/17384/ [accessed 29 June 2016].

governmental and faith-based organisations committed to the conduct of free, fair and credible elections, field approximately 2 000 observers at polling and counting stations.[103]

The IEC also publish an assessment report on each election with recommendations for improvements. This report is usually made available to those who participate in party liaison committees.[104]

Citizen evaluations

Electoral authorities should be widely regarded as credible by their electorates. While electoral integrity is central to ensuring that the results reflect the general will, and that citizens can exercise their right to change their government and hold incumbents accountable, citizen perceptions about the freeness and fairness of elections are also crucial to democratic legitimacy. Research shows that citizen perceptions of the integrity of their elections have an effect on their perceptions about the supply of, and satisfaction with democracy in countries like Kenya and South Africa.[105] In this regard, EMBs can play a vital role in building public trust in electoral processes. This in turn, generates support and legitimacy for the political system.

The IEC is widely regarded as an efficient and independent body and remains one of the most trusted national institutions. Voters have provided exceptionally favourable evaluations of the IEC's performance and the conduct of officials at voting stations over the past few elections. An IEC/Human Sciences Research Council (HSRC) 2014 voting day survey found that an overwhelming 97% voiced satisfaction with the quality of services rendered by IEC officials, while 70% reported that they took fewer than 15 minutes to reach their voting stations, and 98% found the voting procedures inside the voting station easy to understand.[106] Results from the voter participation survey (VPS) and an election satisfaction survey (ESS) also show an overwhelming endorsement of the electoral commission by voters over the past local government elections.[107]

While the IEC enjoys a solid public reputation, two separate public opinion surveys found that the institution has experienced a decline in public confidence in recent years; a

---

103 Democracy in Africa Research Unit (DARU) at the Centre for Social Science Research, University of Cape Town (2012) *The Open Society Monitoring Index Round 2 2012.* Cape Town: Open Society Foundation for South Africa. Available at http://osf.org.za/wp/publications/OpenSocietyMonitoringIndexRound2_2012. pdf [accessed 30 June 2016].

104 Independent Electoral Commission (2014) Roles, Mandates and Challenges. IEC presentation to the Portfolio Committee on Home Affairs, National Parliament, Cape Town, 19 August 2014. Available at https://pmg.org.za/committee-meeting/17384/ [accessed 29 June 2016].

105 Schulz-Herzenberg C, Peter Aling'o P & Gatimu S (2015) The 2013 general elections in Kenya: The integrity of the electoral process. *Institute for Security Studies Policy Brief 74.* Pretoria: Institute for Security Studies; Schulz-Herzenberg C (2015) South African citizen perceptions of electoral integrity across three elections: 2004, 2009, 2014. Presentation at the Electoral Integrity Conference 2015, hosted by the Hanns Seidel Foundation and the Electoral Integrity Project, Cape Town, 22–24 June 2015.

106 Struwig J, Roberts BJ, Gordon SL, Davids YD & Marco J (2014) *Election Satisfaction Survey (ESS).* Report by the Human Sciences Research Council (HSRC) Democracy, Governance and Service Delivery (DGSD) Research Programme. Pretoria: HSRC.

107 Struwig J, Roberts S & Vivier E (2011) A vote of confidence: Election management and public perceptions of electoral processes in South Africa. *Journal of Public Administration* 1(46): 1122–1138.

likely consequence of the Tlokwe municipality leasing scandals that confronted the electoral body in the years before the 2014 elections. Both events had raised questions about the IECs ability to conduct impartial and transparent elections. An IEC/HSRC survey found that trust had declined from 72% in 2009 to 63% in 2015.[108] The Comparative National Elections Project (CNEP) public opinion post-election surveys shows a decline in positive trust ratings for the IEC dropped from 58% in 2004, to 53% in 2015.

Citizen perceptions about the freeness and fairness of elections are also crucial to democratic legitimacy. When asked by CNEP surveys to rate the freeness and fairness of the most recent national election, an overwhelming majority of respondents across past three general elections agreed 'the election was free and fair', or with just minor problems. However, the data shows a decline in a 'free and fair' verdict from 81% in 2004 to 71% in the 2009 elections and dropping again to 68% in the 2014 elections. That over 68% of South Africans still rates the conduct of the elections favourably, and felt them to be free and fair, reflects a positive performance by the IEC and provides a constructive platform upon which to address lowering levels of institutional trust.

When asked 'How accurately did the announced results of the election reflect the way the people of this country actually voted?', we see similar declines in accuracy ratings. In 2004, 80% of respondents thought the election results to be accurate, which declined to 74% in the 2009 elections and to 71% in the 2014 elections.

The integrity of the electoral process also depends on the ability of voters to exercise their right to vote in the absence of manipulation or intimidation. Generally, political party members adhere to the strict rules that prohibit party campaigning or materials around election polling stations. The data shows little evidence of voter experiences of political coercion. The CNEP survey asks respondents a battery of questions about their personal experiences during the elections. Respondents are asked if they or someone they know personally was prevented from:

- Registering to vote;
- Attending an election event such as a campaign rally;
- Voting because their name was not on the voters' roll;
- Voting due to fear or intimidation;
- Offered reward or compensation; and
- Pressured to support a particular party.

The data shows no more than 5% of respondents ever reporting on any of these incidents across the past three general elections. This suggests that the declines in integrity perceptions regarding trust, ratings of freeness and fairness and the accuracy of results cannot be easily attributed to negative incidents experienced by voters personally during the electoral process.

---

108   Roberts B, Struwig J, Gordon S, Davids YD & Marco JL (2014) *IEC Voter Participation Survey 2013/14: Key Findings*. Report prepared for the Electoral Commission of South Africa. Pretoria: Human Sciences Research Council.

Recommendations

An assessment of the available evidence suggests that the IEC's successful performance since its inception in 1993 is attributable in large part to the well-defined and detailed constitutional and legislative framework within which it operates. It is also due, however, to the noticeable improvements in the implementation of election management over the years. The IEC can boast several laudable achievements. For example, its numerous dispute resolution mechanisms, including the party liaison committees, the code of conduct, voting station party agents, and the Electoral Court, have all proved critical to ensuring low levels of political conflict and free and fair elections. The IEC should continue to find ways to support and strengthen these mechanisms, especially as elections become increasingly contested.

The IEC should also strive to preserve its institutional independence and impartiality in forthcoming years. In doing so it can also simultaneously address its weakened credibility brought about by a decline in public trust. First, the independent selection committee must expedite the commissioner appointment process to ensure full representivity and constitutionality amongst its five commissioners. Second, the selection of commissioners must remain independent, and the recommendations of both the multiparty parliamentary committee and independent selection committee must remain central to the final decision-making process. The IEC can also further protect its institutional credibility by prioritising non-partisan and impartial behaviour among its senior officials. This should be reinforced through a transparent and accountable ethics framework to manage conflicts of interests; not dissimilar to those that govern elected officials.

In terms of election administration, the IEC should explore the benefits of introducing automatic registration in South Africa. While automatic registration does not oblige voters to participate at the polls, it will likely lessen the costs of registration for many, and ultimately, can encourage an increase in voter turnout. The IEC should continue to prioritise addressing the infrastructural disparities in voting stations found in many rural areas across South Africa. The commission will also need to grapple with the potential costs and benefits of introducing electronic voting migration in future elections; to be weighted against other priorities that compete for the national budget. Furthermore, the IEC will need to urgently address a growing perception that temporary election staff particularly union members recruited to voting stations, are not adequately trained. A comprehensive training programme must be implemented for all temporary election staff, and must emphasise their statutory responsibilities. Moreover, the IEC must expedite, and make public, its recommendations in its anticipated report on the thorny issue of the employment of union members as temporary IEC staff at elections.

Electoral integrity also presupposes a degree of political competition and a level playing field during the campaign period. It is during this time that many voters make up their minds about which party to support. Before the 2016 municipal elections commence, the IEC must actively consider new regulatory mechanisms to manage new forms of voter manipulation and intimidation that curb freedom of political association and expression in South Africa. These regulations can be communicated and promoted through the party liaison committees to ensure political parties subscribe to the principles of the voter's right to non-interference and freedom of political association and expression. In line with the principle of openness and transparency, the IEC can also provide far more public information on public funding to political parties to ensure voters are kept informed of how parties use and spend their funds, and any violations and subsequent sanctions.

Finally, the IEC is suitably positioned to provide a unique and informed perspective on several complex debates that all pivotal to the fairness of electoral politics in the country. The commission can, and should, bring to bear its considerable intellectual resources to inform contemporary discourses on the current 90% proportional 10% equitable ratio allocation of public funds; the future regulation of private party funding; and the possible consequences of electoral reform.

11
ZAMBIA

Dr Njunga-Michael Mulikita

This chapter assesses the performance of the Electoral Commission of Zambia (ECZ) in organising free, fair, transparent and credible elections in Zambia since 1991 when Zambia made the transition from a one-party polity to open, competitive, pluralist politics.

Political history

Zambia, formerly Northern Rhodesia, gained independence from Great Britain in 1964. Three periods have defined the history of modern Zambia. From 1964 to 1972, the First Republic laid the groundwork for the first set of multiparty elections. The Second Republic, which lasted from 1973 to 1990, institutionalised a one-party system. The Third Republic saw the re-introduction of multiparty elections in Zambia.

1964–1972: The First Republic

The first two multiparty elections of 1964 and 1968 marked the birth of the First Republic. Following his victory in the 1964 elections, Kenneth Kaunda of the United National Independence Party (UNIP), became the first president of the Republic of Zambia.[1] UNIP was born out of the split of the Northern Rhodesian African National Congress (ANC) in 1958. After the split, UNIP and the ANC formed the first government of the country in 1962.

Although the Constitution of Zambia provided for a pluralist political system, UNIP retained dominance throughout the First Republic. Kaunda and his party secured a victory in both the presidential and parliamentary elections in 1968. The introduction of a single-party system in 1973 entrenched UNIP domination of the political landscape in Zambia.[2]

---

1   Katotobwe ABC (1996) The impact of plurality voting system on Zambian politics. MSc Dissertation submitted to the Department of Government, London School of Government & Political Science. p. 16.
2   Mbao M (2007) The politics of constitution making in Zambia: Where does the constituent power lie? Draft Paper presented at African Network Law Conference on Fostering Constitutionalism in Africa, Nairobi, Kenya, April 2007. p. 7. Available at http://www.ancl-radc.org.za/sites/default/files/Constitution%20 Making%20in%20Zambia%20by%20Melvin%20Mbao.pdf [accessed 14 July 2016].

1973–1990: The Second Republic

The one-party system established at the end of the First Republic limited competition in the National Assembly elections. Although UNIP had supremacy over parliamentary decisions, real power lay in the hands of the presidency. Kaunda was re-elected in 1973, 1978, 1983 and 1988.[3]

Elections under one-party state regime

Under the one-party state regime, candidates for election to the office of president and to the National Assembly had to be UNIP members. The person elected by the party's general conference, attended by party delegates from provinces, was to be adopted as the sole candidate for election as republican president. A recommendation by the Mainza Chona Constitutional Review Commission for primary elections to be held and for up to three candidates to be allowed to contest for the presidency (which was also incorporated into the Constitution of Zambia Bill, No 28 of 1973) was rejected by the party.[4] Efforts to challenge Kaunda for the party at the 1978 general conference by the former leader of the ANC, Harry Mwaanga Nkumbula, former vice-president and former leader of the proscribed United Progressive Party (UPP), Simon Mwansa Kapwepwe, and businessman Robert Chiluwe were thwarted by an amendment to the party constitution. The amendment required candidates to have been party members for at least five years and to raise two hundred supporters from each province to back their nomination. Kapwepwe was disqualified by the five-year membership requirement. Nkumbula and Chiluwe failed to raise two hundred supporters from each province.[5]

All registered voters could vote in the presidential and parliamentary elections. At the primary stage of parliamentary elections, however, only party officials were eligible to vote. For presidential elections, only one candidate, Kaunda, was nominated and voters were required to vote 'yes' or 'no', for approval or disapproval, respectively. He was declared winner after receiving 51% or more of the valid votes cast.

Primary elections were introduced for the National Assembly elections. The top three candidates to go through primaries were eligible to stand for election in a constituency. Primaries enhanced the role of grassroots party organs in the choice of candidates as the latter were generally local people. Article 75 of the republican constitution allowed the party central committee to vet (or veto) candidates who had won primaries if they were found undesirable. In 1978, 30 candidates, including six serving members of parliament (MPs), were vetoed. This system tended to arouse ill-feeling among vetoed victors and

3   EISA Observer Mission Report (2011) *Zambia Presidential, Parliamentary and Local government Election, 20 September 2011*. Johannesburg: EISA. p. 2.

4   Kaela LCW (2002) Zambia. In: T Lodge, D Kadima and D Pottie (eds) *Compendium of Elections in Southern Africa*. Johannesburg: EISA. pp. 379–380.

5   Ibid.

their supporters. At times, the party appeared to use it to facilitate the success of favoured candidates and to punish 'black sheep'.[6]

Election campaigns were controlled by the party. For presidential elections, the machineries and resources of the party and government were mobilised to campaign for 'yes' votes for the presidential candidate. Campaigning for 'no' votes was not tolerated. Senior party officials guided the campaign for the National Assembly elections. They would introduce the candidates at public rallies and invite them to canvass for votes. Candidates were expected to follow the party line and not to criticise its policies. Campaigns, therefore, tended to focus on personalities rather than issues. As a result, the National Assembly elections were heavily contested. 'Autonomous' ad hoc electoral commissions were responsible for the supervision and conducting of elections, as well as the delimitation of constituencies.[7] They also had the power to make regulations. The president appointed three commissioners; High Court judges were conventionally appointed chairs and the elections office (in the office of the prime minister) was headed by the director of elections.[8] The director of elections was responsible for executive functions pertaining to elections. In reality, the electoral commissions of the Second Republic were not autonomous as the constitutionally prescribed monopoly over political power exercised by UNIP did not allow for it.

The Kaunda government reintroduced multiparty elections following (i) public dissatisfaction with progressive economic decline and military coup attempts in 1988 and 1990; and (ii) local and international calls for political liberalisation. Subsequently, article 4 of the Constitution of the Second Republic was repealed in order to accede to the demands of the opposition.

Return to multipartyism

The transition to multiparty democracy was the culmination of a number of developments both at home and abroad. The transition was largely a result of widespread protests sparked by a deteriorating economy, which the army attempted to silence through a failed coup attempt in 1990. A number of people were killed, especially during the 1990–1991 protests. The protests were spearheaded by a coalition of civil society organisations (CSOs), including trade unions, business associations, professional and student bodies, and churches. Internal protests were aided by global events at the time. An important external factor was the dramatic collapse of communism in Eastern Europe and the former Soviet Union, which unleashed the new 'winds of Perestroika and Glasnost' sweeping across Africa.

In the wake of these pressing factors, Kenneth Kaunda accepted the need for reform.[9] He promised a referendum on multiparty democracy. The popular demand was that he

6   Kaela LCW (2002) Zambia. In: T Lodge, D Kadima and D Pottie (eds) *Compendium of Elections in Southern Africa*. Johannesburg: EISA. pp. 379–380.
7   Ibid.
8   Interviews with SACCORD & FODEP revealed this point.
9   Mulikita NM (2003) A False Dawn? Africa's post-1990 democratisation waves. *African Security Review* 12(4). Available at https://www.issafrica.org/pubs/ASR/12No4/Mulikita.pdf [accessed 14 July 2016].

amends the 1973 Constitution by deleting the article which declared Zambia a one-party state. In November 1990, President Kaunda appointed a constitutional review commission under the chairmanship of the respected lawyer and academic, Professor Patrick Mvunga. The commission was to enquire, determine and recommend a system of political pluralism that would ensure the separation of the powers of the legislature, the executive and the judiciary (to enhance the role of these organs) and to look into the composition and functions of the various organs of the state and recommend modalities of their operation.

Shortly thereafter, Kaunda reached a compromise agreement with the nascent opposition and a constitutional amendment was passed, expunging article 4 from the constitution and thus paving the way for the formation of political parties. In the meantime, the Mvunga Commission held public hearings in most of the country's major centres. Some of the petitioners who appeared before that commission submitted that the constitution should be debated and adopted by a constituent assembly or a national conference to affirm its legitimacy.

In its report, the Mvunga Commission concluded that 'there was no need for a Constituent Assembly since there was in place a legitimate and lawfully constituted National Assembly'. The commission therefore recommended that the constitution should be adopted and enacted by parliament. The Kaunda administration did not accept most of the commission's recommendations. As for the emerging opposition forces – particularly the newly formed Movement for Multiparty Democracy (MMD) and the labour movement – they did not accept the draft constitution appended to the commission's report. To his credit, Kaunda was prepared to accept a compromise constitutional text agreed to at an inter-party dialogue between the ruling UNIP and the MMD.

The document agreed to at the inter-party talks was eventually enacted into law as the Constitution of Zambia Act, which came into force on 30 August 1991.

1991 constitution establishes an electoral commission

As part of the transition towards the landmark 1991 elections, on 24 August 1991 the National Assembly approved a new election law[10] that established an electoral commission with the responsibility of conducting the elections (article 76). The members were to be appointed by the state president and implemented by an election directorate, a body of civil servants in Lusaka.[11]

---

10 The Constitution of Zambia Act, which came into force on 24 August 1991; Motsamai D (2014) Zambia's constitution-making process: Addressing the impasse and future challenges. *Institute for Security Studies (ISS) Situation Report*. Available at https://www.issafrica.org/uploads/SitRep2014_15Jan_2.pdf [accessed 14 July 2016]; Republic of Zambia (1991) Zambia Constitution. Adopted on: 24 August 1991. Available at http://www.wipo.int/edocs/lexdocs/laws/en/zm/zm052en.pdf [accessed 14 July 2016].

11 Rakner L and Svåsand L (2003) Uncertainty as a strategy: Electoral processes in Zambia 1991–2001. *CMI Working Paper* 2003 (13). p. 14. Available at http://www.cmi.no/publications/file/1738-uncertainty-as-a-strategy.pdf [accessed 14 July 2016].

For the most part, the electoral commission relied on electoral regulations derived from previous practice in Zambia.[12] Due to the perceived bias towards UNIP, the electoral commission was heavily criticised by the opposition, as well as local and international election observers. The alleged lack of independence and impartiality stemmed partly from commission members' insecure tenure as the president could remove them. Criticism was also raised against the chairman of the electoral commission for being biased in favour of UNIP.[13] The perception that the commission was biased was understandable because of the deep mistrust the nascent opposition party, the MMD, bore towards the Kaunda government as Zambia made the uncharted transition from autocratic one-party rule to a multiparty dispensation.

The 1991 elections marked Zambia's official return to multipartyism. Frederick Chiluba of the MMD, a coalition of civic organisations, emerged as the winning candidate with 75.8% of the popular votes.[14] Domestic and international observers judged the elections to be largely fair and transparent. Thereafter, Zambia was plagued by rising levels of unemployment and poverty. Ultimately, the implementation of structural adjustment programmes did not lead to the much-awaited improvement in living standards of ordinary Zambians.

The MMD retained power with the re-election of the incumbent President Chiluba in the 1996 elections, although there were socio-economic challenges, concerns over internal democracy within the ruling party and controversy over a constitutional amendment that excluded Chiluba's closest rival, former President Kaunda, from contesting the presidential election. A state of emergency was declared in late 1997 after a small group of army officers falsely claimed to have overthrown the government. Kaunda was briefly detained on accusations of having had prior knowledge of the coup attempt. There was a sharp decrease of political freedom between 1996 and 2001.

In June and July of 1996, a shady group called the 'Black Mamba' was blamed by the government for a spate of bomb blasts in Zambia that killed one person and seriously injured another. Eight UNIP officials, including its vice-president, Senior Chief Inyambo Yeta, were arrested in connection with the bombings in June and charged with treason and murder. The trial provided little evidence to suggest that these UNIP members were involved in any violent conspiracy against the state. It appeared that they were detained solely because of their political affiliation. They were acquitted of all charges by the High Court in November.[15]

---

12 Kaela LCW (2002) Zambia. In: T Lodge, D Kadima and D Pottie (eds) *Compendium of Elections in Southern Africa*. Johannesburg: EISA. pp. 379–380.

13 Ibid.

14 Though the 1991 election and the peaceful transfer of power gave rise to optimism regarding democratic consolidation in Zambia, Lise Rakner observes: 'Zambia's democratization process had stagnated and maybe even reached a critical point in terms of continued stability.' Rakner L, Rocha Menocal A & Fritzal V (2007) Democratization's third wave and the challenges of democratic deepening: Assessing international democracy assistance and lessons learned. Working Paper 1 for Irish Aid. Available at http://www.odi.org/sites/odi.org.uk/files/odi-assets/publications-opinion-files/241.pdf [accessed 14 July 2016].

15 Human Rights Watch (1996) Zambia: Elections and human rights in the Third Republic. *Human Rights Watch* 8(4A). Available at https://www.hrw.org/reports/1996/Zambia.htm [accessed 27 July 2016].

Judicial independence came under attack from government supporters in 1996, especially after the Supreme Court struck down provisions of the Public Order Act (POA), finding that requiring permits for meetings was in contravention of the Zambian peoples' constitutional rights. One particular focus of these attacks was the championing of exclusivist ethnic politics, with the judiciary characterised as being mainly from the Eastern Province of Malawi. Leaders of opposition parties and civic groups also had their nationality status challenged by government officials.[16] Internal squabbles erupted within the MMD over Frederick Chiluba's attempt to run for a third term. The disagreement over Chiluba's bid led to the expulsion and resignation of a number of senior members of the MMD. The nomination of Levy Mwanawasa as the MMD presidential candidate resulted in a split. Michael Sata, then secretary general of the MMD, left the party to establish the Patriotic Front (PF).[17]

2001 elections

Zambia organised the third tripartite elections on 27 December 2001. Because of the late start of voter registration, the ECZ registered only 56% of eligible voters. Anderson Mazoka of the United Party for National Development (UPND) and Levy Mwanawasa of the ruling MMD were the two major contestants in the presidential race. The National Assembly and local government elections were a fierce contest between the ruling party and the UPND.

Among other controversies, for instance, was the tabulation of results at district level and the transmission of the results to the national results centre.[18] Discrepancies were picked up between results announced at constituency level and those announced by the ECZ at the national results centre. There was no record of invalid ballots on some results sheets. Furthermore, the accuracy of the results was challenged given the small margin between the two leading presidential candidates. Ninety-six hours after the polls, the ECZ announced the official results amidst protests in Lusaka. Levy Mwanawasa, the winner of the presidential election, obtained 28.69% of valid votes, while his main challenger, Anderson Mazoka, received 26.76%.[19] Following the loss of its parliamentary majority ten years after its rise to power, the MMD was able to regain control in parliament with the eight presidential appointees, by-election victories and dubious alliances. PF candidate Michael Sata received a lowly 3.4% of the vote.

---

16 Ibid.

17 EISA Observer Mission Report (2011) *Zambia Presidential, Parliamentary and Local government Election, 20 September 2011*. Johannesburg: EISA. p. 3.

18 Ibid.

19 Mulikita NM (2002) Good governance in Zambia's public administration: Challenges & opportunities. p. 7. Available at http://unpan1.un.org/intradoc/groups/public/documents/CAFRAD/UNPAN009299.pdf [accessed 14 July 2016].

2006 tripartite elections

Tripartite elections took place on 28 September 2006. Three out of 11 registered political parties contested the presidential election. The three main contesting parties were the ruling MMD, the PF and the United Democratic Alliance (UDA), a coalition between the UPND, the Forum for Democracy and Development (FDD) and UNIP. The leader of the UPND, Anderson Mazoka, died in a Johannesburg hospital on 24 May 2006. The UPND was beset by internal power struggles after the loss of its leader. Following the selection of businessman Hakainde Hichilema as new leader of the UPND, the UDA subsequently nominated Hichilema as its candidate for the presidential election. With 42.98% of the valid votes, Levy Mwanawasa of the MMD secured his re-election for a second and final term as the President of Zambia. The MMD won 50% of the seats in the National Assembly. Michael Sata of the PF and Hakainde Hichilema of the UPND scored 29.37% and 25.32% of the popular vote respectively. A total of 709 candidates from 13 political parties contested the National Assembly elections. A total of 4 095 registered candidates stood in the local government elections. Women made up 15% of the National Assembly election candidates, whereas less than 10% of the candidates running for local government elections were women. In the National Assembly elected in 2006, only 14.6% of members were women.[20]

2008 presidential by-election

Two years after his re-election in 2006, incumbent President Levy Mwanawasa passed away in France on 19 August 2008 after a stroke. As a result, an unprecedented presidential by-election was held in Zambia on 30 October 2008. Rupiah Banda, then acting president of the MMD, emerged as the presidential candidate of the ruling party following his nomination by the party's National Executive Committee.[21] Four candidates, namely Rupiah Banda of the MMD, Michael Sata of the PF, Hakainde Hichilema of the UPND and Godfrey Miyanda of the Heritage Party (HP) contested the presidential by-election. The candidature of Rupiah Banda was boosted by the endorsement of a number of opposition parties: the National Democratic Focus (NDF) (of Benjamin Mwila, who withdrew from the presidential race), UNIP, the All People's Congress Party (APC), the Reform Party (RP), the Forum for Democracy and Development (FDD), the United Liberal Party (ULP), the National Democratic Party (NDP), the New Generation Party (NGP) and the National Revolutionary Party (NRP). Allegations of vote rigging and an outbreak of rioting preceded the announcement of the final results. With 40.63% of the

---

20 Ibid.
21 Simutanyi N (2010) The 2008 presidential elections in Zambia: Incumbency, political contestation and failure of political opposition. Paper presented at the CMI/IESE Conference on 'Election Processes, Liberation Movements and Democratic Change in Africa', Maputo 8–11 April 2010. Available at www.cmi.no/file/?1016 [accessed 14 July 2016].

votes, Rupiah Banda was declared the winner of the election. Michael Sata and Hakainde Hichilema obtained 38.64% and 19.96% of the popular votes respectively.[22]

2011 tripartite elections

On 23 September 2011, the commission announced the results of 2011 tripartite election. In the presidential race, the results given were 1 170 966 (42%) votes to the leader of the opposition party, Michael Sata of the PF, and 987 866 (36.1%) to the incumbent, Rupiah Banda of the MMD.[23] Sata was announced the winner with seven constituencies outstanding.[24] The UPND performed well in Southern Province, as expected in view of Hakainde Hichilema being a member of the Tonga-speaking people who are in the majority in the province. Hakainde garnered 506 763 votes, accounting for 18% of the total number of votes cast.[25]

In the parliamentary results of 148 contested seats, the PF won 60 (40.1%), with the MMD a close second with 55 (37.2%), leaving the UPND trailing with 28 (19%). Of the remaining five seats, three were taken by independents, and one apiece went to the FDD and the Alliance for Democracy and Development.[26]

2015 presidential by-election

On 28 October 2014, Zambian President Michael Sata died while in London, where he was seeking medical care after months of reports of poor health. Sata was the second Zambian President to die while in office.

The Electoral Commission of Zambia, as was the case in 2008, managed to organise a free, transparent and credible election within 90 days as prescribed by the constitution. Voter turnout was at an all-time low in the 2015 by-election. The voter rolls updated from the 2011 election had 5 166 084 Zambians registered to vote. Of these, only 1 671 662 Zambians cast ballots in the election, resulting in the lowest voter turnout in an election on record: 32.4%. The last special by-election held in Zambia also saw a very low turnout. In 2008, only 45.4% of the 3.9 million registered voters cast ballots.[27] A more startling comparison, however, is that the 2015 election had even lower turnout than the 1973 election — during Zambia's single-party era — when turnout was 39.4%. The electorate

22 Ibid.
23 ECZ (2011, 28 September) 2011 Presidential Election Results. Public Notice. Available at http://www.elections.org.zm/media/28092011_public_notice_-_2011_presidential_election_results.pdf [accessed 14 July 2016].
24 Hogan J (2011) Zambia: Cobra becomes King in a telling result. *African Arguments*. Available at http://africanarguments.org/2011/09/26/zambia-election-2011-cobra-becomes-king-at-last-by-jack-hogan/ [accessed 14 July 2016].
25 ECZ (2011, 28 September) 2011 Presidential Election Results. Public Notice. Available at http://www.elections.org.zm/media/28092011_public_notice_-_2011_presidential_election_results.pdf [accessed 14 July].
26 ECZ (2011) Tripartite elections: Summary of allocation of national assembly seats. Available at http://www.elections.org.zm/media/summary-allocationofnationalassemblyseats.pdf [accessed 14 July 2016].
27 ECZ (2008) 2008 Presidential Election: National Results Totals. Available at https://www.elections.org.zm/media/national_summary1.pdf [accessed 27 July 2016].

was split between Edgar Lungu, (Michael Sata's successor and PF candidate) and the UPND's Hakainde Hichilema. When the final votes were counted, Lungu had edged out Hichilema by less than 2% of the vote. None of the other nine candidates managed to win as much as 1% of the national vote.[28]

All in all, both local and foreign observers of the by-election praised the ECZ for high levels of professionalism and impartiality in staging an election that broadly reflected the will of the Zambian electorate.

Framework of the ECZ

Constitutional and legal framework

The commission is enshrined in the constitution. The Constitution of Zambia declares:

> There is hereby established an autonomous Electoral Commission to supervise the registration of voters, to conduct Presidential and Parliamentary elections and to review the boundaries of the Constituencies into which Zambia is divided for the purposes of elections to the National Assembly.[29]

Article 76 provides for the promulgation of the various legal instruments to govern the management and administration of elections in the country, while article 77 provides for the delimitation and management of the constituency boundaries.[30] To this effect, the constitution provides the commission with legal backing in terms of its core mandate to the election process and provides for the collaborative use of other pieces of legislation, such as the Electoral Commission Act No. 24 of 1996, which provides for the establishment of the full-time Electoral Commission of Zambia.

The legal framework underpinning the work of the ECZ is backed by the following legislation:
- The 1996 Constitution of Zambia;
- The 1996 Electoral Commission Act;
- The 2006 Electoral Act; and
- The 2011 Electoral Code of Conduct and Regulations.

All these pieces of legislation form a constitutional, legal and regulatory framework for the commission to function and fulfil the mandate for which it was set up. These instruments of legislation enable the commission to perform its obligations in all the three phases of the electoral process.

---

28 Dionne KY & Mulikita NM (2015) The 2015 presidential by-election in Zambia. *Electoral Studies* 38: 130.
29 The Constitution of Zambia, article 76.
30 EISA Election Observer Mission (2006) Zambia: Presidential, Parliamentary and Local Government Elections, 28 September 2006. Available at https://www.africaportal.org/dspace/articles/eisa-election-observer-mission-report-zambia-presidential-parliamentary-and-local [accessed on 14 July 2016].

Composition

Under the constitution, the chairperson and members of the electoral commission are appointed by the president and subject to ratification by the National Assembly.[31] The commission consists of five full-time members. That means the 'Chairperson and not more than four other members constitute the Commission'.[32]

'The Chairperson shall be a person who has held, or is qualified to hold, high judicial office or, any other suitably qualified person.'[33] Apart from this formulation (article 4 of Electoral Commission Act), neither the Constitution of Zambia nor the Electoral Commission Act explicitly outlines the criteria that guide the president in his/her appointments of commissioners. Members of the commission are

> appointed for a term not exceeding seven years, subject to renewals and ratification by the National Assembly; provided that the first members shall be appointed for periods ranging from two to five years in order to facilitate retirement by rotation.[34]

According to the Act, a commissioner may resign upon giving one month's notice in writing to the president. Article 5(3) of the Electoral Commission Act gives the president the power to remove a commissioner if the commissioner is insane or otherwise declared to be of unsound mind, or if the commissioner is declared bankrupt.[35] Financial bankruptcy may make commissioners susceptible to bribery and perceptions of corruption, whether justified or not, cast into doubt the integrity of the commission. Under the Electoral Commission Act (1996), the president is authorised to dismiss commissioners. The president is not obliged to explain his/her decision to any other authority.

Currently the commission is composed of:

- Justice Esau Chulu, formerly a member of the commission;
- Justice Christopher Mushabati, who also serves as a member of the Judicial Complaints Authority;
- Fredrick Ng'andu, a legal scholar;
- David Matongo; a former member of parliament; and
- Emily Sikazwe, a gender and civil society activist.[36]

---

31 The Electoral Commission Act, article 4(3).
32 Ibid.: article 4(2), sub articles (a) & (b).
33 Ibid.: (4).
34 Ibid.: article 5(1).
35 Ibid.: article 5(3). Kangali C (2016, 26 January) Ex-ECZ official convicted. *Times of Zambia*. Available at http://www.times.co.zm/?p=77700 [accessed 14 July 2016].
36 Commissioners work on a full-time basis. Some informants expressed reservations over having full-time commissioners when there is a full-time secretariat headed by a full-time chief executive officer. They spoke of the likelihood of turf wars between the commissioners and director.

The commissioners are men and women of unimpeachable integrity. However, the constitutionally prescribed 'imperial' position of the president in appointing and removing commissioners has always raised questions regarding the ability of commissioners to resist subtle political pressures from the head of state to rule in favour of the ruling party in electoral contestation.[37]

The constitution further vests the ECZ with the mandate for the delineation of constituency boundaries for parliamentary seats. Under article 77(4) 'the boundaries of each constituency shall be such that the number of inhabitants is as nearly equal to the population quota as is reasonably practicable'.

The Electoral Commission Act authorises the commission to perform the following functions:

- Registration of voters;[38]
- Delimitation of boundaries for electoral districts;
- Voting operations;
- Vote counting;
- Announcement of election results; and
- Initiating legislation pertaining to the conduct of elections.[39]

The electoral code of conduct provides guidelines on how election disputes/petitions are to be handled by the commission and the stakeholders involved. Against this background, the commission has ventured to work in close contact with the stakeholders. In August 2011, 75 conflict management committees (CMCs), one for each district and one for national level, were established.[40] These committees comprise political parties, civil society and state law enforcement agencies. The leadership is appointed by the ECZ and this body coordinates with district conflict management committees (DCMCs). As for post-election petitions, the law provides that a full bench warrant be submitted to the Supreme Court of Zambia 14 days after swearing in of the declared winner in a presidential election. Whereas, in a parliamentary election petitions must be submitted to the High Court within 30 days of the particular declaration; if there is an allegation of corruption, an extra 30 days are available. The procedures for election petitions are in line with international standards.

37 Chipenzi M, Kaela LCW, Madimutsa C, Moomba JC, Mubanga, H, Muleya N & Musamba C (2011) *The State of Democracy in Zambia*. Lusaka: Pro Print Limited. p. 28.
38 Though the ECZ is mandated to register voters, it is the Department of National Registration, Passport and Citizenship, under the Ministry of Home Affairs which issues National Registration Cards whose possession is prerequisite for obtaining of Voter Cards under National Registration Act, available at http://www.parliament.gov.zm/sites/default/files/documents/acts/National%20Registration%20Act.pdf [accessed 27 July 2016].
39 EISA Election Observer Mission (2006) Zambia: Presidential, Parliamentary and Local Government Elections, 28 September 2006. Available at https://www.africaportal.org/dspace/articles/eisa-election-observer-mission-report-zambia-presidential-parliamentary-and-local [accessed on 14 July 2016].
40 See European Union Election Observer Mission (EU EOM) (2011) General elections, 20 September 2011. p. 32. Available at http://www.eueom.eu/files/pressreleases/english/eueom_zambia_final_report_en.pdf [accessed 14 July 2016].

As there is no legal instrument empowering the commission to monitor political party funding, the commission therefore remains toothless as to monitor how and from where political parties get their funding.[41] Further, the auditor general's office does not even obligate political parties to produce financial records and to be audited. It is the office of the registrar of societies that is mandated to ensure political parties submit financial and activity reports. Zambia's amended constitution, which was signed into law by President Edgar C. Lungu on 5 January 2016, has a provision for state funding of political parties with seats in the National Assembly.[42]

The commission possesses its own building (Elections House) in the capital city of Lusaka. In a symbolic way, this demonstrates its autonomy, as it is not located in the district/enclave that houses the bulk of government ministries and departments.

Administration

Article 12(1) of the Electoral Commission Act empowers the commission to appoint the director of the ECZ. Article 12(2) states that the

> Director shall be the Chief Executive Officer of the Commission and shall be responsible for the –
> (a) Management of the Commission; and
> (b) Implementation of the decisions of the Commission.

Article 12(3) of the act states: 'The Director shall be assisted by such staff as the Commission may appoint, by statutory instrument, on such terms and conditions as the Commission may determine.'

Staff members are not civil servants; they are employees of the ECZ who are hired by the commission. They all serve on fixed-term contracts, which may be renewed or not renewed by the commission.

Funding

Funding remains one of the major challenges of the commission. The ECZ is expected to do more and more, whilst having to manage perennial resource constraints. Government has the responsibility of funding the commission by making resources available through the treasury. In this regard, the government has tried to bring stakeholders on board to help finance some of the activities of the ECZ. In 2009 the commission received a four-year

---

41 For detailed analysis see EISA Election Observer Mission (2006) Zambia: Presidential, Parliamentary and Local Government Elections, 28 September 2006. p. 22. Available at https://www.africaportal.org/dspace/articles/eisa-election-observer-mission-report-zambia-presidential-parliamentary-and-local [accessed on 14 July 2016].

42 Republic of Zambia (2015) The Constitution of Zambia. Amendment Bill. Available at http://www.parliament.gov.zm/sites/default/files/documents/bills/National%20Assembly%20Bill%2017-2015.PDF [accessed 14 July 2016].

fund (2009–2012) of USD 22.9 million from the United Nations (UN), together with its stakeholder, the department of national registration, passport and citizenship (DNRPC) to:

- Improve capacity of the ECZ;
- Improve implementation of continuous voter registration;
- Digitalise of the voter register;
- Review the legislative framework;
- Facilitate participation of women in the electoral process;
- Enhance effective media monitoring mechanisms;
- Enhance civic, voter education, and domestic observation programmes; and
- Enhance the capacity of inter-party dialogue.

Funding to the commission will need to be scaled up if the activities outlined in the electoral phase or cycle are to be realised.

Independence

By law, the commission is an autonomous body and as such, it is in essence supposed to operate as an independent body, free from interference of the central government. The commission has, in the past, made positive reforms which have enhanced their electoral integrity in the eyes of the voting public. These reforms include improved training for poll workers on a merit basis; election result management, including posting election hardcopy results for each polling station at each polling station; accelerated preliminary election result management; and real-time website posting of election results. The commission has also held stakeholder meetings in the election cycle.

However, the commission still remains fragile as its chairperson and its commissioners' appointments remain in the hands of an 'imperial' president, who at the time of an election is most likely one of the presidential candidates, and in a scenario where his/her party has the majority MPs in the National Assembly. Most stakeholders surveyed contended that this compromises the operations of the commission as an independent body.

Reporting and accountability

On an annual basis, the ECZ issues reports that outline its major accomplishments and shortcomings. These reports are open to scrutiny by the general public, political parties, CSOs, media bodies, academics and the National Assembly. The commission is required to submit its reports to the ministry of justice. Commissioners and the director of the commission are obligated to give submissions to the parliamentary committee on legal affairs, governance, human rights and gender matters. At these hearings, the ECZ has been very candid in pointing out legal, constitutional and resource constraints that impede the body from more efficiently managing electoral processes in the country.[43]

---

43 See http://www.parliament.gov.zm/sites/default/files/documents/committee_reports/SECOND%20

As times are changing and technological advancement is growing rapidly, there is an urgent growing need for updated information and communications technologies (ICT) in the commission. As the electoral cycle requires technology to fulfil the mandate of the commission, the ECZ and the DNRPC managed to receive USD 22.9 million in funding from the United Nations Development Programme (UNDP) for technical assistance and capacity building (2009–2012). The funding is to be used to improve:

- Institutional capacity of the ECZ;
- Implementation of continuous voter registration; and
- Digitalisation of the voter register, among others.

The commission, therefore, has made positive strides in the area of ICT as it has continued to network with other regional, continental and international election management bodies (EMBs), as evidenced by Zambia sending its representatives to various ICT capacity building forums. Enhanced deployment of ICTs in Zambia's electoral processes has, by and large, remained a challenge because the commission ultimately depends on the central government for funding. The commission has recognised the strategic importance of technological advancement and noted that technological failures have marred elections through the delayed transmission of results as some polling stations have no mobile network, are inaccessible by road, etc.[44] This has put the commission in an awkward position as stakeholders have cited this as a tool for vote rigging.

Interactions with stakeholders

Political parties

The major mechanism which regulates the interaction between the ECZ and political parties is the political parties liaison committee.[45] The committee at national level, is composed of the director of the ECZ, the heads of departments of the ECZ, one representative of each political party registered with the registrar of societies and the ECZ public relations officer who serves as secretary.

The committee's operations are governed by the following terms of reference (ToRs):

(a) To be a forum for consultation and co-operation between the Commission and registered political parties on all electoral matters.

(b) To promote harmony, trust and confidence among stakeholders in the electoral process.

REPORT%20FOR%20LEGAL%20AFFAIRS.pdf [accessed 27 July 2016].

44 ECZ honorable chairperson briefed a researcher on plans to enhance the use of ICT to facilitate speedier transmission from all polling stations throughout the country to national command centre during tripartite elections, 22 October 2015.

45 ECZ/Political Parties Liaison Committee. Available at http://www.elections.org.zm/media/t._o._r._-_political_party_liason_committee.pdf [accessed 4 August 2016].

(c) To enhance members' understanding of the role of the Electoral Commission and the political parties in the process

(d) To share knowledge, skills and strategies of participation in the electoral process and acknowledgement of dissenting view points.[46]

The committee provides a forum for regular exchange of views or information between the ECZ and political parties. By so doing, the commission has enabled political parties to build their confidence in the ECZ as an honest broker in Zambia's electoral process. The chairperson of the ECZ revealed that meetings of the committee are enthusiastically attended by political parties. The author deduced that the motivation behind political parties' enthusiasm for meetings of the liaison committee are the sitting allowances that the ECZ pays to political party representatives.[47]

The media

The media has played a pivotal role in the management of elections in Zambia since independence. Articles 11 and 20 of the Zambia Constitution guarantee the freedom of expression, including the freedom to hold opinions, communication and receive ideas and information without interference. The Electoral Act 27(2) establishes that all candidates and parties have the right to have their campaigns and manifestos reported on by all of the public media in a balanced manner. The key regulations for media coverage of elections are outlined in the code of conduct of 2011 (regulations 13, 14 and 15) which has an extensive list of obligations for media regarding their coverage of the campaign.

In Zambia, the media, especially state-owned media, is seen as creating a highly polarised environment which has led to selective campaign coverage of the parties and their campaigns in some of the mass media monitored by the European Union Election Observer Mission. This means that a specific obligation is placed on the public radio and television channels of the Zambia National Broadcasting Corporation (ZNBC) to allocate time to all political parties for political party broadcasts. However, this has not been adhered to as the ruling party has been dominating state-owned media. During the 2011 general elections, the ZNBC's coverage of opposition political parties was unbalanced and resulted in the PF boycotting election-related programming produced by publicly owned media.

In Zambia, several media personnel have been accused by both opposition and ruling party cadres of biased reporting, especially in the run-up to the 2011 general tripartite elections.[48] Evidence shows that public media tend to favour the party in government. Commercial radio and television have had wider and more balanced coverage of the candidates and the political parties, with key commercial broadcasters demonstrating

---

46 Ibid.

47 Ibid.; Interview with the Honorable Chairperson of the Electoral Commission of Zambia; 22 October 2015.

48 Chipenzi M, Kaela LCW, Madimutsa C, Moomba JC, Mubanga, H, Muleya N & Musamba C (2011) *The State of Democracy in Zambia.* Lusaka: Pro Print Limited. p. 55.

a more equitable balance between key candidates and their political parties. Muvi TV allotted 34% of their airtime to the PF, 20% to the MMD, 16% to the UPND, 9% to the National Restoration Party (NAREP), and divided the remaining coverage between the smaller political parties.[49]

As a result, the ECZ has engaged the media through the Media Institute of Southern Africa (MISA) and the security agencies with regard to the protection of journalists covering political events in the electoral process.[50] The commission has also worked with the accreditation of the media to cover ballot paper printing, transportation of ballot papers to polling stations and coverage of tabulation of results, among others. It should be mentioned that the commission has fewer mechanisms of monitoring the media as it is also faced with other logistical issues. However, by virtue of engaging with media bodies such as MISA, there are norms of election reporting standards which are adhered to (i.e. media houses refraining from partisanship in their operations).

Lastly, the ECZ has stressed that it is of the understanding that the media is a vehicle which can be used to afford the electorate with information necessary to make informed choices about who to elect into positions of authority. Further, on the basis of existing legislation, the commission has emphasised and outlined the role of the media in the election process, namely:

- Playing a watchdog role;
- Vehicle for voter education; and
- Instrument for peace building.[51]

Security agencies

The electoral process is one that should start from the time the victorious party or candidate at any level assumes power. This is due to the nature of the process, the number of stakeholders involved and other intricacies, which if overlooked, would compromise the credibility of the EMB. The role of security wings cannot be over-emphasised as they are the enforcers of Public Order Act during elections. The Zambia Police Service (ZPS) is one of the most important partners as the ECZ has no enforcement mechanism to sanction violators of the electoral code of conduct. The ZPS has established an election programme to re-train police personnel on rules of engagement. The ZPS has also involved political parties, the ECZ, the media, the church and civil society representatives in electoral conflict prevention. Its courses include public order management and the electoral code of conduct. Some training is done, in collaboration with the European Union (EU), on police response in critical situations. In addition, the ZPS is in the process of establishing an early warning

---

49 European Union Election Observer Mission (EU EOM) (2011) General elections, 20 September 2011. Final Report. Available at http://www.eueom.eu/files/pressreleases/english/eueom_zambia_final_report_en.pdf [accessed 14 July 2016].
50 MISA has lauded the ECZ for being open and transparent in its management of elections.
51 See 'Role of the Media in the Electoral Process'. Available at https://www.elections.org.zm/media_role.php [accessed 27 July 2016].

centre as a central point for receiving all electoral-related incident reports or complaints from the public on security issues relating to the conducting of polls countrywide.

The securing and transportation of ballot boxes is managed by officers of the ECZ. The duty of the ZPS is to simply provide physical protection to ECZ personnel as they move ballot boxes from polling stations to the national command centre in Lusaka.

However, the ZPS is not without flaws. It has been noted in past elections that the capacity of the ZPS to maintain public order remains open to question. Moreover, uncertainty surrounding the validity of some arrests of opposition supporters calls into question the ZPS' impartiality in performing its duties.[52] This can be evidenced by the Bangweulu parliamentary by-election campaigns which were marred by violence resulting in the PF's secretary general allegedly opening fire on a member of the opposition party, the UPND.[53]

Electoral dispute resolution

Election periods have been volatile in Zambian history. Skirmishes are reported in almost every election. There have been inter-party clashes, exchange of insults, disruption of election campaigns and the abuse of state resources, mostly by the party in power. Against this background, the ECZ has established complaints management committees (CMCs). The mandate of the CMCs is to act as a mediator in all the electoral-related disputes. The CMCs operate at both national and district level, comprising stakeholders such as the ECZ itself, political parties, civil society, Zambian police, the ministry of justice and the anti-corruption commission. The CMCs are mandated to resolve disputes within 24 hours, failing which cases should be referred to the courts of law. In addition, appeals against decisions taken by voter registration officers are to be lodged with the ECZ. According to the Electoral Act, electoral offenses are encompassed as: bribery, impersonation, exerting undue influence, publishing false statements about candidates, inciting disorderly conduct at an election meeting, misuse of a ballot papers, etc. The CMCs are regarded by many stakeholders as a step in the right direction, however, their deficiency is that they have no legal backing.

Human rights instruments

Zambia has signed relevant international agreements on the protection of human rights, including the Universal Declaration of Human Rights (UDHR, 1948), the International Covenant on Civil and Political Rights (ICCPR, 1966), the International Convention on the Elimination of Racial Discrimination (ICERD, 1996) and the Convention on Elimination of all Forms of Discrimination against Women (CEDAW, 1979). As a member of The African Union (AU) and the Southern African Development Community (SADC),

---

52 A UPND representative said police tend to target opposition party cadres, whilst those of the ruling party act with impunity.
53 Nyirenda C (2015, 11 August) Police probe political violence. *Times of Zambia*. Available at http://www.times.co.zm/?p=64771 [accessed 14 July 2016].

Zambia has also ratified the African Charter on Human and Peoples' Rights (ACHPR 1986), with its protocol on the Rights of Women, the African Union Declaration on the Principles Governing Democratic Elections in Africa, as well as the African Charter on Democracy, Elections and Governance, adopted in 2007.[54]

In addition, Zambia has committed to the SADC Principles and Guidelines Governing Democratic Elections and the SADC Declaration on Gender and Development. These international and regional instruments are not directly enforceable in the courts of Zambia unless incorporated into national law by statute of the National Assembly.

Zambia is also a member of the Electoral Commissions Forum of SADC (ECF-SADC).[55] The ECF-SADC's main aim is to promote close cooperation among member bodies in order to develop a democratic culture and a responsive electoral process in the region and to promote conditions conducive to free, fair, transparent and accessible elections.[56] Through the ECF-SADC, the ECZ has been involved in sending election observer missions to member countries in the SADC region. These election observer missions also play a role in knowledge sharing and learning from other experiences as they are governed under the umbrella of:

- Principles for Election Management, Monitoring and Observation (PEMMO) in the SADC region; and
- Principles and Guidelines Governing Democratic Elections in the SADC region.

These regional instruments set benchmarks for running and managing transparent and credible elections. The ECZ has also worked with the EU on different occasions in the quest to enhance its election management and administration capacity through internationally set standards. The commission has been sending representatives to attend seminars under the auspices of regional EMBs. During elections, the ECZ also collaborates with other players, such as the European Union Election Observation Mission, the Carter Center, the Common Market for Eastern and Southern Africa (COMESA), the African Union, etc.

However, as much as Zambia has signed an impressive range of regional and international good governance and human rights treaties, transformation of these commitments into domestic legislation has moved at a slow pace, as noted by stakeholders. This has compromised the operations of the ECZ much to the dissatisfaction of other players. For example, the electoral code of conduct is seen by many stakeholders (political

---

54 European Union Election Observer Mission (EU EOM) (2011) General elections, 20 September 2011. p. 7. Available at http://www.eueom.eu/files/pressreleases/english/eueom_zambia_final_report_en.pdf [accessed 14 July 2016].

55 Friedrich Ebert Stiftung, Electoral Commissions Forum of SADC Countries (2010) Report on the regional workshop on principle of election management, monitoring and observation in the SADC region (PEMMO) and roles played by stakeholders, 10–11 November 2010. p. 10. Available at file:///C:/Users/User/Downloads/regional%20workshop%20report%20on%20election%20instruments-%20nov%202010.pdf [accessed 14 July 2016].

56 Ibid.: p. 11.

parties, the media, etc.) as theoretically providing a good regulatory framework for the conduct of campaigns and for regulating the behaviour of stakeholders throughout the electoral process, but that it has proved an inadequate and weak deterrent of poor conduct due to the lack of substantive enforcement mechanisms.[57]

Evaluation and assessment

Interview with stakeholders suggest that the image of the ECZ has incrementally improved, from its rather inauspicious beginnings in 1996 to an EMB which now enjoys credibility and a good standing both locally and internationally. The commission was able to perform 'mission impossible' in both 2008 and 2015 when, it had to organise presidential elections within 90 days to give the Zambian electorate the opportunity to elect successors to late Presidents Levy Mwanawasa and Michael Sata.

Impartiality and autonomy

Studies undertaken by academics and reports from both local and international domestic observer missions have questioned the impartiality of the ECZ. As indicated earlier, although the constitution provides for an autonomous electoral commission, the members of the commission, including its chairperson, are appointed by the president, who has an interest in the outcome of the elections. After the 2001 elections, the EU Observer Mission questioned the impartiality of the ECZ in its report on the elections. The Carter Center was undiplomatically candid in its evaluation of the ECZ, concluding that:

> the ECZ and government failed to administer a fair and transparent election and address electoral irregularities that clearly could have affected the outcome of a close race; that the 27 December presidential, parliamentary and local government election results were not credible and could not be verified as accurately reflecting the will of Zambian voters; and that consequently the legitimacy of the entire electoral process was questionable.[58]

However, in 2006, the ECZ had heeded the criticisms offered by the EU and Carter Center Observer Missions and effected improvements in electoral administration. Thus, the Zimbabwe Election Support Network Observer Mission observed:

> The Zambian election administration was not only characterised by openness and transparency of the entire electoral process but was also all inclusive as any Zambian who had attained the age of eighteen could vote as long as such person

---

57 Respondents representing UPND, FODEP, SACCORD and ECZ staff members expressed frustration over a lack of enforcement of the code of conduct.

58 Carter Center (2002) *Observing the 2001 Zambia Elections*. p. 12. Available at https://www.cartercenter. org/documents/1135.pdf [accessed 14 July 2016].

had registered to vote. The Zambian electoral laws do not discriminate against people of foreign descent who were born in that country.[59]

The Report concluded:

> The Zambian tripartite elections offer an invaluable lesson, not only to Zimbabwe, but to the rest of Africa ... Poorly run and bogus elections have often been a source of conflict on the continent and the manner in which the Zambian elections were run offers hope that Africa may at long last be beginning to shake off its image of being regarded as a dark continent.[60]

By the time the ECZ organised the 2011 tripartite elections, the EMB demonstrated that it had corrected its shortcomings as highlighted in the reports by international observer groups. The EU Observer Mission observed:

> These presidential and parliamentary elections were organised in a transparent and credible manner according to the observations of both the EU EOM and other international and regional election observation missions that were present.

The EU Observer Mission went on to say:

> The Electoral Commission acted with impartiality organising these elections in a transparent and professional manner in accordance with its mandate. It demonstrated competence in planning for key stages of the electoral process and this was reflected in its delivery and organizational preparation.[61]

The ECZ has taken cognizance of the perception that it may not be perceived to be truly autonomous and independent by opposition political parties and CSOs. Thus, in its response to the draft constitution prepared by the technical committee drafting the Zambian Constitution in 2012, the ECZ stated:

> To consolidate the independence of the Commission and adhere to good international practice, the Commission should be called the Independent Electoral Commission of Zambia (IECZ) and should have legal personality.[62]

---

59 Zimbabwe Election Support Network (2006) Zambia 2006 Tripartite Elections Report. pp. 2–3. Available at http://aceproject.org/ero-en/regions/africa/ZM/Zambia%20Tripartite%20Election%20report.doc/view [accessed 14 July 2016].

60 Ibid.: 5.

61 European Union Election Observer Mission (EU EOM) (2011) General elections, 20 September 2011. p. 3. Available at http://www.eueom.eu/files/pressreleases/english/eueom_zambia_final_report_en.pdf [accessed 14 July 2016].

62 ECZ (2012) *Comments and Recommendations by the ECZ on the Electoral Provisions Relating to the First Draft of the Zambian Constitution Submitted to the Technical Committee Drafting the Zambian Constitution,*

The commission also proposed that the power of identifying and recruiting members of the commission should be transferred from the presidency to an ad hoc committee. This proposal is not new. It reinforces the recommendation of the Mungomba Constitutional Review Commission in 2005:

> ... the Constitution should provide for the recruitment and appointment of the Electoral Commissioners by advertisement and selection by a panel of independent experts consisting of one member of the Supreme and Constitutional Court appointed by the Chief Justice, a member of the Public Service Commission, a member of the Judicial Service Commission, a representative from LAZ and the Ombudsman.[63]

Code of conduct

Statutory Instrument No. 52 of 2011 is a legal document that provides for an electoral code of conduct. The current electoral code was issued in 2011.[64] The code guarantees rights and freedoms of both the electorate and contestants. It forbids bribery, corruption, intimidation and violence. However, experience in Zambia has shown that the code is violated with impunity, particularly by the cadres of the ruling party.[65] The main opposition party, the UPND, was adamant that during the 2015 presidential by-election, the ruling PF cadres ripped up campaign posters of the UPND and used 'pangas' and other weapons to intimidate opposition party members. The UPND representative accused the ZPS of turning a blind eye towards these violations of the code of conduct.[66]

Decentralisation

One of the constraints on more effective electoral administration that the ECZ chairperson, political parties and CSOs have cited was the absence of the ECZ at provincial and district levels.[67] The EU Electoral Observer Mission in 2011 made the observation:

> The lack of permanent and decentralized structures at provincial or district level did however limit the Electoral Commission's capacity to directly manage events. Reliance on seconded administrative structures both fuelled mistrust

17–18 July 2012. Lusaka: ECZ. p. 4.

63 Republic of Zambia (2005) Report of the Constitution Review Commission, 29 December 2005. Available at http://www.ncczambia.org/media/final_report_of_the_constitution_review_commission.pdf [accessed 14 July 2016].

64 ECZ (2011) Electoral Code of Conduct. Lusaka: ECZ.

65 Chipenzi M, Kaela LCW, Madimutsa C, Moomba JC, Mubanga, H, Muleya N & Musamba C (2011) The State of Democracy in Zambia. Lusaka: Pro Print Limited. p. 28.

66 This point was made by a representative of the UPND, 19 October 2015; Chikondi Foundation (CF), Foundation for Democratic Process (FODEP) and Zambia National Women's Lobby (ZNWL) (2005) Preliminary Statement on the 20 January 2015 Presidential Elections. Golden bridge Hotel, Lusaka, Wednesday 28 January 2015. Available at aceproject.org/ero.../preliminary-statement-on-the-20-january-2015/.../fil [accessed 14 July 2016].

67 Interview with the Honorable Chairperson of the Electoral Commission of Zambia, 22 October 2015.

> questioning the Electoral Commission's independence, as well as reduced its
> ability to control all aspects of the process.[68]

Thus, in administering elections, the ECZ cannot manage alone. The commission sub-contracts officers under the ministry of local government and housing (MLGH) to work as agents of the ECZ. Though the ECZ mounts training programmes for MLGH staff to serve as electoral/polling officers, the ECZ chairperson stressed that the commission would be much happier if the EMB established a presence at provincial and district level countrywide. The ECZ has already submitted this reform proposal to the executive for necessary action. It is, however, reassuring that decentralisation of the commission is recognised by article 238 of the draft constitution which states: 'There is established the Electoral Commission of Zambia which shall have offices in Provinces and progressively in districts.'[69]

Commissioners and ECZ management

Consultations with stakeholders (political parties and CSOs) revealed a certain degree of discomfort with the relationship between full-time commissioners and the full-time ECZ administration headed by the director. An authoritative study on the state of democracy in Zambia[70] found that there is a perception that commissioners are answerable to the party in power in order for them to remain in their positions. The study also reveals that there is a perception that commissioners are given 'big cars and fat gratuities' to make them loyal to the party in power.[71] CSOs surveyed, namely the Southern African Centre for the Constructive Resolution of Disputes (SACCORD) and the Foundation for Democratic Process (FODEP), indicated their discomfort with full-time commissioners supervising the ECZ director and administration on a day to day basis.

'Is there not the possibility that Commissioners may subtly pressure the ECZ to make administrative decisions, which the Director may not really be comfortable with?' they wondered aloud. Both CSOs said this arrangement of full-time commissioners occupying offices at Elections House was contrary to good corporate governance.

Budget

The ECZ's inordinate dependency on government funding emerged as a factor among CSOs and opposition political parties in their perception of the ECZ not being a truly

---

68 European Union Election Observer Mission (EU EOM) (2011) General elections, 20 September 2011. Available at http://www.eueom.eu/files/pressreleases/english/eueom_zambia_final_report_en.pdf [accessed 14 July 2016].

69 Republic of Zambia (2015) The Constitution of Zambia. Amendment Bill. Available at http://www.parliament.gov.zm/sites/default/files/documents/bills/National%20Assembly%20Bill%2017-2015.PDF [accessed 14 July 2016].

70 Chipenzi M, Kaela LCW, Madimutsa C, Moomba JC, Mubanga, H, Muleya N & Musamba C (2011) *The State of Democracy in Zambia*. Lusaka: Pro Print Limited.

71 Ibid.: 28.

autonomous EMB. This apprehension is consistent with the Carter Center Election Observer Mission's observation in 2001:

> ECZ's lack of funding and government delay in disbursing election funds tend to undermine ECZ ability to properly administer the electoral process. Such tactics create an uneven playing field for candidates and their parties thereby fuelling mistrust of ECZ.[72]

Voter registration

There are no openly discriminatory or unreasonable criteria to register as a voter in Zambia. To vote, a person must be a Zambian citizen, at least 18 years old and in possession of both a national registration card and a voter card, and have their details included in the voter register. There appears to be broad confidence in the integrity of the voter register. However, there remain some anomalies. Currently by law, it is the DNRPC which issues national registration cards (NRCs) that must be displayed by an eligible voter in order to register as a voter. Whilst the ECZ has embraced modern ICT methods in voter registration, the DNRPC has tended to lag behind in issuing of NRCs.[73] Furthermore, the ECZ is constrained from expeditiously removing deceased voters from the voter register, because it has no access to the DNRPC database. During the survey, an opposition UPND representative accused the DNRPC of concentrating the issuance of NRCs in strongholds of the ruling party (PF), but claiming resource and logistical constraints when it came to the issuance of NRCs in areas inhabited by UPND supporters, thereby precluding UPND supporters from voter registration.[74] The UPND representative said this was proof of the PF's grand scheme to rig the 2016 general elections. On 14 September 2015, the ECZ commenced the process of updating the voter register with a target of capturing a total of 1.7 million new voters.[75] The ECZ has, with the latest ICT innovations, developed a robust voter registration methodology which captures biometric features of voters. The ECZ is thus able to detect instances of double registration.[76]

---

72 Carter Center (2002) *Observing the 2001 Zambia Elections*. Available at https://www.cartercenter.org/documents/1135.pdf [accessed 14 July 2016].

73 Prior to the 2011 general elections, a new mobile system of voter registration was introduced that employed digital registration kits with a capability of capturing thumbprints for biometric and facial portrait data storage, see European Union Election Observer Mission (EU EOM) (2011) General elections, 20 September 2011. p. 11. Available at http://www.eueom.eu/files/pressreleases/english/eueom_zambia_final_report_en.pdf [accessed 14 July 2016].

74 Interview with UPND representative.

75 Extended voter registration comes to an end (14 December 2015). *Lusaka Times*. Available at https://www.lusakatimes.com/2015/12/14/extended-voter-registration-comes-to-an-end/ [accessed 14 July 2016]; ECZ (2015) Update on Voter Registration by the Chairperson of the Electoral Commission of Zambia, the Honorable Mr. Justice Esau E. Chulu, during a stakeholders meeting on Thursday, 12 November 2015. p. 3. Available at http://www.elections.org.zm/media/update_on_voter_registration_by_the_chairperson_of_the_electoral_of_zambia.pdf [accessed 14 July 2016].

76 Interview with the secretary of the ECZ, 2 December 2015.

Developing a reliable results system

Since the 2006 elections, the ECZ has been developing a reliable results system to guarantee integrity and reliability in the collection, aggregation and publication of results from polling stations right up to the national tallying centre in Lusaka. Thus, during general and by-elections, counting is done manually at polling stations and the results are then delivered to a totalling centre where results from all polling stations in a constituency are totalled and then transmitted electronically to the national command centre. The results are announced at polling stations in full view of agents that represent the political parties taking part. These agents are required to authenticate the results by signing the results sheets. The sheets are displayed publicly at polling stations to enhance transparency. During an interview with the chairperson of the ECZ, he gave the assurance that the ECZ is using ICT to explore modalities and strategies to enable the ECZ to announce results of a general election within 48 hours.[77]

Electoral dispute resolution

A major challenge that the ECZ must confront is the backlog of electoral petitions that have come to characterise elections in the country. Article 93(2) of the Electoral Act requires that electoral disputes are adjudicated by the High Court of Zambia. The ECZ has no power in settling electoral disputes. Article 102(1) of the Act states: 'An election petition shall be tried and determined by the High Court within one hundred and eighty days of the presentation of the election petition.'[78] Experience shows that the High Court is very slow in disposing of electoral petitions. The executive director of election monitoring watchdog FODEP revealed that by October 2015, eleven petitions from the 2011 elections were yet to be disposed of by the High Court.[79]

Convenience of election date

The holding of general elections during the rainy season has created formidable logistical challenges for the ECZ. Because of difficult terrain in remote parts of the country, delivery of electoral materials has been extremely slow and transmission of results equally problematic. Delays in the announcement of results can fuel speculation and rumours of election rigging that can lead to outbreaks of deadly violence. Additionally, holding elections during the rainy season has been cited as a cause of voter apathy, as evidenced most recently by the very low voter turnout during the 20 January 2015 presidential election. An authoritative assessment of voter turnout during the 2011 general election observed:

> Timing of elections is also critical to voter turnout since as most rural dwellers derive their livelihoods from agriculture, if elections are held during the farming

---

77 Interview with Honorable ECZ chairperson, 22 October 2015.
78 Electoral Act, No. 12 of 2006.
79 Interview with FODEP director, 15 October 2015.

season, most voters will be busy in their fields. Equally it is not advisable to hold elections during the rainy season or during times of normal floods.[80]

Thus, the ECZ advised that the draft constitution which has been tabled to the National Assembly incorporate the following clause:

> ... the election should be held on the second Tuesday of August, instead of the last Thursday of September, because schools are on recess in August and in the event that there is a second ballot, there will be adequate time to hold elections before the rainy season.[81]

Conclusion

The evidence obtained from stakeholders and secondary data surveyed, portray a picture of an EMB which has incrementally improved from its rather inauspicious beginnings in 1996 to one which now enjoys credibility and high standing both locally and internationally. The fact that Zambia has remained peaceful since 1991 (when the 'landmark/referendum' election that marked the transition from single-party rule to open, pluralistic and competitive multiparty politics was staged) indicates that the ECZ has performed satisfactorily as the guardian of elections in Zambia.

Another message that stakeholders articulated was that the leadership of the ECZ has played a major role in building confidence among stakeholders in the electoral process. There was consensus among all informants surveyed that the unimpeachable integrity and impartiality of former ECZ chairperson, Irene Mambilima, did much to build the stature and moral authority of the ECZ. At moments of uncertainty (such as in 2008 when the country went to the polls to elect a successor to late President Mwanawasa, in 2011 when the then opposition PF was claiming victory over the MMD, and in 2015 when Zambians went to the polls to elect late President Sata's successor) Mambilima's firm but impartial leadership helped Zambia to veer away from the spectre of violence and anarchy.

Recommendations

To consolidate the independence of the commission and adhere to good international practice, the commission should be called the Independent Electoral Commission of Zambia (IECZ) and should have legal status.[82] It is recommended that an ad hoc committee

---

80 UNDP/ECZ (2012) *Voter Turnout Survey of the 2011 Tripartite Elections in Zambia Final Report.* Lusaka: UNDP/ECZ. p. 82.

81 ECZ (2012) *Comments and Recommendations by the ECZ on the Electoral Provisions Relating to the First Draft of the Zambian Constitution Submitted to the Technical Committee Drafting the Zambian Constitution, 17–18 July 2012.* Lusaka: ECZ. p. 4.

82 ECZ (2012) *Comments and Recommendations by the ECZ on the Electoral Provisions Relating to the First*

should be appointed by the president to recruit and select commission members. The committee should consist of the following persons:

- One judge appointed by the chief justice;
- One member of the Civil Service Commission nominated by the chairperson of the Civil Service Commission;
- One member of the Judicial Service Commission nominated by the chairperson of the Judicial Service Commission;
- The ombudsman; and
- Three representatives from faith-based organisations (FBOs) and CSOs.

The committee should advertise the names of all shortlisted candidates for public scrutiny, after which such names should be submitted to the president for appointment subject to ratification by parliament. The composition outlined above comprises entities and persons who are broadly perceived to be impartial and non-partisan, thereby introducing transparency and openness into the selection and appointment of ECZ commissioners.

The electoral code of conduct needs to be revisited to enable the ECZ to enforce it. Currently, it is not clear whether it is the ZPS or the anti-corruption commission that has legal mandate to enforce the code.

In regard to speedy settlements of electoral disputes, the Electoral Act should be amended to provide for the establishment of electoral tribunals or ad hoc courts to deal with the plethora of petitions that has marred Zambia's electoral system. The ECZ can take cognizance of the best practices in the framework of the ECF-SADC.

The executive should take the necessary legislative and administrative measures to facilitate the decentralisation of the ECZ into provinces and districts. It was made clear by respondents from the ECZ and stakeholders that the lack of ECZ presence at both provincial and district levels hampers the work of the commission, because short-term staff from the ministry of local government and housing are subcontracted to carry out ECZ core mandates.

The ECZ's composition which provides for full-time commissioners when there is a full-time director of the commission needs reconsideration. Some stakeholders (CSOs) said this practice may not be consistent with good corporate governance norms and practices. Consideration should be given to reform which would de-link commissioners from the day-to-day operations of the commission, so the director and full-time staff can professionally and assertively perform their functions.

Government needs to ensure a competent and neutral ECZ to assure the electorate of free and fair elections. This should be achieved by the ECZ owning its budget. The appointment of its chairperson and commissioners by parliament, and not the president, should further enhance its independence from the executive (president).[83]

Draft of the Zambian Constitution Submitted to the Technical Committee Drafting the Zambian Constitution, 17–18 July 2012. Lusaka: ECZ. p. 4.
83 UNDP/ECZ (2012) *Voter Turnout Survey of the 2011 Tripartite Elections in Zambia Final Report.* Lusaka:

The ECZ should explore modalities and strategies of introducing an electronic voter register which should allow people to vote anywhere in the country.

Apart from requiring citizens who have reached the voting age to produce NRCs in order to be registered as voters, the law should be amended to enable citizens to use other bona fide identity documents, such as valid passports and driver's licences, in order to register as voters.

The Government of the Republic of Zambia must take the necessary legislative and administrative measures to synchronise the registration of voters by the ECZ with the issuance of NRCs by the DNRPC, to rebut conspiracy theories about pre-election rigging and disenfranchisement of voters in certain regions of the country.

The ECZ must investigate new technologies to speed up the announcement of results.

The ECZ must embark on continuous voter education and registration and involve civic leaders and other stakeholders.

The ECZ must ensure the timely announcement of results (within 24 hours) to avoid election-related violence. The law, as it stands, does not specify a time limit within which results must be announced. Article 74(1) of the Electoral Act No. 12 of 2006, states only that, 'the Commission shall determine and declare the result of an election by adding together the results received from all polling stations'.[84] Article 74(3) further adds that, 'the Commission may determine and declare the result of an election without having received the results of all polling stations'.[85]

Government must incorporate a permanent election date in the constitution that will emerge from the protracted constitution-making process (1993–2015). The practice in Zambia has been for the head of state to announce the date of the general election. However, the amended constitution which received presidential assent on 5 January 2016, contains the general election date which will be on the second Thursday of August after the expiry of a five-year term.[86]

UNDP/ECZ.

84 ECZ, Electoral Act No. 12 of 2006.

85 Ibid.

86 President Lungu observed, 'With the constitution making process taking place in parliament I hope that this will be the last time an individual is allowed be the one to set the date of elections. It is like holding the entire country at ransom.' Constitution bill published (2015, 3 August) ZNBC. Available at http://www.znbc.co.zm/?p=18337 [accessed 27 July 2016]; Adamu P (2015, 18 December) Zambia: ECZ ready to hold elections under new constitution. *Zambia Reports*. Available at http://allafrica.com/stories/201512180814.html [accessed 14 July 2016].

12

ZIMBABWE

Dr Charity Manyeruke

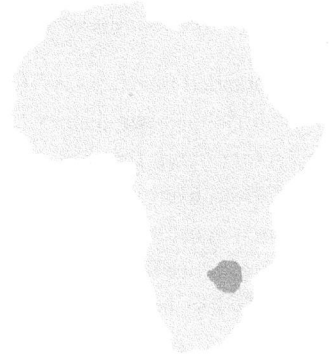

Introduction

This chapter examines the Zimbabwe Electoral Commission (ZEC), Zimbabwe's own electoral management body (EMB), with a view to assessing its contributions to the management of elections. The grand objective is to determine the extent to which the ZEC's decision-making and activities adhere to the precepts of impartiality, integrity, transparency, efficiency and effectiveness. These are the key principles that determine democratic outcomes.

Electoral politics in Zimbabwe started with the internal settlement election of 1979. This is the moment when the majority of Zimbabweans were initiated into the practice of elections; it is also where post-independence electoral institutions and practices originate. The institution of the Electoral Supervisory Commission (ESC), the Elections Directorate (ED), a bicameral parliament and practices such as adult suffrage, inviting international observers and polling procedures can be traced to that election. The electoral system used for that election was one of proportional representation (PR) based on the party list system; according to which, seats in the National Assembly were allocated in proportion to the number of votes that each contesting party won in each of the country's eight provinces. This is the first time in the electoral history of this country that the PR system was used. A threshold of 5% was used for allocating seats in each province. The PR system was again used in the 1980 independence general elections, but was abandoned in the 1985 elections and replaced with the first-past-the-post (FPTP) system reminiscent of the colonial era politics. This has been the electoral system used in all subsequent elections until the introduction of the hybrid system under the new constitution adopted in February 2013. The current situation combines the PR and FPTP systems.

By the 1985 general elections, nationalists who delivered independence began to realise that the PR system was being used by the minority to prevent complete power transfer from the whites to the Africans. However, it should also be noted that mainstream nationalists, in particular Robert Mugabe and Joshua Nkomo, had always been sceptical of the PR system, so they accepted it in 1980 on the basis of pragmatism, given the urgency with which elections were held in February 1980. 'Their preference for the first-past-the-post electoral system was made known during the 1979 Lancaster Conference and that they intended rewriting the Electoral Act with the view of introducing the constituency based single-member district (SMD) system if they won the independence elections'.[1] On the other hand, the shift to the current practice (a combination of PR and FPTP) may have arisen from the need to balance different political forces who took part in drafting the new constitution. It represents a compromise struck to reflect the opposition's long-known preference for the PR system and maintaining ZANU-PF's position on FPTP. Moreover, a hybrid arrangement enables the country to benefit from the advantages of both systems at once. In 1980 the government established a tripartite electoral management structure, consisting of the Delimitation Commission (DC), responsible for the delimitation of single member electoral districts, the ESC, whose responsibility was to supervise the conduct of elections, and the registrar general (RG) of elections. Critical functions were assumed by the registrar general of elections who had a range of responsibilities, namely: registering voters, compiling the electoral registers, conducting the actual voting and vote-counting, and announcing the results. The RG's office administratively fell under the ministry of home affairs. The ED was also formed to provide support to the RG. The ED was a logistical committee made up of representatives of several government ministries and departments. This election management structure was heavily criticised because of its highly centralised composition and perceived partisanship.

For example, 'the two commissions – the DC and the ESC – were appointed by the president, who, although he was required to consult the Chief Justice and the Judicial Services Commission (JSC), was not compelled to abide by their recommendations'.[2] One major distinguishing feature of the structure was that it was controlled by the central government. Sachikonye notes that allegations by opposition parties revolving around irregularities, rigging and partisanship also undermined credibility of the structure to conduct free, fair and credible elections. Election management was riddled with institutional, legal and constitutional challenges, which lead to disagreements on electoral outcomes.[3]

Due to the real and perceived weaknesses highlighted, and also in compliance with regional and sub-regional instruments (particularly African Union [AU] and Southern African Development Community [SADC] principles and guidelines on democratic elections), national consensus on the need for an independent election body culminated in the establishment of a new structure. This was thought to be a structure that would be insulated from political interference. The result of this political soul searching was the formulation of the Zimbabwe Electoral Commission Act which established the ZEC in

1   Sithole M & Makumbe J (1997) *The ZANU PF Hedgemony and its Incipient Decline. African Journal ofPolitical Science* 2(1): 24. Available at http://pdfproc.lib.msu.edu/?file=/DMC/African%20Journals/pdfs/political%20 science/volume2n1/ajps002001007.pdf [accessed 6 August 2016].
2   Musanhu B (2009) *Zimbabwe: A New Era in Election Management.* Strömsberg, Sweden: International IDEA. pp. 33. Available at http://www.idea.int/publications/emd/upload/EMD_CS_Zimbabwe.pdf [accessed 5 August 2016].
3   Sachikonye LM et al. (2007) *Consolidating Democratic Governance in Southern Africa: Zimbabwe.* South Africa, Johannesburg: EISA. p. 44.

2005 (legally supplanting the ESC through Constitutional Amendment No. 17). The DC was disbanded through Amendment No. 18, transferring its functions to ZEC. Through further electoral reforms initiated in 2007, the registrar general continued to be in charge of voter registration but under the supervision of ZEC, the Electoral Court was also established. Under the amended constitution, the Zimbabwe Electoral Commission Act was repealed and its contents transferred to the Electoral Act. By and large, internal political developments and Zimbabwe's international obligations as a member of international organisations explain the current state of election management frameworks.

Legal framework

There are various legal instruments which provide for the management of elections in Zimbabwe. The legal instruments range from the constitution, acts of parliament, statutory instruments, treaties, protocols, regulations, guidelines and codes of conduct.[4] The Zimbabwean legal framework on elections provides exclusive right to vote in referenda and elections to every adult Zimbabwean citizen. The Referendum Act, unlike the Electoral Act, does not impose the requirement of registration as a voter for a citizen in a referendum. Intensive voter registration must take place at least 30 days after the promulgation of the voting day. While the legal requirement was adhered to by the ZEC, the significance and quality of voter education provided needed to be assessed. Lovemore Madhuku argues that it is therefore important for the dates of elections to be set by the law, preferably in the constitution itself, and not proclaimed by the president.[5] This will enable the ZEC to have adequate planning and preparation time for the intensive mandatory voter education. Over the years, Zimbabwe has steadily incorporated regional and international legal instruments for elections. There is room, however for more electoral reforms to be implemented in order to promote the efficiency and effectiveness on the management of elections in Zimbabwe. Some of the key reforms recommended are: regular engagement of key stakeholders in order to improve perceptions of the independence of the Commission; increasing transparency in all the administrative processes, including

---

4   Combined the legal instruments are inclusive of: Constitution of Zimbabwe Amendment (No. 20) Act, 2013; Electoral Act (Chapter 2:13); Referendum Act (Chapter 2:10); Electoral Act (Chapter 2:01); Electoral Regulation 2005, Statutory Instrument 21 of 2005; Electoral Accreditation of Observers Regulation 2013 Statutory Instrument 89 of 2013; Electoral (Nomination of Candidates) Regulations Statutory Instrument 88 of 2013; Electoral (Special And Postal Voting Regulation 2013) Statutory Instrument 84 of 2013; Electoral (Votes Registration Regulation 2013) Statutory Instrument 69 of 2013; The Electoral Commission Media Coverage of the Elections, 2008 Statutory Instrument 33 of 2008; SADC Principles and Guidelines Governing Democratic Elections; Principles and Guidelines on the Independence of Election Management Bodies; Principles for Elections Management, Monitoring and Observation in the SADC Region of 2003; The African Charter on Human and Peoples' Rights on Women in Africa (African Women's Protocol) and The African Union's Declaration on the Principles Governing Democratic Elections in Africa (Durban Declaration).
5   Madhuku L (2014) A critique of the legal framework that governed the 2013 referendum and harmonised elections. *All-Stakeholders Review Conference on the 2013 Referendum and Harmonised Elections* Harare: ZEC. pp. 10–12.

recruiting of staff during elections; diversification of the sources of funding in order to strengthen operations of the ZEC; integration of user-friendly modern ICT in the voting process; enhanced accessibility to the voters roll for all citizens; continuous update of the voters roll; discontinuation of the use of voter registration certificates on the polling day (which present potential for abuse); widened reach of voter education in all local languages; and enhancement of working relations with other electoral supporting institutions and service providers.

Institutional framework and operations

Commission members

The Constitution of the Republic of Zimbabwe Amendment No. 20[6] provides for the establishment and composition of the Zimbabwe Electoral Commission. The ZEC chairperson is appointed by the president after consultation with the Judicial Service Commission and the Parliamentary Committee on Standing Rules and Orders. According to the constitution, the chairperson of the ZEC must be a judge, former judge, or person qualified for appointment as a judge. The other eight members are appointed by the president from a list of at least 12 nominees submitted by the Parliamentary Committee on Standing Rules and Orders. The members of the electoral body must be citizens of the country, and must be chosen for their integrity, experience and competence in the conduct of affairs in the public or private sectors. Members of the ZEC are appointed for a six-year term and may be re-appointed for one further term, limiting the maximum period that one can serve to 12 years.

The involvement of parliament enhances independence of the ZEC since it creates loyalty to the people. The term-limits provide security of tenure to the commissioners thus allowing them to discharge their functions impartially. A commissioner of the ZEC may be removed from office only when the member concerned is unable to perform the functions of his or her office because of physical or mental incapacity; has been grossly incompetent and has been guilty of gross misconduct.[7] The removal procedure appears fair enough since it involves a number of institutions and a tribunal. It guards against the arbitrary dismissal of commissioners.

The ZEC's mandate includes, among other things, preparing for, conducting and supervising all parliamentary and presidential elections and national referendums; directing and supervising the registration of voters, and supervising the completion and storage of the electoral register; designing, printing and distributing ballot papers; accrediting election observers; establishing and operating polling stations; and conducting and supervising voter education. As an independent commission, together with other commissions, the ZEC was charged with the role of safeguarding democracy through a system of the

---

6 Constitution of the Republic of Zimbabwe Amendment No. 20 (2013)
7 Section 237 of the Constitution.

government's abuse of power in check, ensuring accountability as well as strengthening constitutionalism.[8] However, the ZEC is charged with the role of safeguarding democracy, checking against government's abuse of power, ensuring accountability and strengthening constitutionalism.

Section 11 of the Electoral Act makes provisions to ensure the independence, impartiality and professionalism of commissioners, staff and agents of the ZEC. In this regard, ZEC commissioners, employees and agents should: exercise their function in a manner that promotes conditions conducive to free, fair and democratic elections and referendums; ensure that the secrecy and integrity of voting at elections and referendums is respected and shall not interfere, directly or indirectly, with a voter exercising their rights under the Electoral Act; maintain strict impartiality in their functions and they shall not do anything that may give rise to reasonable apprehension; assist accredited observers to exercise their functions under this Act; and safeguard all ballot boxes, ballot papers and other electoral documentation and material entrusted to the custody of the ZEC. They may not: divulge, make private use of, or profit from any confidential information gained through their role within the commission; hold or seek appointment, election or nomination to any political office; perform any work for a political party; or knowingly wear any badge or article of clothing that is associated with a party or candidate.

There is a gender balance in terms of appointments to the ZEC, which is commendable in the spirit of attaining gender equity in high-level decision-making bodies in Zimbabwe. The commission's current chairperson is Justice Rita Makarau, the deputy chairperson is Emmanuel Magade. Over the years, the commissioners who have been appointed are of different professional backgrounds, thus enriching the ZEC with wide expertise. In 2013 there were four lawyers (including the chairperson) a manager, two educationists, one political scientist and one social scientist. Two of the lawyers resigned after the harmonised elections of July 2013.[9] Commissioner Mkhululi Nyathi resigned on 31 July, the day of the elections, stating 'I do not wish to enumerate the many reasons for my resignation, but they all have to do with the manner the Zimbabwe 2013 harmonised elections were proclaimed and conducted.'[10] Geoff Feltoe also resigned from the ZEC saying his time was up and he was returning to the University of Zimbabwe, where he teaches law.[11] Resigning from the ZEC as they did is professional and acceptable. However, there is need to interrogate the issues that led to the resignations since some people in Zimbabwe viewed these resignations as protests against the integrity of the ZEC. Exit interviews must always be carried out

---

8   Fombad C (2016) Seperation of powers in African constitutionalism. In D Matyszak (ed.) *The Reconstitution of Zimbabwe's Electoral Commission: From Bad to Worse.* Oxford: Oxford University Press. p. 1.

9   Makoni P (2014) The Impact of the Composition and Staffing of the Zimbabwe Electoral Commission on its Performance. *Politeia* 33(3): 24–25.

10 ZEC commissioner resigns over rigged election (2013, 3 August) *Nehanda Radio.* Available at http://nehandaradio.com/2013/08/03/zec-commissioner-resigns-over-rigged-election/ [accessed 6 August 2016].

11 Shoko J (2013, 6 August) Zimbabwe: Top electoral commission officials resign. *The Africa Report.* Available at http://www.theafricareport.com/Southern-Africa/top-electoral-commission-officials-resign-in-zimbabwe.html [accessed 6 August 2016].

when a ZEC commissioner resigns in order to improve the election governance framework and processes.

In the period before 1 March 2007, the ZEC had no permanent secretariat and it operated with seconded personnel from government ministries. This meant that the ZEC was at the mercy of the executive arm of government, which posed serious challenges to its autonomy and effectiveness. The seconded personnel had allegiance to two masters at the same time which naturally affected perceptions on the autonomy of the EMB. As of 2014, the ZEC's secretariat had a staff complement of 440, led by the chief elections officer (CEO), who is appointed by the commission to manage its affairs and property, as well as supervise other employees.[12] The CEO has full accounting powers as provided for in the Electoral Act. Prior to 2016, the ZEC's funds were disbursed through the ministry of justice, legal and parliamentary affairs which in a way compromised the independence of ZEC since the ministry is part of the executive. The full accounting powers that ZEC now has means that it draws funds directly from the consolidated revenue fund. This is a commendable development which enhanced the ZEC's independence.

The ZEC has ten permanent provincial offices headed by a provincial elections officer who reports to the CEO. In addition, the commission has physical presence in all the districts in the country, which are headed by a district elections officer. Although it is present in all the provinces in the country, the 2014 Evaluation Report on the ZEC by Rushdi Nackerdien noted a gap in providing these decentralised offices with the training and transportation needed for them to be able to improve quality of services to the public.

The ZEC secretariat has three divisions. The administration and finance section is headed by a deputy Chief Elections Officer (CEO) whose key responsibility is to oversee the administration, finance, human resources, security and information services. In addition, the position interfaces with the legal, and internal audit units which are under the CEO. The finance section was separated from the administration section and the two operate separately as stand-alone divisions with the former being headed by an acting deputy CEO. The other division is operations, which is responsible for the management of elections and referendums, election logistics, voter education, publicity campaigns and image promotion. This division is headed by a deputy CEO and has four departments, namely: public relations, polling and training, voter education and election logistics. The third division of the secretariat is the inspectorate, which is headed by the chief inspector, responsible for monitoring and evaluating the implementation of the electoral processes and systems and to carry out research. During electoral periods, the ZEC can request seconded staff from the Public Service Commission, the Health Services Board, local authorities, or any other state institution. The seconded personnel is then trained by the ZEC to ensure it meets its institutional values and standards. This structure is sufficient for the ZEC's mandate. However, staff have to be continuously capacitated to adapt to

---

12 Makoni P (2014) The Impact of the Composition and Staffing of the Zimbabwe Electoral Commission on its Performance. *Politeia* 33(3): 25–26.

emerging trends of running elections and in the use of technology. An evaluation report for the ZEC[13] shows that its staff have adequate competency in managing elections in Zimbabwe. The staff have a good combination of age, profile, academic qualifications, EMB and election experience, and 97% of the ZEC's staff have experience in managing at least two major elections.[14]

The ZEC implemented its first strategic plan from 2010 to 2015. The identified strategic challenges after implementation of this plan included the need for timely constitutional alignment of laws; the need for sufficient and timely financial resourcing of the institution and processes; entrenching the independence and credibility of the ZEC; the need to increase support from donors in the form of financial and technical assistance; and increasing constructive engagements with diverse stakeholders.

Nomination of candidates

The Electoral Act provides clear and detailed procedures to be followed on the nomination of candidates, nomination fee, determining when the poll is to be held, withdrawal of candidates, death of a candidate, and pre-polling day substitution in certain circumstances resulting from withdrawal or death of a candidate.

A candidate for election as a member of the National Assembly is nominated by means of a separate nomination paper in a prescribed form, which should be signed by no fewer than five persons who are registered on the voters' roll for the constituency in which the candidate seeks election. This nomination paper shall be counter-signed with the acceptance of the candidate or his or her chief election agent. In the form, the candidate specifies a distinctive symbol, which he or she wishes to appear on the ballot paper in conjunction with his or her name, the candidate's political party or specifying if standing as an independent candidate.

The Electoral Act is very explicit about all the requirements for the nomination of candidates. The nomination of candidates for the office of president, and members of the National Assembly and local authorities is held in a public court, commencing at 10h00 and ending at 16h00. The nomination officer presides over the court and he decides on whether the candidate is duly nominated or not for the election stipulated by the Electoral Act.

The Electoral Act details the offences on the nomination of some candidates and the expected punishment. For example, forging any signature purporting to be that of a nominator receives a fine and/or imprisonment. In such a case, a candidate shall be disqualified from being nominated for election as a member of parliament for a period of five years from the date of conviction.

---

13 ZEC (2014) *Identifying of the Zimbabwe Electoral Commission Needs Gaps*. Harare: ZEC.
14 Author's own compilation from an evaluation report done by Rushdie Nackerdien in October 2014, 'Identification of the Zimbabwe Electoral Commission Needs Gaps', Zimbabwe Electoral Commission, Harare.

Over the years, candidates have been disqualified by the Nomination Court or Electoral Court on appeal for various reasons. In the 2013 harmonised elections, some candidates faced problems getting signatures from registered voters to support their candidature since voter registration was not yet complete. This problem was also experienced in the 1995 elections. A few political parties experienced instances where they had two candidates for the same constituency. This has normally led to some aggrieved candidates filing their papers as independents. An example is that of Jonathan Samukange of ZANU PF in the Mudzi constituency who stood as an independent in the 2013 harmonised elections. The MDC-T failed to resolve its double candidature in the Dangamvura-Chikanga constituency in Manicaland province. ZANU PF also fielded two candidates for the Bikita West constituency. It is imperative that political parties engage the ZEC to conduct their primary elections, which are sometimes characterised by contestation and intimidation[15]. It is equally useful to computerise the Nomination Court processes for speedy capturing of candidates' details. It is also important that candidates are given adequate time to prepare for the Nomination Court, for the ZEC to process papers after the Nomination Court, and for the appeals to be heard by the court. According to the Electoral Act, a period of 14 days is given for candidates to prepare; that is, from proclamation of dates of an election to the sitting of the Nomination Court. In the past elections, particularly before 2000, elections were characterised by 'resignations' or 'defections' of some candidates to ZANU (PF), thus creating logistical problems for the electoral body, particularly in printing the ballot papers. More time can be given to candidates to prepare for the Nomination Court and for the ZEC to process the papers before the polls.

Voter education

Voter education is concerned with encouraging and motivating voters to participate in elections and teaching them how they should prepare themselves for voting. Voter education is carried out by the ZEC and its approved voter education partners. Section 40B(1) of the Electoral Act requires that the commission provide adequate, accurate and unbiased voter education; and ensure that the education provided by partners is adequate and not misleading or biased in favour of any political party. The ZEC is expected to produce its own voter education materials for use in the process. The ZEC may, however, permit any person or organisation to assist in providing voter education.

Generally, voter education is regarded as having improved since 1980. It is, however, still inadequate. For example: in 2013, the Zimbabwe Election Support Network (ZESN)[16] stated that the ZEC deployed only two voter educators per district who could not have been expected to deliver voter education adequately throughout the areas of their jurisdiction. Considerable improvements were noted towards the end of voter registration in the 2013 harmonised general elections where the ZEC conducted a door-to-door campaign in an

---

15 Mukuta F (ed.) (2014) Report on the All Stakeholders Review conference on the 2013 Referendum and Harmonised Elections. Harare: ZEC.
16 ZESN (2013) *Report on the 31 July 2013 Harmonised Elections.* Harare: ZESN. p. 30.

attempt to educate voters in every ward about the electoral process. The high numbers of voters who get turned away on polling days, voter apathy, and spoilt papers show that voter education still needs to be improved by the ZEC.

A study carried out in Gweru for the 2008 and 2013 harmonised elections by Dewa and Muchemwa show that voter education in that district was limited and inadequate. Many residents eligible to vote did not register to vote. The study argues that the inadequate voter education and limited duration therefore culminated in an electorate with insufficient information. According to this study, voters were turned away for reporting in wrong wards, bringing wrong documentation and non-appearance on voters' rolls. It was noted that the limitedness of voter education hindered the people previously labelled 'alien' from regularising their citizenship and registering as voters.[17] These authors quote the Catholic Commission for Justice and Peace (CCJP) in 2013 who claimed that '"ZEC voter educators lacked entry strategies and some of them were seen just waiting at public places and asking people whether they have identification documents, registered as voters and whether they know how to vote". The ZEC educators who managed to call meetings lacked group dynamics and community mobilisation skills resulting in a handful people attending.'[18]

The ZEC complies with the Electoral Act by partnering with civil society organisations (CSOs) such as Citizen Participation Forum, Gweru East Development Trust, Musasa Project, Institute of Young Women Development and Habakkuk Trust, among others on voter education. The ZEC is however criticised for accrediting these organisations very late, thus hindering their effectiveness in assisting with voter education. Funding from the ZEC for voter education was also received late in the 2013 harmonised elections. Uncertainty over the date of the election must have attributed to this late start by the ZEC in terms of engaging its partners. Forward planning could limit some of these constraints. The determination of the proclamation date, sitting of the nomination court and the fact that the campaign period is a prerogative of the executive often creates problems for the ZEC in terms of adequate time being allowed for its planning and implementation of processes. A major criticism laid against ZEC on voter education, which requires urgent attention and action, is the aspect of reaching out to marginalised groups. Farai Mukuta, the executive director of the National Association of Societies for the Care of the Handicapped (NASCOH) reported in 2013 that people with disabilities were not catered for during the voting process. About 800 000 potential voters, who are visually impaired did not receive voter education materials as the ZEC did not produce adequate brailed voter education materials. He also reported that there were no sign language interpreters for those with impaired hearing. The physically challenged still continue to face problems of failing to cast their vote because of long distances.[19] The ZEC can also increase its voter education

17 Dewa D and Muchemwa T (2014) The Voter Education 'Ghost' in Zimbabwean Harmonised Elections of 2008 and 2013: What can be done? Case of Midlands, Gweru District. *International Journal of Research in Humanities and Social Studies* 1(1).

18 Ibid.: 48.

19 Mukuta F (ed.) (2014) Report on the All Stakeholders Review conference on the 2013 Referendum and Harmonised Elections. Harare: ZEC.

and reach out to churches that have negative beliefs about voting. Most importantly, the ZEC should conduct voter education throughout the electoral cycle and the government must provide adequate funding for voter education.

Registration of voters

The registration of voters is an important element in any electoral system which an EMB must handle efficiently and effectively since it can ensure fairness and credibility of an election. The Electoral Act of 1990 and the preceding amendments established the registrar general of elections and constituency registrar who were responsible for managing voter registration and voters' rolls for every constituency. However the ESC was generally responsible for the supervision of voter registration which was carried out by the registrar general of elections. Each constituency registrar was in charge of voter registration and had the custody of the voters' roll for his/her constituency.

Voter registration procedures were amended recently by the General Laws Amendment Act No. 3 of 2016, whose intention among others was to align the electoral law with the constitution. According to this act, voter registration is conducted by the ZEC through its voter registration officers (who are employees of the ZEC and may be appointed to this office conjunctively with any other office as an electoral officer) or any persons whom the ZEC appoints to assist in voter registration. A voter registration officer is appointed for such locality as the commission may determine, including (but not limited to) a constituency, district or ward. Voter registration officers exercise the functions conferred upon them under the general supervision and direction of the ZEC. A person seeking registration as a voter can approach any of the registration offices of the commission for registration as a voter during the period specified in section 17A(2) of the Electoral Act.

The voters' roll has always been availed to the political parties and candidates upon request in print form; however, more recently it is available in electronic form. This has been a contested issue, with political parties and candidates requesting to have access to the electronic copies in an editable and analysable format. It is widely believed that the irregularities which appear on the voters' roll can easily be rectified when the public has access to the electronic copies in an editable and analysable format. The irregularities that continue to be cited over the years are, for example: names appearing on the roll with an incorrect or missing national registration number; incorrect spelling of people's names; deceased people's names appearing on the roll; and names appearing several times on the same roll. Opposition political parties and some non-governmental organisations (NGOs) have always cried foul over the issue saying that it is a deliberate attempt by the ruling party to rig elections. The director of the ZESN in September 2014 argued that it was impossible to have a fair election as long as the voters' roll is not clean. She doubted whether the voters' roll could be clean for the 2018 election.[20] However, the registrar

20 Mahlanga B (2014, 15 September) Impossible to have clean voters' roll by 2018 – ZESN. *NewsDay*. Available at https://www.newsday.co.zw/2014/09/15/impossible-clean-voters-roll-2018-zesn/ [accessed 6 August 2016].

general of elections and subsequently the registrar general of voters always called on people to inspect the voters' roll for any inaccurate information and allow for corrections. It is, however, a positive development that the ZEC now has the mandate of carrying out voters registration, and has complete control and management of the voters' roll. This is because the commission's accountability to the electoral system has increased and should put in place measures to improve any areas of concern noted in the past by various stakeholders.

The ECS was often criticised for not being very effective on its responsibility of overseeing the voter registration process. The registrar general of elections provided reports to the ZEC regarding the registration of voters and the conduct of the elections as the commission required from time to time. This lack of tightness in electoral regulations rendered the ESC's supervision to be regarded as weak and therefore undesirable. It is now required that the ZEC have complete control of the electoral processes and immediately address electoral concerns rather than well after it receives the reports from the registrar general of elections, as was the case with the ESC.

The ZEC is now responsible for voter registration with effect from 22 May 2013 as provided by the Constitution of Zimbabwe Amendment Act No. 20. All previous voter functions are now conferred upon the ZEC under the Electoral Act, including: the functions of registering voters; compiling voters' rolls and registers; ensuring the proper custody and maintenance of voters' rolls and registers; and all other connected functions, provided that the ZEC may give such instructions to the former registrar general of voters, in his or her capacity as the registrar general of births and deaths, the registrar general of citizenship and the registrar general of national registration, as will ensure the efficient, free, fair, proper and transparent conduct of any election or referendum.[21] A most celebrated electoral reform introduced in 2012 is that the voter registration is now conducted by the commission. The Electoral Act states that the ZEC shall maintain, in printed and electronic form, a voters' roll for each ward constituency, containing the names of all registered voters who may vote in the ward and constituency.[22] The voters' roll is regarded as a public document and open to inspection by the public, free of charge, during ordinary office hours at the office of the ZEC or the constituency registrar, where it is kept.

In order to have the requisite residence qualifications to be registered as a voter in a particular constituency, a claimant must be resident in that constituency at the date of his or her claim. Transfer of registration is allowed, subject to fulfilment of the requirements in the Electoral Act.

There are various perceptions as to how the EMBs in Zimbabwe have fared over the years. In the 2000 election, for example, the ZESN[23] reported that the registration process was relatively smooth, despite the well acknowledged problems of limited time and lack of voter registration cards. The Catholic Commission for Justice and Peace in

---

21 Section 239(j) of the Constitution of Zimbabwe Amendment Act No. 20.
22 Section 20(1) of the Electoral Act.
23 ZESN (2000) *Report on the 2000 Parliamentary Elections Zimbabwe 24–25 June 2000.* Harare: ZESN. p. 66.

Zimbabwe[24] observed that in the July harmonised elections, voters with registration slips were allowed to vote even if their names did not appear in the voters' roll, whilst others were not allowed to vote in some polling stations. The SADC Observer Mission[25] observed that some stakeholders raised concerns about the inadequate time allocated to register to vote. Registration was divided into two phases. The first phase lasted 21 days; this was followed by a mandatory 30 day registration from 10 June to 9 July 2013. Given similar issues in elections conducted in Zimbabwe so far, the ZEC must keep up the momentum of voter registration throughout the electoral cycle including between elections, and voter education must be carried out continuously. The voters' roll must also be inspected and corrected continuously so that it remains accurate and credible.

Polling stations, voting, infrastructure and environment

According to Section 51 of the Electoral Act (as amended by the General Laws Amendment Act, 2016) it is the responsibility of the ZEC to establish in each constituency as many polling stations as it may consider necessary for the purposes of conveniently taking a poll of the voters of that constituency. The commission is expected to establish a sufficient number of polling stations in each ward of the constituency concerned; receive representations on the issue of polling station locations in any constituency from political parties contesting the election concerned; and may give directions on this matter to any provincial elections officer, district elections officer or constituency elections officer on the basis of such representations.

For any election the Commission ensures that every constituency elections officer is provided with polling booths or voting compartments and ballot boxes, and is expected to provide papers, including ballot papers, instruments for marking ballot papers with the official mark, seals and other necessary items and makes arrangements to facilitate the taking of the poll as the Commission may consider advisable for effectively conducting the election, and the expenditure incurred upon all such acts and things shall be charged upon and paid out of the funds of the Commission obtained from the Consolidated Revenue Fund. Where two or more elections are held concurrently in a constituency, the Commission provides the constituency elections officer concerned with separate ballot boxes for each such election.

The location of polling stations must be readily accessible to any citizen, and no polling station shall be located in a property occupied or owned by a political party or candidate, police station, barrack, cantonment area or any other place that may violate voters' rights or the integrity of the voting process.[26] To ensure that all registered voters are accorded an opportunity to cast their vote, polling stations open from 07h00 to 19h00, but must

---

24 Catholic Commission for Justice and Peace in Zimbabwe (2013) *Election Observation Report for 2013 Harmonised Elections Zimbabwe.* Harare: The Catholic Observer. p. 39.

25 SADC (2013) *Report of the SADC Election Observation Mission to the Harmonised Elections in the republic of Zimbabwe Held on 31 July 2013.* Gaborone: SADC. p. 11.

26 Section 51(1b) of General Laws Amendment Act (2016).

remain open for a continuous periods of 12 hours. The presiding officer shall permit every voter who, at the time fixed in terms of this section for the closing of the polling station concerned, is in the queue of persons waiting to cast their votes, to record his or her vote before closing the polling station.[27] For the purpose of enhancing transparency, the ZEC is required to furnish all contesting parties with information as to where and by whom the ballot papers were printed, their total number and the number distributed to each polling station.[28] The ballot papers are also recorded before commencement of the poll at each polling station.[29]

In terms of the general principles provided for in the Electoral Act,[30] voting methods must be simple, accurate, verifiable, secure and transparent. The ZEC is also called upon to maintain strict impartiality in the exercise of any function related to elections.[31] The ZEC shall arrange for the obtaining of voting compartments and ballot boxes, and provide papers (including ballot papers) instruments for marking ballot papers with the official mark, seals and other necessary things to ensure credibility of the process.[32] Separate ballot boxes are to be provided for concurrent elections.[33] The expenditure incurred upon all such acts and items shall be charged upon and paid out of the funds of the commission obtained from the consolidated revenue fund. In addition, the ZEC may appoint a member of its staff or one other person to be the constituency elections officer for each constituency for the purposes of the election.[34] At the request of the ZEC, the Public Service Commission and the Health Services Board and the responsible authority of any statutory body or council shall second to the ZEC such persons in the employment of the state, the statutory body or the local authority, as the case may be, as are necessary hold such offices and perform such functions as the ZEC may direct during an election. The presiding officer must check the ballot box within 30 minutes of commencement of voting and satisfy himself or herself that the box is empty. He must also show representatives of parties in the electoral contest, before closing and sealing the box. The ballot box closed and sealed shall not be opened unless for the purpose of vote counting.[35] During the actual voting, no other person is allowed into the polling station other than voters admitted to cast their votes, electoral officers, candidates, election agents, police officers on duty, accredited observers and such other classes of persons as may be prescribed.[36]

The security of votes is also provided in the Electoral Act. The commissioner general of police is mandated to ensure that sufficient numbers of police are available in the immediate vicinity of each polling station to provide order and ensure observance of the

---

27 Ibid.: section 53.
28 Ibid.: Section 52A of the Electoral Act
29 Ibid.
30 As amended by SI 85 of 2013, Section 3(e).
31 Electoral Act, Section 11(c).
32 Section 52(1) of the Electoral Act.
33 Section 52(1)(a) of the Electoral Act.
34 Section 10 (4)(a) and Section 10(4)(a) ss. 1 of the Electoral Act.
35 Section 54 of the Electoral Act.
36 Section 55(2) of the Electoral Act.

law; the commissioner general of police must not, however, interfere with the electoral process. In actual fact, during polling, police officers will be under the command of the presiding officer who directs and instructs them.[37] Voting is done by ballot, and the ballot paper bears the name of all candidates in alphabetical order, candidates' symbols and passport size photograph of the candidate.[38] Before the voter receives the ballot paper and secretly expresses his or her choice in the voting compartment, the presiding officer must mark the paper with the official mark. Illiterate or physically challenged voters can also be assisted to cast their votes by people of their choice, or a presiding officer in the presence of two other persons who may be a police officer on duty and a ZEC employee. The person rendering assistance shall only do so once and need not be a registered voter.[39]

At the close of voting, ballot boxes are sealed in the presence of candidates and or their agents and observers; and spoilt, unused, counterfoils of ballot papers and assisted voters are accounted for. Thereafter, ballot papers are opened and vote counting begins in the presence of candidates and or their agents and observers at the respective polling stations. The presiding officer shall also display the results outside the polling station. The results are in turn transmitted to the ward, constituency, provincial and national centres. At all levels, ZEC officials conduct their duties in the presence of candidates or their agents. The idea of involving agents is to ensure that they verify figures on the returns at each stage of the process. The verification entails that agents check whether the figures transmitted at all levels tally with the ultimate results. It seeks to uphold the integrity of the outcome.

The Electoral Act also provides for postal voting, a right enjoyed by employees of government or their spouses serving outside Zimbabwe, and unable to vote on the day of the election in their respective constituencies,[40] provided they make such an application in terms of section 73.

From the above provisions, it is plausible that the amended Electoral Act seeks to promote the integrity of elections by securing the ballots and ballot boxes and also involving agents at all critical stages of the process. Under the current system, it would be very difficult for any party to steal the election, as was allegedly suspected. The security procedures and breakage of ballot seals would be apparent to any observer or agent. The ballot boxes used are translucent, which all parties may inspect to their satisfaction. The source and number of ballot papers distributed is well known by all stakeholders well in advance. The official mark on the ballot paper given to the voter before the vote is cast makes the whole process even more transparent. This is especially so during ballot counting when ballot papers which do not bear the official mark are rejected if they exceed 5% of the votes cast at that polling station. The reconciliation process done at the end of the voting process, accounting for each ballot paper as well as the requirement to have a list of assisted voters

---

37 Section 55(7) of the Electoral Act.
38 Section 57 of the Electoral Act.
39 Section 59(2) of the Electoral Act.
40 Section 72 of the Electoral Act.

will increase the transparency of voting. With all these and other security provisions, it is difficult to foresee how the ballots can be tempered with.

Equally, it is difficult to conceal electoral fraud when it happens. It will be for all to see. Perhaps, what can be manipulated are the voters themselves during the campaign period and not the voting process itself which is too transparent. The continued emphasis on processing results from the polling station upwards is also meant to ensure that results are not unduly delayed. This could be a direct consequence of the delay endured in the announcement of the 2008 presidential election results by ZEC, which then raised serious integrity questions. Polling stations are made public in advance, and every candidate knows their actual location, where they will station their agents. The traditional talk about ballot boxes coming from somewhere is difficult in the sense that the ZEC has to account for each ballot box according to the number of polling stations gazetted for each election. More refreshing is that throughout the provisions relating to polling stations and voting, there is no direct role of the security institutions except the police who will be under the command of the presiding officers to maintain law and order throughout the voting and counting process.

The SADC Election Observer Mission (SEOM) observed in the 2013 elections that counting was conducted procedurally and transparently. The mission witnessed the counting of votes in the polling stations. It also observed that electoral officers and party agents signed the polling station return in the presence of observers and each party agent received a copy of the polling station return. The mission also observed isolated incidences of political intoleration. The SEOM observed that 304 890 people failed to vote after being turned away at various polling stations across the country. Some of the reasons noted by SEOM for people being unable to vote are: others found their names in wards they do not reside in; not appearing on the voter roll at the polling stations; bringing improper documents such as expired passports, torn or illegible documents; underage voters; and those registered after the closure of the voter roll.[41]

Information technology

In some developing countries, EMBs are in the process of integrating ICT in voter registration to enhance sustainability and effective use of electronic systems with biometric data analysis functionality. In developed countries, some have already developed synergies between voter registration and other national registration systems. In the case of the ZEC, this revolution is yet to happen. The ZEC is, however, expected to develop relevant expertise and is responsible for the use of technology with regards to electoral process. Recently, the commission expressed intentions to adopt the biometric system[42] but

---

41 SADC (2013). *Report of the SADC Election Observation Mission to the Harmonised Elections in the republic of Zimbabwe Held on 31 July 2013*. Gaborone: SADC.

42 Chidza R (2016, 11 May) 'Zec to adopt biometric voting for 2018'. *Zimbabwe Situation*. Available at http://www.zimbabwesituation.com/news/zimsit-m-zec-to-adopt-biometric-voting-for-2018-newsday-zimbabwe/ [accessed 15 October 2016].

questions of implementation immediately come to the fore because of the broader macro-economic context in the country.

Codes of conduct

The Electoral Act provides for a code of conduct for election agents and observers and a code of conduct for political parties and candidates, which are informed by the principles for election management, monitoring and observation in the SADC region, principles and guidelines for managing democratic elections in Southern Africa and the African Union's declaration on the principles governing democratic elections in Africa. These codes of conduct provide the behavioural standards that are expected by various people during elections. According to the code of conduct for election agents and observers, no observer or agent shall wear any apparel sporting a prohibited symbol or apparel indicating any affiliation with another candidate or political party participating in the poll. Only the prescribed number of candidate's election agents may be present at the counting of votes. The code of conduct for political parties and candidates provides that all political parties and their members and supporters must promote conditions conducive to free, fair and democratic elections conducted through a secret ballot in a climate of democratic tolerance in which political activity may take place without fear, intimidation or reprisals.

Despite the detailed provision in the law on the expected conduct by various electoral players, some political parties, agents, candidates and ordinary people continue to flout these regulations. This is despite the existence of explicit forms of punishment for violation. Some incidences of violence and voter intimidation have been recorded during electoral campaigns in some parts of the country over the years. The ZEC, through its voter education programmes, should emphasise the need for political tolerance in all elections. Independent bodies such as the Human Rights Commission and the National Peace and Reconciliation Commission should assist on enhancing the culture of political tolerance throughout the electoral processes.

Electoral dispute resolution mechanisms

The ZEC is inevitably faced with disputes throughout the electoral process, as a result of contestation in the fight for political power. The legal framework on elections makes the ZEC's task better in terms of facilitating the management of electoral conflicts. The ZEC is mandated by the Constitution of Zimbabwe to receive and consider complaints from the public and to take such action in regard to the complaints as it considers appropriate.[43] The Electoral Act further provides for conflict resolution mechanisms in relation to the conduct of elections. Remedies for electoral malpractices are also available.

The Electoral Court has exclusive jurisdiction to hear appeals, applications and petitions in terms of the Electoral Act. It can review any decision made by the ZEC or any other person under the Act. The Electoral Court does not have jurisdiction to try any

---

43 Section 239(j) of the Constitution of Zimbabwe Amendment Act No. 20.

criminal case. Judgments, orders and directions of the Electoral Court are enforceable in the same way as judgments, orders and directions of the High Court. Section 162 of the Electoral Act provides that the chief justice appoints at least two judges of the High Court to be judges of the Electoral Court after consultations with the Judicial Service Commission and the judge president of the High Court, for such period as he or she may specify in the appointment. This provision seems to fly in the face of section 183 of the constitution which prohibits a person from being appointed as a judicial officer of more than one court. There is need for alignment of section 162 of the Electoral Act with the constitutional provision.

In the 2013 harmonised elections, the Electoral Court dealt with at least 31 appeals against decisions of the Nomination Court.[44] The Nomination Court appeals were mostly against decisions made by the Nomination Court presiding officers in accepting or rejecting nomination papers from some prospective candidates. Some parties had filled in two candidates in one constituency, with candidates having duly signed forms. Some candidates' nomination forms were rejected for failure to produce original documents or police clearance. The court cleared all the cases but the finalisation of the cases left very few days for the ZEC to print ballot papers; this also created logistical challenges for the commission to manage special voting. A total of 41 election petitions were filed with the Electoral Court after the announcement of the 2013 harmonised elections. The Electoral Court has been criticised for failing to expeditiously clear electoral cases in past elections held in Zimbabwe before 2013. The chief justice is highly commended for having designated 24 magistrates to adjudicate over cases involving politically motivated violence and intimidation in the 2013 elections. This is in line with section 182 of the Electoral Act which now provides that every election petition shall be determined within six months of the date of its presentation. Most observer missions in Zimbabwe's elections such as the SADC, AU, SADC Parliamentary Forum, and ZESN commended the ZEC for facilitating the dispute resolution management mechanism through the multiparty liaison committees which are established and provided in the Electoral Act.[45] These committees consist of a national multiparty liaison committee, a constituency multiparty liaison committee and a local multiparty liaison committee.

The national multiparty liaison committee consists of a commissioner of the ZEC as the chairperson, two representatives of each political party, or independent candidates contesting the election. The function of a multiparty liaison committee is to hear and attempt to solve any disputes, concerns, matters or grievances relating to the electoral process including allegations concerning non-compliance with the code of conduct.[46] The decisions of the committee are arrived at by consensus. The multiparty liaison committees must, however, be strengthened by broadening the membership to include other stakeholders, since this process provides an informal means of resolving conflicts and

---

44 ZESN (2013) *Report on the 31 July 2013 Harmonised Elections.* Harare: ZESN.
45 Section 160B of the Electoral Act.
46 Section 160C of the Electoral Act.

helps to reduce escalation of conflicts during elections. The multiparty liaison committees should be operational throughout the electoral cycle so as to provide a platform for continuous engagement.

It is important to note the law provides for the appointment and functions of a special police liaison officer and special investigation committee. In every general election, the commissioner-general of police in consultation with the Zimbabwe Human Rights Commission, appoint a senior police officer for each provincial centre who becomes the special police liaison officer responsible for the expeditious investigation of cases of politically motivated violence or intimidation within that province which come to the attention of the police, a multiparty liaison committee, the ZEC, or the Zimbabwe Human Rights Commission during the election period. To assist each special police liaison officer, the Zimbabwe Human Rights Commission, in consultation with the ZEC, establishes a special investigation committee for each provincial centre, chaired by a Zimbabwe Human Rights Commissioner or a member of the staff of the Zimbabwe Human Rights Commission, and consisting of the special police liaison officer for the province in question. Two representatives of each political party contesting the election are also selected by the party concerned; provided that an independent candidate contesting a presidential election is entitled to select two representatives to represent him or her on the committee.

The Electoral Commissions Forum of SADC (SADC-ECF) countries noted that for the 2013 elections, there were no incidents of violence, harassment, or intimidation brought to the attention of the mission. The SADC Parliamentary Forum Mission observed that in the 2013 elections, there was general peace, tranquility, harmony and a high degree of political tolerance throughout the electoral process. The mission argues that the political environment was conducive to whoever wanted to vote.[47] They attribute this to the political leadership of the contesting political parties, which preached a message of peace and unity throughout the whole process. They argue that this greatly facilitated free movement of people during the entire electoral process. The SADC argues that for the same elections, the ZEC conducted its work in a transparent, orderly and professional manner.

Accreditation of observers and media personnel

Election observers play an important monitoring role in electoral processes. There is an inherent relationship between the accreditation of observers and the principles of transparency and integrity espoused in the Electoral Act. Integrity and transparency also determine and enhance whether elections are free and fair. Invitation of observers helps to improve citizens' perceptions of electoral integrity and it encourages sharing lessons through recommendations made by observers.

In Zimbabwe, the accreditation of observers, monitors and media personnel is done by the ZEC. Under the Electoral Act, observers are accredited by the observers

---

47 SADC Parliamentary Forum (2013) Mission Report: Election Observer Mission to the 31 July 2013, Zimbabwe Harmonised General Election.

accreditation committee, which consists of: the chairperson of the commission, who chairs the committee; three commissioners designated by the commission; one person nominated by the office of the president and cabinet; one nominated by the minister of foreign affairs; one nominated by the minister of justice, legal and parliamentary affairs; and another person nominated by the minister responsible for immigration. This committee can recommend to the commission the accreditation of individuals of foreign countries, individuals representing local organisations, and eminent persons from within Zimbabwe who have applied to be accepted as observers.[48] Recommendation for accreditation can be made on: invited individuals representing bodies that exercise functions similar to those of the commission; individuals representing foreign countries, or international organisations and foreign eminent persons who have been invited by the minister of foreign affairs to observe an election; and individuals representing local organisations and eminent persons from within Zimbabwe invited by the minister to observe an election.

The Act specifies the time period in which applications for accreditation as an observer must be received by the commission. For all elections, applications for accreditation must be made no later than the fourth day before the first day of polling in a proclamation.

A person does not practice as an observer unless they have reported to the observer accreditation committee at a time and place notified by the committee; having received a copy of, or been made aware, of the contents of the code of conduct; and having paid the prescribed accreditation fee, upon which the accredited observer will be issued with a certificate. It is from this point that an accredited person can observe the election process, in particular the conduct of polling, the counting and collation of votes, and the verification of polling station returns. An accredited observer can bring to the attention of the ZEC any irregularity in the conduct of the poll, as well as to provide the commission with a comprehensive review of the election.[49]

The issue of accrediting observers in Zimbabwe's elections has been contentious, particularly since the 2000 election when some observers were viewed by the ruling party as openly siding with the opposition. EISA observed that:

> After weeks of prevarication over the issue of election observers for Zimbabwe's forthcoming presidential election, the government finally ordered the head of the Union (EU) Observer Mission, Pierre Schori, to leave the country. The EU retaliated by imposing 'smart sanctions' on President Mugabe and his close associates, which include a travel ban and an assets freeze, and withdrawing the remnants of the EU observer mission. Pierre Schori, who is Sweden's ambassador to the United Nations, was expelled after the Zimbabwean government refused to accept his credentials as head of the EU Observer Mission. The Zimbabwean government had invited individual EU members to observe the presidential

---

48 Section 40H(2) of the Electoral Act.
49 Section 40G(c) of the Electoral Act.

election, but had rejected observers from Britain, Germany, the Netherlands, Sweden, Finland and Denmark, which President Mugabe accuses of supporting the opposition Movement for Democratic Change (MDC).[50]

The imposition of sanctions on the country by the west also resulted in retaliation through the denial of mostly western observers. The ruling party has always argued that Zimbabwe is a sovereign country and decides who comes to observe its election. In 2009, the minister of justice, legal and parliamentary affairs, Patrick Chinamasa, reportedly said the government would not invite election observers from western countries to monitor a presidential run-off unless western sanctions against Zimbabwe are lifted. Main opposition MDC leader Morgan Tsvangirai, who claimed victory in the 29-March elections, said he would only be part of the run-off if international observers and media were given full access to ensure the vote is free and fair. Elphas Mukonoweshuro, (the late) who was the international affairs secretary of the MDC, said that the government's pronouncement was contemptible.

In the 2013 elections, observers came from the AU; the SADC; the ECF-SADC peer review forum; the SADC Parliamentary Forum; individual countries inside and outside of Africa; over 5 000 others from Zimbabwe's civil society groups/NGOs; and the protestant, Catholic, evangelical and indigenous churches in Zimbabwe and the Southern Africa region. All observers (in pre- and post-election statements) concluded that both the election campaign and actual vote were peaceful. The SADC Observer Mission deployed 170 teams of observers with 573 observers throughout the ten provinces of Zimbabwe. The teams comprised SADC members of parliament, civil servants, and civil society organisations, and the project was chaired by Bernard Membe, Tanzania's foreign affairs minister. This was the largest observer mission ever deployed by the SADC. President Mugabe declined to invite western observers, citing the sanctions as proof of their bias against him and his party. Western embassies' staff were, however, allowed to freely view the polling taking place in the vicinity of Harare.[51]

In the past, accreditation of election observers was centralised to three centres; thus creating enormous logistical and financial challenges for observer groups. The 2013 election is commended for having decentralised accreditation to ten provincial capitals.

Notably, however, there have been few international groups from outside Africa observing elections in Zimbabwe. The country should open up observation of its elections to any observers, in order to enhance transparency and acceptance of the electoral results, unless there are security concerns for such observer(s).

---

50 EISA (2002) Foreign observers and the 2002 Zimbabwean presidential election. Available at https://www.eisa.org.za/wep/zim2002om3.htm [accessed 6 August 2016].

51 ACLJ (n.d.) A reflection on Zimbabwe's 2013 elections. Available at www.aclj.org/united-nations/reflection-zimbabwe-2013-elections [accessed 6 August 2016].

Stakeholder collaboration

The ZEC collaborates with a number of stakeholders in the electoral processes. In its 2014 review, the ZEC noted that there was a concerted effort in the 2013 elections to manage its stakeholders throughout the electoral cycle. To build rapport and trust with stakeholders, in 2013, the ZEC held several consultative meetings with political parties, CSOs, faith-based organisations, traditional leaders, the security sector, government departments and the media. In 2013 alone, the ZEC held five consultative meetings with political parties, members of the defence forces, civil society and media from the 7–10 July.

The ZEC had two major collaborations with cooperating partners. The agreement between the ZEC and UNDP covered the period 2011-2012 with USD 3.5 million earmarked for improving institutional, administrative and operational systems. This led to the identification and establishment of a unified ZEC headquarters, among other notable achievements. Another important agreement was with EISA worth ZAR 12.5 million or USD 1.995 million and it focuses on establishment of multiparty liaison committees, training political parties, etc. These programmes have increased the ZEC's ability to engage with key stakeholders across a wide variety of audiences.

The ZEC extended its capacity to building key institutions involved in supporting the running of elections. In 2013, the ZEC provided the District Development Fund with USD 730 000 to upgrade damaged roads, bridges and water supplies. During the same period, the ZEC disbursed USD 38 562 635 to the Zimbabwe republic police and USD 15 083 938 to the registrar general of voters for use during the elections. Such institutions assist in ensuring that voter registration, voting and other electoral processes are undertaken efficiently and effectively. In addition to donor relations, the ZEC also liaises with the judiciary, the ministry of justice, legal and parliamentary affairs, parliament and many other relevant institutions.[52]

The electoral body has initiated and conducted stakeholders meetings to review its performance from 19–24 March 2014. An all-stakeholders review conference was held to assess the 2013 referendum and harmonised election.[53] A stakeholder's feedback meeting was also convened by the ZEC on 16 October 2015 to get responses on the Marondera Central constituency polling station-specific voter registration and voting exercise. The stakeholders' engagement meetings were conducted within the spirit of building confidence among players in electoral processes. The ZEC should take these forums seriously and make decisive steps in implementing recommendations made, as they provide an invaluable mirror in which the ZEC's performance is also assessed.

In 2014, the ZEC was elected as president of the ECF-SADC for a two-year term. The position implies that the ZEC has to lead by example on how it conducts its affairs in order to provide best practices to other SADC EMBs during its tenure. Its conduct on leading the regional body can raise its profile higher and increase the faith of ordinary

---

52 ZEC(2014) *Report on the All-Stakeholders Review Conference on the 2013 Referendum and Harmonised Elections*. Harare: ZEC.
53 Ibid.

Zimbabweans in the electoral processes. Since electoral processes are dependent on a multitude of stakeholders, cutting across political parties, media, civil society, government ministries and departments, courts, election observers and the electorate, it is therefore essential for the ZEC to continuously improve its stakeholder management mechanisms and styles.

Communication and media

Section 160J of the Electoral Act covers the conduct of mass media during election period. During an election period, broadcasters and print publishers are obliged to treat all political parties and candidate equitably in their news coverage. Inaccuracies in the reports on the elections in their news media should be rectified without delay and with due prominence. News media is expected not to encourage violence or hatred against any class of persons.

Section 160K of the Electoral Act provides that by request of the ZEC, the Zimbabwe Media Commission and the Broadcasting Authority of Zimbabwe are to monitor the Zimbabwean news media during the election period to ensure that political parties, candidates, broadcasters, print publishers and journalists observe this legal requirement. No one is prevented from monitoring news media and reporting during an election period.

According to Makumbe,[54] a free and fair electoral process is virtually impossible to attain without the active participation of an economically healthy, free and effective mass media. The issue of control and ownership of media affects fairness of elections. Since independence, Zimbabwe has witnessed an increase in mass media institutions; newspapers such as the *Daily News, Newsday, The Herald, The Financial Gazette, The Chronicle* and *The Manica Post*. The electronic media consist of both public and private media. The Zimbabwe Broadcasting Corporation (ZBC) has monopoly over television in terms of national broadcasting. However, as a result of internet satellite availability, the public has direct access to multiple channels of broadcasting. The major problem in terms of accessing internet and satellite broadcasting is the high user fees. The major problem faced by the ZEC is that 'the media itself could be said to be instigators of hate speech whose net effect could be the poisoning of the electoral environment'.[55]

The ZBC owns and controls four radio stations (Radio Zimbabwe, National FM, Power FM and Spot FM) and has a good national coverage. It does, however, experience transmission problems in some areas, particularly around the borders. Internet live-streaming and digitisation by the broadcaster is, however, now assisting problems which existed. STAR FM and ZI-FM radios also covered elections, particularly the 2013 harmonised elections since they are fairly new players in broadcasting. The establishment of these radio stations which are quasi- government and independent respectively, has brought in new spaces for broadcasting electoral issues. Since 2000, the media environment

---

54 Makumbe J (2000) *Behind the Smokescreen: The Politics of Zimbabwe 1995 General Elections.* Harare: University of Zimbabwe Publications. p. 185.

55 ZEC (2014) *Report on The All Stakeholder Review Conference on the 2013 Referendum and Harmonised Elections.* Harare: ZEC. p. 11.

in Zimbabwe has been reported, by some observer missions, to be extremely polarised and 'nearly all of the independent media have an adversarial relationship with the government while the state-owned media are fiercely pro-government'.[56] Reports issued on the 2013 elections, by some observers, including a ZESN Report,[57] state that: 'The state controlled publications tend to report favourably on ZANU PF and negatively on other parties. The opposite is true of the private media that favours the MDCs and other parties that are not ZANU PF.'

However, over the years, the public broadcaster, ZBC has always indicated that there is no uptake of available slots or advertisement time by the candidates. This could be attributed to advertising costs. The Media Alliance of Zimbabwe was concerned by what it termed:

> blatant bias by the ZBC, firstly by reporters wearing party regalia while reporting to the nation. Secondly, monitoring reports by the Media Monitoring Project Zimbabwe (MMPZ) have noted a continued trend of positive reporting for ZANU PF and persistent negative reports for the MDC-T . A worrying trend in the last few weeks has also been the lack of clarity and monitoring of political advertising on the ZBC, where adverts mocking and discrediting the Prime Minister are aired on television and radio. The adverts are however not clearly identified as adverts, nor indicate who placed the adverts as such going against Clause 160H(1)(c) of the Electoral Act that states that every advert should be clearly identified as such. MAZ is also worried by the increase in cases of assault and harassment of journalists following the proclamation of the 31 July elections. [58]

Opposition parties feel that they do not get sufficient or fair coverage by the ZBC during elections. The ZBC should have more interface with political parties during elections, especially on news coverage where the issue of costs for advertising do not arise. It should be emphasised that political parties should have events during the electoral cycle worth being categorised as news for them to be covered. No news, remains not news. As a state broadcaster serving the interests of the public at large, the role of the ZBC is to ensure that voters are able to make an informed choice by providing fair, balanced, accurate and objective coverage of candidates, parties and all related electoral processes. In order for the commission to take ZBC to task on its expectations, a budget should also be provided to the ZBC by the ZEC so that it can enforce some of its programmes. The ZEC can sponsor programmes on the ZBC to allow candidates to debate on their election manifestos. It is

56 SADC Parliamentary Forum. (2001) *Norms and Standards for Elections in the SADC Region.* Windhoek: SADC Parliamentary Forum. p. 1.
57 ZESN (2013) *Report on the 31 July 2013 Harmonised Elections.* Harare: ZESN. p. 31.
58 Media Alliance of Zimbabwe (2013, 24 July) Statement on the state of the media ahead of the 31 July harmonised elections.

expected, however, that the ZBC's digitisation programme will improve both its capacity on coverage and transmission.

A number of recommendations have been submitted to the ZEC on how it can strengthen its role with regards to media. Some of the recommendations are that the ZEC must revise its media code of conduct in consultation with relevant stakeholders; the revision should also take into consideration existing codes such as the SADC guidelines on reporting elections; the ZEC should use the expertise of existing media organisations for independent monitoring of the media conduct; the ZEC should set up and publicise a public complaints mechanism to allow citizens to submit their complaints on the conduct of media.[59]

Evaluation of credibility

This section presents the various comments made by stakeholders on the integrity of the ZEC. On the appointment of new ZEC commissioners in July 2016, the ZESN's director, Rindai Chipfunde, said the conduct of the commissioners should enhance the integrity of the ZEC in the administration of electoral processes. She argues that it is important for the EMB to be independent from governmental, political and other partisan influences on their decisions. As a principle, impartiality can be enforced through behaviour, attitudes and engagement with all stakeholders. The electoral processes must be managed in a manner that does not disenfranchise stakeholders.[60] The *Zimbabwe Independent* wrote an article entitled 'ZEC integrity still doubtful' in February 2013. The paper argued that the ZEC's credibility took a knock in 2008 when it spent five weeks withholding results of the first round of the presidential election which President Mugabe had lost.[61] ZEC indicated that it recruits all its employees on professional basis and they have no connections to the security sector except as provided by law. According to Madhuku, the appointment of ZEC commissioners was seconded by the three political parties in the inclusive government, namely, ZANU PF, MDC-T and MDC led by Welshman Ncube. He said ZEC must be independent, or at least seen to be independent. Madhuku said the appointment of ZEC Commissioners was not done in terms of the law as they were selected by political parties.[62] However, the Minister of Justice, Legal and Parliamentary Affairs, Emmerson Munangagwa applauded ZEC when he said 'I am pleased at the frankness of ZEC to public scrutiny'.[63]He also commended ZEC for organising a workshop to expose themselves to public scrutiny for the benefit of future elections.[64]

59 ZESN (2013) *Report on the 31 July 2013 Harmonised Elections.* Harare: ZESN. p. 34.
60 Sibanda M (2016, 10July) New ZEC commissioners face uphill task. *Daily News.* Available at https://www.dailynews.co.zw/articles/2016/07/10/new-zec-commissioners-face-uphill-task [accessed 6 August 2016].
61 ZEC integrity still doubtful (2013, 15 February) *Zimbabwe Independent.* Available at http://www.theindependent.co.zw/2013/02/15/zec-integrity-still-doubtful/ [accessed 6 August 2013].
62 www.newsday.co.zw, 'Political parties overshadow ZEC independence, credibility, March 20, 2014.
63 Ibid.
64 Ibid.

Opposition leaders have under their umbrella, Coalition of Democrats (CODE) in July 2016, called for a free and fair election, managed by the international community, which can be SADC, AU, and or UN singularly or together. CODE argues that ZEC is heavily partial and cannot hold a credible, free and fair election. ZEC should however manage Zimbabwe's elections but should continue to enhance its credibility.[65]

Dumiso Dabengwa lodged a complaint at the High Court in 2013, arguing that the ZEC had failed, since 2012, to give him the consolidated national voters' roll in an electronic format which makes it possible for him to analyse the document. On April 2016, the ZEC then responded to Dumiso Dabengwa that they had an electronic copy of the voters' roll, but not in the form that can be analysed or which you can use a search facility.[66] The ZEC must provide the voter's roll in an electronic form which can be analysed.

A study by the Zimbabwe Democracy Institute (ZDI)[67] called on the inclusive government to immediately take measures to demilitarise the ZEC secretariat to restore its independence for it to credibly run crucial election set for 2013. The report called upon the SADC to ensure fresh recruitment of ZEC employees and ensure they have no connections to the security sector.[68] The ZEC must conduct interviews for its secretariat in public, especially for its senior officers to enhance its credibility by raising public confidence, just as the interviews for judges in the judiciary are held in public

On the polling operations, the Common Market for Eastern and Southern Africa (COMESA)[69] concluded that polling stations allowed easy access to voters, observers and monitors/party agents, guaranteed secrecy to vote. The COMESA mission argued that where voter-identification problems occurred, electoral officials recorded and handled such cases in a manner that ensured that voters with valid documentation were accorded the right to vote even if their names did not appear in the voters' roll. The mission concluded that the election took place in an environment of peace and tranquility. The mission argues that it did not witness any occurrences that compromised the integrity of the vote cast. COMESA argues that the process took place in an environment which was transparent and secure enough to guarantee the freedom of the vote and respect the will of the voters.[70]

In 2013, the AU observer mission head Olusegu Obasanjo said the elections were free, honest and credible. SADC observer mission head and Tanzania Foreign Minister Bernard Membe said 'Zimbabwe should be congratulated for holding a free and peaceful

65 www.radiovop.com, 'Opposition Leaders Want AU Body To Take Over ZEC Job, 29 July 2016.

66 The Legal Monitor (2013, 27 May) Dabengwa fumes ... shoots at ZEC conduct, doubts credible polls. Harare: Zimbabwe Lawyers for Human Rights. Available at: http://archive.kubatana.net/docs/hr/zlhr_legal_monitor_issue_194_130529.pdf [accessed 6 August 2016].

67 Zimbabwe Democracy Institute (ZDI) (2013) Confronting security risks for Zimbabwe civil society ahead of elections. *ZDI Policy Briefing Paper* No. 2. Harare: ZDI

68 ZEC cannot deliver free and fair elections: Harare ZDI. *Zimbabwe Independent*. Available at http://www.theindependent.co.zw/2012/12/21/zec-cannot-deliver-free-and-fair-elections-zdi/ [accessed 6 August 2016].

69 COMESA (2008) Official preliminary statement by the COMESA Electoral Observer Mission in 2008 Harmonised Elections for the Republic of Zimbabwe.

70 Ibid.

harmonised election.'[71] The mission, however, noted that 'there were logistical challenges that made it impossible for 26 160 out of a total of 65 956 registered members of the disciplined forces and electoral officers to cast their vote'.[72] Botswana, however, initially rejected that the poll was credible and in early August 2013, called for an audit of the election results. The Southern African Regional Society and Social Movements observer mission said these elections were heavily compromised and fall far short of meeting the SADC principles and guidelines governing democratic elections.

In July 2016, the ZEC chairperson, Justice Rita Makarau, said the election management body is implementing a raft of measures aimed at making Zimbabwe's electoral system more transparent and credible. [73]The reforms include a robust and efficient biometric voter registration exercise that would eliminate the dead and absent from the voters' roll. She said the polling station-based voter registration exercise would, among other issues, result in the reduction in the number of ballot papers per polling station and reduce chances of double voting. She said that the reforms, some of which are mandatory, were driven by the new constitution, recommendations from observer missions in previous elections, as well as engagement with other stakeholders. Justice Rita Makarau also said that the ZEC was ready to engage stakeholders and political parties on a monthly basis with a view to building trust and confidence in the electoral process. These proposed reforms were welcomed by the People's Democratic Party, the MDC, other political parties, the Women's Coalition, faith-based organisations and CSOs – just to mention a few. It is, however, hoped that the ZEC will walk the talk on its willingness to continue the reforms which will improve its credibility.

Electoral Resource Centre executive director Tawanda Chimhini has said that there is progress in electoral reform, but that it is piecemeal and inadequate. In his view, more needs to be done by the country heads for the 2018 elections. However, he also noted that there has been marked improvements in voter registration since the ZEC took over the process.[74]

The Commonwealth observer mission in 2000 found the polling and counting procedures to be transparent and fair. It found no major problems with the secrecy of the ballot and complaints by party agents and voters were few. Presiding officers, constituency registrars and their staff were conscientious in addressing their responsibilities and worked hard to meet the requirements of a complex and demanding process. The mission found out that delays in the tabulation and counting of results suggest that the authorities had not

---

71 African Union Commission (2013) Report of African Union Election Observation Mission to the 31 July 2013 Harmonised Elections in the Republic of Zimbabwe.

72 Moyo H (2013, 9 August) SADC, AU withhold credibility stamp. *Zimbabwe Independent*. Available at http://www.theindependent.co.zw/2013/08/09/sadc-au-withhold-credibility-stamp/ [accessed 6 August 2016].

73 Chifera (I (2016, 19 July) Zimbabwe Electoral Commission set to implement sweeping reforms. *VOA Zimbabwe*. Available at http://www.voazimbabwe.com/a/zimbabwe-electoral-commission/3424852.html [accessed 15 October 2016].

74 Sibanda M (2016, 21 July 2016) Civil society, election stakeholders meet. *Daily News*. Available at https://www.dailynews.co.zw/articles/2016/07/21/civil-society-election-stakeholders-meet [accessed 15 October 2016].

anticipated the scale of voter turnout, and consideration should be given to dealing with this situation in future elections.[75]

The ZESN[76] argues in its observer mission report that the following factors seriously compromised the credibility and fairness of 31 July 2013 harmonised elections: inadequate and delayed voter education; an inadequate and flawed voter registration process; failure to provide the voters' roll to political parties and stakeholders on time; chaotic special voting; and the high numbers of assisted and turned-away voters.

A survey carried out by Mass Public Opinion Institute (MPOI) and Afrobarometer in 2005 showed that more than 66% of a sample did not trust the national election administration in the 2005 election[77]. Sachikonye[78] notes that, in 2008, the long delay in announcement of the first round of presidential election results meant that public confidence in the electoral process plummeted further.

Whilst lessons can be learnt by the ZEC on issues raised by its stakeholders which has a bearing on its integrity, this paper finds it worthwhile for Zimbabwe and SADC member-states to reflect on these various reports given by different parties, especially with issues raised by Mbeki, Mathlosa and Mandaza.[79]

Matlosa[80] notes with concern that election monitoring and observation which should essentially represent good practice in consolidating and nurturing democratic governance into a blatant political conditionality of aid donors. He claims that both bilateral and multilateral aid agencies and governments are using monitoring and observation exactly the same way that political pluralism and adjustment were used in the late 1980s and early 1990s to apply a carrot and stick pressure to developing countries to achieve their strategic interests. Mandaza[81] agrees with Matlosa that, recently, the conflict between Zimbabwe and the EU over the election observation is a reflection of the desire of the European Union and the western world in general – to assert its global superiority, power and hegemony in Africa and the third world. Thabo Mbeki giving a lecture at the University of South Africa on 23 August 2013, referring to the 2013 elections said that so, we still don't know what was the substance, what is the substance of all the allegations made which Washington and London and Brussels have used to say the elections were not credible. We don't know in reality, the only reason they were not credible is because Robert Mugabe got elected. That's all. [82] This view together with those of Mathlosa and Mandaza cited above show that

75 Commonwealth Observer Group (2000) The Parliamentary Election in Zimbabwe 24–25 June 2000. The Report of the Commonwealth Observer Group.

76 ZESN (2013) *Report on the 31 July 2013 Harmonised Elections*. Harare: ZESN.

77 Afrobarometer & Mass Public Opinion Institute (MPOI) (2006) support for democracy and democratic institutions in Zimbabwe. *Afrobarometer Briefing Paper* No. 27. Harare and Cape Town.

78 Sachikonye L (2011) *When a State turns on its citizens, 60 years of Institutionalised Violence in Zimbabwe*. Harare: Weaver Press. p. 82.

79 Matlosa K (2002) Election monitoring and observation in Zimbabwe: Hegemony versus sovereignty. *African Journal of Political Science* 7(1): 130.

80 Ibid.: 130.

81 Mandaza I (2002, 22–28 February) The Schori Affair. *The Zimbabwe Mirror*.

82 Former South African President Thabo Mbeki's lecture at UNISA's Thabo Mbeki African Leadership Institute (TMALI), delivered in Tshwane on 23 August 2013.

the issue of election monitoring and observation has become value- laden. It is therefore important not to view it as an end in itself but a means to an end. Beyond observation during elections, all variables and processes in an election must be considered in deciding whether an election is free and fair. An election does not start with proclamation. It is an everyday affair, it is a part of life where democracy and governance are entrenched or undermined by what happens every day in a political system. Adherence to the constitution, other laws and regulations, promoting democracy on a daily basis will count in the final analysis of whether an election was free and fair. It can be concluded that a lot has been said about the ZEC's credibility. Some stakeholders praise the ZEC, others speak about its compromised credibility. Both groups, however, give recommendations on how to improve the ZEC's.

Conclusions and recommendations

The electoral management system in Zimbabwe has improved since independence. The improvements came from the multidimensional requirements submitted by its stakeholders such as observer missions, civil society, political parties, national, regional and international institutions and researchers in general, election candidates and the electorate. The recommendations or complaints resulted in major and notable improvements being instituted by the EMB's resulting in amendment to the law, including the constitution. The establishment of the ZEC as an independent commission was a major milestone in terms of electoral reforms implemented in Zimbabwe since independence.

The issues raised by the various stakeholders in Zimbabwe included: the lack of independence of the commission; inadequate polling stations; the voters' roll that suffers credibility deficit; delay in announcement of overall election results (in 2008); selective invitation and accreditation of poll observers, including the media; failure to hold parties accountable on compliance with ground rules of elections; biased media coverage by the public broadcaster with no access to the public broadcaster; no mechanisms for the diaspora vote; use of registration certificates as a result of un-updated voters' rolls; poor preparedness for the special voting facility (in 2013); inappropriateness of the indelible ink; and lagging behind in electoral technologies to allow for convenience, efficiency and reduce costs in elections.

Recommendations have been made by various stakeholders including academics, observers, political parties, civil society, students, the electorate, various interest special groups and the diaspora. Some of these recommendations have been discussed in this chapter. The following represent the principal recommendations as understood from this case study.

- The recruitment of the ZEC's secretariat must be done publicly and transparently, especially for senior posts, just like in the judiciary.
- ICT-driven voter registration must be done by the ZEC instead of unnecessarily sticking to manual registration.

- Voter education and registration must be done continuously by the ZEC. Voter education must cover all stakeholders, taking into account their special needs.
- Registration slips must not be used as proof of registration on polling day. This means that this law must be repealed by the legislature.
- The registration process must close in good time to allow for the updating of the voters' roll so that it is accurate on election day.
- Online dissemination of information must be done by the ZEC in order to increase its coverage and reach new voters.
- The ZEC must intensify its engagement with the media to ensure fair coverage on elections since media houses control their own editorial policies. The ZEC relies on the good will of the media and thus continuous engagement and training is recommended.
- Observation of elections in Zimbabwe should be open to all stakeholders except institutions where national security considerations may disqualify certain applications.
- Government must ensure the timely release of adequate resources to the ZEC.
- There is the need to establish permanent stakeholder liaison committees capable of solving conflicts throughout the electoral cycle.
- The voters' roll needs to be continuously edited to ensure it is up-to-date, in accordance with the civil registry.
- The election date must be provided by law in order to reduce conflicts concerning its determination.

www.ingramcontent.com/pod-product-compliance
Lightning Source LLC
Chambersburg PA
CBHW080354030426
42334CB00024B/2877